TOLSTOY'S LETTERS
VOLUME I

Tolstoy's Letters

Volume 1: 1828–1879

Selected, edited and translated by
R. F. CHRISTIAN

FABER & FABER

This edition first published in 2015
by Faber & Faber Ltd
Bloomsbury House, 74–77 Great Russell Street
London WC1B 3DA

Printed by Books on Demand GmbH, Norderstedt

All rights reserved
Selection, English translation and editorial matter © R. F. Christian, 1978
Preface © Rosamund Bartlett, 2010

The right of R. F. Christian to be identified
as author of this work has been asserted in accordance
with Section 77 of the Copyright, Designs and Patents Act 1988

This book is sold subject to the condition that it shall not, by way of
trade or otherwise, be lent, resold, hired out or otherwise circulated
without the publisher's prior consent in any form of binding or cover other than
that in which it is published and without a similar condition including this
condition being imposed on the subsequent purchaser

A CIP record for this book is available from the British Library

ISBN 978–0–571–32407–1

CONTENTS

VOLUME I

Preface to the 2015 Edition		vii
Preface to the First Edition		ix
The Letters		
I	1828–1851, Letters 1–9	1
II	1852–1855, Letters 10–33	19
III	1856–1862, Letters 34–112	55
IV	1863–1869, Letters 113–152	175
V	1870–1879, Letters 153–252	223

VOLUME II

VI	1880–1886, Letters 253–306	337
VII	1887–1894, Letters 307–402	411
VIII	1895–1902, Letters 403–494	513
IX	1903–1910, Letters 495–608	627
Index		719

PLATES

Between pages 144 and 145

1. The four Tolstoy brothers, 1854
2. Tolstoy's sister Marya as a girl
3. Valeriya Arsenyeva
4. Tolstoy with a group of writers, 1856
5. L. N. Tolstoy, self-photograph, 1862
6. S. A. Tolstaya, 1862
7. Tanya Behrs (Kuzminskaya)
8. A. A. Tolstaya ('Granny')
9. A. A. Fet
10. N. N. Strakhov
11. N. N. Gay
12. N. A. Nekrasov, 1861
13. V. P. Botkin
14. A. I. Herzen
15. L. N. and S. A. Tolstoy with eight of their children, Yasnaya Polyana, 1884
16. L. N. Tolstoy on the road from Moscow to Yasnaya Polyana, 1886
17. V. G. Chertkov
18. L. N. and S. A. Tolstoy with seven of their children, Yasnaya Polyana, 1892
19. The Tolstoy family, Yasnaya Polyana, 1903
20. L. N. Tolstoy telling his grandchildren, S. A. and I. A. Tolstoy, a fairy tale about a cucumber, 1909
21. Aylmer Maude with Tolstoy's daughter Tatyana Sukhotina and her daughter Tanya
22. Tuckton House colonists, Christchurch, Hampshire, 1907
23. Tolstoy's house at Yasnaya Polyana

Plates 1, 3, 4, 5, 7, 8, 10, 11, 13, 15, 18, 19, L. N. Tolstoy State Museum, Moscow; 2, 6, 9, 12, 14, 17, 20, Society for Cultural Relations with the USSR, London; 16, P. Birukoff, *The Life of Tolstoy* (Cassell & Co. Ltd, 1911); 21, grand-children of Aylmer Maude; 22, Alfred Brandt Esq.; 23, Novosti Press Agency, London.

PREFACE TO THE 2015 EDITION

Tolstoy's literary activities famously began in the venereal diseases clinic of Kazan University in the spring of 1847, when he was eighteen years old. During the month that he spent in the clinic, in almost complete isolation, he started keeping a diary. To begin with, Tolstoy regarded his diary as a record of his hopelessly optimistic self-improvement programme. Later it became an outlet for his creative and philosophical reflections, and as such comprises an indispensable companion to his published writings, both fictional and otherwise.

Keeping a diary, for Tolstoy, was not the deeply private affair it is for most people, even if it started out that way. In the all-too-brief week between Tolstoy's proposal and marriage to Sonya Behrs in September 1862, he felt it incumbent upon him to give his young fiancée his diaries to read. The vivid realism which is the hallmark of Tolstoy's fiction is matched by the frankness of his diary entries, but he did not feel he should conceal anything in his past from his future bride.

As an innocent and inexperienced eighteen-year-old girl, who had seen little of life, Sonya was deeply shocked and upset by what she later termed his 'excessive conscientiousness', particularly when it came to reading about his sexual history with peasant girls. Nevertheless, she went ahead with the marriage and before long she and her husband were regularly and sometimes frenetically reading each other's diaries. It was a habit kept up until the very last months of Tolstoy's long life in the summer and autumn of 1910, when his deteriorating relations with Sonya led him to try for the first time to keep a diary for 'himself alone'.

Tolstoy did not keep a diary regularly throughout his life, for sometimes he transferred his exploration and articulation of psychological processes to his fictional works. Since his diaries span his entire adult life, however, they are indispensable reading for anyone seeking to look behind the scenes of the great novels and become better acquainted with their creator.

The same is true of Tolstoy's letters, and his epistolary output was, as one might expect, equally prodigious – there are 8,500 letters published in the Russian edition of his *Complete Collected Works*. Tolstoy wrote thousands of letters, to all manner of people, from persecuted peasant sectarians exiled to Siberia to the Romanovs, eventually addressing both *muzhik* and Tsar as 'Dear brother'.

The most touching letters Tolstoy wrote were to his immediate family – his wife Sonya, his children, his 'aunt' and surrogate mother Tatyana Alexandrovna ('Toinette'), his sister and brothers. The most important letters he wrote were to his closest friends. First there was his distant relative Alexandra Andreyevna, a lady-in-waiting at Court, for whom he had the deepest respect and affection until his defection from the Orthodox Church. Then there was the shy and retiring Nikolay Strakhov, who worked at the Imperial Library in St Petersburg, but the most frequent recipient of Tolstoy's letters was the aristocratic Vladimir Chertkov, his devoted follower. Chertkov was instrumental in disseminating Tolstoy's religious ideas in translation, and thousands of people, from a dizzying array of faiths, felt compelled after reading them to write to the 'Sage of Yasnaya Polyana' for his advice on how to live their lives. Tolstoy tried to reply to them all.

It will be a long time before we have full English editions of the fourteen volumes of Tolstoy's diaries and the twenty-five volumes of his letters in the *Complete Collected Works*. In the meantime, we can be eternally grateful to R. F. Christian, doyen of Anglophone Tolstoy studies, for doing all the hard work for us. The result of Professor Christian's scrupulous work is four manageable volumes containing faithful translations of the most important of Tolstoy's diary entries and letters. Rendered into supple English, they are enhanced by judicious and helpful annotations, and introductions which draw on Professor Christian's deep knowledge, the fruit of a distinguished career of studying and writing about Tolstoy. It is hard to see how these invaluable editions can be surpassed.

Rosamund Bartlett

Rosamund Bartlett is the author of Tolstoy: A Russian Life *(Profile Books).*

R. F. Christian's four volumes of Tolstoy's Diaries *and* Letters *are all available in Faber Finds.*

PREFACE TO THE FIRST EDITION

Lev Tolstoy was unquestionably the most prolific letter-writer of all the great Russian novelists of the nineteenth century. Thirty-two volumes of the monumental ninety-volume Soviet edition of his works are devoted exclusively to his letters and their annotation. The final volume appeared as recently as 1958, and brought the total of published letters to over 8,500. More have come to light since then, but many have been irretrievably lost, especially those written in youth and middle age. By contrast, the vast majority of his later letters have survived, thanks to his copying machine, the efficiency of his secretaries and the devotion of his wife and daughters, although many of them are repetitive and predictable in content, and tend to be merely a conventional channel for supplying advice to the hundreds of people from all over the world who sought it.

Nobody would claim that Tolstoy was an accomplished exponent of epistolary art. He was no 'letter-writer's letter writer'. Nevertheless it is remarkable that there has never been a comprehensive selection of his letters in English, and that comparatively few of them have been translated in full, although extracts are frequently quoted in the standard biographies. The only two collections of note belong to the 1920s, and are both out of print: *Tolstoy's Love-letters*, translated by S. S. Koteliansky and Virginia Woolf, London 1923, (one assumes that Virginia Woolf's role was a passive one), and *The Letters of Tolstoy and his Cousin Countess Alexandra Tolstoy*, translated by L. Islavin, London 1929. Both are seriously marred by their translators' inadequate command of English and are inevitably unrepresentative. When the Athlone Press suggested to me as long ago as 1971 that the time was ripe to remedy the situation, I was at first reluctant and apprehensive. Eventually, however, a re-reading of Tolstoy's correspondence persuaded me that the idea was a good one, and that it might even be possible to produce a volume in time to commemorate the 150th anniversary of his birth in 1978. The task has been a long and difficult one, and I am only too well aware of the limitations of a book, the writing of which has spanned so many years and been so frequently interrupted.

When I began to consider how many letters to translate and on what basis to select them, it soon became apparent that the great majority fell roughly into one of three main categories. First there were those to do with Tolstoy the writer, his views about his own work and the works of other writers. Secondly there were those which concerned Tolstoy the thinker in a broader sense, and expressed his attitude to the times he lived in, contemporary social problems, rural life, industrialisation, education, and more especially in later life, religious and spiritual questions. Thirdly there were the letters which were more loosely to do with Tolstoy the man, the main stages of his biography, his relations with his family and friends, and the growth and development of his own personality. Inevitably

Preface to the First Edition

there was much overlapping between these three categories, but they did at least provide a rough and ready criterion for deciding what to select or reject. My final choice is bound to be criticised by those who would like to see more of the artist and less of the man, or more of the thinker and less of the moralist. Nevertheless, it has been made in the hope that it will provide something of interest for as many people as possible, that it will complement the existing biographies of Tolstoy, and that it will stimulate other admirers of Tolstoy to produce a companion volume based on extracts from his copious diaries and notebooks.

From the first of my three categories, I have selected and translated some of Tolstoy's letters to his fellow Russian writers: Turgenev, Nekrasov, Fet, Saltykov-Shchedrin, Ostrovsky, Pisemsky, Herzen, Gorky, Andreyev and Korolenko, as well as such lesser known authors as Panayev, Grigorovich, Boborykin, Annenkov and Ertel. It is disappointing that there were so few distinguished European writers among his correspondents, although my selection does include letters to Shaw, Wells, Romain Rolland and Rainer Maria Rilke. Needless to say, it is not solely, or indeed mainly in his letters to other authors that Tolstoy expressed his views on literature and art. They are just as likely to be found in his extensive correspondence with the critic and philosopher Strakhov and the art critic and librarian Stasov, or in letters to complete strangers. As 'literary criticism' they leave much to be desired. Tolstoy himself never concealed his distaste for 'books about books', especially those written by professional critics, and on at least one occasion declared that 'of all the boring things in the world, criticism is the most boring'. Behind this attitude lay the belief that the critic's job was superfluous as long as literature was honest, for then it would make its impact without the need for interpretation. The only quality required of art, he wrote to Strakhov, was a negative one—'not to lie'; and he congratulated his fellow writer Leskov on writing truth, not fiction, and on making the former more entertaining than the latter. In later life he became increasingly prone to regard the function of art as moral edification and didacticism, and in a letter to the artist Gay in 1887 he stated unequivocally that in order to compose a work of art 'a man needs to know clearly and without doubt what is good and what is evil, to see plainly the dividing line between them and consequently to paint not what is, but what should be'. This is a relatively late opinion, but there is ample evidence in Tolstoy's earlier letters that moral criteria profoundly affected his literary judgements and his conception of the meaning and purpose of art as, for example, when he wrote to Nekrasov in 1856 of the superiority of love to hatred in literature, or complained to Fet in 1860 about Turgenev's lack of humanity or sympathy for his characters, and the artistic shortcomings which he believed were the result. Tolstoy was looking for the man behind the writer, and when he told Gorky in a letter of 1900 that he liked his writings, but that he liked *him* better, he was paying him the greatest compliment he could.

Apart from the morally coloured critical *obiter dicta* scattered throughout Tolstoy's correspondence, one can also discern from it his views about the various genres of literature and his marked preference for prose fiction (as long as it was truthful and not invented!), to drama or poetry. He confessed to Golokhvastov in

Preface

1876 that he was prejudiced against drama and that he was not a good judge of it. In 1887, when his own play *The Power of Darkness* was being staged, he told the dramatist Potekhin that he understood nothing about the theatre or dramatic art—and it would be wrong to attribute this remark solely to false modesty. As for poetry, he refers several times in his letters to his dislike of it, and while this opinion needs to be carefully qualified, and while we know that he greatly admired and often returned to the poetry of Fet, Tyutchev and Pushkin in particular, it is certainly true that his literary tastes were rather circumscribed and that he had something of a blind spot for anything not written in prose. This is confirmed by the well-known letter he wrote to a Petersburg bookseller in 1891 with a list of the books which had made the greatest impression on him at different periods of his life. It is very heavily weighted on the side of the eighteenth- and nineteenth-century prose classics of Russian, French and English literature, and more particularly the fiction of his own lifetime. Elsewhere in his letters Tolstoy makes occasional references to prose genres, especially the novel, which bear out his remarks late on in life to Goldenweiser about the need for artists to create their own form, and about the difficulty of fitting any outstanding Russian prose work of the first half of the nineteenth century into the conventional categories of novel or *novella*. It is true that in an unguarded moment, when writing to Nekrasov about his first 'story', *Childhood*, he did use the word 'novel'; but he refused to apply the term to *War and Peace*, and in a letter to Strakhov of 1873 he actually described *Anna Karenina* as his 'first novel'. His terse statements, however, are not supported by any reasoning, and one can only conclude that Tolstoy had no interest in academic problems of classification, but preferred simply to abide by his early and unhelpful observation, made while writing *War and Peace*, that 'we Russians, generally speaking, don't know how to write novels in the sense in which the genre is understood in Europe'.

In reading through Tolstoy's letters which have to do with literature, one finds that the most useful passages concern his own works. By contrast, his comments on what he is reading are sparse and laconic—especially in the case of foreign literature, where a novel is often classified as simply 'good 'or 'stupid'. They are also coloured, as already indicated, by his estimate of a writer's moral worth, with the result that Turgenev is roughly treated ('*Asya* is rubbish'), while George Eliot is highly esteemed, and the Gogol of *Selected Passages from a Correspondence with Friends* is rapturously hailed as 'our Pascal'. Students of Tolstoy's own fiction and drama, however, cannot ignore his letters, even though they are less rewarding than those of Chekhov as a source of literary self-revelation. He has some interesting things to say about the changes made in *Childhood*, the idea behind *Three Deaths*, and the artistic shortcomings of *Family Happiness*. His correspondence with Bashilov, the first illustrator of *War and Peace*, contains a number of pertinent remarks about the drawings of the major characters and the way Tolstoy envisaged them. The letters to the proof-reader Bartenev reveal some of the minor corrections and alterations by which Tolstoy set so much store, while miscellaneous letters to the poet Fet, the publisher Katkov and the historian Pogodin are all important for what they say about the focal point of the novel, the use of French, the relevance and content of the digressions or about Tolstoy's views on history. In the 1870s he wrote several letters to Strakhov about *Anna Karenina*—the genesis of the novel, its architecture, and in particular the passages in it with which he was dissatisfied. The architecture of the novel is also the subject of an interesting letter to Rachinsky in 1878, while the correspondence with Katkov is not confined to the controversial Part 8, but also includes a short but important letter to do with the scene of Anna's intimacy with Vronsky, which Tolstoy refused to change. There are some worthwhile *obiter dicta* on *The Power of Darkness* and the interpretation of the role of Akim, on *Master and Man* and on *The Kreutzer Sonata*. Later still, the letters about *Hadji Murat* are a good illustration of Tolstoy's concern for historical accuracy and his conscientious approach, even as an old man, to the serious business of writing fiction.

If one learns something of Tolstoy the writer from his correspondence, one learns more about Tolstoy the thinker, of whom Bertrand Russell wrote in one of his more irresponsible moments that 'it is the greatest misfortune to the human race that he has so little power of reasoning'. For the last third of his life, however, his letters are less valuable in the sense that they often repeat what has been said elsewhere in his numerous articles and public pronouncements. Some of them indeed are 'open letters', intended for public consumption, while others which were addressed to tsars or government ministers were inevitably publicised, whatever their author's original intention. This was not the case, of course, before his so-called 'conversion', and it is not surprising that his earlier correspondence should contain sentiments which he was later to find abhorrent—pleasure at joining the army, desire for promotion and military decorations, the joy of hunting, and even a short-lived enthusiasm for founding an 'art for art's sake' journal in order to mould public taste. What *is* surprising, however, is the fact that so many of Tolstoy's mature opinions are to be found in embryonic form at a very early age. It cannot be said too often that his 'conversion' was not a sudden *volte-face*, the sour grapes of a man growing too old to enjoy the pagan, sensual and materialistic pleasures of life, and devoting his last years to saving his soul and making his peace with God. The germ of almost everything that came to fruition in his thinking and writing after 1880 can be found in one or other of his letters of the previous thirty years: his pacifism, his rejection of capital punishment, his hostility towards state institutions and bureaucratic practices, his unconventional views on primary and secondary education, his distrust of university professors, doctors and journalists, his hatred of big cities and an urban society based on the buying and selling of property, his painful awareness of the contrast between his own material well-being and the poverty surrounding him and his concern to justify his art in terms of its usefulness to the community as a whole. There are many such pointers in Tolstoy's earliest letters to the direction in which his thoughts were leading him, but none are so obvious, perhaps, as those which indicate his attitude towards death and the meaning of life. His description of his brother Nikolay's death is harrowing in the extreme, and it was almost certainly his constant obsession with the phenomenon of mortality which impelled Tolstoy to seek a religious solution to the purpose of existence which would reconcile him to the bitter but inevitable fact that he too must die. The stages of his religious quest can be followed in his correspondence with Countess Alexandra Tolstaya, to whom he confided his innermost thoughts and who was, unlike himself, an orthodox believer, comparatively untroubled by doubts. What is revealed in these letters is Tolstoy's absolute conviction of the paramount importance of religion, his impatience with Orthodox ritual and dogma, and his belief that the essence of Christian feeling is love and unselfishness and that these qualities were not only the most desirable virtues in themselves, but were conspicuously lacking in those adherents of official Orthodox Christianity with whom he was most familiar.

The third category of letters are those which concern in a more general way Tolstoy the man and his biography, rather than his literary, social or religious views. Naturally enough, the most interesting ones are those to his wife and children, his brothers and sister, his prospective fiancée Arsenyeva, his 'aunt' Tatyana Yergolskaya, his cousin Alexandra Tolstaya and his devoted disciple and intimate friend for the last twenty-five years of his life, Vladimir Chertkov. Reading them chronologically, one sees Tolstoy first as a student at Kazan University, then very briefly as a landowner, before volunteering for service in the Caucasus, and later joining the army and fighting in the Crimean War. This period of his life, up to the fall of Sevastopol, is best reconstructed from his letters to Yergolskaya and his brother Sergey, which reveal him as enthusiastic, restless, self-centred, vain, but at the same time very unsure of himself and of his vocation. He writes of the scenery and of local customs; of the military actions he is engaged in and his companions; of his dissipation and venereal disease; his first tentative efforts at writing a novel; and his dreams of an idyllic future at Yasnaya Polyana.

In the years between his discharge from the army and his marriage in 1863, his correspondence includes a series of long letters to Arsenyeva which give a fascinating picture of Tolstoy, the would-be domestic tyrant, planning future happiness according to his own rules. His letters advise her to go for a walk every day and to put on her corsets and stockings by herself. They reproach her for her bad taste in hats. They plan the details of ideal married life with scrupulous and pedantic care, recommending where to live in summer and winter, how many rooms their apartment should have, what the husband should do to make his peasants happy, what he should teach his wife, and how she should divide her time between music, reading and helping her husband! These well-intentioned, but tactless and patronising letters shed much light on Tolstoy's personality, as do his letters from abroad and those which tell of his imminent 'renunciation' of literature, and his rural and educational pursuits. But what is of especial interest to Tolstoy's biographers is his correspondence with his devoted wife and daughters and his wayward and unruly sons, from which he emerges, perhaps, as a better husband than a father. His loyalty to his wife, despite the widening rift between them, never wavered until the last year of his life, but his feelings for his children were by no means always affectionate. With his daughters, who were much closer to him than his sons, one

Preface to the First Edition

readily senses his jealousy and possessiveness. He could never reconcile himself to the fact that they might wish to get married, and when they did, he could not refrain from pointing out to them the disadvantages and dangers of married life or making them aware of the unsuitability of their prospective husbands. With his sons, his relations were much more strained. To Andrey and Misha in particular he often had hard things to say about their laziness, debauchery and drinking habits, and some of his reproachful letters run to more than ten pages in length. Andrey is even rebuked for the idiotic whining of his noisy gramophone! The shadow of Tolstoy's overpowering personality lay heavily on those nearest to him, and for all his basic kindness and concern for their welfare, his desire to mould them in his own image frequently got the better of his wish to help them with the benefit of his own experience and advice.

Tolstoy's letters to Chertkov and their annotation take up five volumes of the ninety-volume Jubilee Edition of his works. Although they are biased towards religious and spiritual matters and therefore particularly relevant to Tolstoy as a thinker, they are full of fascinating glimpses of his personality and his rapidly changing moods, veering from blind devotion to his dedicated disciple, to barely concealed exasperation at his pernicious influence on Tolstoy's family life. Of particular interest are the letters to Chertkov in 1910, which, together with those to his wife and children in the same year, provide essential source material for the tragic story of Tolstoy's final homeleaving and lonely death on the railway station at Astapovo. As I have stated elsewhere, it is my belief—however controversial—that in the last resort Tolstoy was a great writer because he was a great man, and I would like to justify my selection and translation of this small fraction of his enormous correspondence by the clues it may give to the enigma of this tormented, struggling, often exasperating man who never abandoned the search for the meaning of life and remained to the end of his days a seeker and a visionary.

My translations are based on the texts printed in Volumes 59–90 of the ninety-volume 'Jubilee Edition' of Tolstoy's works (Moscow 1928–58), or in Volumes 17 and 18 (both Moscow, 1965) of the recent twenty-volume collection edited by N. N. Akopova, N. K. Gudzy, N. N. Gusev and M. B. Khrapchenko. In cases where the text appears to be defective, or where there are *loci obscuri*, I have consulted the original manuscripts in the Tolstoy Archives in Moscow. Letters written in French to other Russians, such as those to Tatyana Yergolskaya, have been translated into English, but I have retained the original French and German when Tolstoy was writing to a Frenchman or a German, in order to give some impression of his written command of those languages. My selection also contains a number of letters which Tolstoy wrote in English, and this fact is indicated at the beginning of the text. The great majority of the letters which I have chosen to include have been translated in full, but I have felt justified from time to time in omitting self-contained introductory or concluding paragraphs not relevant to the part of a particular letter which I wished to translate, and I have indicated the number of lines of the Jubilee Edition text which have been omitted. In a very few cases there are omissions within the translated text itself, due to a gap in the manuscript or the illegibility of Tolstoy's handwriting. In fewer than a dozen instances I have left out passages which either have no relevance to the content of the letter or would require copious annotation (for example, a list of people's names). All these omissions have been clearly indicated, and in no way affect the sense of the text. Where vulgar or obscene words occur in the original, I have preferred to follow the old-fashioned Soviet editorial practice of not reproducing them in full.

All the letters have been grouped chronologically into nine chapters, each prefaced by a short introduction. Biographical notes have also been provided for all Tolstoy's correspondents. I have erred on the generous side with the textual annotation, which is intentionally biased towards Tolstoy and his family, and the most important people in his life. In order to avoid elaborate cross-references, however, a footnote is generally given only when a person or thing is first introduced, and on other occasions it will be necessary to consult the index first of all.

My transliteration system closely follows the one outlined by Dr R. Hingley in his preface to Volume 3 of the *Oxford Chekhov* (O.U.P. 1964), pp. xi–xii. Like him, I have transliterated Russian e after vowels or a soft sign and as the first letter of a word by *ye*, and the Russian ё by *yo* except after ж, ч, ш and щ where it appears as *o*. I have also used the English *y* for all nominal and adjectival endings in -ий and -ый, and have omitted the soft sign altogether. However, the Russian combination кс has been reproduced as *x* rather than *ks* (e.g. Alexander, Alexey, Maxim etc.), and in the case of Alexander the conventional English spelling has been preferred. With all other Christian names, the Russian form has been retained in order to preserve as far as possible the Russian flavour and pronunciation, while avoiding the outlandish Aleksandr: hence Nikolay not Nicholas, Sergey not Serge, Andrey not Andrew and—rather regretfully—Pyotr. The spellings Hippolyte, Anatole, Pierre and Louise have been kept for the characters in *War and Peace*. In cases where Russian surnames and place-names have become standardised in English in a form which is not consistent with my transliteration system (e.g. Moscow, Petersburg, Tchaikovsky), I have followed conventional usage. With adjectives derived from place-names, I have kept the adjectival form where it denotes a small village—even Russians cannot always be sure of the noun from which the adjective derives—but have used nominal forms in all other cases (hence Yepifensky and Masalsky villages, but the Oryol, not the Orlovsky region).

If a Russian surname is clearly of foreign origin, I have spelt it in the way in which it is normally spelt in the language of origin (Eichenbaum, not Eykhenbaum, Goldenweiser not Goldenveyzer, Rees not Ris). When a Russian's surname is preceded by *gospodin* or *gospozha*, the Russian words have been translated by Mr, Mrs or Miss as the case may be, but M., Mme and Mlle have been retained when reference is made to a French man or woman. Russian terms for weights and measures and for certain institutions (*verst*, *sazhen*, *zemstvo* etc.) have not been converted into English equivalents, but have been explained where necessary in the notes. Copeck and rouble are spelt in the conventional English way.

Preface to the First Edition

Tolstoy's own spelling, whether in Russian or the major European languages, left something to be desired. Soviet editors have seen fit to make corrections, where necessary, in his letters written in Russian, and I have followed their example with those in French and English. Errors of grammar and syntax, however, have not of course been corrected in the French and English texts. Tolstoy's punctuation was also idiosyncratic and inconsistent, and this fact, together with the different conventions of the Russian and English systems, will, I hope, justify my policy of taking liberties with commas and semi-colons for the sake of ease of reading. I have also ventured to italicise a few words in order to give them the emphasis in English which is given by the freer word order of Russian.

Round brackets have been used wherever Tolstoy used them; square brackets for all editorial comment or explanation. Russian words occurring in a letter written in French to a Russian (for example, the letters to Yergolskaya) are indicated by the use of angle brackets ⟨ ⟩. The hyphen in 25–8 August at the head of a letter indicates that it was written between those two dates. The stroke in 25 August/ 6 September means that the date is given in both the old and the new styles. Unless otherwise mentioned, Russian dates are given in the old style, which in the nineteenth century was twelve days in arrears of Western Europe.

A word of explanation is needed about standard formulae which commonly occur at the beginning and the end of letters. The expression *mily drug* has been translated 'dear friend', except when addressed to Tolstoy's wife and family, in which case I have used 'my dear'. As far as possible I have used 'cordial' or 'cordially' to translate formulae involving *dusha*; 'heartily' or 'with all my heart' for set expressions containing *serdtse* or *izo vsekh sil*; and 'yours affectionately' for the common *vas lyubyashchy*. Despite a certain awkwardness in English, I have translated *zhmu ruku* by 'I press your hand', and have qualified it by the words 'in friendship' or 'as a brother' when it is combined with *druzheski* and *bratski*. Similarly *Je vous baise les mains mille fois* has been rendered literally and not paraphrased. While these are not ideal solutions and will jar on some readers, I have at least tried to be consistent and to accept the fact that nineteenth-century epistolary usage in Russia and France was more flamboyant and less inhibited than in England.

A marked feature of Tolstoy's style, whether as a novelist or a letter-writer, is his fondness for repeating the same word, when most other writers would, for the sake of variety, have employed a near synonym. I have tried to reproduce this feature by deciding on one particular equivalent for a commonly recurring word or phrase and retaining it throughout; for example, 'firstly' for *vo-pervykh*, rather than 'in the first place' or 'first of all'. Needless to say, this is not always possible in every context in English (and even if it were, absolute consistency would be extremely difficult in a work which has taken four years to complete), and so I have sometimes translated *otritsayu* as 'repudiate' or 'renounce' as well as 'deny'; *ispolnyayu* as 'carry out' as well as 'fulfil'; or *radi Boga* as 'for God's sake', 'for goodness sake' or 'for the love of God', according to the situation in which it occurs and the person being addressed. I am aware that at times I have sacrificed good English in order to

Preface

capture the Tolstoyan flavour; at other times I have been guilty of 'improving' the original in the interests of readability, especially when an error of grammar or syntax on Tolstoy's part is obviously due to carelessness or a slip of the pen, and no useful purpose would be served by concocting a comparable grammatical blunder in English.

After much deliberation, and in the absence of any generally agreed alternatives, I have erred on the side of caution in keeping the unfortunate titles *Russian Conversation* and *Notes of the Fatherland* for the Russian periodicals widely known in English by these names. I have, however, replaced the familiar but clumsy *A Library for Reading* by *Reader's Library*. *Russky Vestnik* is translated as *Russian Herald* (not *Messenger*), and *Russkiye Vedomosti* as *Russian Gazette*. I have preferred 'gentry' to 'nobility' as the translation of *dvoryanstvo*, and have rendered *gimnaziya* by the now unfortunately obsolescent 'grammar school'.

I would like, in conclusion, to express my sincere thanks to Mr Paul Medlicott and Miss Doris Bradbury who helped me considerably at different times with my task of translating and annotating the letters, checked many facts for me and made valuable suggestions. I would also like to thank Mrs Pamela Marshall and my daughter Jessica Christian for typing my manuscript. The Carnegie Trust and The University of St Andrews gave me a travel grant to enable me to visit the Tolstoy Museums in Moscow and Yasnaya Polyana, and I gratefully acknowledge their assistance. Finally I would like to thank the many scholars in the Soviet Union who gave me their time and help during my visits in 1972 and 1975, and who made it possible for me to consult the manuscript material which I wished to see.

St Andrews, 1975   R. F. Christian

I
1828–1851

Lev Nikolayevich Tolstoy was born on the family estate of Yasnaya Polyana, some 130 miles to the south-west of Moscow, on 28 August 1828, the fourth of the five children of Count Nikolay and Countess Marya Tolstoy. His mother died in 1830, and seven years later the family moved to Moscow where his father died in 1837. His father's sister, Alexandra Ilinichna Osten-Saken, became the children's legal guardian after their grandmother's death in 1838, and when she died in 1841 the guardianship passed to another sister, Pelageya Ilinichna Yushkova, who insisted that the Tolstoy family should live with her in Kazan. This was Tolstoy's home for the next six years. In 1844 he entered the University of Kazan to study oriental languages. A year later he transferred to the Faculty of Law, but a dissolute life and the contraction of venereal disease led to his withdrawing from the university in 1847 without graduating, on grounds of 'ill health and domestic circumstances', and he returned to Yasnaya Polyana to devote himself to the upkeep of his newly inherited estate and the welfare of his serfs. In 1848 he left the country for Moscow, and a new round of debauchery. The following year he moved to Petersburg, but after a brief period in the Faculty of Law at the University of Petersburg and the accumulation of considerable gambling debts, he soon returned to Yasnaya Polyana and opened a school for the peasant children on his estate. For the next two years he continued to live in the country (with excursions into Tula and Moscow society), devoting much time to music, cards and gymnastics, and making his first serious attempts at writing. In 1851 he wrote *A History of Yesterday*, which remained unpublished, translated most of Sterne's *Sentimental Journey* and began to write *Childhood*. In April 1851 he set off for the Caucasus with his eldest brother, Nikolay, who had joined the army after graduating from the University of Kazan in 1844 and was returning to his unit from leave. Soon after arriving in the Caucasus, Tolstoy took part as a volunteer in an expedition against a local village, and towards the end of the year he moved to Tiflis in order to prepare for examinations which would enable him to enter the army as a cadet.

Tolstoy's earliest surviving letter dates from 1844, and for the whole period from 1844 to 1851 fewer than sixty are extant, the great majority to T. A. Yergolskaya, and to Tolstoy's second oldest brother Sergey.

1. To T. A. Yergolskaya

1. To T. A. YERGOLSKAYA

Tatyana Alexandrovna Yergolskaya (1792–1874) was related to the Tolstoy family through the Gorchakovs. After her parents' death she was brought up by Tolstoy's grandmother, Pelageya Nikolayevna Tolstaya (*née* Gorchakova), together with Tolstoy's father, Nikolay Tolstoy. She fell in love with Nikolay at an early age, and continued to love him even after his marriage and early death. Two short poems written by Nikolay to 'Tatenka' before his marriage indicate that he returned her feeling, and the fact that he did not marry her was undoubtedly due to the lack of social and material advantage of such a match—or so his son surmised much later, attributing the decision to Tatyana, who always advised Tolstoy to marry well, that is advantageously. Her own life was entirely devoted to Nikolay Tolstoy and his family, and most of it was spent at Yasnaya Polyana.

In 1836, some years after the death of his first wife, Nikolay Tolstoy proposed to Tatenka and asked her to be a mother to his children. She refused the offer of marriage—according to Tolstoy because she was unwilling to spoil her 'pure, poetic relations with him [Nikolay Tolstoy] and with us'—but promised to care for the children. When Nikolay Tolstoy himself died a year later, 'tante Toinette', as she was called by the children, assumed responsibility for the family, although she was not their legal guardian. Tolstoy recalled that she often addressed him as 'Nicolas', his father's name, which he found a touching indication of her love for them both. In 1841, however, all the children went to Kazan to live with their new guardian, Pelageya Yushkova, whose attitude to Yergolskaya was coloured by the fact that her husband had proposed to Yergolskaya—and been rejected—before he proposed to her.

Despite their temporary separation, tante Toinette's influence on Tolstoy at an important formative period of his life was enormous, as he often recalled later. She was a woman of deep religious feelings, which were more private and mystical than church-oriented, and while she accepted most Orthodox dogmas, she firmly refused to believe in the everlasting torment of sinners. Tolstoy recalled in a conversation with Chertkov in 1884 that he, too, had rejected this point of dogma as a boy. He also claimed that she taught him the pleasure of a solitary, unhurried way of life; that she was the first to acquaint him with one of his favourite sayings, 'Fais ce que dois, advienne que pourra', and—no less important—that she encouraged him to 'faire des romans' long before he wrote anything for publication. After he began publishing, she was always one of his staunchest admirers and supporters. (One of Tolstoy's early projects, dating from 1851, was to write the story of tante Toinette's life.) She also made some more frivolous suggestions for Tolstoy's life which he later recalled with disapproval as being totally out of keeping with her true character: (1) to become an aide-de-camp, preferably to the Emperor; (2) to have an affair with a married woman of good social standing ('rien ne forme un jeune homme comme une liaison avec une femme comme il faut'); (3) to marry a wealthy woman with a big estate and many serfs. Yergolskaya's attitude towards

1. To T. A. Yergolskaya

serfdom was one of unquestioning acceptance—although her own treatment of serfs was beyond reproach—and in the late 1850s, when the issue of emancipation was being hotly debated, Tolstoy often became angry with her stubborn and outdated attitudes.

After Tolstoy's marriage, Yergolskaya continued to live at Yasnaya Polyana until her death in 1874. The measure of her influence on Tolstoy, as well as their mutual affection and confidence, is shown by the extent of their correspondence—of which over a hundred letters from Tolstoy, written between 1840 and 1866, have survived, as well as forty-two of hers to him. She knew French better than Russian, and Tolstoy normally corresponded with her in that language.

Tatyana Yergolskaya has also left her mark on Tolstoy's fiction. In *Childhood* the portrait of Nekhlyudov's mother contains certain features of tante Toinette's personality, as does the character of Nekhlyudov's aunt in *Boyhood*. There is no doubt either that some details of her life and position in Tolstoy's grandmother's home were used in creating the character of Sonya in *War and Peace*.

[Original in French]   Kazan, 25–8 August 1845

Although I've been a little slow in writing to you, I am writing all the same; I could have told you a lot of lies about it by way of excuse, but I won't do so; I'll simply say that I'm a worthless fellow who doesn't deserve your love for him—for although he's aware of it, and although he loves you too with all his heart, he has so many faults and is so lazy that he doesn't know how to prove it to you. But forgive him in return for his love for you. We've been in Kazan now for three days;[1] I don't know if this will please you or not but I've changed Faculties, I've become a law student. Personally I find that the application of this science to our private life is easier and more natural than that of any other, and consequently I'm very pleased with the change. Now I'm going to acquaint you with my plans and the sort of life I want to lead. I shan't go into society at all. I shall divide my time equally between music, drawing, languages and my university lessons. May God grant me sufficient resolution to persist with my plans. Auntie dear, I have a request to make to you which I wouldn't have made to anybody else; but I know how kind and indulgent you are. I've promised myself to write to you twice a week, and no doubt you'll write the same number of letters to me as well. If I don't keep my promise, don't punish me, but go on writing to me, ⟨please⟩. For I reckon we shall only have two short conversations a week, and no prolonged ones as we used to have at ⟨Yasnaya⟩ when my manservant was having supper, and if you deny me every letter I haven't deserved...but no, you won't do that, you'll write to me just the same. For my part I've informed you of everything that concerns me: now it will be your turn. Dear ⟨Pashenka's⟩[2] condition interests me greatly. I was compensated for my

[1] 1. Tolstoy had spent the summer at Yasnaya Polyana.
2. The adopted daughter of A. I. Osten-Saken. She died of tuberculosis in 1846, and Tolstoy's interest in her condition presumably refers to this illness.

1. To T. A. Yergolskaya

sorrow at having to leave you by the satisfaction I got from seeing Nikolay³ again. Poor fellow, he's not happy in camp, and he must be extremely embarrassed, particularly since he hasn't a farthing. As for his comrades—Good Heavens, they're coarse fellows, if ever there were any. You only need to see a little of this camp life to be disgusted with military service. If you are at ⟨Yasnaya⟩, Auntie, please send all my old notes that are there with the cart and horses. I kiss Aunt Liza's⁴ hand a thousand times and embrace Polina.⁵ Goodbye, ⟨Auntie dearest⟩,

Lev Tolstoy

2. To COUNT S. N. TOLSTOY

Sergey Nikolayevich Tolstoy (1826–1904) was the second of Tolstoy's three older brothers. He entered the Faculty of Mathematics at the University of Kazan in 1843, and graduated in 1847. He lived on his estate at Pirogovo in the province of Tula until 1855, when he entered military service. Within a year, however, he resigned his commission and returned to live on his estate. In 1849 he took a gipsy from Tula, Marya Mikhaylovna Shishkina, to live with him at Pirogovo, and he had eleven children by her, of whom seven died young. He emerged from his isolated and secluded life with Marya when he fell in love with Tatyana Behrs, Tolstoy's sister-in-law, in the 1860s, but their plans to marry came to nothing when Marya was informed of the situation and her gipsy parents threatened to sue Sergey and cause a public scandal. A further obstacle to the marriage of Sergey and Tatyana was the fact that under Russian law Sergey was considered to be a blood relation of Tatyana's because his brother was married to Tatyana's sister, Sofya Andreyevna, and consequently such a marriage was forbidden. Ultimately it was Tatyana herself who broke off the engagement. Sergey returned to Marya, whom he eventually married in 1867, and he spent the rest of his life with her on his estate, living in social isolation and ruling his family like a despot. Throughout their lives Tolstoy and Sergey remained close friends. In his *Reminiscences of Childhood*, Tolstoy wrote of Sergey: '...Nikolenka I loved, but Seryozha I admired, as something strange and incomprehensible to me. His was a human life, very beautiful, but completely incomprehensible to me, mysterious and therefore particularly attractive.' Tolstoy's son, S. L. Tolstoy, wrote of Sergey in his later years that 'he was not ambitious and preferred to remain free...He made friends with anyone he pleased and did what he liked, or what he considered it necessary to do. He thought little about the consequences of his actions. His life followed the line of least resistance; he let life do with him as it pleased.' One of Sergey's love affairs while at the University of Kazan provided Tolstoy with the material for his story

---

3. Tolstoy's eldest brother.
4. Countess Yelizaveta Alexandrovna Tolstaya (*née* Yergolskaya), sister of T. A. Yergolskaya; married to Count P. I. Tolstoy, first cousin once removed to Tolstoy. Her son Valeryan married Tolstoy's sister Marya in 1847.
5. Tolstoy's aunt Pelageya Ilinichna Yushkova.

2. To Count S. N. Tolstoy

After the Ball. Many of Sergey's characteristics were included by Tolstoy in his portrayal of Volodya, in *Childhood, Boyhood*, and *Youth*, while Sergey's relationship with Tatyana Behrs was the basis for Tolstoy's portrayal of the relationship of Andrey Bolkonsky with Natasha in *War and Peace*. At least 175 of Tolstoy's letters to Sergey have survived, and are invaluable source material for the biography of Tolstoy.

Petersburg, 13 February 1849

Seryozha!

I'm writing this letter to you from Petersburg, where I intend to stay forever. My plans and the reasons for this decision are as follows. A few days after you left, we also set off, in the opposite direction, we—i.e. Ferzen, Ozerov and I. When we arrived here, Ozerov and I put up at the Hotel Napoleon on the corner of Malaya Morskaya and Voznesensky Avenue (I say this so that you should know the address), and I set off next day to see the Laptevs, the Tolstoys, Obolensky and Pushkin;[1] I came across Milyutin,[2] and the Islavins[3] etc., and was introduced to a lot of people, and a lot of people to me. In a word, it's somehow turned out that I've far more friends here than in Moscow—and *of higher quality*...[6 lines omitted]

I have decided to stay on here to take my examinations[4] and then to enter the service, but if I don't pass (and anything might happen) I'll enter the service at the fourteenth rank; I know many second division civil servants who are no worse than you first division people.[5] I must say in short that Petersburg life has a great and good influence on me: it accustoms me to activity, and is an enforced substitute for a fixed time-table. Somehow one can't be idle; everyone is occupied, everyone is busy doing something; you can't find anyone to lead a dissipated life with, and you can't do it on your own.

I know you won't believe that I've changed; you'll say 'that's the 20th time

[2] 1. The Laptevs and the Tolstoys were relatives of Tolstoy. Prince D. A. Obolensky, a friend from Kazan days; later president of the Chamber of Civil Justice in Petersburg, a well-known liberal of Slavophile leanings, and a contributor to several leading journals. M. N. Musin-Pushkin, also a Kazan friend of the Tolstoy brothers, an administrator of the Kazan, and subsequently Petersburg educational authorities, and chairman of the Censorship Committee at the time of the publication of Tolstoy's *Sevastopol in May*. His drastic alterations to the text prompted Nekrasov to write to Tolstoy about the 'revolting mutilation' of his article. Tolstoy refers to him in Chapter 1 of *A Confession*.

2. V. A. Milyutin, a childhood friend of Tolstoy. In *A Confession* Tolstoy recalls the occasion when Milyutin came to announce the discovery made at school 'that there is no God, and that everything they teach us is pure invention'. He later became a professor at the University of Petersburg, and was the author of several articles on social, political and economic themes. He committed suicide at the age of thirty-four.

3. The Islavins, A. M. Islenyev, a landowner of Tula and a close friend of Tolstoy's father, and his wife S. P. Kozlovskaya, whom he married before she was divorced from her first husband. As a result their six children were considered to be illegitimate, and received the name Islavin. A. M. Islenyev is portrayed in *Childhood, Boyhood* and *Youth* as the father of Nikolenka.

4. See Letter 3.

5. The Russian Civil Service and armed forces were based until 1917 on the Table of Ranks, a hierarchy of fourteen official ranks set up by Peter the Great in 1722. Ranks eight to one in progressive order of seniority carried with them a hereditary honorific title, and these are what Tolstoy refers to as 'the first division'.

2. To Count S. N. Tolstoy

you've said it, and there's no good in you, you're the emptiest of fellows'. But no, this time I've changed quite differently from the way I used to change before. Before I'd say to myself: 'I *think* I shall change', but now I see that I have changed, and I say: 'I have changed'.

The main thing is that I'm now completely convinced that one can't live by philosophy and speculation, but must live positively, i.e. be a practical man. This is a big step and a big change: this has never happened to me before. But if one is young and wants to live, there's no other place in Russia but Petersburg; whatever one's bent is, it can be satisfied, and can be developed easily and without effort. As for the means of existence, life here is not at all expensive for a bachelor; on the contrary, everything is cheaper and better than in Moscow. Lodgings are dirt-cheap. Obolensky came round just now and brought a letter he had just received from *brother Dmitry*.[6] *It's dreadful*. I'm sending you the letter; have a look at it yourself. If I hadn't been on such good terms with Obolensky as with Lvov and co., I would have left Petersburg post-haste. He'll drive me out of here sure enough; I'm only waiting for him to write the same sort of letter to Sheremetev[7]—that's what's tormenting me. However, they've promised to send my permit in a few days. And now to business. Do me a favour, send for Andrey[8] and explain to him that I need as much money as possible, firstly in order to live here and secondly in order to settle up my debts in Moscow. If there's not enough grain to provide me with another 800 silver roubles on top of the 250 and 500 which I've already written about, for goodness sake sell Savin wood, and if that's still not enough, get another advance from Kopylov, less interest. If you sell Savin wood, the first condition must be: all money in advance. I need the money, not for my living expenses here, but to pay my debts here and in Moscow which, together with the wretched debt I owe Orlov, amount to 1,200 silver roubles. I'm relying on you, *brother Sergey*, to arrange all this for me, and to try and get permission to sell the wood from the Moscow Trustee Council; and please keep an eye on Andrey Ilich from time to time and on the Yasnaya account books and the grain books. Tell all our folk that *I send my kisses and regards*, and that I may be in the country in the summer, or I may not. I want to take some leave in the summer and do a bit of travelling in the vicinity of Petersburg; I also want to visit Helsingfors and Revel. For goodness sake write to me, if only for once in your life; I want to know how you and all our folk will take the news. Ask them too, from me, to write; I'm afraid of writing to them: it's so long since I did write to them that they're probably angry. I feel particularly guilty about Auntie Tatyana Alexandrovna—tell her from me that I'm sorry. Obolensky sends his regards. You can imagine how Alyosha Pushkin[9] is *lionised* here; however, I haven't seen him yet.

6. Dmitry Nikolayevich Tolstoy exasperated his brothers by his fondness for mixing with the lowest orders of society and his interest in extreme religious and mystical ideas.
7. The reference is unclear.
8. A. I. Sobolev, an emancipated serf who managed the Yasnaya Polyana estate until he was dismissed for drunkenness in 1852.
9. Count A. I. Musin-Pushkin (not to be confused with M. N. Musin-Pushkin in note 1), a childhood friend of Tolstoy. He and his brother appear in *Childhood* as the Ivin brothers.

Please tell Andrey to write to me; it's already a month since I had any news from anyone, not to mention feelings of love, etc. As for money, I haven't a farthing.

I keep wondering how *brother Dmitry* could have taken it into his head to write such a letter, and can think of absolutely nothing in his favour except that he was drunk.

3. To COUNT S. N. TOLSTOY

Read this letter alone.

Petersburg, 1 May 1849

Seryozha,

I expect you're already saying that I'm *the emptiest of fellows*, and you're right. God knows what I've done! I came to Petersburg without any reason, and have done nothing sensible here at all; I've only run through a pile of money and got into debt. It's stupid, intolerably stupid. You wouldn't believe how it torments me. The main thing is the debts, which I *must* pay, and *as soon as possible*, because if I don't pay them soon, I'll lose my reputation as well as my money. For God's sake do something for me—sell Vorotynka[1] to Uvarov or Seleznev without telling our aunts or Andrey why or what for. This is my last resource, and without it I shan't have enough either to live on or to pay into the Trustee Council. Before my next instalment I need 3,500 silver roubles—1,200 for the Trustee Council, 1,600 to pay debts and 700 to live on. I know you'll sigh, but what's to be done? People do stupid things once in their lives. I had to pay for my freedom and my philosophy, and now I've paid...[20 lines omitted]

You probably know that all our troops have taken the field and that part of them (2 corps) have crossed the frontier and are already in Vienna,[2] so they say. I did begin to take the qualifying exams for a higher degree, and passed two of them all right, but now I've changed my ideas and want to join the Horse Guards regiment as a cadet. I'm ashamed to write this because I know that you love me and that all my stupidity and inconstancy will upset you. I even got up several times and blushed because of this letter, as you will do when you read it; but what can I do? The past is over and done with, but the future depends on me.

God willing, I'll turn over a new leaf and become a respectable person one day. I'm putting all my hopes on serving as a cadet; it will accustom me to a practical life, and *nolens volens* I shall have to serve until I'm commissioned. With luck, i.e. if the Guards are in action, I might be promoted before 2 years are up. The Guards take the field at the end of May. I can't do anything just now because firstly, I've no money—I shan't need much (everything is provided)—and secondly my birth certificate is at Yasnaya; tell them to send it as soon as possible. Please don't be

[3] 1. Malaya Vorotynka, a small estate in the province of Tula which formed part of Tolstoy's inheritance when all the property was divided in 1847.

2. On 28 April 1849 the Russian Government declared its support for the Austrian Government in suppressing the Hungarian uprising and sent a detachment of four infantry regiments and one artillery brigade (not two corps, as Tolstoy writes) to assist the Austrians. Tolstoy was wrong in thinking that these troops were already in Vienna.

3. To Count S. N. Tolstoy

cross with me, I feel only too worthless as it is, but carry out my instructions quickly. Goodbye. Don't show this letter to Auntie, I don't want to upset her.

4. To T. A. YERGOLSKAYA

[Original in French]

Kazan,[1] 8 May 1851

Dear Aunt,

Here once again are these two words at the head of a sheet of paper, and here I am once again in difficulties. What am I going to write to you? And yet I have so much to tell you. Our journey has been most successful as regards the weather and the route. We spent two days in Moscow where I visited the Gorchakovs, Andrey[2] and Sergey,[3] and the Volkonskys,[4] and saw Lvov, Koloshin,[5] Kostenka[6] and all the people I like seeing.

I joined the promenaders in Sokolniki park in dreadful weather, that's why I met none of the society ladies I wanted to see. Seeing that you maintain that *I'm a man who's proving himself*, I went among the plebs, into the gipsy tents. You can easily imagine the inner conflict that was waged there, for and against; however, I came out of it victorious, i.e. having given nothing more than my blessing to the gay descendants of the illustrious Pharaohs.

Nikolay finds me a very pleasant travelling companion, except for my cleanliness; he gets angry because I change my underwear 12 times a day, as he puts it. I also find him a very pleasant companion, except for his dirtiness.

I don't know which of us is right.

I wrote to Valeryan[7] from Moscow that I'd won 400 roubles: I'm afraid this might alarm you; you'll believe that I'm gambling, and will do so again. Don't worry, it's an exception that I allow myself only with Mr Zubkov. It's only since arriving in Kazan that I've begun to regain my good humour and I'm taking advantage of it to write to you. All this time I haven't exactly been in a bad humour, but I just wasn't gay. You'll easily guess the reason for it.

You tried not to appear too sad at our departure; I noticed it and I'm grateful to you.

Have you received the portraits—and are you pleased with them?—I completely

---

[4] 1. Tolstoy and his brother Nikolay passed through Kazan en route for the Caucasus, where Nikolay was to be stationed with the 20th Artillery Brigade.

2. Prince A. I. Gorchakov, a cousin of Tolstoy's grandmother; he was an infantry general with whom Tolstoy's father had previously served as an adjutant.

3. Prince S. D. Gorchakov, a member of the branch of the Gorchakov family which served as the model for the Kornakovs in *Childhood* and *Youth*.

4. Probably Tolstoy's cousins Prince A. A. Volkonsky and his wife (the latter is portrayed in *War and Peace* as Princess Bolkonskaya).

5. Probably S. P. Koloshin, a minor author and editor.

6. K. A. Islavin, the youngest son of A. M. Islenyev and, of all his children, the one closest to Tolstoy.

7. V. P. Tolstoy, T. A. Yergolskaya's nephew.

5. To T. A. Yergolskaya

forgot...[Letter continued by N. N. Tolstoy:]...the purse for Mlle Vergani.⁸ Lev has just left to go and see Mrs Zagoskina and I'm finishing his letter. Tomorrow we're going to Panovo, and then we're going to continue our journey as soon as we find a steamship. That's the big problem for us now! At the moment there isn't a boat in Kazan, but one should arrive on the 10th, i.e. the day after tomorrow. As I can't stay in Kazan for long, it could happen that we'll leave by land, which will be rather unpleasant for us. Goodbye, my dear Aunt, I kiss your hand most tenderly; take care of yourself, be happy, and believe in the love of your affectionate and grateful Nikolay, Count Tolstoy.

5. To T. A. YERGOLSKAYA

[Original in French]

Stary Yurt,¹ 22 June 1851

Dear Aunt,

It's been a long time since I wrote to you; but I too have only received a few words from you in Valeryan's letter. ⟨Allow me to reprimand you for this⟩.

I arrived in ⟨Starogladovskaya⟩² towards the end of May, safe and sound, but a little sad. I've seen at close quarters the sort of life that Nikolay is leading and I've met the officers whose company he keeps. The sort of life is not as attractive as it appeared to me at first, for the countryside that I expected to find really beautiful isn't so at all. As the ⟨stanitsa⟩ is situated on low ground there's no view, and then the quarters are bad, as is everything that makes for comfortable living. As for the officers, they are, as you can imagine, uneducated people, but for all that a fine lot, and above all they are very fond of Nikolay. ⟨Alexeyev⟩,³ his superior, is a small, good-natured chap with ⟨reddish-blond hair in a little tuft, with a little moustache and whiskers, who talks in a shrill voice⟩, but a first-rate man, a good Christian slightly reminiscent of ⟨Alex. Serg. Voyeykov⟩,⁴ but not sanctimonious like him. Then there's a young officer, ⟨Buyemsky⟩—a child and a good one at that, who reminds one of ⟨Petrusha⟩. Then there's an old captain ⟨Khilkovsky⟩⁵ of the Ural

---

8. J. Vergani, Tolstoy's sister's governess in Kazan, and in the 1850s governess to the Arsenyevs.

[5] 1. A Chechen settlement near Grozny in the Caucasus. Tolstoy's journey to the Caucasus provided him with much material for *The Cossacks*.

2. Described in *The Cossacks* under the name of Novomlinskaya stanitsa. Stanitsa, a large Cossack village.

3. Commander of the 4th battery, 20th Artillery Brigade, in which Tolstoy also later served. There was some correspondence between them, and six of Alexeyev's letters to Tolstoy have survived.

4. A landowner, and guardian of the Tolstoy children when young. He supervised the division of the inheritance between them in 1847 and is portrayed as the neighbouring landowner to Nekhlyudov in *The Story of a Russian Landowner*.

5. Entries in Tolstoy's diary in 1852 indicate that he eventually became very friendly with both Khilkovsky and Buyemsky. He himself mentions that Buyemsky was the model for ensign Olenin in *The Raid*, while Captain Khlopov in the same story was partly based on Khilkovsky and to a lesser extent on Nikolay Tolstoy.

5. To T. A. Yergolskaya

cossacks, a simple old soldier, but noble, brave and good. I'll admit that at first, a lot of things shocked me in this company, but I've got used to it, without becoming too friendly with a single one of these gentlemen. I've found a happy medium in which there is neither pride nor familiarity; besides, I only had to follow Nikolay's example. Nikolay had hardly arrived before he was ordered to leave for ⟨the Stary Yurt fortress for the protection of the invalids at the Goryachevodsk camp⟩.[6] Not long ago they discovered hot mineral waters of various qualities that are said to be very beneficial for all catarrhal illnesses, wounds, and above all for illnesses of... It's even said that these waters are of higher quality than those of ⟨Pyatigorsk⟩. Nikolay left within a week of his arrival and I followed him, so that we've been here almost three weeks now, and are living in a tent, but as the weather is fine and I'm getting fairly used to this sort of life, I'm quite happy. There are magnificent views here. To mention first the place where the springs are—there is an enormous mountain of stones, one above the other, of which some have become detached and form grottoes of a kind, while others remain suspended at a terrific height, traversed[7] by torrents of hot water which fall noisily in several places and, especially in the morning, cover all the upper part of the mountain with a white vapour that rises continuously from this boiling water. The water is so hot that you can ⟨hard-boil⟩ an egg in three minutes. In the middle of this ravine, on the main torrent, there are three mills, one above the other. These mills are built here in a very special and picturesque way. All day long Tatar women come continually to wash their clothes above and below these mills. I must tell you that they do their washing with their feet. It's like an ants' nest in constant motion. The women are for the most part beautiful and well-formed. The costume of the oriental women is graceful, despite their poverty. The picturesque groups these women form, together with the savage beauty of the place, provide a really wonderful sight. I very often spend hours admiring this scenery. Then again, the view from the top of the mountain is even more beautiful and quite different; but I'm afraid of boring you with my descriptions. I'm very happy to be at the waters, for I'm benefiting from them. I take baths of ferruginous water and no longer feel pains in my feet. I've always had rheumatism, but I believe I caught a chill as well during our journey on the water.[8] I've rarely felt as well as I do now, and in spite of the great heat I'm being very active. The officers here are of the same type as those I've spoken to you about; there are a lot of them. I know them all, and my relations with them are the same. Tell Sergey that I embrace him and that what I've written to you is exactly what I would have written to him, and that I expect a letter from him. He knows very well what might interest me, so he won't have any difficulty in finding something to say. Goodbye, dear Aunt; I kiss your hand.

6. The fortified camp of Stary Yurt near Goryachevodsk ('Hot Springs') had been set up to protect the invalids taking the waters.
7. Liberties have been taken in translating the obscure French syntax here.
8. Tolstoy and his brother travelled by boat from Saratov to Astrakhan.

6. To T. A. YERGOLSKAYA

[Original in French]

Tiflis, 12 November 1851

Dear Aunt,

In 8 days it will be exactly 4 months since I had news from you; but now, at least, I have hopes that your letters are at ⟨Starogladovskaya⟩, and that it's only my absence from there which is the reason why I can't get them. In my last letter of 24 October I informed you that we were on the eve of our departure for Tiflis.[1] We set off in fact on the 25th, and after 7 days' journey—very tedious because of the lack of horses at almost every station, and very pleasant because of the beauty of the country we were passing through—we arrived in Tiflis on the 1st of this month. The next day I called on General Brimmer to present to him the papers I had received from Tula, and my own person. In spite of his German readiness to oblige and all his goodwill, the General has been obliged to turn me down, seeing that my papers were not in order and that I was without the documents which are for the moment at Petersburg and which I must wait for.[2] I am therefore resigned to waiting at Tiflis until the papers arrive; but since Nikolay's leave expired, he left three days ago. You can easily imagine, dear Aunt, how disagreeable this delay is in several respects. Firstly, if my papers don't arrive within a month I'll give up the idea of military service, since I shan't be able to take part this year in the winter campaign, which was my sole desire in joining up. Secondly, the cost of living being excessively high here, my stay in town for a month (perhaps more) and then the journey back will cost me a lot of money—and thirdly, I'm so used to being with Nikolay all the time, that this separation from him, even for a very short time, has been painful for me. It's only now, I confess to my shame, that I've learned to appreciate, respect and love this excellent brother as much as he deserves. All the time, dear Aunt, I keep recalling your excellent advice. How many times did you reprove me when I used to speak slightingly of Nikolay, and you were completely right; I say without any false modesty that in all respects Nikolay is worth far more than any of us. Contrary to all expectations I have found a good Petersburg acquaintance in Tiflis—Prince Bagration—who is a great support to me. He is a man of wit and education. Tiflis is a very civilised town which apes Petersburg a lot and almost succeeds in imitating it; the society here is select and quite large; there is a Russian theatre and an Italian opera, which I take advantage of as far as my slender means allow. I lodge in the German colony—it's a suburb, but it has

[6] 1. Tolstoy went to Tiflis primarily in order to take the examinations for entering the army as a cadet. Nikolay accompanied him.
2. In order to enter military service, it was necessary for Tolstoy to provide papers of resignation from the provincial administration at Tula, of which he was formally a member. Although these papers were only received by him in March 1852, Tolstoy had passed the examination to qualify as a cadet in January, and was engaged in active service at the end of January and throughout February, while attached to the 4th battery of the 20th Artillery Brigade. However, the failure to provide the necessary discharge papers rendered him ineligible to receive a St George Cross awarded to him for bravery in action on 18 February.

6. To T. A. Yergolskaya

two big advantages for me: one that it's a very pretty place, surrounded by gardens and vineyards, which makes you think that you're in the country rather than in town (it's still very nice and warm, and so far there's been neither snow nor frost); the second advantage is that I pay 5 silver roubles a month here for two quite clean rooms, whereas in town you couldn't get similar accommodation for less than 40 silver roubles a month. On top of everything else I get free practice in German. I have books, occupations and leisure time, since nobody comes and disturbs me, so that in short I'm not bored. Do you remember, dear Aunt, a piece of advice you once gave me—to write novels?³ Well, I'm following your advice and the occupations I speak of consist of writing literature.⁴ I don't know if what I'm writing will ever be published, but it's a work which amuses me and which I have persevered too long at to abandon.⁵ There you have an exact account of my occupations; as for my plans, if I don't enter military service, I'll try and find a civilian post here—but not in Russia, ⟨so that people can't say that I'm frittering my time away⟩. In any case I shall never regret having come to the Caucasus—it's an impulsive act which will be to my advantage. Goodbye. I kiss your hand and look forward to hearing from you. Address letters simply to ⟨Tiflis, Georgia⟩.

7. To COUNT N. N. TOLSTOY

Nikolay Nikolayevich Tolstoy (1823–60) was Tolstoy's eldest brother. He entered the Faculty of Mathematics in the University of Moscow in 1839, but transferred to the University of Kazan in 1843. He graduated in 1844 and joined the army, in which he served from 1844 to 1858, except for a period of two years, 1853–5, which he spent on his estate at Nikolskoye-Vyazemskoye, in the province of Tula. He died of consumption, in 1860, at Hyères in the South of France.

Of all his brothers, Tolstoy loved and respected Nikolay the most. He much admired Nikolay's indifference to the opinions of others, his total lack of pretentiousness, and his high moral and intellectual qualities. However, prolonged contact between the two brothers during the early 1850s resulted in a distinct deterioration in their relationship. 'The strangest thing of all about him', wrote Tolstoy, 'is that his great intellect and kind heart have produced nothing good. Some sort of link between these two qualities is lacking.'

After Nikolay's death Tolstoy wrote to A. A. Tolstaya: 'It is not enough that he was one of the best people I have met in my life, that he was my brother, that the best memories of my life are associated with him—he was also my best friend.' Both Turgenev and Fet, among others, have recorded their great liking for Nikolay.

During his lifetime Nikolay published only one work, in 1857, entitled *Hunting*

---

3. Tolstoy writes 'faire des romans'.
4. Tolstoy writes 'faire de la littérature'.
5. *Childhood*, the second draft of which was written in Tiflis.

7. To Count N. N. Tolstoy

in the Caucasus, based on his observations of life and nature in the Caucasus. Turgenev himself praised it.

When Lev Tolstoy was five years old, Nikolay announced to his brothers that he had discovered a secret, which, when it became known, would reveal how everyone might learn to be happy and to love each other and so become members of the 'ant brotherhood'. This secret he declared was written on a 'green stick', buried beside a particular path in the grounds of Yasnaya Polyana. Tolstoy remembered and treasured this legend of the 'ant brotherhood' and the 'green stick' all his life, and before he died he asked to be buried at the very spot that the 'green stick' was supposedly to be found. His wish was carried out.

Tolstoy's portrayal of Captain Khlopov in the story *The Raid* probably owes something to the character and personality of Nikolay; similarly, the portrait of the artillery captain Tushin in *War and Peace* is modelled on Nikolay, as Tolstoy himself noted in 1908.

Tiflis, 10 December 1851

My dear Nicolas,

I received a letter from you today, 10 December. I certainly like you referring to your letter as a *long epistle*. A long epistle on one sheet of notepaper, two words to a line! Your whole letter is like the endings of Mr Micawber's letters:

On
The
Top
Of
etc.

So your letter deserves a reproach for its brevity. Please ne te laisse pas décourager par ce reproche, but write by *every* post. If laziness (oh, baneful passion!) prevents you from doing so, tell Alyoshka, every day the post goes, to take a sheet of paper from your desk (with drawings of devils on, naturally),[1] put it in an envelope and send it to me. At least this will be proof for me that *unknown brigands have not yet made off with your head*.[2] Vanyushka[3] has worn out 3 pairs of shoes walking to the post, and this morning he came in, or rather ran into my room with clenched teeth and an envelope in his hand. Your letter satisfied me in all respects except for the fact that you are silent on certain points which I'm very keen to know about—namely pecuniary matters. I wrote and told you je serai sur les fèves; now I can

---

[7] 1. In his *Reminiscences of Childhood*, Tolstoy wrote of Nikolay: 'When he was not telling stories and not reading (he read a great deal), he used to draw. He almost always drew devils with horns and twirled moustaches...'

2. In his letter to Tolstoy, Nikolay had written: '*Unknown brigands made off with the head of a Georgian prince*', referring to an incident that had occurred at Dushet through which Nikolay had passed on his way to Yekaterinograd.

3. Ivan Vasilyevich Suvorov. In his *Reminiscences of Childhood*, Tolstoy wrote: 'Our guardian-auntie had the very stupid idea of giving us each a boy, with the intention that he should later become our devoted servant. Vanyushka was given to Mitenka.' Later Vanyushka was passed on to Tolstoy, and he accompanied him to the Caucasus where, among other things, he copied out some chapters of *Childhood*. Tolstoy portrayed Vanyushka in *The Cossacks*.

7. To Count N. N. Tolstoy

say je suis sur les fèves. My illness cost me a lot: 20 roubles for the chemist; 20 visits from the doctor, and now cotton wool and a cab every day cost 1.20. I tell you all these details so that you should send me as much money as you can as soon as possible. In my last letter I told you I needed 100 roubles to get away; now I see I shan't manage without 140. Help me as much as you can. Perhaps you think that I'm quite well now. Unfortunately I'm very unwell. La maladie vénérienne est détruite, mais ce sont les suites du Mercure qui me font souffrir l'impossible. Just imagine, my mouth and tongue are completely covered in sores, which prevent me eating and sleeping. Without any exaggeration, this is the second week I've eaten nothing, and I haven't slept a single hour. All these horse doctors and scoundrels! It's a good thing, though, that there are waters here, and, God willing, I'll get better somehow.

I was going to write to you about a very interesting matter, but I'm so tired that I'll go off to bed. I'll write by the next post, or, if I have time, I'll add something more. It's not worth giving the white horse away for 13 roubles. Goodbye. Don't forget to forward all letters from Russia and send me as much money as you can.

8. To COUNT S. N. TOLSTOY and M. M. SHISHKINA

Tiflis, 23 December 1851

My dear Seryozha,

What a shame that you and I don't correspond! What do 20 or 30 grivenniks[1] a year matter, and the few hours devoted to writing to each other? What pleasure we should get. At the present moment I'm so longing to talk any old nonsense to you, that if the envelope cost not 10 copecks but 30 roubles, I'd pay that much. I write and I envy you the pleasure you'll get when you read my letter. Any day now the long awaited order enrolling me as a bombardier in the 4th battery should come, and I'll have the pleasure of standing to attention and watching the officers and Generals ride past. Even now when I walk up and down the streets in my Scharmer coat and my folding hat for which I paid 10 roubles here[2]—in spite of all my dignified appearance in these clothes, I'm so used to the idea of donning a grey overcoat before long that I can't stop my right hand wanting to seize hold of my hat by the springs and let it down. Yes, Masha, if you drive past me in a cab with Wenzel or Gelke, I'll stand to attention by the pavement kerb, and stay in that position until you and Wenzel vanish out of sight. However, if my wish is fulfilled, I'll leave for Starogladovskaya the day of my enlistment, and from there go straight on to join the expedition, where I'll walk and ride about in a sheepskin or Circassian coat and to the best of my ability assist with the aid of a gun in destroying the *perfidious, predatory and recalcitrant Asiatics*. Marie[3] dans sa dernière lettre

---

[8] 1. Grivennik, a ten copeck piece.

2. Scharmer, the best tailor in Petersburg at the time. By 'folding hat' Tolstoy meant a *chapeau claque* or opera hat, with a spring interior.

3. Tolstoy's sister Marya (or Mashenka).

8. To Count S. N. Tolstoy and M. M. Shishkina

me parle de toi et de Masha (la bohémienne). Elle dit 'ma tante m'a dit que pendant son séjour à Pirogovo elle n'a pas une seule fois aperçu *la sultane* et que c'est une preuve de la délicatesse de Serge; moi, dit Marie, je ne vois en ceci qu'une preuve de froideur de la part de Serge et je plains beaucoup la pauvre fille si véritablement elle est délaissée, car je suis persuadée que ce n'est pour l'argent qu'elle s'est donnée et qu'elle aime Serge'.

That's what the pigeon-toed little Mashenka with the big eyes and rickets thought about it recently. How nice, how clever and what a wonderful heart! I entirely agree with her, and although I know that sooner or later you're bound to separate, and the sooner the better for you in some respects, nevertheless when the fine thread, I won't say chain, which binds your lovers' hearts together *breaks*, I shall be sad for the poor *sinner* Masha. What's her belly like?

Masha! Please have a boy and call him Lev, and choose me as his godfather in absence; even if I'm a debt-encumbered, burnt-out landowner, I'll buy some silk for christening robes with my last copeck and send it to you. The main reason I want this is so that when I go to Moscow in 1875 to get my son a job and I call in to see the Gipsies for old times' sake, I may find Lev Lvovich (my godson) there conducting the orchestra.[4] Seryozha, you see from my letter that I'm in Tiflis, where I arrived as long ago as 9 November,[5] so that I've managed to do a bit of hunting with the dogs I bought over there (in Starogladovskaya), but I've seen nothing of the dogs that have been sent down. The hunting here is wonderful! Open fields, marshes full of hares, and islands, not of woods but of reeds, where foxes are to be found. I've been out 9 times in all, 10 or 15 versts from the stanitsa, with two dogs, one of which is excellent and the other worthless, and I caught 2 foxes and about 60 hares. When I get back, I'll try and hunt goats. I've been out hunting wild boar and deer several times with guns, but I didn't kill anything myself. This sort of hunting is very pleasant too, but if you're used to hunting with borzois you can't grow really fond of it. In the same way, if you're used to smoking Turkish tobacco, you can't grow really fond of Zhukov, although it might be argued that it's better.

I know your weakness; you'll probably want to know who my friends were here, and who they are, and what my relations with them are. I must say that this point doesn't interest me at all here, but I hasten to satisfy you. There aren't many officers in the battery and so I know them all, if very superficially, although I'm popular with everyone because Nikolenka and I always have vodka, wine and a bite to eat for visitors. My acquaintance with the other officers in the regiment whom I happened to meet at Stary Yurt (the watering place where I lived in summer) and on the raid I was in, is founded and maintained on the same basis. Although they are decent people, more or less, I always have more interesting things to do without chatting to officers, and so I remain on the same terms with all of them. Lieutenant-Colonel Alexeyev, the commander of the battery which I'm joining, is a very kind, but vain man. I confess I took advantage of this latter defect of his and showed off a bit in front of him—I need him. But I did so

---

4. The misspelling in the original presumably indicates Masha's gipsy pronunciation.
5. In fact he arrived on 1 November.

8. To Count S. N. Tolstoy and M. M. Shishkina

unwittingly, and I regret it. With vain people you become vain yourself. I have 3 friends here in Tiflis. I haven't made any more friends than that, firstly because I didn't want to, and secondly because I haven't had the opportunity—I've been ill almost continuously and I've only been going out for a week. The first friend of mine is Bagration from Petersburg (a comrade of Ferzen). Here he's a very important Georgian Prince; but although he's very kind and often visited me during my illness—I must do him justice—like all Georgians, he's not distinguished by any great intelligence. The second is Prince Baryatinsky.[6] I met him during a raid in which I took part under his command, and then spent a day with him in a fort together with Ilya Tolstoy[7] whom I met here. This friendship certainly doesn't give me much pleasure, for you can understand the sort of footing on which a cadet and a general can be friends. The third friend of mine is a *chemist's assistant*, a Pole who's been reduced to the ranks, a most amusing creature. I'm sure that Prince Baryatinsky never dreamed he would appear side by side with a chemist's assistant in any list whatsoever, but there it is. Nikolenka is on an excellent footing here: both his superiors and his fellow officers love and respect him. Moreover, he enjoys the reputation of a brave officer. I love him more than ever before, and when I'm with him I'm completely happy, and without him I'm bored. How's Mitenka? I had a very bad dream about him on 22 December. Has anything happened to him? I hope you'll answer me and write about him, and yourself and your relations with Masha, and about various little amusing things—about the Chulkovs, the officer who harnessed the blacksmiths, Ovchinnikov, Andrey, the wet-nurse, Pyatakov etc. Yes, and write about Gasha (the Gipsy), and tell her that I imagine myself doing the chukmak-semyak[8] with her and that I hope she thrives for many years. I've completely forgotten Romany, because I've learned Tatar (better than I spoke Romany); when I spoke Tatar at first, I used to fill out sentences with Romany words, but now, when I met a Gipsy girl here, I spoke to her in Tatar from the beginning. The one thing I remember is kamama tu,[9] and I say it to you with all my heart. Goodbye; I can't think of anything else to say. Write what you know about the Perfilyevs[10] and Dyakov;[11] I wrote to them both, but I'm afraid they won't reply owing to their laziness and stupidity. Take my carriage—it's hired—and use it if it's any good to you, and deduct what you like for it from what I owe

---

6. Prince Baryatinsky, after serving in the Caucasus in the 1830s and again in the 1840s, commanded a division there in the early 1850s. During the Crimean War he served on the Turkish front and returned to the Caucasus in 1856 as Governor-General and Commander-in-Chief of the Caucasian Army. When the Caucasus was finally subjugated, he was appointed Field-Marshal. Tolstoy portrayed him as the general commanding the detachment in *The Raid*, and a diary entry of his records his fear that Baryatinsky might recognise himself in the story.
7. A first cousin once removed of Tolstoy.
8. Possibly a dance, although the expression is not known in Romany.
9. Romany for 'I love you.'
10. V. S. Perfilyev, who eventually became governor of Moscow, was friendly with Tolstoy all his life. According to Tolstoy's sister-in-law, Tolstoy included some of his characteristics in his portrait of Stiva Oblonsky in *Anna Karenina*.
11. D. A. Dyakov got to know Tolstoy in Kazan, and according to Tolstoy, their friendship provided him with the material for his description of the friendship between Nikolenka Irtenev and Nekhlyudov in *Youth*.

9. To T. A. Yergolskaya

you. My address is:– Kizlyarsky district, Starogladovskaya stanitsa, H.Q. 4th Battery, 20th Artillery Brigade, Caucasus.

If there's a daguerrotype studio in Tula, please send me your portrait. Please.

Find out in the Assembly of Deputies if my resignation papers have been sent off; if not, see that it's done at once. *It's very necessary*. If you want to boast of news from the Caucasus, you can tell people that Shamil's[12] number two, a certain Hadji Murat,[13] went over to the Russian government the other day. He was the leading horseman (dzhigit)[14] and brave in the whole of Chechnya, but it was a base thing to do. Furthermore, you can tell people with regret that the well-known, brave and intelligent General Sleptsov was killed the other day. If you want to know *was he in pain*, I can't say.

9. To T. A. YERGOLSKAYA

Tiflis, 28 December 1851

[Short extract from a letter begun on 28 December 1851, and finished on 3 January 1852. Original in French]

...3 January. Today at last I've received the order to set off and rejoin my battery, and I'm no longer a ⟨collegiate registrar⟩,[1] but a ⟨bombardier 4th class⟩. You wouldn't believe how much pleasure it gives me. How many people in the same position as me would have considered the greatest of misfortunes what I regard as the most pleasant things in the world. It's not from childishness that I find so much pleasure in donning a soldier's uniform, but I'm happy because at last I've succeeded in something which I've worked for and which I've wanted for a very long time; because nothing detains me any longer in Tiflis, where I'm bored to death; because I know you'll be pleased; and also because I'm happy not to be free any longer. It will perhaps seem strange to you that I desire *not* to be free. For too long I've been free in every way, and it seems to me that this excess of freedom is the main cause of my faults and that it actually is an evil. *Nothing to excess*. That's a principle which I'd be very glad to follow in all things...[25 lines omitted]

12. A disciple of Kazi Mullah, who headed the religious movement known as Muridism among the mountain peoples of the Caucasus. Kazi Mullah preached social justice and equality, and a holy war against the Russians. Under his leadership the various tribes began to unite in opposition to the Russians, but Kazi Mullah was killed in 1831, and Shamil replaced him as leader in 1834. He directed the resistance of the mountain peoples of Dagestan and Chechnya to the Russians from 1834 to 1859, when he was forced to surrender. He died at Mecca during a pilgrimage in 1871.

13. A chieftain of Avaria in central Dagestan. He joined Shamil in 1840, and fought against the Russians until 1851, when he went over to them, after an unsuccessful expedition to Tabarasan and a disagreement with Shamil. In 1852 he was killed in a skirmish with Cossack troops when attempting to return to the hills. His life is described by Tolstoy in *Hadji Murat*.

14. *Dzhigit* which means 'young' in Turkish was used in the Caucasus to describe a skilful and daring horseman.

[9] 1. The lowest (i.e. 14th) rank in the official hierarchy.

II
1852–1855

Tolstoy joined the regular army as a cadet at the beginning of 1852. For the next two years he was attached to an artillery brigade stationed in the Cossack village of Starogladovskaya, on the north bank of the river Terek, in the North Caucasus. Since Georgia had been annexed to Russia in 1801, the Russians had made spasmodic attempts to subdue the mountain tribes living between Georgia and the chain of Cossack forts protecting Russia's southern frontiers, and by the middle of the century Russian troops under the command of Prince Baryatinsky were concentrating their main efforts against the Chechen tribe led by the redoubtable Shamil. Tolstoy took part in a number of expeditions against the Chechens, being nearly killed by a grenade on one of them, and narrowly escaping capture on another. In 1854 he was commissioned and, after leave at Yasnaya Polyana, was transferred to active service on the Danube where the Russian army had been engaged in hostilities against Turkey since the previous autumn. Tolstoy reached Bucharest in March 1854, but saw little fighting. For most of the time he served as a staff officer, but illness and two operations seriously curbed his activities and in September 1854 he returned to Russia in the same month as British and French troops landed in the Crimea. He at once applied to be posted there, and reached Sevastopol in November when the allied siege was already under way. He spent the next year in the Crimea and for a short time in spring 1855 he was in charge of a gun battery on the outskirts of Sevastopol during some of the heaviest fighting of the war. Not long after the fall of Sevastopol, he was despatched as a courier to Petersburg, but shortly afterwards he sent in his resignation from the army, which became effective the following year. Before his release came through, however, he was promoted to the rank of lieutenant for 'outstanding bravery and courage' at the battle of the Chornaya river in August 1855—although on that particular occasion Tolstoy's battery had not been called upon to fire.

Tolstoy's service in the Caucasus, the Danube and the Crimea was by no means a full-time occupation. On the contrary, the story of these years is the story of various leisure activities, travel, reading and writing, debauchery, frequent illness and long periods of idleness, with just sufficient 'action' to provide the raw material for his stories of contemporary life, the Caucasus and its inhabitants, the skirmishes with the mountain tribesmen and the protracted defence of Sevastopol. His first published story *Childhood* appeared in 1852, followed by *The Raid* in 1853 and *Boyhood* in 1854. In 1855 he published *Sevastopol in December*, *Sevastopol in May* and *The Wood-felling*, and *Sevastopol in August* followed in 1856. As he remarked many years later when talking about his military career: 'I didn't become a general in the army, but I did in literature.'

10. To T. A. YERGOLSKAYA

[Original in French]

Tiflis, 6 January 1852

Dear Aunt,

I've just received your letter of 24 November, and am replying to you straightaway (as I've made a habit of doing). Recently I wrote to you that your letter made me cry, and I blamed this weakness on my illness.[1] I was wrong. For some time now all your letters have had the same effect on me. I've always been ⟨crybaby Lyova⟩. Formerly this weakness made me ashamed; but the tears I weep when I think of you and your love for us are so sweet that I let them flow without any false shame. Your letter is too full of sadness for it not to produce the same effect on me. It's you who have always given me counsel, and although unfortunately I haven't always followed it, I would like to act all my life on your advice only. But for the moment let me tell you the effect your letter has had on me, and the ideas that came to me while reading it. If I speak too frankly to you I know you'll forgive me on account of my love for you. When you say that it's your turn to leave us to go and join those who are no more and whom you loved so much; when you say that you ask God to put an end to your existence which seems to you so unbearable and isolated; forgive me, dear Aunt, but it seems to me when you say these things that you offend God and me and all of us who love you so much. You ask God for your death, i.e. the greatest misfortune that could happen to me—(this isn't just talk: God is my witness that the two greatest misfortunes that could happen to me would be your death and that of Nikolay—the two people I love more than myself). What would be left for me if God were to hear your prayer? For whose pleasure should I then wish to become better, to have good qualities, to have a good reputation in the world? When I make plans for happiness for myself, the idea that you will share and enjoy my happiness is always in my mind. When I do something good, I'm satisfied with myself because I know that you'll be satisfied with me. When I behave badly, what I fear most is to cause you sorrow. Your love is everything to me, and you ask God to separate us! I can't tell you the feeling that I have for you—words can't suffice to express it to you and I'm afraid you might think that I'm exaggerating, and yet I weep hot tears as I write to you. It's to this painful separation that I'm indebted for the knowledge of what a friend I have in you and how much I love you.

And am I the only one to have these feelings for you? And yet you ask God for death! You say that you're isolated. I may be separated from you, but if you believe in my love, the thought of it should have been enough to counterbalance your sorrow; for myself, wherever I am, I won't feel isolated as long as I know that I'm loved by you—as I am.

I feel, however, that the sentiment which prompts my words is a bad one—that I'm jealous of your grief. Today one of those things happened to me which

[10] 1. Tolstoy was suffering from venereal disease at the time.

10. To T. A. Yergolskaya

would have made me believe in God if I hadn't already believed in Him firmly for some time.

During the summer in ⟨Stary Yurt⟩, all the officers who were there did nothing but gamble, and for quite high stakes. Since it's impossible not to see each other often when living in camp, I was very often present during play, but despite all entreaties I refrained from joining in for a month. Then one fine day I jokingly placed a small stake—I lost; I did it again and lost again; I had bad luck; my passion for gambling was aroused, and in two days I lost all the money I had as well as what Nikolay gave me (about 250 silver roubles) and on top of that 500 silver roubles for which I gave a note of hand payable in the month of January 1852.[2] I should tell you that near the camp there is an ⟨aul⟩[3] where the ⟨Chechens⟩ live. A young boy (a ⟨Chechen⟩) named ⟨Sado⟩[4] used to come to the camp and play; but as he couldn't count or write things down, there were some scoundrels among the officers who cheated him. For this reason I never wanted to play against Sado, and even told him that he oughtn't to play because he was being cheated, and I offered to play on his behalf. He was very grateful to me for this and made me a present of a purse. As it's the custom of this people to exchange presents, I gave him a miserable gun that I'd bought for 8 roubles. I should tell you that to become a ⟨kunak⟩, that's to say a friend, it's the custom first of all to exchange presents and then to eat in the house of the ⟨kunak⟩. After that, according to the ancient custom of this people (which hardly survives now except in tradition), you become friends for life and death: i.e. if I ask him for all his money, or his wife, or his arms, or his most precious belongings, he must give them to me, and I must refuse him nothing either. Sado made me promise to come to his home and be his ⟨kunak⟩. I went. After having regaled me in their own manner, he invited me to choose anything in his house that I wanted: his arms, his horse, anything. I wanted to choose what was of least value, and took a horse bridle mounted in silver: but he told me I was offending him and made me take a ⟨sabre⟩ which is worth at least 100 silver roubles. His father is quite a rich man, but he keeps his money buried and doesn't give his son a farthing. To obtain money the son goes and robs the enemy of horses and cows, and sometimes he risks his life 20 times over to steal something that isn't worth 10 roubles; but he does it, not from greed, but because it's the thing to do. The greatest robber is highly esteemed and is called ⟨a dzhigit, a *brave*⟩. Sometimes Sado has 1,000 silver roubles, and sometimes he hasn't a farthing. After my visit to him I presented him with Nikolay's silver watch and we've become the greatest friends in the world. Several times he proved his devotion to me by exposing himself to danger on my behalf; but that's nothing to them—it's become a habit and a pleasure. When I left ⟨Stary Yurt⟩ Nikolay stayed on there, and Sado used to go to see him every day and say that he didn't know what would

2. Tolstoy lost this sum to Second-Lieutenant F. G. Knorring, an officer of the 20th Artillery Brigade.
3. Aul, a Caucasian village.
4. Sado Miserbiyev, a Chechen serving in the Russian army. Sado preserved Tolstoy's letters and gifts until his death. He is portrayed as the kunak of Hadji Murat in Tolstoy's story of that name.

10. To T. A. Yergolskaya

become of him without me and that he was terribly bored. I let Nikolay know by letter that my horse was sick, and I asked him to find me one at ⟨Stary Yurt⟩. When Sado learned of this he lost no time in coming to see me and giving me his horse, despite all I could do to refuse it. After the folly I committed of gambling at ⟨Stary Yurt⟩, I haven't touched a card again, and I've continually lectured Sado, who has a passion for gambling and, although he doesn't know the game, always has astonishing luck. Yesterday evening I busied myself thinking about my financial affairs and my debts, and I was thinking how I should go about paying them.

Having thought about these things for a long time, I saw that if I didn't spend too much money, all my debts wouldn't embarrass me and could be paid off little by little in two or three years; but the 500 roubles that I had to pay this month were driving me to despair. It was impossible for me to pay them and at that moment they embarrassed me far more than Ogaryov's 4,000[5] had done previously. My stupidity in having contracted debts in Russia, and then in coming and contracting new ones here was driving me to despair. In the evening when saying my prayers, I prayed to God—and very fervently—to get me out of this unpleasant position. 'But how can I get myself out of this business?' I thought when going to bed. I already pictured to myself all the unpleasantness I would have to endure because of it, ⟨how he would take proceedings against me, how the authorities would demand an explanation from me as to why I wasn't paying, etc. 'Help me Lord', I said and fell asleep.⟩ This morning I received a letter from Nikolay, enclosing yours and several others. He writes: ⟨'The other day Sado came to see me: he had won your note of hand from Knorring and brought it to me. He was so pleased with his winnings, so happy, and he asked me so many times "What do you think, will your brother be glad that I've done this"—that I've grown very fond of him as a result. This man really is attached to you.'⟩

Isn't it astonishing to see one's wish granted like this the very next day? Or rather the only astonishing thing is the divine goodness towards a being who has merited it as little as I. Don't you think that Sado's sort of devotion is wonderful? He knows that I've a brother Sergey who loves horses, and as I've promised to take him to Russia when I go, he's told me that if it should cost him his life 100 times over, he'll steal the best horse there is in the mountains and bring it to him.

Please get someone to buy a ⟨six-barrelled pistol⟩ in Tula and send it to me, also a ⟨musical-box⟩ if it's not too expensive—these are things which will give him great pleasure.

⟨I'm still in Tiflis, sitting by the seaside, waiting for good weather, i.e. money.⟩ Goodbye, dear Aunt. Lev kisses your hand a thousand times.

5. V. I. Ogaryov, the son of I. M. Ogaryov, a friend of Tolstoy's father and a neighbouring landowner of Tula.

11. To T. A. YERGOLSKAYA

[Original in French]   Mozdok, a posting-station half-way from Tiflis,
12 January 1852

Dear Aunt,

Here are some ideas that have occurred to me. I'll try to express them to you, because I've been thinking of you. I find myself much changed morally, a thing that has happened to me so many times. But then I believe it happens to everyone. The more one lives, the more one changes. You have experience; tell me isn't that true? I think that one's defects and qualities—the basis of one's character—will always remain the same, but one's way of looking at life and happiness must change with age. A year ago I thought I would find happiness in pleasure, in movement; now, on the contrary, tranquillity, physical as well as moral, is the state I desire. Indeed, if I picture to myself a state of tranquillity, without boredom but with the peaceful delights of love and friendship—that is the height of happiness for me! But then one only feels the charm of tranquillity after tiredness, and the delights of love after deprivation. Here I've been deprived for some time now of the one as well as of the other, and that's why I yearn for them so eagerly. I *must* deprive myself of them longer still. How long for? God knows. I couldn't say why, but I feel *that I must*. Religion and the experience I have of life (however small it may be) have taught me that life is a trial. For me it is more than a trial, it is also an expiation of my faults.

I rather fancy that the really frivolous idea I had of making a journey to the Caucasus is an idea which I was inspired with from above.[1] It's the hand of God that has guided me—I never cease to thank Him for it; I feel that I've become better here (and that's not saying much, since I've been very bad) and I'm firmly convinced that all that can happen to me here will only be for my good, since it is God himself who has willed it so. Perhaps it's a very impudent idea, but this is the conviction I have all the same. That's why I bear all the hardships and deprivations I mention (they are not physical deprivations—there are none for a fellow of 23 who is in good health) without feeling them, and even with a kind of pleasure, in thinking of the happiness in store for me. This is how I picture it to myself. After an unspecified number of years I am at ⟨Yasnaya⟩, neither young nor old—my affairs are in order, I have no anxieties, no worries—and you still live at ⟨Yasnaya⟩ too. You have aged a little, but are still fresh and in good health. We lead the life that we used to lead; I work in the morning, but we see each other almost the whole day; we have dinner; in the evening I read you something that doesn't bore you; then we talk. I tell you of my life in the Caucasus, you talk to me of your memories—of my father and mother; you tell me ⟨frightening stories⟩ that we once listened to with startled eyes and gaping mouths. We recall the people

---

[11] 1. In fact Tolstoy left for the Caucasus with Nikolay at the latter's own suggestion. Among the reasons Tolstoy later gave was his desire to escape from his debts and from his 'habits'—especially his susceptibility to women.

11. To T. A. Yergolskaya

who were dear to us and who are now no more; you will weep, I will do the same; but these tears will be sweet. We will talk of my brothers who will come to see us from time to time, and of dear Marya,² who will also spend some months of the year at ⟨Yasnaya⟩, which she so loves, with all her children. We won't have any friends—no one will come and bore us and talk gossip. It's a beautiful dream, but it's still not all that I allow myself to dream of. I am married—my wife is a sweet, good, affectionate person; she loves you in the same way as I do. We have children who call you 'grandmama'; you live in the big house, upstairs—the same room that grandmama used to live in; the whole house is as it was in papa's time, and we begin the same life again, only changing roles; you take the role of grandmama, but you are even better; I take the role of papa, but I despair of ever deserving it; my wife, that of mama; the children—our own; Marya—the role of the two aunts, excepting their misfortunes. Even ⟨Gasha⟩³ will take the role of ⟨Praskovya Isayevna⟩.⁴ But we shan't have anyone to take the role that you have played in our family. Never shall we find a soul as beautiful or as affectionate as yours. You will have no successor. There will be three new persons who will appear on the scene from time to time—my brothers—especially the one who will often be with us—Nikolay—an old bachelor, bald, retired from service, as noble as ever.

⟨I imagine how, as in the old days, he will tell the children fairy stories of his own invention; how the children will kiss his greasy (but deserving) hands; how he will play with them; how my wife will go to the trouble to make him his favourite meal; how he and I will recall common memories of time long past; how you will sit in your usual place and listen to us with pleasure; how, as before, you will call us old men 'Lyovochka and Nikolenka', and will scold me for eating with my fingers, and him for not having clean hands.⟩

If they made me Emperor of Russia, if they gave me Peru, in a word if a fairy came with her wand to ask me what I desired; my hand on my heart, I would reply that my only desire is for this to become a reality. ⟨I know you don't like to look into the future⟩, but what harm is there, and it gives so much pleasure. I'm afraid I may have been selfish and made your share of happiness too small. I'm afraid that the misfortunes of the past which have left too sensitive a trace in your heart might prevent you from enjoying this future which would have made my happiness. Dear Aunt, tell me: would you be happy? All that could come to pass, and hope is such a sweet thing.

I'm crying again. Why do I cry when I think of you? They are tears of happiness —I am happy to be able to love you. If every misfortune were to befall me, I would never call myself completely unhappy as long as you existed. You remember our parting at the ⟨Iverskaya⟩ Chapel when we were leaving for Kazan. Then, as if by inspiration, at the moment I was leaving you, I understood all that you meant to us, and although still a child, I was able to make you understand by my tears and

---

2. Tolstoy's sister.
3. Tolstoy's grandmother's maid. She remained in service at Yasnaya Polyana until her death in 1896. She is portrayed as the maid Gasha in *Childhood* and *Boyhood*.
4. The Tolstoys' housekeeper—portrayed as Natalya Savishna in *Childhood*.

12. To T. A. Yergolskaya

some disjointed words what I felt. I have never ceased to love you, but the feeling I experienced at the ⟨Iverskaya⟩ Chapel, and which I now have for you, is quite different, much stronger and more noble than I have ever had at any other time.

I'm going to confess something to you which makes me ashamed, but which I must tell you in order to ease my conscience. Formerly, when reading your letters in which you spoke to me of the feelings you had for us, I thought I saw exaggeration, and only now on reading them again do I understand you—your boundless love for us and your noble soul. I'm sure that anyone other than you reading this letter and the last one would have made the same reproach to me; but I don't fear that from you: you know me too well and you know that perhaps my only good quality is my sensibility. It is to this quality that I am indebted for the happiest moments of my life. At all events, this is the last letter in which I'll allow myself to express such exalted feelings—exalted for those who don't matter to one—but you will be able to appreciate them. Goodbye, dear Aunt; in a few days I hope to see Nikolay again, and I will write to you then.

12. To T. A. YERGOLSKAYA

[Original in French]

⟨Pyatigorsk⟩, 30 May–3 June 1852

Dear Aunt,

I haven't any good reason to excuse my silence, so I'll begin by asking your forgiveness. After I returned from the expedition[1] I spent 2 months with Nikolay at ⟨Starogladovskaya⟩. We led our usual way of life there: hunting, reading, talking, playing chess. During that time I made a very interesting and enjoyable excursion to the Caspian Sea. I would have been completely satisfied with those two months if I hadn't been ill during that time; however, ⟨every cloud has a silver lining⟩: my illness gave me an excuse to go and spend the summer at ⟨Pyatigorsk⟩, where I'm writing to you from.

I've been here for two weeks and am leading a regular, secluded kind of life, with the result that I'm satisfied with my health as well as with my behaviour. I get up at 4 o'clock to go and take the waters, which lasts until 6. At 6 I take a bath and return home. I read or chat while taking tea with one of our officers who lodges next door to me and with whom I share board; after that I sit down and write until midday— the hour at which we lunch. ⟨Vanyushka⟩,[2] with whom I'm perfectly satisfied, feeds us cheaply and reasonably well. I sleep until four; I play chess or I read; I go to the waters again, and when I return, if the weather is fine, I have tea served in the garden and sometimes I spend whole hours dreaming of ⟨Yasnaya⟩, of the tranquil moments I have spent there, and above all of an Aunt whom I love more day by day. The more distant these memories become, the more I love them and am able

---

[12] 1. Against the Chechens in January–February 1852.   2. I. V. Suvorov.

12. To T. A. Yergolskaya

to appreciate them. Although it's sad to think of past happiness, and above all of the happiness which one has allowed to pass by without having been able to profit from, yet I love this kind of sadness, and at times derive from it the sweetest moments.

Since my journey to Tiflis and my stay there, my way of life hasn't changed: I try to make as few friends as possible and to shun the intimacy of those that I have. People have become used to my manner and don't pester me any more, and I'm sure they say I'm a ⟨crank⟩ and an ⟨arrogant fellow⟩. It's not through pride that I behave in this way: it's come about of its own accord; there's too big a gap in education, feelings and outlook on things between myself and those I meet here for me to find any pleasure in being with them. It's only Nikolay who has the talent, despite the enormous difference there is between him and all these gentlemen, to enjoy himself with them and to be liked by all. I envy him this talent, but I feel I couldn't do as much myself. It's true that this kind of life is not made for enjoying oneself; also for a long time now I've stopped thinking of pleasures: I think only of being quiet and content. For some time I've been developing a taste for historical books (this was a point of dispute between us, and one about which I'm now entirely of your opinion); my literary pursuits are also jogging along, although I'm still not thinking of publishing anything. Three times I've rewritten a work I began a long time ago, and I'm counting on rewriting it once more, to be satisfied with it.[3] Perhaps this will be like the labour of Penelope; but I don't find that distasteful: I don't write from ambition, but from taste—I find my pleasure and my usefulness in working, and I work. Although I may be very far from enjoying myself, as I've told you, I'm also very far from being bored, because I'm busy; and apart from that, I enjoy a more delightful and more noble pleasure than that which society could have given me—that of feeling my conscience at rest, of knowing myself and of being able to appraise myself better than I have done, and of feeling good and generous feelings stir within me. There was a time when I prided myself on my intelligence, on my position in the world, on my name; but now I know and feel that if there is something good in me, if I have reason to give thanks to God, it is for a heart which is good, sensitive and capable of love, and which it has pleased Him to give me and preserve in me. It is to Him alone that I am indebted for the sweetest moments I spend and for the fact that, despite the absence of pleasures and society, I am not only content, but often happy. I will soon have been serving for 5 months, so in a month I should have been promoted; but I know that another six months will pass and perhaps more before I receive a rank. My hand on my heart, I am utterly indifferent to this; the only thing that worries me is the journey to Petersburg that I'll have to make, and for which I haven't the means.

⟨I remember your rule that *one mustn't look into the future*—things will work out somehow.⟩

Goodbye, dear Aunt; I'm finishing this letter because it's late; but as the post only leaves in two days' time and a day doesn't pass without my thinking of you, I'll

3. *Childhood.*

12. To T. A. Yergolskaya

probably continue it. So, goodbye for now. What is Aunt Polina doing?[4] Is she well? Is she still satisfied with her way of life?

I think of her often, of her strange life, which must be basically very sad; I tell myself that it's very bad of me to have broken off relations with her, although unwittingly, and I promise myself to write to her, but it's so difficult to begin, or to resume an interrupted correspondence.

3 June. The only way for me to write to you without being tempted to tear up what I've written is not to reread it. It seems to me that sometimes my letter is cold, sometimes stupid, sometimes impassioned; I'm never satisfied with it; I'm so afraid of shocking you, of giving you cause for uncertainty or anxiety on my account, and I do so want my letters to please you.

I've just learned in a letter from Andrey[5] that you are expected at ⟨Yasnaya⟩. I don't know why, but nothing gives me so much pleasure as to know that you are at ⟨Yasnaya⟩; it seems to me that it brings me closer to you, and then my imagination can only picture you in your little room in the wing, on your ⟨little sofa from Pirogovo⟩[6] with the sphinx's heads, in front of your little table that you like so much, and your ⟨chiffonier⟩ beside you, ⟨which contains everything⟩. When we are short of something, Nikolay and I always say ⟨we haven't got Auntie's chiffonier⟩. Get Andrey to show you the letter in which I mention to him the titles of the French books I need, and be so good as to send them to me.

Be so good also as to tell him to send the 100 roubles I told him to obtain to ⟨Pyatigorsk, No. 252 Kabardinskaya village⟩ (that's my address). I'm extremely dissatisfied with Andrey, and have written to Sergey asking him kindly to take charge of ⟨Yasnaya⟩; I've asked him to write and tell me if he'll agree to take a serious interest in my affairs, which becomes more necessary from day to day; judging from Andrey's letters and ⟨the registers⟩, I can see clearly that he only spends his time drinking and stealing. Up to now, either through laziness or for some other reason, Sergey hasn't resolved my uncertainty on this point. ⟨Please take him to task for this.⟩

Goodbye, dear Aunt; I kiss your hand.

And it's you who speak to me of gratitude in your last letter! I assure you, dear Aunt, that despite all the confidence I have in your heart, I thought for a moment that you were making fun of me. The fact is that it would be too ridiculous for me to take seriously from you, to whom we owe everything, words of gratitude for things which don't require the slightest sacrifice on my part. Goodbye, and au revoir, dear Aunt. In a few months, if the good God doesn't interfere with the plans I'm making, I'll be with you, and in a position to prove to you by my attentions and my love that I've deserved in some small way all that you've done for us. My memory of you is so vivid that after having written this, I left off writing for a few minutes and tried to picture to myself the happy moment when I would see

---

4. P. I. Yushkova, at once both a sociable and deeply religious person. Her marriage was not a success, and she was separated from her husband for long periods.
5. A. I. Sobolev.
6. Sergey Tolstoy's estate in the province of Tula.

12. To T. A. Yergolskaya

you again, when you would weep with joy at seeing me and I too would weep like a child as I kiss your hands. Without exaggeration, there's nothing in all my life that I've looked forward to with such impatience and expectation of happiness as I now look forward to that happy moment. I wanted to address this letter to Sergey, but in spite of myself I've let myself be carried away by the pleasure of speaking to you of my feelings, and as the gibes he might make about it would be too painful for me, I prefer to address it to you and ask you to show him only the first page. I'm sure he has a heart no less sensitive than mine, but a certain false shame he has in speaking of his feelings deprives him of the moral pleasure which I feel at this moment in writing to you and thinking of you. The idea that what I'm writing to you might appear exaggerated or ridiculous to a stranger doesn't concern me at all—I'm so convinced that you'll always understand me.

13. To T. A. YERGOLSKAYA

[Original in French]

⟨Pyatigorsk⟩, 26 June 1852

Why have you offended me, dear Aunt? You begin your letter by telling me that your letters probably bore me, seeing that it's so long since I wrote to you. Do you really think that this reason alone could have prevented me from writing to you? If you take that to be the reason, it probably means you don't believe a word of what I write to you, and that you take me for a hypocrite, parading feelings he doesn't have. I haven't deserved such mistrust on your part. If I can't explain to you all the causes of my actions as I could have done in conversation, it's not I who am to blame, but our separation. I believe, dear Aunt, that it's not correspondence which is the best means of making separation less painful, but mutual confidence; and you don't have confidence in me. Since I left you, I've never been troubled by the slightest doubt about your feelings for me; but you have doubts about me, dear Aunt, and you would never believe how much that hurts me. However, I'm talking absolute nonsense; have I the right to doubt your feelings? You have proved them by a whole lifetime of love and steadfastness, whereas I—what have I done? I've caused you grief, I've spurned your advice, I've not known how to appreciate your love. Yes, you have the right to think me a hypocrite and a liar; but you are wrong to do so.

It has always been a point of honour with me not to conceal my behaviour, of whatever kind and to whatever person. You must have done something bad to want to conceal your actions from the eyes of people who don't matter to you. You must have something terrible to reproach yourself with to keep things back from a person you love. God who looks into the depth of my heart and guides it knows that thanks to Him there is no period of my life which I have spent more irreproachably or which has given me more inner contentment than the 8 months between my journey to Tiflis and the present day. I say this not in order to satisfy my vanity, but because I know that if you believe me, it will be pleasant for you to know. Yes, dear Aunt, you have cruelly offended me in believing me to be a hypocrite. I have nothing to hide from anybody, least of all from you.

Now I'm going to try to explain what seems obscure to you about my service affairs, and also the reasons why I haven't done so sooner. ⟨I wrote to you from Tiflis to say that my resignation had not been received, but that in spite of that I had donned a uniform and was setting off for the battery. This is how General Wolf arranged it. He gave orders for a paper to be sent to the battery saying that *'Count Tolstoy has declared his wish to enter the service, but since his resignation has not been received he cannot enlist as a cadet; I therefore instruct you to take him on, with the intention of enlisting him for active service on receipt of his resignation, with seniority dating from the time he is taken on in the battery.'*⟩ I put this paper in my pocket and set off for ⟨Starogladovskaya⟩. I didn't find Nikolay there; he was on an expedition. I donned my uniform and set off to rejoin him; i.e. ⟨I was taken on, but I wasn't yet enlisted.⟩ The missing paper arrived in Tiflis in January, but only reached ⟨Starogladovskaya⟩ in March—i.e. after our return from the expedition.

I wrote that we had returned from the expedition to reassure you on our account, having been indiscreet enough to have written to Sergey that I was intending to go. I wrote that I'd gone as a volunteer, so that you should know that I could hope neither for promotion nor for a cross. I didn't mention this in my letter before last so as not to repeat something equally disagreeable to you as to me—namely that I have persistent bad luck in everything I undertake. During this expedition I twice had the chance to be nominated for the St George Cross, but I wasn't able to receive it because of the few days' delay over this wretched paper. I was nominated for it on 17 February (my name-day), but they had to turn me down because this paper was missing. The list of nominations went off the on 19th, and the paper arrived on the 20th.[1] I frankly confess that of all military honours, it's that little cross alone that I had the vanity to covet, and that this misfortune caused me bitter resentment, the more especially since there's only one time for receiving it, and as far as I'm concerned that has now passed. You can well believe that I concealed the resentment it caused me not only from those who don't matter, but also from Nikolay; for the same reason I didn't speak to you about it either; but now I have had to tell you, since you mistake my discretion for hypocrisy...[17 lines omitted]

14. To N. A. NEKRASOV

Nikolay Alexeyevich Nekrasov (1821–77), poet and editor, was an extra-mural student at the University of Petersburg from 1839 to 1841. His first volume of poetry, entitled *Dreams and Sounds*, was published in 1840. Among his best-known works are *Red-nose Frost* (1864) and *Who Can be Happy in Russia?* (written over the period 1866–76). Towards the end of 1846 Nekrasov, together with I. I.

[13] 1. I.e. March 1852.

14. To N. A. Nekrasov

Panayev, gained control of the journal *The Contemporary*, founded by Pushkin in 1836, and, during the 1850s, the leading Russian literary journal. From 1847 to 1866 he was the publisher and chief editor of *The Contemporary*. Tolstoy was closely connected with the journal until 1859, and entrusted the publication of his *Sevastopol Stories* and of *Childhood*, *Boyhood* and *Youth*, among other works, to Nekrasov. He ceased to publish in *The Contemporary* because of his dissatisfaction with its increasingly radical political bias and the actual presentation of material in the journal. The new political bias was almost certainly related to the fact that in the mid-1850s the writer and critic N. G. Chernyshevsky became one of the editors of the journal. Thirty-three of Tolstoy's letters to Nekrasov have survived, and twenty-nine of Nekrasov's to Tolstoy.

Starogladovskaya, 3 July 1852

Dear Sir,

My request will cost you so little effort that I am sure you will not refuse to grant it. Look through this manuscript,[1] and if it is not fit to publish, return it to me. Otherwise evaluate it, send me what you think it is worth and publish it in your journal. I agree in advance to all the cuts which you may find necessary to make in it, but I want it to be published without additions or alterations.

Properly speaking this manuscript constitutes the first part of a novel—*Four periods of growth*; the appearance of the subsequent parts will depend on the success of the first. If because of its size it cannot be published in one number, please divide it into three parts: the beginning to chapter 17, chapter 17 to chapter 26, and chapter 26 to the end.

If it had been possible to find a good clerk where I live, the manuscript would have been better copied, and I would not have feared the unnecessary prejudice which you will now certainly entertain towards it.

I am convinced that an experienced and conscientious editor—especially in Russia—can always determine in advance the success of a work of literature and the public's opinion about it through his position as permanent mediator between author and reader. Therefore I await your verdict with impatience. It will either encourage me to continue my favourite occupation, or force me to burn all that I have begun.

With the utmost respect,
I have the honour to be, Sir,
Your obedient servant,
L.N.

[Postscript omitted]

[14] 1. *Childhood*.

15. To N. A. NEKRASOV

Starogladovskaya, 15 September 1852

Dear Sir,

I was delighted by the favourable opinion you expressed about my novel,[1] all the more so because it was the first opinion I had heard about it, and because it was actually yours. In spite of that, I repeat the request I made to you in my first letter to evaluate the manuscript, send me the money which you think it is worth or else tell me frankly that it is not worth anything.

The autobiographical form which I have adopted and the forced connection of the subsequent parts with the previous one so inhibit me that I often feel the desire to scrap them and to leave the first part without a sequel.

However, if and when the sequel is finished, I will send it to you at once. In anticipation of your reply, I have the honour to be, Sir,

With true respect,
Your obedient servant,
L.N.

[Postscript omitted]

16. To T. A. YERGOLSKAYA

[Original in French]

⟨Starogladovskaya⟩, 2 October 1852

Dear Aunt,

It's been quite a long time since I received one of your nice letters. God grant, as I hope, that this silence isn't due to anything serious. Perhaps this delay is simply due to the unreliability of the post; however, I feel the need to write to you: it will soothe me. On my return from the waters, I spent a rather disagreeable month because of the inspection that the General was to make. ⟨Marching about and firing off guns wasn't very pleasant, especially since it upset the routine of my life.⟩ Happily that didn't last long, and I've again resumed my way of life, which consists of hunting, writing, reading and talking with Nikolay. I've acquired a taste for shooting, and as it happens that I shoot tolerably well, this occupation takes up 2 or 3 hours of my day. They've no idea in Russia how much game one finds here and how excellent it is. There are pheasants 100 paces from where I live and I kill 2, 3, or 4 of them in the space of half an hour. Besides the pleasure, the exercise is excellent for my health, which, despite the waters, isn't in a very good state. I'm not ill, but I very often suffer from chills: sometimes from a sore throat, sometimes from toothache (which always drags on), and sometimes from rheumatic pains, so that I

---

[15] 1. In August Nekrasov had written to Tolstoy: 'I have read your manuscript (*Childhood*). It has so much of interest in it that I will publish it. Without seeing the sequel I cannot say definitely, but it seems to me that its author has talent. At any rate, the author's general approach, and the simplicity and reality of the content constitute the work's assured merit. If in the succeeding parts (as may be expected) there is more liveliness and movement, then it will be a good novel.'

16. To T. A. Yergolskaya

keep to my room at least 2 days a week. Don't think I'm hiding something from you: I'm just the same as I've always been, with a strong constitution but weak health. I'm reckoning on spending next summer at the waters too. If they haven't restored me to health, they have done me good. ⟨Every cloud has a silver lining.⟩ When I'm not feeling well, I get on with less distraction with the task of writing another novel that I've begun.[1] The one I sent to Petersburg was printed in the September issue of *The Contemporary*, 1852, under the title of ⟨*Childhood*⟩. I signed it L.N., and nobody except Nikolay knows its author. I wouldn't want him to be known either. My promotion is not progressing. Shall I be an officer and shall I go to Petersburg this year? That's what I don't know: perhaps yes, perhaps no. It would take too long to explain why, but the simple truth is that it depends on circumstances. I assure you that it's all the same to me; I didn't make any ambitious plans in coming to the Caucasus, and I'm not making any now: don't go making any for me! I don't even know where you are, but in addressing this letter to ⟨Yasnaya⟩, I'm sure it will reach you. If you're with Sergey, tell him that I feel very much at fault towards him and that I'll atone for my fault by the next post by writing him a long letter. I'm deeply interested in the state of his financial and love affairs. If you're with Marya, kiss her from me and tell Valeryan that I love him and thank him with all my heart. Goodbye, dear Aunt; I kiss your hand, and so does Nikolay. He very much wants to write to you, but you know his trouble. Perhaps what is left of this sheet of paper will tempt him.[2]

17. To T. A. YERGOLSKAYA

[Original in French]

⟨Starogladovskaya⟩, 29 October 1852

Dear Aunt,

I don't understand, nor can I explain to myself your long silence. Have I had the misfortune to deserve it? In that case, forgive me; but don't deprive me of your letters. You wouldn't believe what value they have for me. They give me peace of mind, cheerfulness, courage and a pleasure which I can't convey to you; I read them and reread them 100 times—they mark an epoch in my life. Write to me often, dear Aunt. I have a small reproach to make to you: why do you show people the letters I write to you? I have told you and have written to you that there is nobody I love as much as you, and that I'm convinced that I'm truly loved only by you: that's why the letters I write to you are different from those I write to other people and I wouldn't like everyone to read them. The demon who has taken it upon himself to wreck all my schemes continues his work. Yesterday I received a paper according to which I'm not able to be promoted for 2 years, as from today.

[16] 1. *The Novel of a Russian Landowner*. Notes in Tolstoy's diary relating to this work begin on 10 May 1852, but he only began writing on 23 September. It was eventually published as *A Landowner's Morning*.
    2. A brief note follows from Nikolay.

18. To N. A. Nekrasov

This news distressed me. The happy moment of seeing you again that I thought had come is now postponed for 2 years. Yes, the plans that I made in one of my letters are too beautiful to be realised so soon. All that has happened to me, and that appeared to be unfortunate for me, has been for my good; I hope God will not abandon me and that it will continue to be so in future. The 18 months that I've spent in the Caucasus have made me less bad; I'll try to make good use of the 2 years that I still have to spend here to become better still, worthy of you and of the happiness that I look forward to with you. My health is good; my occupations are still the same; hunting still gives me great pleasure. Last week I killed a boar, which gave me a moment of joy such as I've never experienced before. I presume you are at Pokrovskoye, judging from a letter from the steward; in which case kiss Marya, the children and Valerian from me. Tell Valeryan that I still haven't received the 60 roubles that were mentioned to me; that I beg him to send 300 silver roubles to me as soon as possible (a sum which will suffice me, I hope, until the next harvest); that I'm perfectly happy with his arrangements; that I thank him for all his trouble and that I beg him to continue doing what he has begun so well! Goodbye. I kiss your hand.

18. To N. A. NEKRASOV

[Not sent]

Starogladovskaya, 18 November 1852

Dear Sir,

I was extremely displeased to read in *The Contemporary*, No. IX, a *story*[1] entitled *A History of My Childhood*, and to recognise it as the *novel Childhood* which I sent to you. I made it the first condition of publication that you should *first evaluate the manuscript and send me what you think it is worth*. This condition has not been fulfilled. The second condition was that nothing should be altered in it. Still less has that condition been fulfilled: you have altered everything, starting with the title. Having read this pathetic, mutilated story with the saddest of feelings, I tried to discover the reasons which prompted the editors to behave so ruthlessly towards it. Either the editors set themselves the task of mutilating this novel as much as possible, or else they entrusted the proof-reading, without any checking, to a completely illiterate employee. The title *Childhood* and the few words of the introduction explained the idea of the work; but the title *A History of My Childhood* contradicts the idea of the work. Who is interested in the history of *my* childhood? ...*The portrait of my mama* instead of the *icon of my angel*[2] on the 1st page is the

---

[18] 1. Tolstoy was dissatisfied with the subtitle 'a story' given by the journal, despite the fact that in his diary and letters he himself refers to *Childhood* as 'a story'. The subtitle 'a novel' is not even to be found in Tolstoy's own published edition of the work in 1856.

2. The 'icon of my angel' was changed to the 'portrait of my mama', not by Nekrasov but by the censor, who was also responsible for some of the other changes in the work. Tolstoy restored most of these to the original in the 1856 edition, but a comparison of this edition with the text suggests that he considerably exaggerated the alleged 'mutilation'.

18. To N. A. Nekrasov

sort of alteration which would make any respectable reader give up the book without reading any further. It is not possible or necessary to list all the alterations of this sort; but not to speak of the innumerable scraps of meaningless phrases, the misprints, the incorrectly transposed punctuation marks, the bad spelling or the unfortunate word alterations such as *to breathe* for *to pant* (of dogs), or *dropped to the ground in tears* for *fell* (cattle drop),[3] which prove ignorance of the language, I would mention one alteration which is incomprehensible to me. Why has the whole story of Natalya Savishna's love been omitted, a story which depicted her and the old way of life and which imparted significance and humanity to the character? *She even suppressed her love for the waiter Foka.* That is the meaningless phrase which replaces this passage. The word *délire* in Mimi's note has been translated as *fervour*.[4] The *iron plate* which the sentry strikes is replaced by a *copper one*. It's incomprehensible. I will only say that when I read the work in print I experienced the unpleasant feeling which a father experiences at the sight of his beloved son whose hair has been cut in an ugly and uneven way by a self-taught hairdresser. 'Where did those bare patches and forelocks come from, when he was a fine-looking boy before?' My child was not very handsome to start with, but to make matters worse he has been cropped and mutilated. I can only console myself with the fact that I have the opportunity to publish the whole novel separately under my own name, and to renounce completely the story *A History of My Childhood*, which by rights belongs not to me, but to an unknown employee of your editorial staff.

I have the honour to be, Sir,
Your most obedient servant,
L.N.

19. To N. A. NEKRASOV

Starogladovskaya, 27 November 1852

Dear Sir,

I very much regret that I cannot carry out your wish at once by sending something new for publication in your journal, the more so because I find the terms which you offer me exceedingly favourable and I agree to them in full.[1]

Although I have something written, I cannot send you anything just now, firstly because the success of my first work, such as it is, has inflated my pride as an author and I would wish my subsequent works to be no worse than the first; secondly because the cuts made by the censors in *Childhood* have compelled me to

---

3. The Russian words used here are *pal* and *povalilsya*: the distinction between them cannot adequately be translated into English.

4. Tolstoy's remark that the word *délire* in Mimi's note had been translated wrongly as 'fervour' would suggest that in the original manuscript sent to Nekrasov, Mimi's notes were written in French. The Russian translations were retained in the 1856 edition, although 'fervour' was amended to the correct translation of 'delirium'.

[19] 1. A considerably toned-down version of Letter 18 which Tolstoy considered too harsh. and which he sent to his brother instead of to Nekrasov.

revise a good deal in order to avoid similar ones.[2] Not to speak of trivial alterations, I will mention two which struck me as particularly disagreeable. They are the omission of the story of the love of Natalya Savishna, which depicted to some extent the way of life of the old days as well as her character, and added humanity to her personality; and the alteration of the title. The title *Childhood* and the few words of the introduction explained the idea of the work; but the title *A History of My Childhood*, on the other hand, contradicts it. Who is interested in the history of *my* childhood? The last alteration is particularly disagreeable to me because, as I wrote to you in my first letter, I wanted *Childhood* to be the first part of a novel, of which the following parts were to be: *Boyhood*, *Youth* and *Early Manhood*.

I would ask you, Sir, to promise me, with regard to my writing in future—if you wish to continue to accept it for your journal—not to alter anything at all in it. I hope you will not refuse me this. As far as I am concerned, I repeat my promise to send you the first thing which I consider suitable for publication.

I sign this with my own name, but I ask that it should remain known only to the editors.

With the utmost respect, I have the honour to be, Sir,

Your most obedient servant,
Count L. N. Tolstoy

P.S. Be so kind as to send me a copy of my story if possible.

20. To COUNT S. N. TOLSTOY

Starogladovskaya, 10 December 1852

I know you so well that as soon as I sent off my manuscript, I said to Nikolenka that as soon as it was published, you would certainly write and tell me your comments about it, and I looked forward to them and received them with greater impatience and pleasure than the reviews in the journals. You're afraid that I might become conceited and might lose at cards. It's obvious that we haven't seen each other for a long time. I don't think the thought of cards has entered my head for a year now, while as for the fear that my later works might show a decline, I hope that won't happen, and this is why: I've begun a new, serious and, in my view, useful novel,[1] to which I intend to devote a great deal of time and all my abilities. I set about it with the same feeling with which I used to set about drawing a picture as a child, when I would say, 'I shall spend three months drawing this picture.' I don't know whether the same fate will befall the novel as the picture, but the fact is that I fear nothing so much as becoming a journalistic hack, and in spite of favourable offers by the editors, I shall send to *The Contemporary*—if I send anything—only one story which is almost ready and which will be very bad.[2] It doesn't matter! It will be Mr L.N.'s last work. You wouldn't believe how much bad blood the publication of my story caused me—how many really good things

2. Tolstoy is referring to *The Raid*, originally called *A Letter from the Caucasus*.
[20] 1. *The Novel of a Russian Landowner*.   2. *The Raid*.

20. To Count S. N. Tolstoy

were cut out of it and how many stupid changes made by the censors and the editors. As proof of this I'm sending you the letter I wrote—but didn't send—to the editors in the first moment of vexation. I don't like to think that you might ascribe to me the various banalities inserted by a certain gentleman.

I was reckoning up the other day how soon I might be promoted and able to retire. With a great deal of luck in 1½ years; without any luck in 2 years, and with bad luck in 3. I confess I'm very bored, often sad even, but what can I do? On the other hand this life has been a great benefit to me. Let me have two or three years to spend at liberty once I've got away from here, and I'll know how to spend them well. You are wrong to think that I mightn't like your plan.[3] I dreamed of it a thousand times back in Russia, and it was only because I was afraid of your uncompromising nature that I didn't suggest it to you myself. The one thing I don't like is the fact that you don't want to live in the country; I, on the contrary, dream of nothing but settling down in the country for good, and resuming the way of life I led in Yasnaya after leaving Kazan: i.e. in other words I want to go back to the days of the long-tailed frock-coat. I should know now how to restrain the rashness, self-confidence and vanity which wrecked all my good schemes before. Were it not for this dream, which I hope with God's help to make a reality, I couldn't have imagined a better life than the one which you propose, although I know in advance that I shan't always be under the influence of the feeling which your letter aroused in me. But Nikolskoye, Yasnaya and Pirogovo are not far apart, and your plan could be carried out in the country, and, in my opinion, 10 times better than in any town where we might live without any jobs or responsibilities—simply in order to live somewhere. The *ties* which are a burden to you worry me too. Knowing your character I can't wish or advise anything better than for you to break them at all costs *as quickly as possible. Time is passing.* Only don't go to the Caucasus for that reason. I don't know why, but I shall be happier to go on waiting than to spoil the pleasure by meeting you here in the Caucasus. I'm tied down by my service but you, if you came here, wouldn't remain in Starogladovskaya, where it's nasty and boring. I don't know why, but I don't want that at all.

Where have you been this winter? I know nothing about you. How are your financial affairs? Goodbye. Please let's correspond more regularly. You promised long ago to send me your portrait. I'm still waiting for it.

21. To N. A. NEKRASOV

Starogladovskaya, 26 December 1852

Dear Sir,

I am sending you a short story;[1] if you should wish to publish it on the terms

---

3. In November Sergey had written to Tolstoy suggesting that they might live together 'somewhere'—Moscow, Petersburg, Odessa or even 'abroad'.

[21] 1. *The Raid*. Tolstoy had by now received a very flattering offer from Nekrasov to publish his next work, and his earlier irritation had largely disappeared.

offered to me, be so good as to grant my following requests: do not omit anything, do not add anything, and above all do not alter anything in it. If there is anything in it that you dislike so much that you decide not to publish it without alteration, better delay publication and talk it over.

If, contrary to my hopes, the censors should delete too much in the story, please do not publish it in mutilated form but return it to me.[2] On the last page I have marked with x and * two alternative versions I have given in two places, which I am afraid about on account of the censors; look over them and put them in if you find it a help.

I think that the notes which I have made on the last sheet, or at least some of them, are necessary for Russian readers.

I would also like the divisions indicated by me with a hyphen to be printed like that.

I am sorry that the manuscript is written in such a slovenly and untidy way: it has cost me an awful effort as it is!

In anticipation of your reply and your opinion about my story, I have the honour to be, with the utmost respect, your most obedient servant,

Count L. Tolstoy

22. To COUNT S. N. TOLSTOY

Pyatigorsk, 20 July 1853

I think I already wrote to you that I've sent in my resignation. God knows, however, whether or when it will be accepted now, because of the war with Turkey.[1] This worries me a lot because I've now got so used to the happy thought of settling down in the country before long that to return to Starogladovskaya and wait there indefinitely—as I wait for everything to do with my service—would be very disagreeable. I arrived in Pyatigorsk 1½ weeks ago and I must confess that I expected far more pleasure from seeing Masha and Valeryan than I actually got. Poor Masha does the rounds of the local assembly rooms and finds it very jolly while I, on the contrary, as you can imagine, find it very sad. Sad first of all that she finds pleasure in bad company, and even sadder that she is so taken up with these pleasures that she prefers them to the company of her brother whom she hasn't seen for 2 years. But in spite of that I can't help rejoicing to see her: how sweetly and simply and with what dignity she knows how to behave everywhere. Valeryan of course kissed and embraced me terribly affectionately, and immediately after his embraces fell silent and didn't know what to say to me. One needs to know how elated I was and how much I expected from seeing Valeryan and Masha to understand how keenly disappointed I was. Perhaps as always I was too *susceptible*; but

2. The story was in fact published in mutilated form in *The Contemporary*, 1853, No. 3. Despite the cuts made by the censors, Nekrasov still thought it worth publishing, although it meant disregarding Tolstoy's request.

[22] 1. The Russian armies had crossed the Prut and invaded the Roumanian principalities in June 1853.

22. To Count S. N. Tolstoy

in actual fact during the two weeks I was with them I never heard from either of them—I won't say a tender (I suppose there was some tenderness)—but a heartfelt word, which might have proved that they loved me, or that I meant something in their lives. I write all this to you boldly, without any fear that the same thing might happen when you and I meet. We've already put this to the test many times and it can't be otherwise, because no brothers have as much in common as you and I, and no people understand each other so well...[20 lines omitted]

23. To N. A. NEKRASOV

Pyatigorsk, 17 September 1853

Dear Nikolay Alexeyevich,

I am sending a short article[1] for publication in your journal. I value it more than *Childhood* or *The Raid*, and therefore I repeat for the third time the condition which I lay down for publication—that it should remain in exactly the same form as it is now. In your last letter you promised to conform to my wishes in this respect. If the censors should again make cuts, for goodness sake return the article to me, or at least write to me before it is published. Whether to publish the article under the title at the head of the manuscript or: *A Suicide. The Story of a Billiard Marker*, will depend entirely on your wish.

N. L. inserted above the line means a new line. In anticipation of your reply and your verdict on what I am sending, I have the honour to be, with the utmost respect, your most obedient servant,

Count L. Tolstoy

24. To COUNT S. N. TOLSTOY

Starogladovskaya, 26 November 1853

[15 lines omitted]...*When shall I come back?* Goodness only knows, because for almost a year now I've been thinking only of how I might sheathe my sword, and I can't do it. But since I'm compelled to fight somewhere or other, I would find it more agreeable to fight in Turkey than here, and I've asked Prince Sergey Dmitriyevich about it, and he has written to me to say that he's already written to his brother, but doesn't know what the outcome will be.

In any case by the New Year I expect a change in my way of life which, I confess, bores me beyond endurance. Stupid officers, stupid talk, stupid officers, stupid talk, nothing more. If only there were a single person one could talk to from the heart. Turgenev is right: 'what irony there is in solitude'—you become palpably stupid yourself. Despite the fact that Nikolenka—goodness knows why—went off with the hounds (Yepishka and I often call him a swine for doing so), I go out hunting alone with a pointer from morning till night for days on end. This is my only

---

[23] 1. It eventually appeared under the title *The Memoirs of a Billiard Marker* in *The Contemporary*, 1855, No. 1.

pleasure, and it isn't a pleasure, but a narcotic. You wear yourself out, get famished, come home and sleep like the dead—and a day has gone by. If you get the chance, or if you're in Moscow yourself, buy me Dickens' *David Copperfield* in English and also send me Sadler's English dictionary[1] which is among my books...[23 lines omitted]

25. To T. A. YERGOLSKAYA

[Original in French]

Bucharest, 5 July 1854

Dear and wonderful Aunt,

Can you imagine that it's only yesterday that I received your letter and the one from Dmitry, written on 14 April while still in Kursk. To answer all the letters I receive has become a habit with me, and to answer yours, i.e. to think of you and to chat with you, is one of my greatest pleasures. As I wrote to you—in my last letter, I think—I'm at present in Bucharest and am leading a pleasant and tranquil life there. So I'm going to talk to you of the past—of my memories of Silistria.[1] While there, I saw so many interesting, poetic and moving things that the time I spent there will never be erased from my memory. Our camp was located on the other side of the Danube, i.e. on its right bank, on very high ground in the middle of superb gardens belonging to Mustafa-Pasha, the governor of Silistria. The view from that spot was not only magnificent, but of the greatest interest to us all. Not to mention the Danube, its islands and its banks, some occupied by us, others by the Turks, you could see the town, the fortress and the little forts of Silistria as though on the palm of your hand. You could hear the cannon-fire and rifle shots which continued day and night, and with a field-glass you could make out the Turkish soldiers. It's true it's a funny sort of pleasure to see people killing each other, and yet every morning and evening I would get up on to my ⟨cart⟩ and spend hours at a time watching, and I wasn't the only one. The spectacle was truly beautiful, especially at night. At night our soldiers usually set about trench work and the Turks threw themselves upon them to stop them; then you should have seen and heard the rifle-fire. The first night I spent at the camp this terrible noise woke me up and alarmed me—I thought an assault was taking place—and I very quickly had my horse saddled; but those who had already spent some time at the camp told me just to keep calm; that this cannon-fire and rifle-fire was quite normal and that it was jokingly called 'Allah'. So I went back to bed, but being unable to get to sleep, I amused myself, watch in hand, counting the cannon shots that I heard, and I counted 100 explosions in the space of a minute. And yet, from nearby, all this wasn't at all as frightening as might be supposed. At night, when you could see nothing, it was a question of who would burn the most powder, and at the very

[24] 1. Tolstoy may be referring to Percy Sadler's *Nouveau dictionnaire portatif anglais-français et français-anglais* (Paris, 1844).

[25] 1. Tolstoy arrived in Silistria on 28 May and remained there until the siege was over. He stayed in Bucharest until 19 July.

25. To T. A. Yergolskaya

most 30 men were killed on both sides by these thousands of cannon shots. You'll allow me, dear Aunt, to speak to Nikolay in this letter; for once I've started giving details of the war, I'd like to go on and speak to a man who'll understand me and be able to explain what might appear obscure to you. This, then, is the ordinary spectacle we witnessed every day, and in which I also took part when sent with orders into the trenches; but we also witnessed extraordinary spectacles such as that on the eve of the assault, when they exploded a mine of 240 poods of gunpowder beneath one of the enemy bastions. On the morning of that day the Prince[2] had been in the trenches with all his General Staff (and as the general I'm attached to[3] is part of it, I was there too) to make final arrangements for the next day's assault; the plan—too long for me to be able to explain it here—was so well devised and everything so well prepared that nobody doubted its success.[4] Apropos of this, I must tell you that I'm beginning to feel an admiration for the Prince (but then you should hear the officers and soldiers speaking of him—not only have I never heard him spoken ill of, but he is generally worshipped). I saw him under fire for the first time that morning. You should see this slightly ridiculous figure with his great height, his hands behind his back, his cap on the back of his head, his spectacles and his way of speaking like a turkey-cock. You can see he's so engrossed in the general course of events that he simply doesn't notice the bullets and cannonballs; he exposes himself to danger with such naiveté that you'd say he was totally unaware of it, and you can't help being more afraid for him than for yourself; then again he gives his orders with such clarity and precision, and yet is always affable with everyone. He's a great man, i.e. a capable and *honourable* man, as I understand the word, a man who has devoted his whole life to the service of his country, and not from ambition but from a sense of duty. I'll tell you about one feature of his character which is connected with the history of this abortive assault that I started telling you about. After dinner that same day, the mine was detonated and nearly 500 guns bombarded the fort that we wanted to take and continued to fire all night: this was one of those sights and one of those emotions you never forget. In the evening the Prince and all the rest of the company went back into the trenches to spend the night, so that he could himself direct the assault that was to begin at 3 o'clock in the morning. We were all there, and, as always on the eve of a battle, we were all pretending not to think of the following day as anything more than an ordinary day, while all of us, I'm quite sure, at the bottom of our hearts felt a slight pang (and not even slight, but pronounced) at the thought of the assault.

2. Prince M. D. Gorchakov (brother of Prince S. D. Gorchakov, Letter 4, note 3). In 1854 he was Field-Marshal Paskevich's Chief of Staff. He took command of the siege of Silistria when Paskevich retired, apparently injured, and later replaced General Menshikov as commander at Sevastopol in 1855.

3. Lieutenant-General A. O. Serzhputovsky, commander of the Artillery of the Danube army.

4. The Russian army crossed the Danube in mid-March 1854. Paskevich, however, delayed the start of the siege of Silistria for six weeks, and when it finally began he insisted on attacking Arab-tabia, a stone outwork some distance from the city. The explosion of the mine under the walls of Arab-tabia took place on 7 June, and the assault was prepared for the night of 8 to 9 June.

25. To T. A. Yergolskaya

As you know, Nikolay, the period that precedes an engagement is the most unpleasant—it's the only period when you have the time to be afraid, and fear is one of the most unpleasant of feelings. Towards morning, the nearer the moment came, the more this feeling diminished, and towards 3 o'clock, when we were all waiting to see the shower of rockets let off as the signal for the attack, I was in such a good humour that I would have been very upset if someone had come to tell me that the assault wouldn't take place. Then suddenly, just one hour before the assault was due to begin, an aide-de-camp of the Marshal[5] arrives with the order to raise the siege of Silistria. I can say without fear of error that this news was received by all—soldiers, officers and generals—as a real misfortune, all the more so since we knew through the spies who came to us very often from Silistria, and with whom I very often had occasion to talk myself, that once this fort was taken—something of which nobody had any doubt—Silistria couldn't hold out for more than 2 or 3 days. If anyone could be expected to be upset by this news, it must surely have been the Prince, who, having done everything for the best during the whole of this campaign, sees the Marshal descend on him right in the middle of the action and spoil the whole affair—and then, having the unique opportunity of repairing our reverses by this assault, he gets a counter-order from the Marshal just as he is launching it. Well, the Prince wasn't put out of temper for an instant: on the contrary, this man who is so impressionable was happy to be able to avoid this butchery for which he would have had to bear the responsibility; and throughout the retreat which he directed himself,[6] not wishing to cross [the Danube] except with the last of the soldiers—and which was accomplished with remarkable order and precision—he was more cheerful than he had ever been. What contributed much to his good humour was the evacuation of nearly 7,000 Bulgar families which we took with us to save them from the ferocity of the Turks—a ferocity which I've been obliged to believe in despite my incredulity. As soon as we left the various Bulgar villages that we were occupying, the Turks moved in and, except for the women young enough for a harem, massacred everyone they found there. There was one village that I went into from the camp to fetch milk and fruit that had been exterminated in this way. As soon as the Prince had let the Bulgars know that those who wanted to could cross the Danube with the army and become Russian subjects, the whole country rose up, and all of them, with their wives, children, horses and cattle, came down to the bridge; but as it was impossible to take them all, the Prince was obliged to refuse those who came last, and you should have seen how much that grieved him; he received all the deputations coming from these poor people, he chatted with each of them, tried to explain to them the impossibility of the thing, proposed to them that they cross without their carts and cattle, and, taking upon himself their means of subsistence until they should reach Russia, paid out of his own purse for private vessels to transport them—in a word, he did

---

5. Field-Marshal I. F. Paskevich had only crossed the Danube to lay siege to Silistria on the insistence of the Tsar. He himself was more impressed by the threat of an Austrian attack, and his conduct of the siege was half-hearted.

6. The Russian forces were back across the Danube by 11 June, Paskevich having persuaded the Tsar of the threat posed by Austria.

25. To T. A. Yergolskaya

everything possible to assist these people. Yes, dear Aunt, I would really like your prophecy to come true. The thing that I covet most is to be the aide-de-camp of a man like him, whom I like and respect from the bottom of my heart. Goodbye, dear, kind Aunt—I kiss your hand. Please tell Valeryan to please write to ⟨Pyatigorsk⟩, to Doctor Drozdov, at whose house I've left my telescope, and ask him to send it to me here. Please ask him also to enclose the letter that I left him for Drozdov with this letter and also money to cover the postage costs.

I congratulate Sergey on his birthday. Please tell him that it's bad of him not to have written to me up to now. Although I've done the same myself up to now, I'm less to blame: (1) because I'm the only one who has to write to everyone, and (2) because although I mightn't write to him, he always reads my letters to you, or Nikolay, or Valeryan, whereas I have no news of him except that he's well and that he's gone to Lebedyan. Moreover, I hope that Nikolay, Sergey and Vasenka[7] will think of me when they're together at Beryozovka, and that they will all write to me from there.

26. To T. A. YERGOLSKAYA

[Original in French]

Kishinyov, 17–18 October 1854

Dear Aunt,

It's ages since I wrote to you. Why this silence? I couldn't tell you; there were several reasons. The most important one is that I hadn't any good news to give you about myself. I've been without money for more than 3 months, and it's the first time I've experienced just how very unpleasant this state of affairs is; but since it's over and done with, I won't speak to you about it any more. I'll speak to you about the pleasant side of my situation. Firstly, for almost 6 weeks, we've been in ⟨Kishinyov⟩, a pretty, provincial town which is very lively because of the arrival of the General Staff, and especially because of the arrival a few days ago of the Grand Dukes Nikolay and Mikhail.[1] We live very quietly here, and think only of enjoying ourselves and of the news that reaches us from the Crimea. This news has been cheering of late. Today we learned the news of Liprandi's victory:[2] he has defeated the English and taken 4 of their redoubts and 4 guns.[3] I felt envious for a moment when I learned of this, the more so because nominally I'm attached to the 12th Brigade which took part in this engagement, and because for a week I've been on the point of setting off there. In general, man is never content, and this is true of me particularly; during our continual campaigns abroad I thought only of the joy

---

7. V. S. Perfilyev, whose estate of Beryozovka was in the Lebedyan district of the province of Tambov.

[26] 1. The third and fourth sons of Nicholas I.

2. Lieutenant-General Liprandi fought in the Crimea from 1853 to 1856 and took part in all the major engagements.

3. This action took place at Balaklava on 13 October. Liprandi captured 11 guns, not 4.

of having a rest; now that I enjoy every comfort—good accommodation, a piano, a good dinner, settled occupations, pleasant acquaintances—I dream again of camp life and am envious of those who follow it. Yesterday I interrupted my letter to go to the assembly where I amused myself watching the Grand Dukes dance. They both appear to be extremely good-natured and very fine young men. Liprandi's aide-de-camp arrived at the ball, and it's there that he related the ⟨details⟩ of the affair. I don't know if, where you are, there's such a lively interest in Crimean affairs, but here it's a great occasion when the couriers arrive from Sevastopol. When the news is sad, everyone is sad. Yesterday, on the contrary, you would have said that it was everyone's name-day, so much so that I drank a whole bottle of champagne at supper and returned to the house slightly tipsy, which hasn't happened to me for a very long time. I've been very busy for some time with a project[4] which I won't tell you about until it succeeds, and which I'm working at with great pleasure, because it's something really useful; it was also one of the reasons for my silence. I must write to Valeryan, but I feel I won't have time by this post; so be so good, dear Aunt, as to tell him from me that I'm very grateful to him for the sale of the house[5] (I'd lost any hope of such a good sale) and for sending the money, intended for buying horses and already put to that purpose; but that this consignment in no way changes my previous arrangements, i.e. to receive 600 roubles a year, starting from September; and that, as I've already received 150 roubles, would he please send me, and as quickly as possible, another 150—i.e. ⟨the amount I allowed myself until January. I need the money now because I've paid my debts, and in January I'll receive my salary.⟩ Goodbye, dear Aunt, I kiss your hand, and please forgive this short and ⟨incoherent⟩ letter. Would Valeryan please also buy for me in Moscow out of the 150 roubles I've asked for:

⟨An artillery helmet with the number 12
      ,, ,, ,, half-sabre
and ,, ,, ,, pair of epaulettes with the number 12.
The helmet must be the smallest size.⟩[6]

27. To COUNT S. N. TOLSTOY

Eski-Orda, 20 November 1854

My dear Seryozha,

God knows I've been to blame towards you all ever since I left, and I don't know myself how it happened; sometimes an idle life, sometimes a nasty situation or frame of mind, sometimes war, sometimes a person interrupting etc. etc. But the

---

4. This project was a plan to publish a military journal (see Letters 27 and 29).
5. This house was built by Tolstoy's maternal grandfather, Prince N. S. Volkonsky, and by his own father. It was sold for 5,000 roubles. It was in this house that Tolstoy was born and spent his childhood and early youth. The main part of the house was dismantled and re-erected on the purchaser's estate about 12 miles from Yasnaya Polyana, and only the two wings have survived at Yasnaya Polyana.
6. Tolstoy had been promoted to the rank of Second-Lieutenant in September.

27. To Count S. N. Tolstoy

main reason has been an idle life, rich in impressions. I've learned and experienced and felt so much this year that I simply don't know what to begin to describe, or even whether I can describe it the way I want. I wrote to Auntie, you know, about Silistria, but I won't write to you and Nikolenka like that—I'd like to tell you things in such a way that you'll understand me as I want you to. Silistria is now an old story; now it's Sevastopol, about which I expect you're all reading with sinking hearts, and I was in Sevastopol[1] only 4 days ago. Well, how can I tell you all I saw there, and where I went and what I did and what the French and British prisoners and wounded are saying, and *whether it hurts them and hurts them very much*,[2] and what heroes our soldiers and sailors are and what heroes our enemies are, especially the British. I'll tell all that later at Yasnaya Polyana or Pirogovo; and you'll learn a lot from me in print. How that will be I'll tell you later; but now I'll give you an idea of the state of our affairs in Sevastopol. The town is besieged from one side, the south, where we had no fortifications when the enemy approached it. Now we have more than 500 big calibre guns on this side, and several lines of earthworks, positively impregnable. I spent a week in the fortress and to the last day used to lose my way among these labyrinths of batteries, as though in a forest. More than 3 weeks ago the enemy advanced in one place to within 80 sazhens, but can't get any further; at the slightest advance he's showered with a hailstorm of missiles. The spirit of the army is beyond all description. There wasn't so much heroism in the days of ancient Greece. When Kornilov[3] made the rounds of the troops, instead of saying, 'Hello, lads!', he said, 'If you have to die, lads, will you die?' and the troops shouted, 'We'll die, Your Excellency! Hurrah!' And it wasn't just for effect, but you could see on every face that it wasn't in jest but *in earnest*, and 22,000 men have already kept that promise.

A wounded soldier, almost dying, told me how they took the 24th French battery, but weren't reinforced. He was sobbing. A company of marines almost mutinied because they were to be relieved from a battery where they'd withstood bombardment for 30 days. Soldiers extract the fuses from bombs. Women carry water to the bastions for the soldiers. Many are killed and wounded. Priests with crosses go to the bastions and read prayers under fire. In one brigade, on the 24th,[4] there were 160 wounded men who wouldn't leave the front. It's a wonderful time! But now, after the 24th, we've quietened down—it's beautiful in Sevastopol now. The enemy hardly fires at all and everyone is convinced that he won't take the town, and it really is impossible. There are 3 assumptions: either he's going to launch an assault, or he's diverting our attention with false earthworks in order to

[27] 1. Tolstoy arrived in Sevastopol on 7 November 1854 and was attached to the 3rd light battery of the 14th Artillery Brigade. On 15 November he moved to the village of Eski-Orda, some four miles from Sevastopol.
 2. This phrase apparently refers to a family joke, and is used by Tolstoy in other letters when mentioning people who have been killed or wounded.
 3. Vice-Admiral V. A. Kornilov (1806–54), one of the main participants in the defence of Sevastopol. He was mortally wounded on the first day of the bombardment of Sevastopol.
 4. Tolstoy is referring to the unsuccessful Russian attack on the allies holding the Inkerman Heights. Of the 80,000 Russian troops that took part in the attack more than 10,000 were killed or wounded.

27. To Count S. N. Tolstoy

disguise his retreat, or he's fortifying his position for the winter. The first is least likely and the second most likely. I haven't managed to be in action even once, but I thank God that I've seen these people and am living at this glorious time. The bombardment of the 5th[5] will remain as the most brilliant and glorious feat not only in Russian history but in the history of the world. More than 1,500 guns were in action against the town for two days, and not only didn't force it to surrender, but didn't even force 1/20th of our batteries to stop firing. If people in Russia regard this campaign unfavourably, as I think they do, posterity will exalt it above all others; don't forget that we, with equal or even inferior forces and with only bayonets and with the worst troops in the Russian army (such as the 6th corps), are fighting a more numerous enemy with a fleet as well, armed with 3,000 guns, exceptionally well armed with rifles, and with its best troops too. I make no mention of the superiority of its generals. Only our army could hold its ground and be victorious (we shall be victorious, I'm convinced of that) in such conditions. You should see the French and British prisoners (especially the latter); they're fine fellows every one of them—morally and physically *a gallant lot*. The Cossacks say it's even a pity to cut them down; and side by side with them you should see some chasseur or other of ours: small, lousy and shrivelled-up.

Now I'll tell you how you'll learn from me in print about the deeds of these lousy, shrivelled-up heroes. In our artillery headquarters which consists, as I think I wrote to you, of very nice decent people, the idea arose of publishing a military journal[6] with the aim of maintaining morale in the army, a cheap journal (3 roubles a year) and a popular one, so that the soldiers might read it. We wrote out a project for the journal and submitted it to the Prince.[7] He liked the idea very much and he submitted the project and a specimen copy, which we also compiled, for the Emperor's approval. The money for publication is being advanced by myself and by Stolypin. I've been chosen editor, together with a certain Mr Konstantinov who has published *The Caucasus* and is experienced in these matters. The journal will publish descriptions of battles—not such dull and untruthful ones as in other journals—deeds of bravery, biographies and obituaries of worthy people, especially the little known; war stories, soldiers' songs, popular articles about the skills of the engineers, the artillery etc. This venture of mine pleases me very much: firstly I like the work, and secondly I hope the journal will be useful and not entirely bad. All this is still surmise until we know the Emperor's reply, about which I confess I have my fears: in the specimen copy which was sent to Petersburg we rashly included 2 articles, one by me, the other by Rostovtsev, which were not quite *orthodox*. For this venture I need the 1,500 roubles which are lying in the Department and which I've asked Valeryan to send me. Since I've let the cat out of the bag, tell him about it as well. Incidentally, tell Valeryan that I recently had the

---

5. This was the first bombardment of Sevastopol by the allies, who hoped to demolish the Sevastopol defences very rapidly. The bombardment did not achieve this, and the allies were compelled to resort to formal siege warfare.
6. The idea for the journal arose from a plan to form a society for the education of the military, in which Tolstoy and six other artillery officers were involved.
7. Prince M. D. Gorchakov.

27. To Count S. N. Tolstoy

good fortune to be introduced to his former general,[8] that he's terribly old, that in spite of the fact that he tries to conceal it, I'm convinced that he's on his last legs, and that at Alma he conducted himself as bravely as he did foolishly. By the way, he asked kindly after him.

I'm well, thank God, and I've been living pleasantly and happily since I came back from abroad.[9] Generally speaking my time in the army can be divided up into 2 periods:– abroad it was awful—I was ill, poor and lonely—but this side of the frontier it's pleasant: I'm well and have good friends, although I'm still poor—money simply runs away.

I can't write at all, but on the other hand I'm *proving myself*, as auntie teasingly puts it. One thing worries me: this is the 4th year I've been without female company, and I might become quite coarse and unfitted for family life which I love so much. Goodbye now; God knows when we'll see each other unless you and Nikolenka can think of a way to drop in at headquarters somehow or other from Tambov after your hunting expedition, for the war seems to have dragged on for a long time. As expected, I wasn't promoted during the Silistrian campaign, but I've been made a second-lieutenant in the normal way which I'm very pleased about, for I've got too old a face for an ensign—I felt ashamed.

28. To T. A. YERGOLSKAYA

[Original in French]

Simferopol, 6 January 1855

Dear and Wonderful Aunt,

I know that at the bottom of your heart you can't doubt the love I have for you and which I won't cease to have for you, whatever the circumstances; I know that it's only sorrow which makes you say such cruel words to me, as though you doubted my love which, instead of diminishing, only increases from day to day the more I'm separated from you and the older I become. Your letter of 23 October, which I received on 3 January, hurt me very much. During last summer I wrote more than 5 letters to you, of which half didn't reach you, I see. For heaven's sake, dear Aunt, never put my silence down to indifference; you know better than anyone that that's impossible in my case; you know that the greatest affection I have in my heart is and always will be that which I have for you; so don't wound me by saying that you doubt it, and that *your letters probably don't give me pleasure.* I've told you, and I repeat from the bottom of my heart (I respect you too much to spoil the feeling I have for you by lying) that your letters don't give me pleasure, but that they do me a great deal of good, that I become quite different, I become better, after receiving one of your letters, that I reread them 80 times, that I'm so happy

---

8. Possibly Baron D. Y. Osten-Saken who entered military service in 1804, and took part in all the major campaigns, including the Napoleonic Wars and the Crimean War, when he was commanding officer of the Sevastopol garrison.
9. I.e. Silistria.

28. To T. A. Yergolskaya

when I receive them that I can't sit still, that I would like to read them to everyone, that if I've allowed myself to be tempted by something bad I stop and make plans to become better. For heaven's sake, dear Aunt, once and for all, put down my silence either to the unreliability of the post (which is particularly bad at present) or to the reason that I wouldn't want to make you anxious on my account to no avail, and don't punish me by your silence.

I didn't take part in the two bloody and disastrous battles that took place in the Crimea,[1] but I was at Sevastopol immediately following that of the 24th, and I spent a month there. There's no more fighting in the field because of the winter, which is extraordinarily severe, particularly at present, but the siege still continues. God only knows what the outcome of this campaign will be; but whatever happens, the Crimean campaign should end one way or another within three or four months. But alas! the end of the Crimean campaign doesn't mean the end of the war: on the contrary, it appears that it will last for a long time yet. In my letters to Sergey and Valeryan, I believe I spoke of an occupation I had in mind, and which attracted me a great deal—now that the matter has been decided I can talk about it. I had the idea of founding a military journal. This project which I worked at with the cooperation of a lot of very distinguished people was approved by the Prince and sent to His Majesty for a decision; but since in our country people intrigue against everything, there proved to be some who feared the competition of this journal; besides, the idea of the journal perhaps didn't accord with the government's views, and the Emperor refused.

This failure, I admit to you, grieved me very much and considerably altered my plans. If God wills that the Crimean campaign should end soon, and if I don't receive a position that I'm happy with, and if there is no war in Russia, I'll leave the army to go to Petersburg, to the military academy. I arrived at this plan, firstly because I wouldn't want to abandon literature and it's impossible for me to work at it in these camp-life conditions, and secondly because it seems to me that I'm beginning to become ambitious—not ambitious, but I would like to do good, and to do that one needs to be more than a ⟨second-lieutenant⟩, and thirdly because I'll see you all, and all my friends. Nikolay wrote to me that Turgenev has become acquainted with Marya[2]—I'm delighted. If you see him at their house, tell Varenka[3] that I charge her to embrace him from me and to tell him that although I only know him through his writings, I would have had a great deal to say to him.

Goodbye, dear Aunt. I'm making a number of plans, as always, for the new year, on which I congratulate you with all my heart, and, among them, that of seeing you again in 5 or 6 months is without doubt the one which appeals to me most. I don't

---

[28] 1. The Battles of the River Alma and Inkerman. The Battle of the Alma was fought on 8 September 1854, shortly after the allied landings in the Crimea: the Russian forces under General Menshikov were defeated and retreated to Sevastopol. The Battle of Inkerman was fought on 24 October 1854; the Russians attacked the British on the Inkerman Heights near Sevastopol, but were repulsed after heavy fighting; the Russian casualties totalled 12,000, including six generals.
2. Turgenev met Tolstoy's sister for the first time on 24 October 1854. See Letter 33.
3. Marya Nikolayevna's daughter.

28. To T. A. Yergolskaya

know what will happen to me this year, but I've begun the new year under happy auspices; I'm as sound as a bell; I'm in a good mood; I've received some letters from you and my brothers... You know that I'm a little superstitious, and I hope and expect something fortunate to turn up almost any moment. But since there can be no happiness for me without you, I look forward to seeing you again soon.

29. To N. A. NEKRASOV

Eski-Orda, 11 January 1855

Dear Nikolay Alexeyevich,

In my previous letter I wrote to you in passing about the materials I have accumulated for the military journal which it was proposed to publish in the army, and which—the materials—I suggested you should include in your journal; now I will speak about this subject in greater detail. What grieves me about the failure of this journal is not so much the wasted effort and materials, as the idea of the journal, which deserves to be realised, at least in part, if it could not have been realised in full.

The basic idea of this journal was that probably a good half, if not the greater part of the reading public consists of military people, but we have no military literature, excluding official military literature, which for some reason does not enjoy the confidence of the public and so can neither give direction to, nor express the point of view of our military society. We wanted to found a *Leaflet*, accessible to *all* ranks of military society in price and content, which would serve only to express the spirit of the army, while avoiding any conflict with our existing official military journals.

The journal would have been divided into an official and an unofficial part. The first part would have included: (1) News of military events from all theatres of war; (2) Despatches on decorations for services going beyond the general run of distinction; (3) Court martial sentences for shameful actions. The unofficial part would have included: (1) Contemporary and historical stories from military life; (2) Biographies and obituaries of military persons of all ranks; (3) Soldiers' songs; (4) Popular articles on academic branches of the art of war (tactics, artillery, engineering). We got a reply from the Ministry of War—where you will be able to find the detailed project and our sample leaflet—to say that we could publish our articles in *The Invalid*.[1] But judging from the spirit of this proposed journal, you will understand that the articles prepared for it might more readily find a place in *The Agricultural Gazette* or in some *Arabesque*, than in *The Invalid*. For this reason I am asking you to give a place in your journal—not a temporary but a permanent place—to some sections—almost all the unofficial ones. I would undertake to provide each month from 2 to 5, or more, printed sheets of articles of literary worth on military matters, in no way inferior to the articles published in your

---

[29] 1. *The Russian Invalid*, a semi-official magazine of the Ministry of War, with exclusive rights to publish various military materials and communications from the theatres of war.

30. To T. A. Yergolskaya

journal (I say this with confidence—as these articles will not belong to me), and of a point of view which will not cause you any difficulties with regard to the censor.

Our advantages, if you accept my proposals, will be: (1) that our idea of founding a literature which will serve to express the military spirit will begin to be realised and will, I hope, in time assume bigger dimensions; and (2) that our articles will be included in the best journal, which enjoys the greatest confidence on the part of the public.

Your advantages will be: (1) the acquisition of educated and gifted contributors; (2) a growth of interest in your journal; and (3) a partially assured supply of materials for it. The advantages are on your side, and therefore the conditions which I am proposing to you will be harder for you than those which I will assume myself.

I pledge myself to provide you each month with between 2 and 5 printed sheets of articles on military matters, for which you can pay me as much as you wish. You pledge yourself to print at once everything I send you, whatever it is. I admit this condition seems too impudent, and I am afraid you will not want to agree to it. But if you can believe how much I value the quality of the journal to which I have the honour to be a contributor, and recognise some literary taste in me, I hope you will not want to ruin by your refusal what is for us such a mutually advantageous bargain and a project not without general benefit as well.

If your reply is favourable, I will send you for the first month *A Letter about the Sisters of Mercy*, *Reminiscences of the Siege of Silistria*, and *A Letter of a Soldier from Sevastopol*.[2]

So, in impatient anticipation of your reply and agreement to my proposal,[3] I have the honour to be,

Your most obedient servant,
Count L. Tolstoy

30. To T. A. YERGOLSKAYA

[Original in French]

Sevastopol, 7 May 1855

Dear Aunt,

I was 6 versts from Sevastopol when the bombardment began,[1] and the first thought that came to me when I learned what it was was to write to you as soon as the bombardment was over, so that you should know about it from me and not from the papers; but the following day our battery entered the town, and for the

---

2. There is no information available about the content of these articles, nor is it known who their authors were.

3. In his reply to Tolstoy on 27 January Nekrasov expressed his enthusiasm for the whole idea, and his readiness to cooperate, but the promised articles did not materialise, and nothing came of the project.

[30] 1. The French and British bombarded the Sevastopol defences uninterruptedly from 28 March to 10 April.

30. To T. A. Yergolskaya

entire duration of the bombardment it stayed there and is still there now. I was at the bastion,[2] but the devil isn't as black as he's made out to be, I assure you, and this bombardment wasn't as terrible as most people describe it. On the contrary, I would say that it's the most agreeable time that I've had. For the moment everything is more or less quiet: I go on duty at the bastion for 4 days and then I'm free for 12 days, which I spend very agreeably. I have very elegant accommodation, with a piano, looking out on to the boulevard, where there are promenaders and music every afternoon; I've a lot of good friends; the weather is superb; and I've begun to bathe in the sea. So if for some time now I've been such a lazy-bones that I can't even bring myself to write letters, it's not because of the service or because of the dangers, but on the contrary because life here is too agreeable. However, I'd started my letter with the intention of explaining, or rather asking your forgiveness for my silence. Letters take so long to come and go, and to write to you while the bombardment was continuing was distasteful to me, and then the bombardment gradually eased up; and then I received your wonderful letter, from which I see that you've already had news of the bombardment from the papers. All that this proves, however, is that I'm a thoroughly bad fellow, who only deserves your love because of his love for you and not because of his behaviour. I can't tell you how touched I was by your nice letter, in which you refuse to scold me, believing that I'm to be pitied, and try to console me. I haven't gambled any more and I've paid a proportion of my most pressing debts with the 400 roubles I got from Valeryan; but I'm still left with more than 600 which torment me. I think there's no need to tell you that I want to, and try to follow the advice you give me about moderation and activity; and up to now I've nothing more to reproach myself with on this account than a little laziness; but then I've an excuse which I hope will seem sufficiently important to you: it's the kind of life that I've led and am leading, at times in high society, at times in low society, at times in want, at times even in luxury; it's difficult in these circumstances never to deviate from the path you've mapped out for yourself. Goodbye, dear Aunt; I wanted to write a lot, but I'm just being called for dinner, and I don't know if I'll be able to write any more this evening, as I'm on duty. I'll try to write to you more often, but in heaven's name don't fret too much on my account—I assure you that the danger I'm in here isn't too great—and don't wish for my success in the service either—it upsets me too much not to be able to fulfil your wishes in this respect; wish only for my health and happiness—these are the true blessings. As for success, i.e. promotion and honours—I'm not made for them. Can you imagine—I couldn't bring myself to take Aunt Polina's[3] letter to the Prince;[4] I entrusted it to one of my friends to do, and he told me 2 days later that the Prince had left word for me to come to dinner that same day; I went, and he didn't notice me, having probably forgotten what he wanted to tell me, and I'm not the man to call attention to myself. So the only thing that I desired—to be his aide-de-camp—won't come about for the present. But then perhaps everything

2. Tolstoy was at the 4th Bastion, which suffered particularly severely in the bombardment.
3. P. I. Yushkova.
4. Prince M. D. Gorchakov.

is for the best, for with regard to the service I'm perfectly happy in the battery where I am. Goodbye, dear Aunt, I kiss your hand a thousand times.

Lev

31. To I. I. PANAYEV

Ivan Ivanovich Panayev (1812–62), writer and editor. In the 1830s he served in the Ministry of Finance and the Ministry of Public Education, where until 1845 he worked on the editorial staff of the Ministry's journal. In retirement, he devoted all his time to literature. From 1839 he contributed regularly to the journal *Notes of the Fatherland*, and was closely associated with V. G. Belinsky. In 1846 he joined Nekrasov in purchasing *The Contemporary*, and he became editor-in-chief of the journal. Today he is, perhaps, best known for his *Literary Reminiscences* (republished in 1928, by Ivanov-Razumnik). Tolstoy met Panayev in November 1855, and subsequently saw him quite frequently. However, there was never any real friendship between the two men. Six of Tolstoy's letters to Panayev have survived and nine of Panayev's to Tolstoy.

The Belbek river, 14 June 1855

Dear Ivan Ivanovich,

Would you believe that I have to overcome the shame I feel in order to take up my pen and write to you? I'm ashamed that I'm alive and well, and that only one thing—had the reverse been the case—could have served as an excuse for my silence in reply to your 3 letters,[1] letters which are so kind, which thrill me, and which sometimes at moments of proud delusion make me believe in my talent and my importance in literature—something, I confess, which I would very much like to have. I will answer your questions in the previous letter point by point: (1) I did receive the money for *Boyhood*, (2) send the money and books to my old address at Staff Headquarters, and (3)—for each article separately. Unfortunately for me, I promised you too much—my collaborators were lazy when I was in Sevastopol—and now it's about a month since I left, and I know nothing about their articles. I have been ill myself, but despite that I hope to send you, in about 3 days' time, *The Story of a Cadet*[2]—quite a long article, but a Caucasian and not a Sevastopol one—which will be in time for volume No. VII. Believe me, the idea of military articles interests me as much now as before, and in a few days I will go to Sevastopol to spur on Rostovtsev and Bakunin and collect their articles, if they are ready; but real life is too rich in events for anyone to have time to think. Nevertheless, for myself I can vouch for an article every month; but for the others I can't be

[31] 1. During Nekrasov's absence from Moscow, Panayev took sole charge of *The Contemporary*, and he wrote three letters to Tolstoy in April and May on matters connected with Tolstoy's contributions to the journal. In his letter of 3 May Panayev wrote: 'Your participation in the journal is so important that its future is in a sense bound up with your works. Do not deprive *The Contemporary* of them, still less the Russian public which loves and appreciates you so much.'

2. The original title of *The Wood-felling*.

31. To I. I. Panayev

sure. My address is still the same; via the couriers is best, if you have arranged it. If Turgenev is in Petersburg, ask him for permission to inscribe the article *The Story of a Cadet* with the words: dedicated to I. Turgenev. The idea occurred to me because, when I reread the article, I found much involuntary imitation of his stories in it.

With the utmost respect and devotion, I have the honour to be your obedient servant.

32. To T. A. YERGOLSKAYA

[Original in French]

Sevastopol, 4 September 1855

Dear and wonderful Aunt,

On the 27th a great and glorious action took place at Sevastopol.[1] I had the good fortune or the misfortune to arrive in the town on the very day of the assault, so that I was present at the action and even took a small part in it as a volunteer.[2] Don't be alarmed, I hardly faced any danger. The 28th—my birthday—has been for the second time in my life both a memorable and a sad day for me: the first time, 18 years ago, it was Aunt Alexandra's death;[3] now it is the loss of Sevastopol. I wept when I saw the town in flames and the French flags on our bastions, and generally, in many respects, it was a very sad day. Valentin Koloshin, whom I was very fond of here, is missing, and no one knows what has become of him. I'm not writing to his parents because I'm still hoping that he's been taken prisoner. The note that I sent to the enemy camp has still not been answered. I can't explain to myself, dear Aunt, the silence of all those whom I never cease to write to: yourself, Valeryan, Marya, Nikolay, Sergey. Over these last few days the idea of leaving the army has occurred to me more and more often. I see that it would be easy for me; but to take this step I would like to have your approval. And there—but for the desire to please you by reassuring you on my account—you have the chief object of

[32] 1. On 27 August 1855, the allies made a determined assault on the Russian defences at Sevastopol. The allies made twelve attacks, all of which were repulsed with the exception of a French attack under General MacMahon, which gained control of the Kornilov bastion on the Malakhov (Hill). Victory apparently belonged to the Russians. But Prince Gorchakov, realising that it would be impossible to recapture the Kornilov bastion and that therefore the Russian position in Sevastopol was untenable, ordered the complete evacuation of the fortress and city. The Russian forces retreated across the Bay of Sevastopol that same night, blowing up the magazines as they went. Much of the city was burned. The end of the siege heralded the end of the major fighting of the Crimean War. Tolstoy described the capture of the Malakhov in *Sevastopol in August*.

2. Colonel P. N. Glebov recounts that on 27 August Tolstoy came to him, hoping to be of assistance, and that he placed him in command of five battery guns. He writes: '...Tolstoy endeavours to smell powder, but only fleetingly, as a partisan, remaining aloof from all the difficulties and privations which war entails. He moves around to various places like a tourist, but as soon as he hears where the firing is, he immediately appears on the field of battle; the battle over, he goes off again as the fancy takes him, following his nose.'

3. Tolstoy makes two mistakes here: his aunt, Countess A. I. Osten-Saken, died on 30 August 1841; i.e. not eighteen but fourteen years previously, and not on Tolstoy's birthday.

33. To Countess M. N. Tolstaya

this short and ⟨nonsensical⟩ letter. Goodbye, dear Aunt, good and wonderful Aunt, I kiss your hand a thousand times and I swear to you that I never cease to think of you.

Yours,
Lev Tolstoy

33. To COUNTESS M. N. TOLSTAYA

Countess Marya Nikolayevna Tolstaya was born on 2 March 1830, and was Tolstoy's only sister. In 1847, when only 17 years old, she married her second cousin, Valeryan Petrovich Tolstoy—a nephew of T. A. Yergolskaya. Valeryan was 34 at the time. It appears that the first years of her marriage were happy, and between 1849 and 1852 she had four children, although the eldest son, Pyotr, died very young. On 24 October 1854, Marya met I. S. Turgenev, and there began a very close friendship which was to last until 1859. On 29 October 1854, Turgenev wrote to N. A. Nekrasov: Marya is a 'very nice woman—intelligent, kind and very attractive...I like her very much'. And in a letter to Annenkov of 1 November 1854, he admits to having almost fallen in love with her. The heroine of his story *Faust* (1856) is largely modelled on her, and he dedicated the work to her. Her marriage, however, proved to be a disaster. Valeryan was a cynical and dissolute man. Before his marriage to Marya he had had several children by a serf girl on his estate, and he continued this liaison after his marriage. In 1857 Marya left him, declaring that she did not want to be 'the senior sultana in his harem'. Turgenev wrote of this separation to Pauline Viardot: 'She was obliged to separate from her husband, a kind of rural Henry VIII, and very repulsive.' Tolstoy, knowing Turgenev's amorousness and his relations with Pauline Viardot, disapproved of the close relationship between him and Marya; in September 1858 he noted: 'Turgenev is behaving badly towards Mashenka. He's a scoundrel.' Over the winter of 1858–9, Turgenev became increasingly indifferent towards Marya, and the fact that Tolstoy's correspondence with him was broken off in February 1859, for a period of almost two years, was probably due to his disapproval of Turgenev's treatment of her. In 1860 Marya and her children accompanied Tolstoy and Nikolay abroad. She travelled considerably, spending a lot of time in Hyères and Algiers, and eventually settled for a while in Switzerland, where she fell in love with a Swede, Viscount Victor-Hector de Kleen, by whom she had another daughter in 1863. She returned to Russia in 1864, on Tolstoy's insistence. From 1864 to 1889, she lived restlessly, constantly on the move—from Pokrovskoye (the estate she inherited from her husband) to Yasnaya Polyana, to Moscow, and abroad and back again—and in later years devoted much of her time to music. The effect of such a solitary, restless life, wrote Tolstoy's son, Sergey, was to make her 'even more capricious and irritable'. She was an extremely religious person and a devout believer in superstitions and miracles. In 1889 she came under the influence of an elder at the Optina Monastery, and in 1891 she settled in the Shamordino Convent

33. To Countess M. N. Tolstaya

nearby and eventually became a nun. She died of pneumonia in 1912. Tolstoy always remained very close to his sister, and when he finally left home in 1910, he went to visit her at Shamordino. He portrayed her as Lyuba in *Childhood, Boyhood* and *Youth*. Only about 30 of his letters to her have survived.

Petersburg, 20 November 1855

My dear Masha,

This letter will be a muddle, I'm afraid, because it's written in a hurry, but I'm writing it immediately after my arrival[1] and my meeting with Ivan Sergeyevich,[2] just as you wished. When I arrived in Petersburg at 9 o'clock yesterday I immediately went to the baths, having made sure beforehand, however, that Turgenev would be at home until 12 o'clock. After a drink of tea, I hurried round to his place from the baths and met him just as he was leaving to come and see me, since his man had told him that a certain Count Tolstoy, who had just arrived, had sent to ask whether he would be at home. We immediately embraced each other most heartily. He's very nice. We went together to Nekrasov's, where we had lunch and sat and played chess until 8 o'clock. He won 2 games and I only one, but I wasn't in the mood, while he couldn't get the better of me entirely. I'm moving in with him today. He's very insistent, and I want to, but I'm afraid we'll get in each other's way; but still we'll try it.[3] I've got to like him above all because he likes and esteems you so much—you and Nikolenka and Valeryan. Nekrasov is interesting, and there's a lot of good in him, but he hasn't any immediately engaging charm. He's very sickly looking. I'll certainly get his portrait for you. My uniform is ready today and I'm paying official visits. Goodbye, my dearest; write to me and kiss Valeryan and the children. Turgenev kept asking how close the bullets whistled past me, and said that as from yesterday evening he would bring the big guns into action so that I shan't be taken back into the army, while I say that this is what I want too, but that I won't do a thing about it on any account and that if he wants to, he must do it in such a way that I shan't know, otherwise I'll prevent him. Once again, goodbye, my dear; I think I shall have a pleasant and profitable time here, if I don't spoil it for myself, and later on Turgenev promises to accompany me to Tula for the elections.

[33] 1. He returned to Petersburg as a courier, with dispatches concerning artillery operations during the storming of Sevastopol.
2. Turgenev.
3. The two men lived together for a little over a month.

III
1856–1862

The years 1856–62 were difficult and unsettling ones for Tolstoy, with the transition from an irregular active life with no immediate concern for the need to make a living to a more humdrum social round of the town and the search for a regular and a satisfying occupation. On his return to Petersburg in 1856 and his resignation from the army, he threw himself wholeheartedly into the life of the capital, frequenting its literary circles as well as exploring its *demi-monde*. In terms of literary production, the year 1856 was an *annus mirabilis* for him with the publication of five new works: the army tales *Sevastopol in August* and *Meeting a Moscow Acquaintance in the Detachment; A Landowner's Morning* based on his unsuccessful project to free his Yasnaya Polyana serfs; the anecdotal *Two Hussars* in which the 'fathers and sons' theme is humorously exploited; and *The Snowstorm* which grew out of an incident on a journey of Tolstoy's from the Caucasus.

The same year witnessed two important events in Tolstoy's personal life: the death of his younger brother Dmitry and his own infatuation for Valeriya Arsenyeva, the daughter of a neighbouring Tula landowner, which led to many meetings and a lengthy correspondence in which Tolstoy adopted a pedagogical rather than an amorous tone and did not conceal from his prospective fiancée the fact that she fell short of his ideal. His affections soon cooled and the relationship had ended by the beginning of 1857, but it had been important in establishing Tolstoy's ideal of marriage in his own mind, and it provided the basis of his story *Family Happiness* (published in 1859).

In 1857 Tolstoy made his first visit to Western Europe, and spent six months in France, Switzerland and Germany. His first impressions of Paris were favourable, but after witnessing an execution he drastically revised his opinions and hastily left for Switzerland. In Geneva he called on two of his relations, the Countesses Liza and Alexandra Tolstaya, both Maids of Honour at the Petersburg Court. Tolstoy's close friendship ('une amitié amoureuse' he called it) with Alexandra Tolstaya, eleven years his senior, dates from this time, and a voluminous correspondence followed. While abroad Tolstoy worked intermittently on several stories, of which the tendentious and undistinguished *Lucerne* and *Albert* were published in 1857 and 1858 respectively without success.

Returning to Yasnaya Polyana in August 1857, Tolstoy turned his attention energetically to farming and the reform of his estate. In the following year he continued his farming, and also helped to found the Moscow Musical Society. The year 1859 saw a further retreat from literature and a growing interest in education, with the founding of his school for peasant children at Yasnaya Polyana which was to occupy him on and off for the next three or four years. No works of fiction were published between 1859 and 1863, but his experience as a teacher bore fruit in the publication of the educational journal *Yasnaya Polyana*, of which twelve issues appeared in 1862–3 with contributions by himself and his teachers and pupils.

An offshoot of his passionate interest in educational theory and practice was a second visit to Western Europe from July 1860 to April 1861. In Germany he studied modern educational methods and met Froebel's nephew. He revisited France, where he was deeply moved by the death of his brother Nikolay from tuberculosis, and from there he moved on to Italy. In the first four months of 1861 he continued his travels through Europe and paid his one and only visit to England where he heard Dickens lecture on education and Palmerston speak in the House of Commons. In London he met Herzen and in Brussels Proudhon. On his return to Russia he resumed teaching at the Yasnaya Polyana school and was appointed an Arbiter of the Peace to arbitrate in disputes between peasants and their former masters following the Emancipation of 1861. In the same year a police raid was made on Yasnaya Polyana in Tolstoy's absence with the object of unearthing revolutionaries among the student teachers at his school and discovering subversive literature—an incident which provoked a vehement and indignant protest from Tolstoy to Alexander II.

During the years following his discharge from the army, both right- and left-wing journals fought to secure his services and allegiance. He became attached to, and later estranged from the devotees of art for art's sake. He maintained an uneasy personal relationship with Turgenev—until their famous quarrel in 1861 when he challenged Turgenev to a duel—but he associated more with the Slavophiles and the right-wing elements of society, not because he agreed with their politics (in the intellectual debates between Slavophiles and Westerners he gave his allegiance to neither side) but because he liked them better as individuals.

Tolstoy's personal life during the period 1856–62 was overshadowed by the deaths of two of his three brothers and the divorce of his sister. It was also marked by a number of tentative love affairs with women of his own class, casual relationships with prostitutes and a passionate liaison with a married serf who bore him a son. In the late summer of 1862, however, he fell in love with Sofya Behrs, the daughter of a Moscow physician and of a childhood friend of Tolstoy's, and after a very short engagement they were married in Moscow on 23 September 1862. After his marriage Tolstoy continued his teaching for a while, but with less enthusiasm than before. For the first time after a break of three years he resumed his literary activities. He revised and published the long unfinished story *The Cossacks* in 1863, as well as the peasant tale *Polikushka*, and in the autumn of the same year he began to write *War and Peace*. His first child was born—the first of thirteen—and his life now took on a pattern which it was to retain until well after the completion of his longest and greatest novel.

34. To COUNTESS M.N. TOLSTAYA

Petersburg, 14 April 1856

Happy Easter, my dear Masha!

I won't apologise for not having written to you for so long; it's happened so many times before and still hasn't prevented us from loving each other and being assured of it. Still, it's very bad. I'm staying here at present waiting for leave which, they say, won't come through in less than about ten days. I've been terribly keen to get away ever since it began to look like spring in earnest, although I'm not bored here. But don't think that I'm not bored because I have a lot of distractions; on the contrary, work is going rather well here, and I'm doing a bit of writing. How did you find the *Snowstorm*?[1] I'm afraid you didn't like it, and I've been waiting, and still am waiting for your verdict. I wanted to dedicate it to you, but it wasn't worth it. A few days ago now I finished quite a long story called *Father and Son*[2] which I read to Ivan Sergeyevich[3] yesterday. He slapped his thigh and said it was charming, but I must admit I don't trust him much. He's too ready to enthuse. Incidentally he was seriously ill the other day, partly from hypochondria. He's invented some illness called 'bronchitis', but I keep assuring him that bronchitis isn't an illness but a stone, and that even Valeryan has one. I met Grigorovich[4] here and liked him very much, the more so because he respects and values you such a lot. He very much wants to dedicate the first thing he writes to you. How did you like his *Ploughman*?[5] Nekrasov is leaving and I told him to have his portrait done. Furthermore, he promised me several times to put together all his unpublished poems for you, but either because they're not all here, or because they're badly written, he's kept putting it off. Furthermore, on my suggestion, all we writers have been photographed as a group: Turgenev,[6] Grigorovich, Druzhinin,[7] Goncharov,[8] Ostrovsky[9] and I, and I'm sending the group on to you. Ask Natalya Petrovna[10] the meaning of the three terribly vivid and memorable dreams I had these last three days: (1) I was turning a table and the table said to me that I would be married in Moscow and it even named the person, and said I would be very happy; (2) I had a tooth extracted; and (3) I dreamed last night that you had gone

[34] 1. Published in *The Contemporary*, 1856, No. 3.
    2. Published in *The Contemporary*, 1856, No. 5, under the title *Two Hussars*. Not only Turgenev, but also Nekrasov and Chernyshevsky thought very highly of it.
    3. Turgenev.
    4. D. V. Grigorovich (1822–99) wrote many stories about peasant life in Russia, of which the two most influential were *The Village* (1846) and *The Hapless Anton* (1847). Tolstoy first met him in January 1856.
    5. Published in *The Contemporary* 1856, No. 3. Tolstoy wrote to Grigorovich in May 1856 to tell him of the extremely favourable impression the story had made on him.
    6. I. S. Turgenev. See Letter 57.
    7. A. V. Druzhinin. See Letter 37.
    8. I. A. Goncharov (1812–91), civil servant and man of letters, was the author of three major novels, *An Ordinary Story*, *Oblomov* and *The Precipice*, of which the second became a Russian classic and has been translated into many languages.
    9. A. N. Ostrovsky. See Letter 302.
    10. N. P. Okhotnitskaya, an indigent gentlewoman who lived with the Tolstoys.

34. To Countess M. N. Tolstaya

mad, and so had I. Goodbye my dear; a thousand kisses to you, Valeryan and the children. Please reply without delay.

Alexander Gorchakov has been appointed to Nesselrode's post.[11] Dolgorukov, the War Minister, has been replaced.

35. To COUNTESS M. N. TOLSTAYA

Yasnaya Polyana, 5 June 1856

I'm sending you the upright piano; send me the grand piano and *Don Giovanni* as you promised, and some Beethoven and Mozart pieces which you perhaps don't need as well. Oh, yes, and I remember, on my way from the Caucasus or the Crimea I left some old writing of mine with you; if you still have it, send it on to me. I won't go back on my word, and I'll come after St Peter's Day,[1] but wouldn't it be better for you to decide to come to my place now for a few days, and you could come again later? It's so nice at Yasnaya now that it's impossible to leave it. The bathing in the river is excellent, I've only just come away from there. I could arrange a place for you to bathe there too. Think about it. Perhaps Ivan Sergeyevich[2] will come with you as well? Auntie and I kiss you all and don't despair of your coming.

Say Uaaa to Varenka for me, and Uiii to Nikolenka and Uuuu to the little sinner![3]

Please let's meet soon. My business with the peasants is going badly[4]—all the more reason why I can't get away. I got home at 4 o'clock in the morning, everyone was asleep and I settled down on the balcony and read Pushkin's *Don Juan*[5] and was so delighted that I wanted to write at once to Turgenev about my impressions.

I kiss you.

Your brother, Count L. Tolstoy

11. A. M. Gorchakov, a distant relative of Tolstoy, succeeded Nesselrode as Minister of Foreign Affairs in 1856.

[35] 1. 29 June o.s.
2. Turgenev.
3. M. N. Tolstaya's children.
4. On his return to Yasnaya Polyana at the end of May, Tolstoy submitted to his peasants his proposals to transfer them to a quitrent system, with very favourable terms of payment. He wrote of the reception given to these proposals in a letter to Nekrasov of 12 June 1856: 'You can imagine that the Emperor's words about emancipation have reached them with various additions and embellishments, and as a result of their vague idea about whom the landowners' land belongs to, they have rejected my very favourable proposals on the pretext that their elders didn't sign any undertakings and they won't either. I'll tell the Slavophiles what I think about the dignity and sanctity of the meetings of the commune. Stupid nonsense.'
5. The principal character in Pushkin's 'Little Tragedy' *The Stone Guest*.

36. To N. A. NEKRASOV

Yasnaya Polyana, 2 July 1856

I'm keeping my word and writing again, more particularly because I want to tell you my impressions about the 6th issue of *The Contemporary*. Well, my Kazan comrade's story was a disgrace,[1] and *The Contemporary* was a disgrace as well; I can imagine how *The Petersburg Gazette* will attack the unfortunate Bervi, and deservedly so. You had good cause to try and keep quiet about this work and to smile your cat-like smile when it was mentioned. I don't think such rubbish has ever been published in *The Contemporary* before—and not only *The Contemporary*—not in Russian or in any other language, I would think. Perhaps I'm exaggerating, but that was my impression. It's like *The Staff of Righteousness*,[2] only the language is worse. I wanted to laugh, only it hurt, like laughing at a close relative. Read it yourself, I'm sure you haven't done so. A semelfactive and iterative aspect in the same sentence very often produce such an unpleasant German impression. And then the content and everything, the devil only knows what it all means. The only thing I discovered from it all was that our dear comrade lived in a Mordvinian village and [...] a white-haired Mordvinian woman who wouldn't [...] and a housemaid.[3] This is the sole feeling which permeates the whole work. Read it yourself with this in view and it will all be comprehensible to you. But why! It's incomprehensible.

I also disliked very much the article about *Russian Conversation*,[4] which *you* didn't write. Although I entirely agree with the idea of the article, obscurely and clumsily expressed as it is, why did they abuse Filippov and all of them in an obscene manner and then say: we want the argument to be conducted in a gentlemanly way. It's like saying: Be so good as to [...]. And then I'm completely *ignorant of*, and want to remain *ignorant of*, what postulates and categorical *imperatives* are.[5] No, you made a big mistake in letting Druzhinin[6] leave your coalition. Then one could rely on the criticism in *The Contemporary*, but now it's a disgrace, thanks to this gentleman who smells of lice.[7] You can just hear his

[36] 1. *In the Backwoods*, written by V. V. Bervi, (1829–1918), a former friend of Tolstoy at the University of Kazan. Bervi's later works include *ABC of the Social Sciences* (1871) and *The Position of the Working-Class in Russia* (1872). Both works were banned. Tolstoy objected to the ponderous style and coarse naturalism of the story.

2. *The Staff of Righteousness*, the Works and Compositions of Afanasy Anayevsky. For the Benefit of Lovers of Literature (1852). *The Contemporary* had published a caustic review of it.

3. All Soviet editions of the letter refrain from publishing the actual words used by Tolstoy here, which may reflect the crudity of Bervi's story.

4. Tolstoy is referring to an article written by Chernyshevsky and published in *The Contemporary*, 1856, No. 6, in response to the publication of the first issues of the Slavophile journal *Russian Conversation*. He exaggerates the harshness of Chernyshevsky's criticism.

5. Chernyshevsky had written that good criticism should observe certain 'postulates' and 'categorical imperatives of scholarship', among which he listed particularly the importance of not remaining 'ignorant of' the facts. Tolstoy follows Chernyshevsky in using the gallicism *ignorirovat*, meaning literally 'to ignore' or 'to disregard'.

6. See Letter 37.

7. Chernyshevsky.

36. To N. A. Nekrasov

unpleasant, reedy little voice uttering stupid, unpleasant things and getting more and more worked up because he can't talk properly and his voice is nasty. It's all Belinsky![8] But Belinsky spoke for everyone to hear, and he spoke in an angry voice because he was angry, but this man thinks that in order to speak well you need to speak insolently, and to do that you need to be angry. And he'll go on being angry in his little corner until someone looks him straight in the face and says 'shut up'. Don't think that I'm speaking about Belinsky to be quarrelsome. I'm convinced, on cool reflection, that as a man he was charming and as a writer remarkably useful; but precisely because he stood out from the ordinary rank and file, he produced imitators who are repulsive. There is a firmly established opinion, not only in our criticism, but in our literature and even in society, that it's very nice to be *angry, irritable* and *malicious*. But I find it very nasty. People like Gogol more than Pushkin. Belinsky's criticism is the height of perfection; your poetry is the best loved of any by modern poets. But I find all this nasty, because an irritable and malicious man is not in a normal state. A loving man is quite the reverse, and only in a normal state can you do good and see things clearly. Consequently I like your most recent poetry which contains sadness, i.e. love, and not bitterness, i.e. hatred. There is never any bitterness in a sensible man, least of all in you. One can put on airs, one can pretend to speak with an accent, and even acquire the habit. Sometimes it's fashionable. And bitterness is terribly fashionable with us. People praise you and say: he's an embittered man; they even flatter you about your bitterness, and you succumb to it all. Although it's possible that I haven't recognised the author of the article on *Russian Conversation*, it does occur to me that while *you* certainly didn't write it, you supplemented it and were very pleased with it. Be as cross as you like with me if you don't agree with me, but I'm convinced that what I've written is not just a verbal polemic, and there's a lot more I'd like to talk to you about on the subject, but there isn't time.

I'm getting on with *Youth*, but it's going badly and sluggishly. On the other hand it's so nice here that I wouldn't want to leave for ages. There's no need now for the paper I asked you for,[9] I've got the money. Or rather there is, but I can send the money at once. Goodbye, and please write back.[10]

Just fancy that it's only now that I'm in the country that I've remembered the Longinov business and realised how stupidly and badly I behaved over the whole affair.[11] And now I sincerely ask your forgiveness, as I shall ask Longinov's when

---

8. V. G. Belinsky (1811–48)—the outstanding Russian literary critic of the first half of the nineteenth century, 'the father of the Russian intelligentsia'. His outspoken radical views, his passionate concern with the social significance of art and his graceless and verbose style of writing all aroused the hostility of the literary purists of the 1850s, with whom Tolstoy was on friendly terms.

9. Paper for a separate edition of *Childhood* and *Boyhood*.

10. Nekrasov replied to Tolstoy on 22 July, with a letter defending Chernyshevsky, and pointing out that it is only possible to have a healthy attitude towards reality if that reality is itself healthy. Tolstoy wrote again at the beginning of August in a much more subdued tone.

11. A reference to a quarrel with the literary historian Longinov, which nearly led to a duel, after Tolstoy had accidentally read some offensive remarks about himself in a letter from Longinov to Nekrasov.

37. To A. V. Druzhinin

I see him. I'd like to tell him the whole story too. Do you agree that I should tell him about the letter? I ask now without any blood-thirsty intentions.

As I was on my way through Moscow I walked past him, looking him majestically in the eyes. It's a strange thing how for two months I could have failed to understand all the stupidity, if not much worse, of this affair, as I do now. Please tell Davydov to send me *The Newcomes* in English—part 4 and any later ones there are—I have 3 parts—and *Little Dorrit*. Please reply. Kiss Druzhinin from me and tell him I'm going to write to him, and perhaps he will write; and can you tell me what's happening to Ostrovsky and how to write to him?

If you see Longinov do me a favour and explain how things are and show him what I've written to you if you like.

37. To A. V. DRUZHININ

Alexander Vasilyevich Druzhinin (1824–64), critic, author and translator. He served in the army, and later in the Ministry of War, until his retirement in 1851. His first work of fiction, *Polinka Sachs*, was published in 1847, and enjoyed considerable success. Druzhinin translated several of Shakespeare's plays, and his critical articles on Dr Johnson, Boswell, George Crabbe and Sir Walter Scott were highly esteemed. Druzhinin emerged as a leading critic in 1849, and was closely associated with *The Contemporary*. However, his staunch adherence to the principle of 'art for art's sake' brought him into conflict with the editors of *The Contemporary*, and with Chernyshevsky, who, in contrast, expounded the fundamentally democratic nature of art and its socially educative role in life, and in the autumn of 1855 Druzhinin ceased collaboration with *The Contemporary*, and became editor of the *Reader's Library*. Tolstoy was on particularly friendly terms with Druzhinin in 1856 and 1857. Together with the two critics, Botkin and Annenkov, Druzhinin exercised a considerable influence on the formation and development of Tolstoy's aesthetic views. Nine of Tolstoy's letters to Druzhinin have survived, as have fourteen of his to Tolstoy.

Yasnaya Polyana, 21 September 1856

Your letter made me very happy, dearest Alexander Vasilyevich; particularly as I've been intending to write to you with every day that passes and, quite genuinely, have been thinking of you practically every day. Firstly I've been thinking of you because I like you very much and respect you, again quite genuinely, and secondly, because I wanted to ask you for assistance. I hope to carry out your request,[1] and would do so straight away were I not bound by a promise I made to Krayevsky to give him the first thing I have ready to publish.[2] For the last issue means for December, doesn't it? The thing for Krayevsky is already in preparation; but I have

---

[37] 1. In his letter, Druzhinin had requested a short article or story about the Caucasus for his journal, *Reader's Library*.

2. A. A. Krayevsky (1810–89)—journalist, and editor of *Notes of the Fatherland* and *The Voice*. Tolstoy was preparing *A Landowner's Morning* for publication in the former journal.

37. To A. V. Druzhinin

something almost ready for you that was written for the *Military Journal* which we intended to publish³—only a tiny Caucasian episode, it's true, and I borrowed a little from it for *The Wood-felling*, so it will need to be revised.⁴ This isn't so as to coax you to do the service I'm asking of you—it's simply that it's awfully pleasant for me to do something pleasant for you and, after receiving your letter, and even before, I regretted that hasty contract with *The Contemporary*.⁵ This is my request. I've written the first half of *Youth*, which I promised to *The Contemporary*. I haven't read it to anyone and I've been writing solidly, so that I simply can't judge it at all—everything's confused in my head. It seems to me, however, without being modest, that it's very bad—particularly the careless language, the long-windedness, etc. This seems to me to be so because when I write something alone, without reading it to anyone, I usually think that what I'm writing is both excellent and very bad; but now I'm far more inclined to think the latter. But I'm in complete agreement with you that once one has embraced literature, one can't trifle with it, but must devote one's whole life to it, and so, since I hope to write more that is good in the future, I don't want to publish anything that is bad. This then is my request. I'm sending you the manuscript—read it and give me your strict and frank opinion: is it better or worse than *Childhood* and why, and is it possible to improve it by revising it, or should it be discarded. The latter course seems to me to be best, because having once made a bad start and having worked at it for 3 months, I'm absolutely fed up with it.

But enough of all this. My address is simply Tula. I'm living in the country, and waiting for money in order to go to Petersburg and abroad. I've been hunting, writing, reading a lot, travelling about from village to village, and have fallen a little in love with a certain country lady, but I'm sitting at home because I'm ill, and very seriously. I've had inflammation of the chest, and before recovering from it I caught a chill again, and am not at all well just now. Goodbye, dear Alexander Vasilyevich; since yesterday I've been looking forward to writing to you, and there was quite a lot to say, but now I'm so tired and I've such pains in my chest, that I'm stopping. Please write; I'll send you *Youth* by this post: keep it by you, and don't show it to anyone, and only pass it on to Panayev if your verdict is favourable and if I write to you again.

Yours truly affectionately,
Count L. Tolstoy

P.S. My regards to the dear general⁶ and to everyone who remembers me. If, contrary to expectations, it should only be necessary to delete a little in *Youth*, then do so where you think it necessary.

3. See Letter 27.
4. Tolstoy is referring to a fragment written in 1852 entitled *A Journey to Mamakay Yurt*. As it had been used for *The Wood-felling*, Tolstoy abandoned it and wrote a new story for Druzhinin, *Reduced to the Ranks*, which was published in *Reader's Library* in 1856, No. 12, under the title *Meeting a Moscow Acquaintance in the Detachment*.
5. This refers to a binding agreement between the editors of *The Contemporary* and Tolstoy, Turgenev, Ostrovsky and Grigorovich, under which the latter all undertook to publish exclusively in *The Contemporary* for a four-year period from 1857.
6. Y. P. Kovalevsky (see Letter 84).

38. To V. V. ARSENYEVA

Valeriya Vladimirovna Arsenyeva (1836–1909). On the death of Vladimir Mikhaylovich Arsenyev in 1854, Tolstoy became the guardian of his children— Valeriya, Olga, Yevgeniya and Nikolay. In this capacity, he frequently visited the Arsenyev estate at Sudakovo, some five miles from Yasnaya Polyana, and in the summer of 1856, when Valeriya was twenty years old, he fell in love with her. There can be little doubt that Tolstoy's approaches to Valeriya were largely prompted by the advice of his old friend, D. A. Dyakov, and by his own growing attachment to the ideal of marriage and a family life. An entry in Tolstoy's diary of 15 June 1856, records both Dyakov's advice and one of Tolstoy's earliest reactions to Valeriya: 'The trouble is she has no bones and no fire—just like noodles.' This comment is in many ways characteristic of Tolstoy's extremely critical attitude towards her. For him, marriage was a matter of the utmost importance: although there were moments when he apparently succumbed to the natural charms of Valeriya, his relationship with her was conditioned by his ideal image of a woman and a wife. From 15 June onwards, he was a frequent visitor to the Arsenyev estate, and he constantly confided his thoughts and reactions to his diary:

18 June. Valeriya chatted about clothes and the coronation. Frivolity with her appears to be not a transient, but an enduring passion.
26 June. Valeriya in a white dress. Very sweet. Spent one of the pleasantest days of my life. Do I love her seriously? And can she love for long? Those are two questions I would like to solve for myself, but can't.
28 June. Valeriya is terribly badly educated, and ignorant, if not stupid.
30 June. Valeriya is a wonderful girl, but I definitely don't like her. And if we see each other often in this way, I might suddenly marry her. That might be no misfortune, but quite unnecessary, and I don't want to...
12 July. Valeriya was nicer than ever, but her frivolity and lack of concern for anything serious are horrifying.
10 August. Valeriya and I talked of marriage; she's not stupid and is unusually kind.

On 12 August 1856 the Arsenyevs left for Moscow to attend the festivities marking the coronation of Alexander II. That evening Tolstoy wrote in his diary: 'She was unusually sweet and simple. I would like to know—am I in love or not?' On 17 August he wrote to Valeriya in Moscow: '...to my surprise I feel sad without you'; and he adds: 'However, in your absence, the thought that you'll return a little older comforts me; for youth, when it verges on childishness, is a failing, though a very sweet one...' Valeriya did not reply to his letter, but wrote to T. A. Yergolskaya apparently (the letter has not survived) recounting her social activities and her own successes in society. Tolstoy responded with a further letter, written on 23 August, in which he sarcastically deprecated high society and her enjoyment of it. He ended the letter: 'So, although I'd very much like to come to Moscow to make myself cross looking at you, I won't come, but I'll wish you all

38. To V. V. Arsenyeva

possible vainglorious joys with their usual bitter endings, and remain your most humble and most unpleasant servant, Count L. Tolstoy.' He subsequently regretted the harsh tone of the letter, and on 8 September wrote an apologetic letter to Valeriya. The Arsenyevs returned to the country on 24 September, and the relationship of Tolstoy and Valeriya resumed its former course. Oblique references to the possibility of Valeriya's infatuation with a Frenchman, Mortier (her music tutor when in Moscow), had the effect of increasing Tolstoy's interest in her for a while. However, entries in his diary for the month of October continue to record the ceaseless fluctuation of his feelings for her: from being 'almost in love with her' (24 October) to extreme irritation with her, and vexation that somehow he had been edged into the position of a 'sort of fiancé' (28 October). Finally, at the beginning of November, Tolstoy left for Moscow, partly, no doubt, to escape from his ever-growing commitment to Valeriya, and partly to test his feelings for her through a prolonged period of absence. His letters to Valeriya from Moscow and Petersburg provide a fascinating and informative account of the continuation of the relationship, of Tolstoy's conflicting attitudes and moods, and of his doubts and hesitations. At the same time, they clearly reveal his views on marriage and the ideal that he had formed of what a woman and a wife should be.

Twenty of Tolstoy's letters to Arsenyeva have survived, but none of hers to Tolstoy.

Moscow, 2 November 1856

I arrived last night and have just got up, and I rejoiced to feel that my first thought was of you and that I was sitting down to write, not in order to keep a promise, but because I really wanted to. Throughout the journey, your favourite, *the foolish man*, got completely out of hand and talked such nonsense and made such absurd, though delightful, plans that I began to be afraid of him. He reached the point of wanting to go back in order to return to Sudakovo, to say a lot of foolish things to you and never to part from you again. Fortunately I've long since got used to despising his arguments and paying no attention to him. But when he started arguing, his friend the good man whom you don't like also began to argue and tore the foolish man to shreds. The foolish man said that it was foolish to risk the future, to test oneself and to lose even one moment's happiness. 'You know you're happy when you're with her, looking at her, listening and talking', *the foolish man* said, 'so why deprive yourself of this happiness? Perhaps you've only a day, only an hour left to live, perhaps you're so constituted that you can't love for long and this is after all the strongest love you're able to feel if you would only abandon yourself to it freely. Then again isn't it nasty of you to respond with such cold, deliberate feelings to her pure, devoted love?' *The foolish man* said all this, but the good man, although a little confused at first, replied to all this as follows: 'In the first place you're lying when you say you're happy with her. True, I feel pleasure in listening to her and looking into her eyes, but this isn't happiness, nor even a worthwhile pleasure, excusable in a Mortier,[1] but not in me; then again I often feel

---

[38] 1. Louis Henri Stanislav Mortier de Fontaine (1816–83)—a pianist and composer. He

38. *To V. V. Arsenyeva*

miserable when I'm with her; but the main thing is that I'm not losing my happiness, as you call it, at all, but am happy with her even now when I can't see her. As for what you call my cold feelings, I can tell you that they're a 1,000 times stronger and better than your feelings, although I do keep them in check. You love her for the sake of your own happiness, but I love her for the sake of her happiness.' This is how they argued, and the good man is right a 1,000 times over. Love him a little. If I were to give way to the foolish man's feelings and to yours, I know that all that would come of it would be a month's tumultuous happiness. I was giving way to them just now before I left and I felt that I was becoming bad and dissatisfied with myself: I could say nothing to you except foolish words of endearment, of which I'm now ashamed. There will be time for that, and a happy time. I thank God that He suggested the idea to me and confirmed me in my intention of going away, because I couldn't have done it by myself. I believe that He guided me for the sake of our mutual happiness. It's excusable for you to think and feel as *the foolish man* does, but it would be disgraceful and sinful for me. I already love in you your beauty, but I'm only beginning to love what is eternal in you and forever precious—your heart, your soul. Beauty one can get to know and love in an hour, and cease to love just as quickly, but the soul one has to learn to love. Believe me, nothing on earth comes without hard work, not even love, the most beautiful and natural of feelings. Forgive me this foolish comparison: to love as *the foolish man* does is to play a sonata without keeping time, without accents, with the pedal always down, but with *feeling*, giving no true pleasure thereby either to oneself or to others. But in order to allow oneself to give way to the feeling of the music, one must first hold oneself in check, work and work hard—and believe me there is no pleasure to be had in life without doing so. Everything is acquired by hard work and privation. But the harder the work and the privation, the higher the reward. And the hard work ahead of us is enormous—to understand each other and to retain each other's love and respect. Do you really think that if we had given way to *the foolish man*'s feeling we should have understood each other now? We might have thought so, but later we would have noticed a huge gulf, and having wasted our feelings on foolish endearments we should have nothing left to fill it up with. I guard my feelings like a treasure, because they alone are capable of uniting us firmly in all our views on life, and without this there is no love. In this respect I expect a great deal from our correspondence; we shall discuss things calmly; I shall try to fathom every word of yours and you will do the same, and I don't doubt that we shall understand each other. All the necessary conditions exist—there are feelings and honesty on both sides. Argue, contend, teach me, ask for explanations. I suppose you'll say we understand each other as it is. No, we only trust each other (sometimes when I look at you I'm ready to agree that Il n'y a rien de plus beau au monde, qu'une robe brochée d'or), but we're not agreed yet about many things. On the journey I was turning over in my mind 1,000 things, letters and conversations. In my next letter I shall write to you about plans for the way of life of the

performed in Petersburg and Moscow from 1853 to 1880. Arsenyeva was his pupil for a short period in the autumn of 1856.

38. To V. V. Arsenyeva

Khrapovitskys,[2] then about your relatives, and about Kireyevsky,[3] your relations with whom are more unpleasant to me than those you had with Mortier, and about Vergani and a million problems which aren't so important for the way we solve them, as for the extent to which we agree when discussing them.

I dreamed last night that Seryozha[4] had embarrassed you in some way, and you had become pock-marked and snub-nosed as a result of this embarrassment, and I was so frightened that I woke up. Now I'm giving rein to the foolish man. I remember a few of our unfinished talks. (1) What is your favourite prayer? (2) Why did you ask me whether I wake up at night and remember the past? You meant to say something and didn't finish. I remember you with particular pleasure in 3 guises: (1) at a ball, when you hop up and down rather naively on the same spot and hold yourself terribly erect; (2) when you speak in a weak, sickly voice, grunting a little; and (3) on the bank of the Grumant pond as you cast your line, in a bad temper, wearing Auntie's enormous knitted boots. The foolish man always visualises you with particular fondness in these three guises. Hasn't Mlle Vergani got a spare portrait of you, or couldn't you get the one back from Auntie? I'd very much like to have it. As for me, there's nothing for me to write about, since I haven't seen anyone yet. If your health isn't good, please write to me about it in detail; you weren't well the last two days. If dearest Zhenechka[5] were to write a few lines to me about this, and about your frame of mind, with her customary frankness, she would make me very happy. Please *go for a walk* every day, whatever the weather. It's excellent, any doctor will tell you. And wear a corset, and put on your stockings yourself, and generally make various improvements of that kind in yourself. Don't despair of becoming perfect. But all this is trifling. The main thing is—live in such a way that when you go to bed you can say to yourself: today (1) I did good to someone and (2) I became a little better myself. *Please, please* try to plan the day's occupations in advance and to check up on yourself in the evening. You'll see what a tranquil but great pleasure it is to say to yourself every day: today I've been better than yesterday. Today I managed to do my threes against fours smoothly, or I understood and experienced to the full a good work of art or poetry, or, best of all, I did good to someone and made him love and thank God for me. This is also a pleasure for you yourself, but now you know that there's a person who'll forever love you more and more for all the good things you can easily acquire, simply by overcoming laziness and apathy. Goodbye, dear lady; the foolish man loves you, but in a foolish way; the good man est tout disposé and loves you with the most ardent, tender and eternal love. Answer me as fully, frankly and seriously as you can. My regards to your people. Christ be with you, and may He help us to understand and love each other well. But however all this may end, I shall always thank God for the real happiness I'm experiencing

2. The Khrapovitskys, the name Tolstoy gave to himself and Valeriya when discussing their relationship.
3. N. V. Kireyevsky (1797–1870), a relation of the Arsenyevs, and a former hunting companion and acquaintance of Tolstoy's father.
4. Possibly Sergey Tolstoy.
5. Vergani.

thanks to you—the happiness of feeling myself better and more upright and more honest. God grant that you may think the same.

39. To V. V. ARSENYEVA

Petersburg, 8 November 1856

Dear Valeriya Vladimirovna,

'What has been will never be again,' said Pushkin.[1] Believe me, nothing is forgotten, nor passes away, nor recurs. Never again shall I experience that calm feeling of attachment to you, of respect and trust, that I experienced up until your departure for the coronation. Then, I gladly gave way to my feeling, but now I am afraid of it. I've just written you a long letter,[2] which I've decided not to send to you, but will show you some time later. It was written under the influence of hatred for you. In Moscow a certain gentleman, who doesn't know you, told me that you are in love with Mortier, that you visited him every day, that you are corresponding with him. It was very unpleasant for me to hear this, and I coldly thought over many, many things and wrote about them in the letter which I'm not sending. *That*, the Mortier affair, was the infatuation of a cold nature which is not yet capable of loving, and this one is too; the one has passed off a little under the impact of time and a further infatuation, the other one hasn't yet, but you are still not capable of experiencing love. Indeed, if you think carefully which was the truer and the stronger, you yourself will admit, if you want to be sincere, that the first was the stronger and by far. In the first, you sacrificed much and even acknowledged your love to yourself and to others; in the second, on the contrary, you are sacrificing nothing. The only reprieve is time and more time. How nice it would be if you lived for a while in Moscow!...I await your letters avidly. I'm bored, sad, miserable, unsuccessful in everything—everything is abhorrent. But on no account will I see you until I feel that the foolish man's feelings have entirely passed off, and that I trust you absolutely as before. I've seen your dear Auntie[3] and [...][4] and Dolgorukova, who's marrying Aprenin.[5] It's incomprehensible how you can live with these people without being disgusted. I feel malice towards you because I can't help loving you, and so I don't want to write any more. I'll carry out your commissions today and send the books tomorrow. My regards to your family. Goodbye then simply; and forgive me my peevishness—it's not only I who am to blame for it. Two things I beg of you: work hard, work at yourself, think harder,

[39] 1. A line from *The Gipsies*.
   2. This letter has survived—it is much more harsh and jealous. Tolstoy asked her suspiciously how far her relations with Mortier had gone, claimed that she had lost his respect and trust, and argued that since she had some reason to think that he might propose to her, she should show no interest in anyone else.
   3. Shcherbacheva.
   4. One word undecipherable.
   5. Tolstoy's writing 'Aprenin' is a mistake. It should be Apreyaninov (S. A.), who married Y. D. Dolgorukova, the daughter of Prince Dolgorukov, Ambassador to Teheran and later a member of the Senate.

39. To V. V. Arsenyeva

and assess your feelings sincerely and be sincere with me in a way most unfavourable to yourself. Tell me everything that was, and is, bad in you. I involuntarily assume too much good in you. For instance, if you were to tell me the whole history of your love for Mortier, with the certainty that that feeling was good, and with regret for that feeling, and even if you were to say that you still loved him, it would be more agreeable to me than the indifference and seeming disdain with which you speak of him, and which demonstrates that you are not looking at him dispassionately, but under the influence of this new infatuation. You say and think that I'm cold, and calculating: but God grant you may not go through as many painful things as I've gone through these last 5 months. Well, goodbye and Christ be with you; try not to get angry with me for this letter. I'm not afraid of revealing myself as I am, although I'm very bad, what with my indecisiveness, doubts and every sort of nastiness; you do likewise. You see, the main question is whether we're able to get on together and love each other; for this purpose we need to express all that is bad in us in order to know whether we're capable of coming to terms with it, and not to hide it, so that we shan't be unexpectedly disappointed afterwards. It would be painful for me now, terribly painful, to lose that feeling of infatuation that you have for me, but it's really better to lose it now than to reproach myself for ever for a deception which could cause you unhappiness. If the ladies of Petersburg and Moscow, old and young, interest you, I can tell you that so far they simply don't exist for me at all.

Yours,
Count L. Tolstoy

40. To V. V. ARSENYEVA

Petersburg, 9 November 1856

It's so painful for me to think about my letter to you yesterday, dear Valeriya Vladimirovna, that now I don't know how to begin this letter, and it's not enough for me to think about you—I so much want to write. I'm sending you some books; do try to read them; start with the short ones, the tales—they're charming—and write and tell me your *sincere* opinion. As regards Nikolenka,[1] I haven't been able to do anything yet; I'll send him a book by the next post. Belavin is absolutely the same, and is an indescribable scoundrel, and it's sinful to think with indifference that a nice girl is going to marry him. Write and tell me if it's true about the wedding, and I'll then write to Lazarevicheva. In all this time I've only seen my literary friends,[2] a few of whom I like; but I avoid my social acquaintances, and haven't seen any of them so far. Today I worked the whole evening with Ivan Ivanovich[3] and for the first time am very pleased about it. Yes, I'm writing about

---

[40] 1. N. V. Arsenyev, Valeriya's younger brother. Tolstoy was helping with the arrangements for his admission to the Imperial College of Law (see Letter 42).

2. In Moscow Tolstoy met Ostrovsky, Botkin and Grigoryev, and in Petersburg, Druzhinin, Panayev, Polonsky and Goncharov.

3. I. I. Sakharov, Tolstoy's copyist.

40. To V. V. Arsenyeva

myself because, under the influence of that letter, you perhaps not only feel a silent hatred towards me, but may even have no feelings whatsoever. I'm also sending you Turgenev's Tales;[4] read them too, if it's not a bore—again, in my opinion, they're nearly all charming, but all the same come out with your opinion frankly, however absurd it may be. *Wage nur zu irren zu träumen!*—Schiller said.[5] It's terribly true that you must make mistakes boldly, firmly and resolutely, and only then will you get at the truth. Well, yes, for you this is still incomprehensible and premature. Why don't you write to me; if only such nasty letters as mine, why don't you write? Kostenka's[6] better than I expected him to be. A big change has come over him; texts from the Holy Scriptures aren't a joke any more; he's recently come to understand the great thing that good is happiness; you remember, I often used to ask you about this. You'll come to understand it too, but only with time, and—sad to say—this great truth can only be understood through suffering, and he has suffered; but you haven't lived yet: you haven't experienced enjoyment and suffering, but only gaiety and sadness. Some people never know either enjoyment or suffering—moral, of course—all their lives. It often seems to me that you are such a person, and it hurts me terribly. Tell me, if you understand the question clearly: are you like that or not? But at any rate you're a nice, a really nice, a terribly nice person. Why don't you write to me? I can't bring myself to write all I wanted to write to you about the Khrapovitskys' way of life, without some response from you, and particularly to my second letter. However, to tell the truth—my hand on my heart—I'm already thinking of you much less now, and more calmly, than I did in the early days, but even so, more than I have ever thought about any other woman. Please answer me this question as sincerely as you can in every letter: *to what extent and in what way do you think about me?* My special feeling for you, that I haven't felt for anyone else, is this: as soon as something unpleasant, big or small, happens to me—a failure, a blow to my self-esteem etc.—I remember you that very second and think—'it's all nonsense—there's a certain young lady, and nothing else matters to me'. It's a pleasant feeling. How are you? Are you *working*? For goodness sake write to me. Don't laugh at the word work. *To work* wisely, usefully, with the object of doing good, is excellent; but even doing work of the simplest and most futile kind, planing a small stick, anything—this is the first condition of a good, moral life and, therefore, of happiness. For instance—I was *working* today, my conscience is easy, I feel a small, modest self-satisfaction and because of this I feel that I'm good. Today I wouldn't have written you such a malicious letter as I did yesterday for anything; today I feel friendliness towards the whole world, and towards you the very feeling I would like to feel forever. Ah, if only you could understand and feel and reach through suffering, as I have done, the conviction that the only possible, the only true, everlasting and supreme happiness comes from three things: work, self-denial and love! I know this, I have this conviction in my soul, but I only live in accordance with it for some 2 hours in the course of a year; you, however, with your honest nature, you could give yourself

4. *Tales and Stories*, published in three parts in 1856.
5. A line from *Thekla*.   6. K. A. Islavin.

40. To V. V. Arsenyeva

wholly to this conviction just as you are capable of giving yourself wholly to people—Mlle Vergani etc. And 2 people united by this conviction, yes, that's the height of happiness. Goodbye; words can't prove this, rather is it inspired by God when the time comes. Christ be with you, my dear, truly dear Valeriya Vladimirovna. I don't know what you have given me more of so far: moral suffering or enjoyment. But I'm so foolish at moments like this, that I'm grateful for both.

Do write every day, for goodness sake. However, if there's no need to, don't write; or no: when you don't feel like writing, just write the following sentence: *Today, such and such a date, I don't feel like writing*, and send it. I'll be glad of it. For goodness sake, don't think up your letters, don't re-read them; you see, I who could show off like that in front of you—and do you really think that I don't want to flirt with you?—I only want to show off my honesty and sincerity in front of you; but *you* have all the more reason to do that yourself—I know many women more intelligent than you, but I've never met one more honest. Besides, too great an intellect is repugnant, but the more honesty there is, and the more complete it is, the more one loves it. You see, I so ardently wish to love you that I'm teaching you how to make me love you. And really the main feeling I have for you is not love as yet, but a passionate longing to love you with all my heart.

Do write, for goodness sake, as quickly, as fully and as incoherently and clumsily —and therefore as sincerely—as you can.

It's possible to live perfectly on earth if one is able to work and to love, to work for what one loves, and to love what one is working at. I embrace darling Zhenechka most heartily. Also the Pindigashki[7] a little. I press Olga Vladimirovna's[8] hand most heartily.

Tell Natalya Petrovna that O. Turgeneva[9] wasn't thinking of getting married. If you should happen to want to write something to me and are hesitant about doing so, *please* hint at it. All questions must be cleared up boldly. I drop many hints to you, even coarse ones, but you never do.

41. To V. V. ARSENYEVA

Petersburg, 11 November 1856

It's your friend Ivan Ivanovich's[1] fault that the books are two days late. Of Turgenev's Tales, don't read *The Jew* or *Petushkov*: they're not for young ladies; among them I particularly recommend: *Andrey Kolosov*, *The Backwater* and *Two Friends*. Of the English ones—*Nicholas Nickleby* and *La foire aux vanités*. There's

---

7. Tolstoy's name for children generally. Here he means Valeriya's younger brother and sister.
8. Valeriya's sister.
9. O. A. Turgeneva, a distant relative of Turgenev, who at one time intended to marry her. She was the model for Tatyana, the heroine of Turgenev's novel *Smoke*. Tolstoy knew her well.

[41] 1. Sakharov.

a book each for Shmigaro and Zhurzhenka.² When you've read Turgenev's Tales, send them to Auntie. The sonata is the one I have spoken to you of more than once—it's not difficult. The Rondo and Largo are particularly fine. I terribly want to write to you, and there's a lot to say, but I can't bring myself to do so—I'm still waiting to hear from you. Are you really not going to marry Gromov?³ If you did, it would be quite like a French novel. I moved today to a flat: at the corner of Bolshaya Meshchanskaya and Voznesenskaya, No. 14, Blum House. If it interests you to know in what state my thoughts about you are, I must announce with regret that the *diminuendo* after Moscow has nearly passed, and a *crescendo* is beginning again now. Do write to me for goodness sake. Why don't you write? Goodbye, dear lady, and Christ be with you.

Count L. Tolstoy

42. To V. V. ARSENYEVA

Petersburg, 12–13 November 1856

I feel I'm being foolish, dear lady, but I can't help it, and although I still haven't received a single line from you, I'm writing to you again. It's now past 12 o'clock at night, and you know yourself how this time disposes one to tenderness and, therefore, to foolishness. I'll write to you about the future way of life of the Khrapovitskys, if it's to be their fate to live on earth. The way of life of a man and a woman depends (1) on their inclinations, and (2) on their means. Let's consider them both. Khrapovitsky, a man morally old, who did many foolish things in his youth for which he has paid with the happiness of the best years of his life, and who has now found for himself both a purpose and a vocation—literature—at heart despises society, adores a peaceful, moral, family life and fears nothing in the world so much as a dissipated social life, in which all good, honest, pure thoughts and feelings perish and in which you become the slave of social conventions and creditors. He's already paid for his delusions with the best years of his life, so that this conviction of his is not just talk, but a conviction born of the painful experience of life. Dear Miss Dembitskaya¹ has experienced nothing of all this as yet: happiness for her is a ball, bare shoulders, a carriage, diamonds, acquaintance with gentlemen-in-waiting and generals' aides-de-camp etc. But it so happens that Khrapovitsky and Dembitskaya seem to love each other (perhaps I'm lying to myself, but I do terribly love you again at this moment). So these two people with opposite inclinations have, it seems, fallen in love with each other. How then must they arrange matters so as to live together? Firstly they must make concessions to each other; secondly the one whose inclinations are less moral must make more concessions. I would be prepared to live all my life in the country. I would have 3 occupations: love for Dembitskaya and concern for her happiness, literature, and

2. Valeriya's brother and sister.
3. An architect from the Tula Province. There is no evidence of any 'affair' between Gromov and Arsenyeva.
[42] 1. This is the name Tolstoy gives to Valeriya in his correspondence.

42. To V. V. Arsenyeva

managing my estate in the way I understand it, i.e. fulfilling my duty towards the people entrusted to me. The one disadvantage about all this is that I would involuntarily fall behind the times, and that's a bad thing. Miss Dembitskaya dreams of living in Petersburg, going to 30 balls a season, entertaining her fine friends at home, and going for drives along the Nevsky in her carriage. The middle course between these two requirements is a life of 5 months in Petersburg, without balls, without a carriage, without unusual attire with lace trimming and point d'Alençon, and *completely removed from society*; and 7 months in the country. Khrapovitsky has an income of 2,000 silver roubles from his estate (i.e. if he doesn't squeeze the last penny out of the unfortunate peasants, like everyone else); he also has about 1,000 silver roubles a year from his literary work (but this is uncertain, for he might become stupid or be unhappy and not write anything). Miss Dembitskaya has a disputed promissory note for 20,000 roubles from which, if she were to receive it, she would have about 800 roubles interest—all told, under the most advantageous conditions, a sum of 3,800 roubles a year. Do you know what 3,800 roubles means in Petersburg? To live in Petersburg for 5 months on that money, it would be necessary to live on a 5th floor, have 4 rooms, have a woman cook, not a chef, and not dare to think of having a carriage and a poplin dress with point d'Alençon lace or a blue hat, for such a hat jurera with everything else. With those means it would be possible to live in Tula or Moscow, and even occasionally show off in front of the Lazareviches, but merci for that. We could also live on a 3rd floor in Petersburg, have a carriage and point d'Alençon lace, hide from our creditors, tailors and tradesmen, and write to the country to say that all the instructions I gave for the relief of the peasants were rubbish, and that the last penny must be squeezed out of them, and then go ourselves to the country and stay there for years feeling ashamed and getting cross with other, and for this too—merci! I've experienced it. There's a different sort of life on the 5th floor (poor but honest), in which everything that might be spent on luxury is spent on domestic luxury, on the decoration of the small flat on the 5th floor, on a cook, on the cuisine, on wine, so that our friends might enjoy coming to that 5th floor, on books, music, pictures, concerts, quartets at home, but not on superficial luxury to astonish the Lazareviches, flunkeys and blockheads (12 November).

Goodbye, I'm going to bed; I press your dear hand and think about you far too much. I shall continue tomorrow. Now I shall write in my little yellow book, again about you. I'm a fool.

13 November. I shall continue this letter another time when I've heard from you; just now it somehow doesn't interest me, and I've something else on my mind. I'm writing to you for the last time. What's the matter with you? Are you ill? Do you have a bad conscience again about something on my account, or are you ashamed of the relations that have been established between us? Whatever it is, write me a line. At first I was affectionate, then I was angry, and now I feel I'm already becoming indifferent, and thank God! Some instinct has long been telling me that nothing will come of this except your unhappiness and mine. It's better to stop in time. I'm sending you a programme about admission to the preparatory class in

Jurisprudence. Everything is there. When you submit an application in May, write on it that the documents formerly sent by me are already with the Council of Jurisprudence. Notice, that in order to qualify for entry Nikolenka[2] has to learn to read and write German, which he appears not to know. The person who takes him there will provide the guarantee. When I love you, I often want to come to you and tell you everything I feel; but at times like this, when I'm angry with you and feel completely indifferent, I want even more to see you and to speak to you about everything that has boiled up inside me, and to prove to you that we can never love each other, and that no one is to blame for this except God and ourselves, if we go on deceiving ourselves and each other.

In any case, for the sake of the true God, I implore you by the memory of your father, and all that you hold sacred, be frank with me, absolutely frank, and don't allow yourself to be carried away.

Goodbye, and may God grant you all that is good.

Yours,
Count L. Tolstoy[3]

43. To V. V. ARSENYEVA

Petersburg, 19 November 1856

Thank you very much, darling, for your letters. I've received three; I haven't received the portrait, but don't worry: nobody can or will see either the letters or the portrait. This is my 7th letter I'm writing. Your last letter moved me very, very much, and I felt ashamed that I had hurt you. What can I do? It's better all the same than if I'd concealed this doubt within me. I'll answer point by point. (1) You judge Kireyevsky well, but not altogether sincerely—you're afraid to understand my idea, which is that he is rich and you are poor; he is your uncle and godfather and so might think you are hoping to receive money from him. If I were in your place, I would firmly make up my mind never to receive anything from him, and only then would I love and respect him if he deserved it. (2) You say that you're ready to sacrifice *everything* for a letter from me. God forbid that you should think such a thing, and there's no need to say it. Included in this *everything* is *virtue*, which one can't sacrifice, not just for a worthless creature like me, but for anything in the world. Think about it. Without respect for *good*, above all else, one can't live happily on earth. (3) Your habit of waking up at nights is good and very sweet. (4) Why did Ostrovsky's comedy make you gloomy?

(5) Zhenechka's[1] postscript is cruel. Do you really get so agitated, in fact, that you turn to fortune-telling and nonsense of that sort? Avoid all such upsetting remedies and especially idleness. Don't say that a golden age is dying. On the

2. N. V. Arsenyev.
3. Tolstoy followed up this letter with a further and rather more affectionate one on 17 November in which he acknowledged receiving two 'sweet, good, honest' letters from Valeriya and apologised for his two previous letters.

[43] 1. Mlle Vergani.

43. To V. V. Arsenyeva

contrary, we are both living, and living with the same good feelings as God grant we may live with ever after. (6) Don't think, darling, that no one has ever loved you as your father loved you. You deserve a great and powerful love and therefore you will have it. That's how the world is ordered. (7) Don't write about and don't commit the folly of coming to Petersburg, but if you're well off for money, go and spend at least a month in Moscow, and then, perhaps, come to Petersburg.

(8) For goodness sake, don't think I'm so perfect; you embarrass me terribly by it. If I'm so intelligent, it's no merit of mine; on the other hand, my heart is tainted with doubt, distrust and all sorts of nastiness. If there is something in me that one can love, it's honesty when it comes to feelings. I have never deceived you, and never will deceive you. You are a different matter: you have a fresh nature, untainted with doubts; if you love, you love, if you hate, you hate; you will never understand much that interests me, but on the other hand I shall never attain the height of love which you can attain if only you won't force or deceive yourself. So it's I who must feel myself unworthy of you, and not you of me, darling. And I do feel it. But it's just this difference in our characters, which really won't change—and if it were to change, it would be so much the worse,—it's just this difference that is terrible for our future. This is what we must reconcile ourselves to: I—to the fact that a great part of the intellectual interests which are the main ones of my life will remain alien to you, despite all your love; and you—you must reconcile yourself to the thought that you will never find in me that fullness of feeling which you will give to me. Although only for short times and in fits and starts, my feelings can be much stronger even than yours, and my respect and gratitude for your love, while it lasts, will not weaken for a second. One thing that can firmly unite us is a true love of good, which I have attained with the intellect, and you will attain with the heart. So it seems to me; but God grant that it might be as you dream, when you walk up and down the drawing room with your hands behind your back. My strength, for which you love me, is the intellect; your strength is the heart. Both these things are good, and we'll try to develop both of them with each other's help: you will teach me to love, I will teach you to think. How is it you understand the necessity for work and love in life, yet don't understand self-denial? Isn't work self-denial? And love? You say yourself in the letter before last that you feel you loved me selfishly. It's very true; only it means you didn't love me at all. It's impossible to love for one's own pleasure, rather one loves for the pleasure of another. But why explain to you what your excellent heart already knows. Please don't stop writing to me about your occupations, and in more detail: what you've been reading, what you've been playing, and for how many hours. Please don't waste the evenings. Take yourself in hand. Not simply so that the evenings' occupations will be useful to you, but so as to teach yourself to overcome bad tendencies and laziness. I stopped here and thought for a long time about your character. Your principal defect is weakness of character, and all the other minor defects come from it. Cultivate strength of will. Take yourself in hand and fight persistently against your bad habits. It's boring to teach Zhurzhenka[2]—be sure to

2. Yevgeniya Vladimirovna Arsenyeva, Valeriya's younger sister.

43. To V. V. Arsenyeva

make yourself do it. Without work, everything and—most important—happiness, is impossible. And I'll jump for joy to read about your successes over yourself. For goodness sake, go for a walk and don't sit for long in the evening; take care of your health. Zhenechka says you're getting thin—that's not good. I'll come in January almost certainly.[3] That I want to come and terribly want to come immediately and never go away again—that you must believe, for I never lie to you in this respect, rather the contrary. Three days ago I spent the evening at Turgeneva's—Olga Alexandrovna's—she's a sweet girl, and I couldn't help comparing her with another girl I know. No, so far I know no one better than this other girl: she's both better to look at, and her heart is the best in the world, and she plays better; only the first girl has read more, is more mature, and loves and understands poetry more. I ask myself incessantly: am I in love with you or not, and I answer: no, but something draws me to you; it always seems that we should be close to each other as people, and that you are my best friend. This, I think, is how the Khrapovitskys should live. Their means are small, but such that with hard work and practical skill, which *he* doesn't possess at all, and of which *she* has little (so it would be very desirable for her to develop it in herself), the Khrapovitskys can live 5 months in town and 7 months in the country, and in both places poorly, but honestly. The 5 winter months they can spend abroad one year, and in Petersburg the next, and then abroad again etc. But in Petersburg or abroad without fail, so that neither of them will fall behind the times, or become provincialised, which is its own sort of unhappiness. And not to fall behind the times—not in the sense of knowing what hats and waistcoats are being worn, but of knowing what remarkable new book has come out, or what question is preoccupying Europe, or of not buying and selling people or collecting quitrent from the peasants, when every student already knows that it's shameful, etc. In Petersburg, the Khrapovitskys can, without going into society, have a small circle of acquaintances chosen not from people who are simply comme il faut and who are like dogs, but from intelligent, educated and good people. This item is particularly important for Mrs Khrapovitskaya who, on account of her youth, loves a lot of new acquaintances and requires nothing from them except that they should be comme il faut and not blockheads. In this respect Mr Khrapovitsky is, on the contrary, convinced that this is not enough and that one should be as careful as possible in the choice of acquaintances, because it's no misfortune to be acquainted with one shallow person, but if you are acquainted with 30, then, without doing you any harm, they will, by their visits and invitations alone, deprive you of the freedom of loisir and poison your life. Besides, Mr Khrapovitsky thinks that he, with his literature and dear Mrs Khrapovitskaya, and Mrs Khrapovitskaya, with her music and Mr Khrapovitsky, won't be bored on their own at home. The Khrapovitskys will use all their means, however much they increase, on domestic luxury—on the arrangement of rooms, on pictures, on music, on food and wine—so that home will be the most cheerful place of all, and Mrs Khrapovitskaya will be primarily engaged in this. When living in Petersburg or

---

3. Tolstoy stayed in Petersburg until 12 January 1857, when he moved to Moscow. On 29 January he set off on his first journey to Western Europe, without seeing Valeriya meanwhile.

43. To V. V. Arsenyeva

abroad, the Khrapovitskys will see little of each other, because both society and occupations will distract them both; and because of this they won't bore each other so quickly; on the other hand in the country, where they'll try not to see a single outsider, they'll bore each other to their heart's content. But there won't be any silent hatred, because they'll both have occupations there as well. That's the most important thing of all. Mr Khrapovitsky will carry out his very long-standing intention—in which Mrs Khrapovitskaya will no doubt support him—to make as many of his peasants as possible happy;[4] he will read and write and study and teach Mrs Khrapovitskaya and call her 'poppet'. Mrs Khrapovitskaya will occupy herself with music and reading, and, sharing Mr Khrapovitsky's plans, will help him in his main activity. I imagine her as a little Benefactress to the peasants, going to their huts in a poplin dress with her black head of hair, and returning every day with the consciousness that she has done a good deed and waking up at night satisfied with herself and wanting the dawn to come quicker in order to live again and do good, for which Mr Khrapovitsky will adore her more and more, ad infinitum. And then they will go to town again, and will live an abstemious, quite arduous life again with hardships and regrets, but on the other hand with the knowledge that they are good and honest people, and that they love each other with all their hearts, having good friends who will love them both warmly, and each having his own favourite occupation. Perhaps it will sometimes happen that when returning in an old hackney carriage from seeing some modest friend, they will go past a lighted house where there's a ball, and a Strauss orchestra can be heard playing wonderful waltzes. Perhaps Mrs Khrapovitskaya will sigh deeply at this and grow pensive, but she really must get used to the idea that this pleasure will never really be hers to experience. On the other hand, Mrs Khrapovitskaya can be quite confident that few, very few, perhaps not a single one of those she envies at this ball, has ever experienced her pleasures,—tranquil love, friendship, the charm of family life, a friendly circle of nice people, poetry, music and her chief pleasure—the consciousness of not living in vain in the world, of doing good and having nothing to reproach herself with. Everyone has his own pleasures, but the highest pleasures given to man are the pleasure of the *good* that he does, and of pure *love and poetry* (l'art). But having once chosen this path, the Khrapovitskys must firmly believe that it's the best path, that it's not necessary for them to travel by any other one; they must support one another, pause, point out to each other the pitfalls, and with the help of religion which points to the same path, must never stray from it. For the slightest faux pas destroys everything, and you can't regain a happiness that is lost. And there are many of these faux pas: *coquetry*, and in consequence of its mistrust—jealousy and malice; *jealousy* without reason; *triviality* which destroys love and trust; *secretiveness* which implants suspicion; *idleness* which makes you bored with each other; a *hot temper* which makes you say things to each other like

---

4. This 'intention' of Tolstoy dates back to the summer months of the years 1847–9 when he lived at Yasnaya Polyana, and when, for the first time, he attempted to realise some of his ideas for improving the conditions of the peasants. Tolstoy's work, *A Landowner's Morning*, to a large extent records his experiences of the time, although it reflects also the relationship of Dmitry Tolstoy with his peasants.

43. To V. V. Arsenyeva

little boys who never grow up; *carelessness* and inconsistency in one's plans; and the main thing—*extravagance* and prodigality, as a result of which one's affairs are thrown into disorder, one's good spirits are demoralised, plans disrupted, peace and quiet destroyed, aversion for each other generated—and so goodbye!

It's a hard path, yes; but it's a delightful one, and it alone leads to true happiness; so it's worth while working at yourself and doing away with all those underlined reasons for making 'faux pas'.

And if it's too hard, then I advise the Khrapovitskys to act like this: to live in Petersburg, not on the fourth floor but on the first, to have 30 dresses made for Mrs Khrapovitskaya, to attend all the balls, to entertain at home all the aides-de-camp to generals and royalty and be proud of it, and to drive along the Nevsky in their carriage. I advise Mrs Khrapovitskaya to play the coquette, and Mr Khrapovitsky to play cards, then, having disgraced themselves, to flee from their debts to the country, and to become hateful to each other, and…

All this is very, very easy: you've only to stop putting pressure on yourself, and it happens of its own accord; and, once they've strayed from the first path, it's very easy for the Khrapovitskys to end up on this one. And doubtless they will do so if they stray, for Mr Khrapovitsky has a feeble and unpractical nature, and so has Mrs Khrapovitskaya. But the first path—what a happy, charming dream it is! If I were now sitting with you at Sudakovo in a little corner of the drawing-room, I would say a very great deal to you. However, perhaps you yourself understand the charm of this dream. If you do, don't forget one thing,—I'm speaking after serious thought and from experience of life,—*there is no middle course, choose one of the two*: either choose the first in all its severity, repeating to yourself every day, every minute that I want to go along this path, or else you will involuntarily end up on the second, in a slough, in which 999 people out of 1,000 get stuck. I've sat for a long time over this letter; I haven't so much written as thought, and it's already 2 o'clock. About myself—I can tell you that I'm well and I'm working[5]—what on doesn't interest you yet—that I see very few people and still haven't paid any visits to anyone and won't do so until December. I haven't managed to get the portrait done today. I will tomorrow. Goodbye, my darling, work at yourself, be firm, take courage, study, and love me just the same, only a little more calmly. I'm so happy at the thought that there is you who loves me, that I don't know what would become of me if you suddenly told me that you didn't love me. Please, don't try to. I embrace Zhenechka, press Olenka's hand, and kiss Natasha's hind legs. Ivan Ivanovich[6] went to see *The Huguenots*[7] yesterday: he didn't like it very much; but Alyosha[8] found it wonderful!

5. Tolstoy was currently working on his story, *Reduced to the Ranks*.
6. I. I. Sakharov.
7. An opera by Meyerbeer, written in 1836.
8. A. S. Orekhov, Tolstoy's valet. He had been with Tolstoy in the Caucasus, Silistria and Sevastopol.

44. To V. V. ARSENYEVA

Petersburg, 23–4 November 1856

I've just received your wonderful, glorious, perfect letter of 15 November. Don't be cross with me, darling, for calling you this in my letters. The word exactly fits the feeling I have for you. Just *darling*. And how many times when chatting with you I terribly wanted to call you this—not any other name—just this. This letter must be short unless I get carried away, because I've such a lot of work to do of the most pressing and tormenting kind, and as a result I haven't slept for several nights. You know we've concluded a contract with *The Contemporary* to publish our things there, starting in 1857, but I've promised something for Druzhinin[1] and for Krayevsky[2] for *The Notes of the Fatherland*, and these have to be written for 1 December. For Druzhinin I've somehow managed to write a short story, but the thing for Krayevsky isn't going well; I've written it, but am not satisfied myself; I feel it needs revising, but there's no time and I'm not in the mood, but I'm working nevertheless. On the one hand I must keep my word, on the other—I'm afraid of damaging my literary reputation which, I confess, I value very much, almost as much as a certain lady you know. I'm in a foul mood, I'm dissatisfied with myself, and therefore with everyone in the world; I'm in a bad temper; why did I give my word? I want to work on my old things—but I'm disgusted, and as ill luck would have it, plans for new works which seem delightful keep coming into my head. This is the mood your last letter found me in, and it comforted me entirely. Nothing else matters as long as you love me and are as I wish, i.e. perfect; and from your letter it seemed to me that you both loved me and were beginning to understand life more seriously and to love the good and to find pleasure in watching yourself and going forward along the path to perfection. This path is endless; it continues in the next life and is delightful, and it is the same one on which you find happiness in this life. May God help you, my darling; go forward, love, love not only me but the whole of God's world, people, nature, music, poetry, and everything that is delightful in it, and develop your mind so as to be able to understand the things that are worthy of love on earth. Love is one's main vocation and happiness on earth. Although what I'm going to say doesn't entirely fit in with our conversation, there's another great reason why a woman ought to develop herself. Besides a woman's vocation to be a wife, her chief vocation is to be a mother, and in order to be a *mother* and not a *wet-nurse* (do you understand this distinction?), development is necessary. Don't be cross, darling (I do terribly enjoy calling you this) at the remarks I'm going to make to you. (1) You always say that your love is pure, elevated etc. In my opinion, to say my love is elevated etc., is the same as saying that my nose and eyes are very nice. This must be left for others to judge, not you.

(2) In your excellent supplement to the Khrapovitskys' plan of life, it's bad that you want to live in the country and travel to Tula. God forbid! The country ought to be a place of seclusion and work, as I wrote in my letter before last, and nothing

[44] 1. *Reduced to the Ranks.*   2. *A Landowner's Morning.*

44. To V. V. Arsenyeva

else, but you wouldn't be able to stand such a country life, and Tula acquaintances breed provincialism, which is terribly dangerous. Both the Khrapovitskys will become provincials and will silently hate each other for being provincials. I've seen examples of it. I've even felt a silent hatred for Auntie,[3] mainly for her provincialism. No, my dear, the Khrapovitskys will either see no one, or else the best society in the whole of Russia, i.e. the best society not in the sense of royal favour and wealth, but in the sense of intellect and education. They will have rooms on the 4th floor, but the most remarkable people in Russia will gather in them. God forbid that because of this we should be rude to our Tula friends and relatives, but we must keep them at a distance, we don't need them; and I told you that relations with people we don't need are always harmful.

(3) Alas! You are deluding yourself that you have taste. That is, you may have, but you haven't any tact. For instance, a certain style of dress, like a pale blue hat with white flowers is splendid; but it suits a lady riding a trotter in English harness or walking up a staircase with mirrors and camellias; but in a modest 4th floor environment, a hansom-cab etc, such a hat is ridiculous, while in the country or in a springless carriage—goodness me! Then there's a certain type of woman, something like Shcherbacheva,[4] or even much worse, who, in this kind of élégance, bright colours, dishevelled coiffure and anything unusual—ermine mantillas, crimson cloaks, and so on—will always outdo you, and the only result will be that you will look like them. Both girls and women who haven't lived much in big cities always make this mistake. There's another kind of élégance—modest, shunning anything unusual, bright, but very particular over small things, over details such as shoes, collars, gloves, clean nails, a neat hairstyle etc., for which I stand as firm as a rock, as long as it doesn't take up too much attention from serious things, and which any man who loves refinement can't help but love. The élégance of bright colours etc., is excusable, although ridiculous, in an ugly young lady, but for you with your pretty little face it's inexcusable to make such a mistake. If I were you, I would take simplicity as the rule for your attire, but with the strictest refinement in all the smallest details.

And (4) WALKS ROUND THE SHOPPING ARCADE!!! Good Lord! But all this wouldn't matter if you were dreaming even of going to study music in the Tula arms factory, and it would be nothing in comparison with the wonderful sincerity and love which your letters breathe. For goodness sake, don't let my remarks spoil your best quality—sincerity. Who's Olenka[5] in love with? Can't you say? It's looking at you that's made her lose her head. Goodbye, till tomorrow. I've received a note for 1 rouble, which must be the portrait, and tomorrow, when I receive it, I'm afraid I'll become foolish, even more foolish than I am now. I'm sorry I haven't had mine done, I haven't had time. When there's really a lot to write, there isn't time, and to write to you gives me great pleasure. Goodbye, darling, darling, a thousand times darling—whether you're angry or not, I've written it all the same. Christ be with you.

3. T. A. Yergolskaya.   4. V. V. Arsenyeva's aunt.   5. Olga Arsenyeva.

44. To V. V. Arsenyeva

Just now, after finishing my work for the day which is a torture for me, and which I wrote to you about, I opened a book and read a wonderful thing—Goethe's *Iphigenia*. It's impossible for you to understand (perhaps you'll understand in time) the indescribably great pleasure one feels from understanding and loving poetry; but the point is that the immense pleasure I felt for some reason made me remember you, and want to write to you: *darling*, and nothing more. I haven't received your portrait yet, but I'm sending mine, and have already given it to Ivan Ivanovich.[6] It will soon be a month since I saw you, but I still think of you in almost the same way—sometimes with mistrust and malice, but for the most part with foolish love. However, I do nothing to test my feeling. Since I went away, I've been leading a much more secluded life than at Yasnaya. From 1 December I'll plunge into every sort of distraction, and see what happens. I'll come to see you no earlier than the holidays, and even that's not for sure. At present I'm still working for the December issues; my main task—to revise *Youth*—I haven't started yet: it will take up the whole of December. Did you go to the ball? Won't you go to Moscow to take some lessons from Mortier? Both these things are very, very necessary, and I advise you a thousand times to do them. Please, darling, do so. How's the music? I often dream that, when I return to dear Sudakovo in 5 weeks' time and chat with you beside the fire, you'll sit down at the piano and suddenly stagger me with your exceptional progress. If you're not lazy, you can do this. Goodbye, darling, dearest lady, I press your dear hand; Christ be with you. I'll probably write again tomorrow. Write, write as before, only with more details of your occupations—what you're reading, and how, and what you like.

To the charming Zhenechka—Ooha!
To the Pindigashki—Oohi!
To the love-stricken Olenka—O—okh!
Shall we have to live in grief for long
Bearing cruel sorrows?
What do you think? I think—not for long.

I remember—my letter to you yesterday was foolish; for some reason I was terribly conceited.

45. To V. V. ARSENYEVA

Petersburg, 27–8 November 1856

Yesterday I received the second of your letters, written after preparing for communion, and today the first. I don't know whether it's because the letters aren't nice, or because I'm beginning to change, or because you mention Mortier in your last one, but the letters haven't made such a pleasant impression on me as the first ones. I congratulate you[1] with all my heart and am glad you are taking it so seriously.

---

6. I. I. Sakharov.

[45] 1. It was the custom in the Orthodox church to congratulate a person on receiving communion. The Russian word translated by 'preparing for communion' literally means 'fasting',

45. To V. V. Arsenyeva

There's one thing wrong—you must talk less, so as to feel more. And you mustn't be too carried away by the hope that everything will begin afresh, and that by means of this sacrament you are severing the links with the past. It helps a great deal in life and purifies one spiritually, but not in the way you think. For instance, the fact that you say that after preparing for communion you'll keep a watch on yourself, exert yourself and work hard (I'm adding this for you)—is excellent, and may God help you in these thoughts, but the Mortier affair remains the Mortier affair. The first thing wrong, as I see it, is that you spend your time idly. That's bad. Yesterday I was at O. Turgeneva's and heard a Beethoven trio there, which is still in my ears—enchanting. I can't see a woman without comparing her with you. This lady is perfect in every way, but I just don't like her; but one must give her her due. Can you imagine?—I learned from her aunt that she gets up at 7 o'clock in Petersburg and plays until 2 o'clock every day, and she reads in the evening, and really she has made enormous progress in music, although she has less talent than you have. The second thing wrong, and terribly wrong, is that you didn't invite Mortier to come to Tula and Sudakovo. I told you—told both you and Zhenechka —that it's essential for you to see him so that your relations can be broken off, but you don't want to believe me. Try not to be annoyed and imagine that I'm jealous, but just try calmly to put yourself in my position and see with my eyes. Mrs Dembitskaya was in love with Passe-passe[2]—she herself admitted this to Zhenechka. Don't sigh, it isn't a calamity—it's actually rather nice. Mrs Dembitskaya is convinced that Passe-passe is passionately in love with her. Their relations were *interrupted*, but were not *broken off*. Understand me, I'm absolutely convinced that you now feel nothing for Passe-passe, but this hasn't been proved to him; the last he knew was that you were well disposed towards him. Don't you understand that for him the most difficult half of the path has already been covered. Remember how you and I talked beside the piano about what would happen if you fell in love, and you said this couldn't happen because you wouldn't allow yourself to reach the degree of intimacy and reciprocity that is essential for love to be dangerous. It's true. And you understand—you and Mortier have reached the point where he has the right to think either that you loved him, or that you are the sort of woman who is capable of loving many men, and as a result of this your parting and your dry letter with its fabrications won't put an end to your relations and you can't set Khrapovitsky's mind at rest. And it is actually only your relations with Mortier that disturb Khrapovitsky. Why does he enjoy talking to you of your love for dearest Islavin?[3] Why, if he's to be Mrs Dembitskaya's husband, should he (if the necessity should arise) send Mrs Khrapovitskaya off on a 2 years' journey with Islavin, etc., without any qualms? But Mortier's another matter. Mrs Dembitskaya is convinced that he loves her, and he, Mr Khrapovitsky, who has lived in the world longer than she has, knows what this *exalted* love means—it's nothing more than a desire to kiss the little hands of a pretty girl, you understand? This is

and includes a period of fasting, as well as attendance at certain church services, and making one's confession.
2. Mortier.   3. K. A. Islavin.

45. To V. V. Arsenyeva

proved both by Werther, and by the fact that he never thought of what might be best for Mrs Dembitskaya, but even in music, the one thing where he might have been useful, he frightened and harmed her by his stupid flattery. Besides, this is the kind of love which turns terribly quickly from servility into impudence. I'm a man, and

28 November

I know all this. Of course, I can't forbid anyone to feel this sort of love for my wife, and it's not dangerous when there's nothing in common between her and him; but when the first half of the journey has been covered, then it is dangerous. And dangerous in this sense that if Mr Mortier were to write a love letter to my wife or kiss her hand, and she were to hide this from me (and who is preventing him now?), then if I loved my wife, I would shoot myself, or if not, I would get a divorce instantly and flee to the ends of the earth simply out of respect for her and for my name, and from disappointment over my plans for the future. And this isn't just talk; I swear to you by God that I know it as I know myself. Because of this I'm so afraid of marriage that I look at it too sternly and seriously. There are some people who think when they get married: 'Well, if I should fail to find happiness here, I still have my life ahead of me'; but this thought never occurs to me, I'm staking everything on this one card. If I don't find complete happiness, I shall ruin everything, my talent, my heart; I'll become a drunkard and a gambler; I'll steal, if I haven't the courage to cut my throat. But to you these are little jokes, a pleasant feeling, *tender, exalted* etc. I don't love what is tender and exalted, I love what is honest and good. Try calmly to put yourself in my place and think—and ask Zhenechka for her advice—whether I'm right or not in wanting you and Mortier to be in the relationship of music teacher and pupil. Perhaps this is difficult, but it can't be helped, and I repeat—to lie to him in your letters (how is it you didn't feel this when you were preparing yourself for communion?) is to humiliate yourself, to be afraid of him. It will be very jolly for Khrapovitsky to run away from Mortier, in case his wife should suddenly melt away at the expression of his passion. Khrapovitsky has a rule and sticks to it—not to have any enemies, not to have a single man in the whole world whom it would be painful for him to meet; but you who love him want to put him in this vile, humiliating position. Try to see it from my point of view: you have a good heart and if you love me, how is it that you can't understand this? To be jealous is humiliating enough, but of Mortier…

You think that the lecturing is over—no, let me have my say. For three days you didn't venture to tell me something which you know interests me very much, and then you tell it me as though you're proud of your action. Why, this is the first condition of even the slightest friendship, not to mention *exalted* and *tender* love! I wasn't joking when I said that if my wife made me a surprise—a cushion, some sort of trinket—and kept it a secret from me, I would run away from her next day to the ends of the earth, and we would become strangers. I can't help it, I'm like that, and I neither conceal it nor exaggerate it. Think carefully—can you love such a monster while you hesitate over a matter so close to your heart and mine! Believe me, I don't act like that with regard to you. Since I left, there's nothing I can't tell you straight out, and I do tell you, and will tell you, everything that might interest you. It's principally because of this that I love my relations with you—because they sustain me on the path to all that is good. What you ask me about priests reminded me of something I've long wanted to say to you. Whatever our future relations may be, *let us never speak* of religion and everything that concerns it. You know I'm a believer, but it's very possible that my faith differs greatly from yours, and this question should not be touched upon, especially by people who want to love each other. I rejoice to look at you. Religion is a great thing, especially for women, and it's something you have. Guard it, never speak of it and, without going to extremes, fulfil its dogmas. Busy yourself more and more, school yourself to hard work. This is the first condition of happiness in life. Goodbye, dear Valeriya Vladimirovna, I press your dear hand most heartily. Before receiving your last letters, I thought that instead of putting ourselves to the test by our letters, we were only agitating each other even more. Well, this letter, it seems, isn't of that kind. In a day or two I'll finish my work[4] and plunge into society.

Goodbye; Christ be with you, dear lady.

46. To COUNT S. N. TOLSTOY

Petersburg, 5 December 1856

My dear Seryozha,

From my letter to Auntie, who I think is staying with you, you'll discover various details about me and my relations with the *guests*,[1] which I wrote for your benefit as well. I confess I'm hurt by your terribly unjust indignation against the *guests*. Your arguments about their circumstances are forceful and justified, but the question is, are there inner virtues which redeem this? You say there aren't, and you say so on the basis of personal lack of sympathy towards, and superficial observation of the *guests* at a most unfavourable period. But despite that, I'm very close to going and marrying a *guest*, although on no account will I do so before June. The one thing that can deter me is for her to fall in love with someone or for me to fall in love with someone before then; for the feeling I have for her, however wavering and imperfect, is just the same here as it was in summer and autumn. My main feeling is a staunch love of a certain sort of family life to which this girl conforms better than anyone I have ever known. You are wrong to think that this love of family life is a dream which I'll grow sick of. I'm a family man by nature; even as a young man I had just the same tastes, but still more so now. I'm as convinced of this as I am that I'm alive. The only question is whether she is the sort of person I think she is, but you can't tell that now because not only have you not observed her but, apart from your habitual contemptuous manner with women, you have also shown antipathy towards her. In your opinion—although it's a funny thing to

4. Tolstoy finished writing *A Landowner's Morning* on 29 November.
[46] 1. The Arsenyevs.

46. To Count S. N. Tolstoy

say—the wrinkles on her neck and some *spider* or other absolutely prevent her from being a good wife. You pronounce sentence at once without appeal because of the spider, but this sentence is also a spider in its own way. But enough of this, let's talk about other things which I know interest you. Davydov's edition of my *Military Tales*[2] has brought me nothing yet. Davydov is a rogue, and it's been a lesson to me; he says it hasn't paid for itself yet, while *Childhood* and *Boyhood*[3] have already done so, and I've received over 300 roubles and will receive the same again in a month's time and so on up to 3,000. My resignation has come through and in a few days I'll be putting on a tail coat. It'll cost me about 350 roubles but fortunately I've written 4½ printer's sheets for the *Reader's Library* and *Notes of the Fatherland* which will supply the money.[4] I learned the other day that the Emperor read my *Childhood* to his wife and wept. Apart from the fact that this is flattering to me, I'm glad that it makes amends for the slander which well-wishers put abroad about me and brought to the notice of their Majesties and Highnesses, namely, that I composed a Sevastopol song and walked round the regiments teaching the soldiers to sing it. That sort of thing smacked of the fortress[5] in the last reign, and even now, perhaps, the Third Department has a note of my name and I shan't be allowed abroad.[6] Are you going to the Caucasus, and if so when? Please write back. Goodbye. For the next couple of weeks I have urgent work to do revising *Youth*.

47. To V. V. ARSENYEVA

Petersburg, 7 December 1856

Yesterday I received your 2 letters—of 1 December and 29 October at once—and read both letters through several times. These letters in which you advise me to go to Andalusia and tell me that I should love you together with your weaknesses, and that you love to flirt and to please, and that a 14- or 35-year old woman can take my road, etc., etc., these letters are delightful. If either of us were married, or if your father would on no account give you to me in marriage, then (and I say this in all seriousness, with God as my witness) I would give free rein to my feelings, for me there would be no past and no future, and I would passionately—so passionately that you yourself would begin to say: calm down!—fall in love with you. But consider this carefully: our objective, you know, isn't solely the enjoyment of love —for this one has to give free rein to one's feelings and not think of anything at all. Our objective, besides that of loving, is also to spend our lives together and fulfil all the obligations that marriage entails; and for this one has to work on oneself a great deal and make great changes both before and after. Let's assume I'm an

---

2. A. I. Davydov, a bookseller and publisher, had published a volume of *Military Tales* containing *The Raid*, *The Wood-felling* and *The Sevastopol Stories*.
3. A volume containing *Childhood* and *Boyhood* was published in 1856.
4. The stories *Reduced to the Ranks* and *A Landowner's Morning*.
5. The Peter and Paul Fortress in Petersburg where political prisoners were confined.
6. The Third Department, the Tsarist secret police. In the event, Tolstoy was obliged to furnish an explanation to a senior officer.

47. To V. V. Arsenyeva

egoist, but for 6 months already I've been struggling with myself continually, and changing my favourite habits; you're not an egoist, but you only want to love, to enjoy this most wonderful blessing in the world, and for this you not only don't want to work on yourself, but you don't even want to sacrifice the smallest pleasure. Do you really think that in your place I couldn't do what you do, i.e. melt like noodles, and enjoy the best feelings in the world, and then, as for what happens afterwards, say—'that's your affair'? But despite that, you're still nice, terribly nice, with your honesty and your tenderness, which, though I underrate it, I love more than anything in the world. To turn to the future again. I only advise you to occupy yourself with domestic affairs, music, the peasants and reading, so that life will be good for you, but perhaps you'll find other occupations more agreeable to you, perhaps many aren't to your taste...all this is your own affair: you can be a perfect Khrapovitskaya, even walking in the shopping arcade; but it's the business of Khrapovitsky, who loves her and has lived longer, to indicate to her what brings happiness, and not to leave her to seek it for herself—and make all those mistakes that he himself has made. But this is only advice, because whether she reads or walks round the shops will make no difference to him, for better or worse, only to her; but as far as society is concerned, that's another matter. Here it will be for the worse, and very much so, for Khrapovitsky. He has to associate with people he doesn't respect and who disgust and bore him, he has to waste time, alter his whole way of life, and give up what is best in him—his occupations. Let's assume Khrapovitsky is an egoist; still he has never demanded, nor will he demand, anything of that nature from Dembitskaya. In many ways you're right in saying— what's 'dressing like an old woman' got to do with me?—that I demand an impossible perfection and keep setting tasks, each one more difficult than the other, and frightening you too much with these faux pas. But still it's good not to lose sight of *that* road and to try not to deviate from it. But society, of whatever kind, even Tula society, and *that* road, are two incompatible things. Society is a certain faux pas away from that delightful road; and I'll say this en connaissance de cause, even though I were to burn for it. Think seriously about it and, as always, write *frankly*, my most perfect darling. Let's assume that you now agree to this sacrifice as a sacrifice, and I'm sure that as long as other, higher delights are accessible to you, you'll forget to think about the sacrifice and will laugh at it. You're right, given your age and development, to see life as a pleasant diversion, and I'm right to see it as hard work, in which nevertheless there occur moments of high delight; if you are not an empty lady, you'll come round to this, but will you come round soon? Perhaps only when I've already come to see life as a burden (in almost the same way as Zhenechka does). And how is it possible to love one another with differing views on life? It would be possible to if I were married, but it's impossible for us to live together and not suffer every minute. One of two things: either you must work and catch up with me, or I must go back so that we can go forward together. But I can't go back because I know that it's better, brighter and happier ahead. Off you go on the post-horses, I'll help you all I can; you'll find it hard, but on the other hand how happily, peacefully and lovingly (if this is what you need)

47. To V. V. Arsenyeva

shall we walk to the end of the road. And even on the other side of the road it will be so happy, peaceful and loving.

How is it that you say nothing about Dickens and Thackeray? Is it possible you find them boring? And what's this nonsense you've been reading: Notices sur les opéras? And why have you made friends with dear Sashenka? What a weak-willed lady you are! She's a nobody—and it's an excellent thing that you're not irritated by anyone—but this *contact* is bad for you. In consequence of this contact, ideas and convictions which you ought to shed with time are taking root in you. Consequently it will only be the more difficult for you to part from them. I sent you a book by the last post—read this delightful thing.[1] That's where one learns how to live. One sees differing views on life and on love—you might not agree with any of them, but then one's own views become wiser and clearer. I'm *lecturing* again; but what can I do?—I can't understand relationships with a person I love without doing so. And you sometimes lecture to me, and I'm terribly glad when you're right. And this is what love is. It isn't kissing poppet's hands (it's disgusting even to say this)—it's opening one's soul to one another, checking one's ideas against the ideas of the other, thinking together, feeling together. Goodbye, my darling, I press your hand, and embrace Zhenechka and the Pindigashki.

48. To V. V. ARSENYEVA

Petersburg, 12 December 1856

It's already 2 days since I received your last letter, and all the time I've been undecided whether to reply to it or not, and how to reply. Like cures like; you need a wedge to drive out a wedge. I'll again be as frank as I can. After careful thought, I'm convinced that my letter really was rude and bad, and that you could and should have been offended on receiving it. But still, I won't take it back. It wasn't a fit of jealousy, but a conviction which I expressed too rudely but which I still adhere to. As regards your letter, this is what I thought: either you have never loved me, which would be excellent both for you and for me, because we're too far apart from each other; or you pretended to, and did so under the influence of Zhenechka, who advised you to rouse me by your coldness. It seems to me that il y'a du Zhenechka here. Mais c'est un mauvais moyen with me: j'envisage la chose trop sérieusement pour que ces petits moyens naifs puissent avoir prise sur moi. Je vois depuis longtemps le fond de votre coeur, and these little wiles don't hide it from me, but only obscure it. When I say that it would be excellent if you have never loved me, I say it sincerely too, and furthermore, although I felt it before, your *last* letter particularly brought it home to me. You're angry that *I'm only able to give lectures*. But don't you see, I write to you about my plans for the future, my ideas as to how one should live, and what I understand by good etc.: all these are the ideas and feelings most precious to me, and I write about them almost with tears in my eyes (believe me); but to you it's all *lecturing and boredom*. Well, what

[47] 1. Goncharov's *An Ordinary Story*.

do we have in common? Man expresses his love according to his stage of development. Olenka's fiancé expressed his love for her by speaking of exalted love; but as for me, I couldn't for the life of me talk such nonsense. Do believe one other thing: that in all my relations with you I was as sincere as I could be, that I felt and still feel friendship for you, that I sincerely thought that you were the best of all the girls I'd ever met, and one with whom I could be happy, if she wanted, and to whom I could give happiness as I understand it. But in one thing I am to blame, and I ask your forgiveness for it, and that is this, that without being convinced whether you wanted to understand me, I somehow involuntarily entered into explanations with you which weren't necessary, and, perhaps, I often caused you pain. In this I'm very, very much to blame; but try to forgive me and let's remain good friends. Love and marriage would bring us only suffering, but friendship, I feel, would be helpful to us both. I don't know about you, but I feel myself strong enough to keep within its limits. Besides, it seems to me that I wasn't born for family life, although I love it more than anything in the world. You know my nasty, suspicious, changeable character, and God knows if anything can change it. Perhaps a powerful love which I've never felt and which I don't believe in. Of all the women I've known, I've loved and still love you the most, but all this is still not enough.

Goodbye; Christ be with you, dear Valeriya Vladimirovna; at least let them know at Yasnaya whether I can still come and see you in January.

Yours,
Count L. Tolstoy[1]

49. To COUNT S. N. TOLSTOY

Petersburg, 2 January 1857

I'm writing you a few words because I'm leaving Petersburg in a few days for Moscow, where I'll spend a couple of weeks, and so will be seeing you soon.

I detect in your letter a certain vexation, even spleen. This is not good at all, and is the result, it seems to me, of a solitary life. Won't you come to Moscow? It wouldn't be at all bad just now. My relations with *the guests*[1] continue, but weigh down on me terribly, and I don't know how to break them off because I feel not merely complete indifference, but vexation and remorse with myself for having gone so far. You say you expect all sorts of about turns from me and you say you know me. But if you expect all sorts of *about turns* it means you don't know me, but have observed inconsistencies in me over certain things and appear to reproach me for them as if I found pleasure in doing incongruous things. I've spent 2 very good months here, and although I've hardly been anywhere, I've seen a lot of my literary friends, read a lot, and listened to music, and I wrote for the first month. But I need a little of everything, and although I dearly love these literary friends—

---

[48] 1. Following this letter, there was an interruption in the correspondence for about three weeks. Tolstoy received a letter from Arsenyeva on 29 December and replied to her on 1 January with what he described in his diary as a 'short and dry' letter.

[49] 1. The Arsenyevs.

49. To Count S. N. Tolstoy

Botkin, Annenkov and Druzhinin—still all *clever* conversations are already beginning to bore me although they have been genuinely useful to me. My two stories in *Notes of the Fatherland* and the *Reader's Library* have, it seems, had little success, which was only to be expected as they were written in a hurry. *Youth* has already been printed, but the censors have mutilated it, for they've become stricter again since Nekrasov's poems and the incident that followed them.[2] My books are selling, but not too well. About 700 copies of *Childhood* have been sold, and about 500 of the *Military Tales*. I intend to go out and see *the guests* in Moscow. Goodbye, and don't be angry with me for being the sort of person I am. I kiss Auntie's hand and will send her my portrait which I think she wanted to have, by the next post. *Notes of the Fatherland* has been sent to Yasnaya, and I'll send the *Reader's Library* with my story in it as soon as I get it.

A Happy New Year!

Yours,
Count L. Tolstoy

50. To T. A. YERGOLSKAYA and COUNT S. N. TOLSTOY

[Original in French]

Moscow, 14 January 1857

Dear Aunt,

I received my passport for going abroad, and came to Moscow to spend a few days with Marya, and then go on to ⟨Yasnaya⟩ to put my affairs in order and say goodbye to you. ⟨But now I've changed my mind, particularly on Mashenka's advice, and have decided to stay here with her for a week or two, and then travel direct to Paris via Warsaw. You probably understand⟩, dear Aunt, ⟨why I don't want to—and ought not to—come to Yasnaya, or rather to Sudakovo now. I seem to have behaved very badly towards Valeriya, but if I were to see her now, I would behave even worse. As I wrote to you, I am more than indifferent towards her, and feel that I can't deceive either myself or her any more. And were I to come I would perhaps begin to dupe myself again through weakness of character.⟩ Do you remember, dear Aunt, how you made fun of me when I told you that I was leaving for Petersburg in order to prove myself. And yet it's to this idea that I'm indebted for not having caused the unhappiness of the young lady and myself. For don't think that it's got anything to do with inconstancy or infidelity—I haven't been attracted by anyone else during these two months—but quite simply I saw that I was deceiving myself and that not only have I never had, but I never shall have the slightest feeling of true love for Valeriya. The only thing that grieves me very much is that I've wronged the young lady, and that I won't be able to say goodbye to you before leaving. I expect to return to Russia in July, but, if you

---

2. Chernyshevsky had published several of Nekrasov's poems with a sharp political bias in *The Contemporary*, 1856, No. 11. The censor informed the editor that if anything similar happened again, the journal would be closed down.

want me to, I could come to Yasnaya to embrace you, as I'll have time to get your reply in Moscow. In any case, goodbye; I kiss your hand, and beg you ⟨(this is not just talk)⟩ never to believe that I have changed or could change towards you and not love you, as always, ⟨with all my heart⟩.

⟨Please, Seryozha, answer me at once, won't you come to Moscow now?[1] That would be the best thing of all. In that case I'd wait for you; otherwise,—and if it's what Auntie wants—I'll make a stealthy detour and come to Pirogovo to say goodbye to you. Goodbye, dear misanthrope; but best of all come and see us without your misanthropy.⟩

51. To V. V. ARSENYEVA

Moscow, 14 January 1857

Dear Valeriya Vladimirovna,

That I'm to blame towards myself and towards you—terribly to blame—there is no doubt. But what can I do? What I wrote to you in reply to your short letter in which you forbade me to write to you was absolutely just, and I can't say more than that. I haven't changed in my attitude towards you, and feel that I'll never cease to love you *the way I did*, i.e. with friendship; I'll never cease to value your friendship more than anything else in the world, because my heart is not, and never has been attracted to any other woman as it has been to you. But what's to be done? I'm not capable of giving you the same feeling as your fine nature is prepared to give me. I've always felt this vaguely, but now our 2 months' separation, a life with new interests, activities, obligations even, which are incompatible with family life, have fully proved this to me. I've behaved badly towards you—I was carried away; but if I were to come to you now and, of course, be carried away again, I would be behaving even worse. I hope you respect me enough to believe that there's not one insincere word in anything I'm writing now; and if so, that you won't cease to love me a little. In a few days' time I'm going to Paris, and when I shall return to Russia —goodness only knows.[1] There's no need to tell you that if you were to write me a few lines, I should be happy and content. My address is: Paris, Rue de Rivoli, No. 206. Goodbye, dear Valeriya Vladimirovna, thank you a thousand times for your friendship and please forgive the pain that it has perhaps caused you. For goodness

[50] 1. Sergey came to Moscow on or about 18 January.

[51] 1. After receiving his passport, Tolstoy went to Moscow on 12 January to make preparations for going abroad. He left for Western Europe on 29 January and deliberately avoided visiting Yasnaya Polyana again for fear of a further meeting with Arsenyeva. From Paris he wrote a further letter to her, similar in tone and content to this one, in reply to one from Arsenyeva in which she appears to have asked the reasons for his change in attitude towards her. He again expressed the hope that they might remain good friends. His last extant letter to her was written in December 1857—again in reply to one from her in which she apparently expressed dissatisfaction with her life. Tolstoy's advice to her was: 'Go abroad, get married, enter a convent, bury yourself in the country, only don't remain for a moment in a state of indecision.' Any hope she may have had of a reconciliation was gone, and shortly afterwards she married a certain A. A. Talyzin, subsequently a Justice of the Peace in Oryol.

51. To V. V. Arsenyeva

sake ask Mlle Vergani to write me a few lines, even if only of abuse. Perhaps it will seem just talk to you, but really and truly I feel and know that you will bring happiness to some good fine man, but, as far as the heart goes, I am not worth your little finger, and would only bring you unhappiness.

Goodbye, dear Valeriya Vladimirovna, Christ be with you; you and I both have a long and splendid road ahead of us, and God grant it may lead you to the happiness that you deserve a 1,000 times over.

Yours,
Count L. Tolstoy

52. To V. P. BOTKIN

Vasily Petrovich Botkin (1811–69), a writer and critic. The eldest son of a Moscow tea merchant, he devoted much time to the study of literature and foreign languages. His involvement in his family's commercial interests and his financial security may have been partly responsible for the fact that he published comparatively little. He was on very friendly terms with Belinsky, and on more than one occasion assisted him with his critical articles. From 1836 to 1850 he published a series of articles and reviews in leading journals, including *Notes of the Fatherland*. His *Letters on Spain*, published in 1847 in *The Contemporary*, brought him wide recognition. Like Druzhinin, Botkin was an adherent of the principle of 'art for art's sake', and his close association with *The Contemporary*, and its editors Nekrasov and Panayev, came to an end with the growing ascendancy within the journal of the views of Chernyshevsky, and his eventual appointment to the board of editors. Tolstoy first met Botkin in January 1856, and a close friendship was established between the two men which was to last until 1862. Tolstoy valued Botkin's literary taste very highly. Sixteen of Tolstoy's letters to Botkin have survived, and nine of Botkin's to Tolstoy.

Moscow, 20 January 1857
Dear Botkin,

I'm travelling on Monday week, i.e. the 28th; I already have a place, and for various reasons I shall not be calling in at Yasnaya Polyana where you were afraid I should stay put. I've been leading a frivolous and not particularly good life here, rather against my wishes, and I shall go on doing so for these next 8 days. I go out in society and to balls, and I would enjoy myself if I weren't overpowered by *clever people*. There are nice men and women sitting in the same room, but there is no chance of reaching them because a clever man or woman buttonholes you and tells you some story or other. The only escape is to dance, which I've begun to do, however strange it may seem to you. But I must confess to dear Pavel Vasilyevich[1] that all this is *not it*. Thank you for your opinion about *Youth*, it is very, very welcome to me because, without discouraging me, it exactly accords with what I

[52] 1. P. V. Annenkov. See Letter 58.

52. To V. P. Botkin

thought myself—that it's *shallow*. I read your article here.[2] If you don't take up criticism seriously, you've no love for literature. There are some readers here who have told me that this isn't criticism, but poetic theory, in which they are told for the first time what they have long felt and not been able to express. Indeed it is a poetic catechism of poetry, and in that sense you have still a great deal to say— you yourself. The Slavophiles are *not it* either. When I meet them I feel that I unwittingly become obtuse, limited and terribly righteous, just as one always speaks French badly oneself with someone who speaks it badly. There isn't that intellectual verve there is with you, my priceless triumvirate of Botkin, Annenkov and Druzhinin, with whom one feels stupid only because one wants to understand and say too much. Ostrovsky, who was full-blooded, exuberant and strong when I met him last year, is still as strong as ever, but has formulated some theory of his own in his flattery-ridden seclusion, and it has gone hard and dried up. S. T. Aksakov says that his *A Lucrative Situation* is feeble.[3] His comedy for *The Contemporary* is ready, and I shall hear it in a day or two. Druzhinin's critical articles are very well liked here, especially by the Aksakovs. His introduction to a critique of Pisemsky is splendid.[4] But what disgraceful rubbish Fuflygin is.[5] God forbid he should treat *The Contemporary* to anything like that. Everyone here is reproaching Turgenev over the Katkov affair for not sending a story.[6] Grigoryev's article about Granovsky[7] is entertaining everyone in the Moscow fashion—i.e. they come out into the ring and fight. For some reason I broke a few lances on Granovsky's behalf, and so it seems I've been written off as having been corrupted by the Petersburg circle. V. A. Bobrinskoy gave Shevyryov a thrashing at Chertkov's over the Slavophile question, that's a fact.[8] Shevyryov is in bed, and they are paying him visites de condoléance. Goodbye, dear Vasily Petrovich, please let us correspond. I cordially embrace Druzhinin and Annenkov. Cordial greetings to Ivan Ivanovich.[9]

Yours,
Count L. Tolstoy

I heard Ostrovsky's comedy. The motifs are all old, and the ideas are shallow. Only the merchant from another town is plausible, but it's all very talented and wonderfully polished.

2. 'The Poetry of A. A. Fet' (*The Contemporary*, 1857, No. 1).
3. Tolstoy read it a few days after writing this letter, and noted in his diary that he thought it was one of Ostrovsky's best works (see Letter 53). S. T. Aksakov, see Letter 53, note 2.
4. Druzhinin's article on Pisemsky's stories contained an attack on the aesthetic views of the revolutionary democrats.
5. The main character in D. V. Grigorovich's story *Relations in the Capital*.
6. Turgenev was accused of publishing his story *Phantoms*, which he had promised to Katkov for *The Russian Herald*, in *The Contemporary* instead, under the title *Faust*. However, in signing a contract to publish all his works exclusively in *The Contemporary*, he had made special provision for fulfilling his promise to Katkov which he had made before the story was even written.
7. Grigoryev's article 'T. N. Granovsky and his Professorship in Moscow' sought to discredit the distinguished historian and leader of the Moscow circle of pro-Western intelligentsia.
8. Count Bobrinskoy, a guards officer, came to blows with the Slavophile professor, Shevyryov, who objected to certain of Bobrinskoy's remarks about the Russian peasantry as being unpatriotic and demeaning. The professor came off worse.   9. Panayev.

53. To V. P. BOTKIN

Moscow, 29 January 1857

Please print my brother's name as Count N. N. Tolstoy.[1] Your letter about him made me awfully glad, and my sister also. But aren't you being too enthusiastic? I've spent an awfully enjoyable 2 weeks here, but so frivolously that I long for solitude with all my heart. I've heard two splendid literary things: S. T. Aksakov's *Reminiscences of Childhood* and Ostrovsky's *A Lucrative Situation*. The first seemed to me as a whole better than the best parts of *A Family Chronicle*.[2] It doesn't have the youthful, concentrating power of poetry, but the uniformly sweet poetry of nature suffuses everything, as a result of which it may sometimes seem dull, but on the other hand it's unusually soothing and impressive in the clarity, authenticity and graceful proportions of its reflection. Ostrovsky's comedy in my opinion is his best work, and those sombre depths which were discernible in *The Bankrupt*[3] are discernible here for the first time since then in the world of bribe-taking officials which the Sollogubs, Shchedrins and company tried to express. But now the last true word has been spoken. As in *The Bankrupt* too, one can discern a strong protest against contemporary life: just as it was expressed there through the young steward, and in *The Misfortune of Being Clever*[4] through Famusov, so it is expressed here through the old bribe-taker, the secretary Yusov. This character is delightful. The whole comedy is a marvel. But...if only the author lived in the wide open world and not in his own little circle, this could have been a chef d'oeuvre, but as it is, there are grave and sad blemishes in it. Ostrovsky is a truly brilliant dramatic writer; but he won't produce anything really brilliant, because his awareness of his own brilliance has overshot the mark. With him this awareness is no longer a force which activates his talent, but a conviction which tries to justify his every action. I have got to know Chicherin[5] better here, and I like him very much. The Slavophiles seem to me not just backward enough to have lost their meaning, but so backward that their backwardness is turning into dishonesty. When I got home the day before yesterday I found Grigorovich here, and I was delighted beyond words—he is wonderful; he has brought three essays with him and has

[53] 1. Nikolay Tolstoy's essay, *Hunting in the Caucasus*, was published in *The Contemporary*, 1857, No. 2. Tolstoy's letter clearly reached Botkin too late, as only the initials N. N. T. were used.

2. Tolstoy had attended readings of *Years of Childhood* and *A Lucrative Situation* at the home of S. T. Aksakov (1791–1859), a sympathetic and sensitive recorder of Russian patriarchial life, and the father of two well-known Slavophile writers Ivan and Konstantin Aksakov. His *A Family Chronicle* (1856) treated the world of his parents and grandparents, while *Years of Childhood* continued the chronicle, dealing with his own fictionalised childhood. In a letter of 29 January 1857 Tolstoy thanked Ostrovsky for sending him a copy of his comedy *A Lucrative Situation* and, after indicating what he thought were its minor blemishes, praised its depth and power, pointing out especially the masterly characterisation of Yusov.

3. The original title of the play that was later called *Among Friends One Always Comes to Terms*.

4. A comedy by A. S. Griboyedov (1795–1829), sometimes translated into English as *Woe from Wit*.

5. B. N. Chicherin. See Letter 81.

stayed on here for 2 days for my sake, so that this letter will arrive before him. He is in raptures about the travel plans. There is a lot more I would like to write to you about, but there are still personal matters holding me up, and I have to go. Goodbye, dear Vasily Petrovich; if you think about it, write to me in Warsaw where I shall spend some time—addressed to me poste restante. If anyone wishes to write to my brother, his address is Kizlyar, Starogladovskaya stanitsa, H.Q. 4th battery, 20 brigade. I'm sending him your letter about him. I heartily embrace our dear friends. I don't know what will come of it, but I terribly want to work and I want to live too. Goodbye, write more often.

Yours,
Count L. Tolstoy

54. To V. P. BOTKIN

Paris, 10/22 February 1857

Yesterday I arrived in Paris,[1] my dear Vasily Petrovich, and found Turgenev and Nekrasov there. They are both wandering about in a sort of fog, moping and complaining about life—they have nothing to do, and are oppressed, it seems, by their respective relations with each other. However, I haven't seen much of them yet. Turgenev's suspiciousness is becoming a terrible disease and, in conjunction with his conviviality and good nature, is such a strange phenomenon. This first impression made me sad, especially since, after my life in Moscow, I've been awfully lebensfroh until now. Germany, which I saw in passing, made a powerful and agreeable impression on me, and I expect to spend some time there and travel about in a leisurely way. Nekrasov returns to Rome today. I'm thinking of going there in a month. This month I hope to finish *Kiesewetter*[2] here; it's grown so much on the journey that it already seems beyond my strength. Perhaps it will be in time for the April issue. Turgenev isn't writing anything; I'm going to pester him, but what will come of it I don't know. Goodbye, dear Vasily Petrovich. This letter doesn't count, but I'm still looking forward to some letters from you, and this is better than nothing. Rue de Rivoli, Hôtel Meurice, No. 149.

You like L. I. Mengden[3]—I'm very glad. It's obvious that it's not just in poetry that our tastes are similar.

[54] 1. Tolstoy remained in Paris until April, except for a short trip to Dijon with Turgenev in March. After witnessing a guillotining, he left Paris for Geneva, and stayed mostly in Switzerland until July. He returned home via Baden-Baden, Frankfurt and Dresden at the end of July.
 2. The original title of *Albert* (1858), based on Tolstoy's friendship with a drunken violinist and composer Kiesewetter.
 3. Hostess of a Moscow literary salon, and a good friend of the Tolstoy family for many years. She translated *The Cossacks* into French in 1878.

55. To D. Y. KOLBASIN

Dmitry Yakovlevich Kolbasin served as an official in Petersburg, and was on friendly terms with the circle of contributors to *The Contemporary* in the 1850s. He supervised the publication of Turgenev's *Tales and Stories* in three volumes (1856), and his *A Sportsman's Sketches* (1859), and also Botkin's *Letters on Spain* (1857). Tolstoy entrusted Kolbasin with various commissions between 1856 and 1859, including the publication of a separate volume, *Childhood and Boyhood*, and there was quite a lively correspondence between the two men during these years.

Paris, 24 March/5 April 1857

I'm terribly ashamed and vexed, dear Dmitry Yakovlevich, that I was afraid to carry out your commission, not knowing the customs' procedures.[1] I've already been living in Paris for more than 1½ months, and I've found so much that's interesting and pleasant here that I don't want to leave. I still haven't replied to what you wrote to me about *A Landowner's Morning*. Thank you for not seeing any evil intention in it. It's very easy for anyone who wants to see it there as well as in *Reduced to the Ranks*. I'm now settling down to work gradually, but it's going slowly—there are so many other occupations. Turgenev seems ill, both physically and morally, and it's painful and sad to look at him. We must hope that the summer and the waters will help him, and I'm waiting impatiently for this. You write to him that he's to tell me that your legs are still intact. I trust that for the time being they remain intact and won't be exposed to danger.[2] The enormous number of Russians gadding about abroad, especially in Paris, seems to me to bode well for Russia in this respect. Not to mention people whose attitude changes completely as a result of such travelling, there's no officer fooling around here with the whores or in the cafés, who's such a blockhead as not to be affected by this feeling of social freedom, which constitutes the main charm of life here, and which it's impossible to judge without experiencing it. If you're not too lazy, let me know some of the literary news: what your brother is doing—I cordially press his hand—and dear Druzhinin whom you so dislike, etc. What's this about *The Son of the Fatherland* going on so?[3] And is there no possibility of sending journals here? How are sales going?[4] Isn't there any money? 500 roubles wouldn't come amiss for me in a month's time. If there is, even if it's a smaller sum, then send me on a letter of credit from the house of Brandenburg and Co. in Moscow, though there must be an office in Petersburg too. Goodbye, dear friend, please drop me a line—I'll reply punctually.

Yours,
Count L. Tolstoy

[55] 1. The reference is to Tolstoy's refusal to take abroad some papers intended for Herzen.
2. Kolbasin had written to Turgenev: 'Tell him [Tolstoy] that my leg is intact, and that it seems it will remain intact until the end of my days.' The meaning is unclear.
3. A reference to an anonymous article on *Youth*, published in *The Son of the Fatherland*, February 1857, and commenting unfavourably on its length and tedium.
4. The sales of *Childhood* and *Boyhood* as a separate volume.

56. To V. P. BOTKIN

Paris, 24–5 March/5–6 April 1857

It's very unfortunate that you are ill, dear Vasily Petrovich; I'm afraid it may upset your plan to go abroad.[1] It seemed to me in Petersburg, and it still seems from your letter, that you don't want to go. Do come, my dearest and wisest friend; of course you and I would meet, and I'm longing to see you and to talk to you. I've been living in Paris for nearly 2 months now, and I can't foresee the time when the city will have lost its interest for me, or the life its charm. I'm a complete ignoramus: nowhere have I felt this so keenly as here. Consequently for that reason alone I can be happy and content with my life here, the more so since I also feel that my ignorance is not beyond redemption here. Then again enjoyment of the arts, the Louvre, Versailles, the Conservatoire, the quartets, the theatres, the lectures at the Collège de France and the Sorbonne, and above all the social freedom of which I had no conception at all in Russia—all this means that I shan't leave Paris, or the village near Paris where I want to settle shortly, for another 2 months at the earliest, when the courses start at the watering-places. It seems that Turgenev really has spermatorrhoea; he's going to take the waters, but it's not yet certain when and where. He's awfully pathetic. He suffers morally, as only a man with his imagination can suffer. I've only very recently managed to organise things so that I can work a few hours a day. The Kiesewetter business is terribly sordid, and this dampens my spirits a little, but still I'm enjoying my work.[2]

I wrote this yesterday and was interrupted, and today I'm writing in a completely different mood. I was stupid and callous enough to go and see an execution this morning. Apart from the fact that the weather has been dreadful here for the last fortnight and that I'm very out of sorts, I was in a vile state of nerves, and the spectacle made such an impression on me that I shan't get over it for a long time. I've seen many horrible things in war and in the Caucasus, but if a man had been torn to pieces before my eyes it wouldn't have been so revolting as this ingenious and elegant machine by means of which a strong, hale and hearty man was killed in an instant. In war it's not a question of the rational will, but of human feelings of passion; but in this case it's cold, refined calculation and a convenient way of murder, and there's nothing grand about it. It's the insolent, arrogant desire to carry out justice and the law of God—justice, which is determined by lawyers taking their stand on honour, religion and truth, and all contradicting each other. With just the same formalities they killed the king, and Chénier[3] and the republicans and the aristocrats and the man (I forget his name) who, a couple of years ago, was declared innocent of the murder for which he was killed. Then the repulsive crowd, the father explaining to his daughter the convenient and ingenious mechanism that does it etc.... The law of man—what nonsense! The truth is that the

[56] 1. Botkin did in fact travel abroad. Tolstoy met him in Turin in June.
2. *Albert*
3. André Chénier (1762–94), one of the earliest of the French Romantic poets. He was alienated by the excesses of the Revolution which he had at first welcomed, and was guillotined for suspected collaboration with the Royalists.

56. To V. P. Botkin

state is a conspiracy designed not only to exploit, but above all to corrupt its citizens. But still, states exist, and moreover in this imperfect form. And they cannot pass from this system into socialism. So what should people do who think as I do? There are other people—Napoleon III for example—who, because they are more clever or more stupid than I, see their way clear through all this confusion; they believe that these lies may contain a greater or a lesser amount of evil, and they act accordingly. Well all right, I suppose such people are necessary. But I can see only what is loathsome in all these repulsive lies; I don't want evil and I can't fathom where there is more of it and where there is less. I understand moral laws, the laws of morality and religion, which are not binding, but which lead people forward and promise a harmonious future; and I sense the laws of art which always bring happiness; but the laws of politics are such terrible lies for me that I can't see in them a better or a worse. All this I felt and understood and recognised today. And this recognition at least to some extent relieves the burden of the impression for me. A whole host of arrests have been made here recently; a plot has been discovered; they wanted to kill Napoleon at the theatre; more people will be killed too before long, but as from today I will certainly never go and see such a thing again, and I will never serve *any* government anywhere. There's a lot more I would like to tell you about what I've seen here, such as the people's poets' club[4] outside town where I go on Sundays. Turgenev was right when he wrote that il n'y a pas de poetry in this people. Their only poetry is political, and it has always been alien to me, especially now. In general I like French life and the French people, but I haven't met a single sensible man here, whether of high society or of the people. Goodbye, dear Vasily Petrovich, forgive me for this foolish letter, I am quite ill today.

Yours,
Count L. Tolstoy

57. To I. S. TURGENEV

Ivan Sergeyevich Turgenev (1818–83) first attracted attention with the serial publication of *A Sportsman's Sketches* (1847–51)—a collection of stories depicting peasant types and individuals, against the background of the Russian countryside. His most successful and important works include: *Rudin* (1856), *A Nest of Gentlefolk* (1859), *On the Eve* (1860) and *Fathers and Sons* (1862)—the latter being the highwater mark of his career. A self-confessed Westerner, he travelled extensively in Western Europe, and was acquainted with a number of leading French writers including Daudet, George Sand and Flaubert. Turgenev never married. He had numerous affairs, but his only life-long attachment was to the Spanish singer, Pauline Viardot, a married woman with a family. Turgenev greeted the appearance

---

4. There were many such clubs in and around Paris at the time. They went by the name of *'goguettes'* (meaning literally: (1) festive mood, (2) small club), and were simple taverns or restaurants where people from the lower and lower middle classes gathered on Sundays to listen to and perform songs. These songs were often of a political or social character, and consequently many of the *goguettes* were suppressed by the authorities.

57. To I. S. Turgenev

of Tolstoy's *Childhood* (1852) with marked enthusiasm, and on reading *Boyhood* (1854), he wrote of Tolstoy as 'Gogol's successor'. Despite their subsequent quarrels, Turgenev hardly modified his boundless admiration for Tolstoy as Russia's greatest writer, but he deeply regretted Tolstoy's later preoccupation with religious and moral questions at the expense of his art, and even on his death-bed wrote to him to urge him to return to literature. The personal relations between the two men were, however, always marred by the absence of mutual understanding or tolerance of each other. Tolstoy despised Turgenev's smooth urbanity and aristocratic liberalism, and believed him insincere, while for his part Turgenev was shocked and exasperated by the more explosive and primitive side of Tolstoy's personality, and his often extravagant behaviour, particularly during the early years; furthermore, he was easily angered by Tolstoy's frank, and often rude, comments and gibes. Their frequent quarrels resulted from the most trivial and petty disagreements, and their reconciliations, despite apparently genuine protestations of mutual affection and respect, were never more than skin-deep. One such quarrel in 1861 resulted in a break in all communication between the two men for a period of seventeen years. The correspondence between the two writers amounted to more than 100 letters; of these, 43 of Turgenev's letters and only 7 of Tolstoy's have so far come to light.

[Not sent][1]   Geneva, 28 March/9 April 1857

I shall write a few words to you, dear Ivan Sergeich, if nothing more, because I was thinking an awful lot about you throughout the journey.[2] At 8 o'clock yesterday evening when, after a vile railway journey, I transferred to the open seat of a stagecoach and could see the road and the moonlit night, all the sounds and smells of the journey and all my sickness and melancholy vanished as if by magic, or rather were transformed into that calm but moving feeling of joy which you know. I did very well to get away from that Sodom. For goodness sake get away somewhere yourself too, only not by railway. The railway is to travelling what the brothel is to love—just as convenient, but just as inhumanly mechanical and deadly monotonous. I didn't travel without good reason, and *somebody* must have drawn a line across my forehead[3] (notice I left on the 28th, our style).[4] I spent a whole wonderful spring moonlit night alone, travelling through Switzerland by stagecoach next to the driver, and when I arrived in Geneva and found the Tolstoys out,[5] I sat all evening alone in my hotel room looking at the moonlit night and the lake, and then I mechanically opened a book, and the book was the Gospels, which

[57] 1. This is a rough draft of a letter which was later sent to Turgenev but has not survived.
2. From Paris to Geneva (8–9 April N.S.).
3. The meaning is not clear. The suggestion that it refers to a dream Tolstoy had after witnessing an execution in Paris, in the course of which somebody scratched his neck, hardly fits in with the context which seems to imply good fortune.
4. In fact he left on 27 March O.S. The 28th of August was his birthday, and he always attached great importance to the date 28th.
5. Countess A. A. Tolstaya and her sister.

57. To I. S. Turgenev

the Société Biblique puts in every room here. And now I feel so terribly happy that I could cry, and I'm glad to feel that in such a mood I constantly think of you and wish you as great, if not greater happiness. I spent 1½ months in Sodom, and there is a great accumulation of filth in my soul: two whores, and the guillotine, and idleness and vulgarity; you are an immoral man, although you live a more moral life than me, but in 6 months a great many things have accumulated in your soul too, which ill accord with it. You really should go for a drive in a stagecoach, or walk all night in the country, bravely shed all the tears which are pent up in you and see how much easier things are, how good they are. Please find out what the relations are between Orlov and Princess Lvova.[6] It seemed to me that your wish is coming true. You are right that Orlov will make a good husband, but if this is not to be, tell me frankly whether it might happen that a girl like her could love me—i.e. I mean by that only whether she wouldn't find it repulsive or ridiculous to think I wanted to marry her. I'm so sure of the impossibility of such a strange thing that it's ridiculous to put it in writing. But if only I could believe in its possibility, I would prove to you that I too can love. You smile ironically, sadly, despairingly. I can—after my own fashion—I feel I can. Goodbye, dear friend, and please don't try to make what I'm writing to you now fit into the general idea you've formed about my personality. A good thing about a man is that you sometimes don't in the least expect him to do what he does, and an old nag will sometimes take a bit between her teeth and bolt off with a fart; in just the same way my present mood is a strange and unexpected, but genuine fart.

Yours,
Count L. Tolstoy

58. To P. V. ANNENKOV

Pavel Vasilyevich Annenkov (1813–87), a writer and critic, had studied at the University of Petersburg, and served for a short period in the Ministry of Finance. In 1840 he travelled abroad, and sent back to Russia a series of letters which were published in *Notes of the Fatherland* from 1841 to 1843. When in Rome, Annenkov lived with Gogol, who dictated to him the first volume of *Dead Souls*. On his second journey abroad, Annenkov accompanied the critic Belinsky. He began his career as a literary critic with the publication in *The Contemporary*, in 1849, of his *Notes on Russian Literature, 1848*. Like Druzhinin and Botkin, he was an adherent of the principle of 'art for art's sake'. He was the editor of the first *Complete Works* of Pushkin, published in 1855–7. From the late 1860s, he spent long periods in Western Europe, only occasionally returning to Russia, and devoting much of his time to writing literary memoirs. His most important contribution of these years

---

6. Tolstoy frequently visited Princess Lvova in Paris where she was staying with her uncle whom he knew. He was for a time attracted by her, and was even advised to marry her by Countess A. A. Tolstaya. Her expected marriage to Prince Orlov, a distinguished government official, did not take place. See also Letter 63.

58 To P. V. Annenkov

was *A Remarkable Decade (1838–48)*. Annenkov was one of the first critics to recognise Tolstoy's talent, and even as early as 1855 he placed him on a level with Turgenev and Goncharov in an article on the latest works of Turgenev and 'L.N.T.' He also wrote two major critical articles on Tolstoy, the first on *The Cossacks* in 1863 and the second entitled 'Historical and Aesthetic Problems in Count Tolstoy's novel *War and Peace*', 1868. Tolstoy first met Annenkov during the winter of 1855/6. Their surviving correspondence is limited to 3 letters from Tolstoy to Annenkov and one from Annenkov to Tolstoy and Turgenev.

Clarens, 22 April/4 May 1857

I am sending you, dear Pavel Vasilyevich, a note from Pushchin[1] with whom I'm living at Clarens, Canton de Vaud, where you should write to me if you wish to make me truly happy.

His note is most amusing, but his stories are a delight to listen to. Evidently this is what the disorderly age of Pushkin was like in general. This Pushchin is a charming and good-natured man. His and his wife's kindness to me here is very touching, and I'm awfully glad that we are neighbours. This is now my 4th week in Switzerland and I'm very pleased with my existence. It's cheap and secluded; it's warm now; the blue Léman and the mountain passes are constantly in view; there are the kind, good-natured Pushchins, of whom I am very fond, and there is work.

The work, however, is going badly. I started that serious thing[2] I once spoke to you about in four different tones, wrote about 3 printer's sheets in each and then stopped, not knowing what tone to choose, or how to blend them, or whether I should drop the whole thing. The point is that I'm rather sick of this subjective poetry of sincerity—this poetry of questions—and it doesn't suit either my purpose or the mood I'm in now. I've plunged into a vast, solid, positive, objective realm, and have gone mad, firstly because of the abundance of objects, or rather aspects of objects which I envisage, and then bceause of the variety of tones in which these objects might be portrayed. I think there is a vague principle beginning to emerge from all this chaos, whereby I shall be able to choose; but so far this abundance and variety amount to impotence. The one thing that consoles me is the fact that I never think of despairing, but my head gets in a greater and greater turmoil. I'll keep to your wise principle of chastity and not show it to anyone, and I'll leave it to myself alone to decide what to choose or whether to drop it altogether.

I haven't read your two articles, but Turgenev was enthusiastic about the first one particularly. Where are you and what are you doing? Please drop me a line. Clarens, Pension Perret. Canton de Vaud.

[58] 1. M. I. Pushchin (1800–69), a former Decembrist, and the brother of Pushkin's close friend. He met Pushkin in the Caucasus in 1828, and Tolstoy persuaded him to record his memories of these meetings for Annenkov, who was writing a biography of Pushkin.

2. *The Cossacks*, at which he worked on and off for a period of ten years. Four draft manuscripts relate to 1857.

58 To P. V. Annenkov

I would write more, but one eye is bandaged because of a stye, and it's difficult to write. Turgenev is due to go to London shortly with Nekrasov, who is also due in Paris now.

Yours,
Count L. Tolstoy

59. To T. A. YERGOLSKAYA

[Original in French]

Clarens, 6/18 May 1857

I have just received your letter, dear Aunt, which found me, as you must know from your last letter, at Clarens in the neighbourhood of Geneva, in the same village where Rousseau's Julie lived. I won't try to describe the beauty of this country, especially at present when all is in leaf and flower; I will only say that it's literally impossible to tear oneself away from this lake and its shores, and that I spend most of my time gazing and admiring while I walk or simply sit at the window of my room. I never cease congratulating myself on my idea of leaving Paris and coming to spend the spring here, although it might have earned me a reproach from you for inconstancy. Truly I'm very happy ⟨and I'm beginning to feel the advantage of being born with a silver spoon in my mouth⟩. There is some charming Russian society here, ⟨the Pushchins, the Karamzins and the Meshcherskys; and they have all, goodness knows why, taken a liking to me; I feel it, and the month I have spent here I have been so nice and happy and cosy that it's sad to think about leaving⟩. All these families are going away in eight days and if my friends ⟨Botkin and Druzhinin⟩ don't come here, I'll go and join them in Florence. I'm waiting for their reply. Goodbye, dear Aunt, I kiss your hand...[13 lines omitted]

60. To V. P. BOTKIN

Lucerne, 27 June/9 July 1857

Dear Vasily Petrovich,

I'm terribly busy; work is in full swing—whether fruitless or not I don't know—but I can't refrain from telling you at least part of what I wanted to talk to you about. In the first place, I've already told you that many things abroad have struck me in such a new and strange way that I've jotted some of them down in order to be able to come back to them at leisure. If you advise me to do so, let me write them down in my letters to you. You know my belief in the need for an imaginary reader. You are my favourite imaginary reader. Writing to you is as easy for me as thinking; I know that any thought of mine and any impression of mine is grasped by you in a purer, clearer and higher form than that in which I expressed it. I know that a writer's working conditions are different, but never mind that—I'm not a writer. The only thing I want when I'm writing is for another man, and one who is dear to my heart, to rejoice at what I rejoice at, to be angry with what angers me, or

60. To V. P. Botkin

to weep the same tears as I weep. I'm not aware of the need to say anything to the world at large, but I am aware of the pain of solitary enjoyment and suffering. As a sample of my future letters I'm sending you one from Lucerne, dated the 7th.

It's not this letter, but another one which isn't ready yet.[1]

What a charming place Lucerne is, and how wonderful I find everything here. I'm living in the Pension Daman on the shores of the lake, only not in the Pension itself but in an attic consisting of two rooms and completely detached from the main house. The little house where I live stands in a garden, and is completely covered by apricots and vines; a caretaker lives downstairs and I upstairs. Horse collars hang in the porch and a little fountain babbles under a shed a short distance away. In front of the windows are heavily laden apple trees with supports, uncut grass, the lake and the mountains. Stillness, solitude and calm. My servant is an old woman with grey hair turning yellowish-white, a little bird-like crop and the most good-natured wrinkled little face. She's as deaf as a post, and speaks such a terrible *patois* that I can't understand a word. She's old and ugly and is perpetually washing, fetching water and doing the heavy work; but she laughs perpetually, and such a child-like, ringing, cheerful laugh that even the two yellow teeth which show when she does so are nice. When I came home yesterday the first person I met was the nice-looking 17-year-old landlady's daughter in a white blouse who was running and bounding along the green avenues like a kitten with another pretty girl, and the second person was the nice old woman who was washing the floors. I asked her where the landlady was. She didn't hear me and said something I couldn't understand. I smiled; she put her hands on her hips and started to laugh, but so splendidly that I began to laugh too. And now, as soon as we meet, we look at each other and laugh, with such a wonderful, summery laugh. Often when I get tired of writing I go out on purpose to see her, and we look at each other and laugh, and I go back to my writing and she goes back to her washing, and we're both very content. Yesterday evening I sat down with a candle in my first little room, which I've made into a drawing-room, and simply doted on my apartment. Two chairs, a comfortable armchair, a table, a cupboard—it's all simple, rural and terribly nice. Bare floors with loose boards, a little window with a white blind, vine leaves and tendrils which look through the window, and in the light of the candle seem like heads when you suddenly look at them askance. And framed in the window beyond them you can see shapely black poplars, and through their leaves the still lake in the moonlit glow; and from the lake the distant sounds of horn music drift across. It's perfect! So perfect that I'll stay here a long time. Do come here, dear friend, after your first course of treatment. We could really begin to live here, and could travel about together. I'll look forward to your reply. The letter about Lucerne I'll send to you as soon as I've finished it. You really must come; I'm going down

[60] 1. Tolstoy added this line to the letter as an afterthought. The 'letter' promised by Tolstoy, but which he never sent to Botkin (see Letter 61), was his story *Lucerne*. In its first draft this work took the form of a letter from abroad addressed to an imaginary reader (i.e. Botkin). Tolstoy completed this draft in just three days (9–11 July). However, on 15 July he returned to the work and substituted for the letter form that of a diary kept by a Prince Nekhlyudov—the hero of several other of his works, including *Boyhood*, *Youth* and *A Landowner's Morning*.

60. *To V. P. Botkin*

the Rhine to Holland you know, and, in your direction, to Ostend[2]—it's really en route; anyway I'll agree to anything in order to be with you. Goodbye.
Yours,
Count L. Tolstoy

61. To V. P. BOTKIN

Zurich, 9/21 July 1857

I'm very much to blame, dear Vasily Petrovich, for having let a whole week go by since receiving your letter, without replying. I was busy, and the Tolstoys came to Lucerne and then I was getting ready to go. As I wrote to you, I'm going down the Rhine to England, but on the way I'll call in to see Turgenev at Sinzig, from where I got a letter from him. Sinzig is on the left bank of the Rhine near Remagen, not far from Andernach. There's a spa there, where his Berlin doctor sent him. Judging from his letter, he's more composed mentally. Fet's poem[1] is charming. Before I'd read your remark about the 2 clumsy verses, I'd made the same remark myself. A pity. On the other hand, 'The air resounds with love and trepidation after the nightingale's song' is charming! And where does this fat, good-natured officer get such incredible lyrical boldness from, the attribute of great poets? The main content of my letter which you couldn't decipher was as follows. I was forcibly struck by a particular incident in Lucerne, and I felt the need to express it on paper. And since in the course of my journey there were many such incidents which I jotted down, the idea occurred to me of recalling them in the form of a letter to you, about which I sought your agreement and advice. I started to write down my Lucerne impressions at once. The result was virtually an article, which I've finished, which I'm almost satisfied with and which I'd like to read to you, but evidently I'm not fated to do so. I'll show it to Turgenev, and if he approves I'll sent it to Panayev.[2] If you want to write, write to Paris poste restante. I'll be in Paris in a month's time, I think. How good it would be if we could bump into each other there. Alas! I've picked up syphilis in Lucerne. So much for my continence! I threw myself at the first woman I came across! I'm having treatment now, and I want to arrange things so that I can stay longer with Turgenev, and wait there until it's quite cleared up.

How are you physically and morally? I hope you are better physically. Morally you can never be in a bad way. But write, if you aren't angry with me (I still think you have been angry since your last letter, and this was the reason for your silence —I wasn't able to hit the right note). Write to London poste restante. It would be sad to lose sight of each other.

If I wrote my first letter so 'uncalligraphically'[3] and confused you somewhat,

2. It was Tolstoy's intention to travel to Ostend to see A. A. Tolstaya; he did not in fact do so, nor did he see Botkin until the spring of 1859.

[61] 1. Fet's poem *Another May Night* was published in *The Russian Herald*, 1857, No. 11. Botkin sent Tolstoy the manuscript of the poem.

2. Botkin, Turgenev and Panayev all reacted unfavourably to Tolstoy's *Lucerne*. They considered it immature, disagreeable, and lacking in any distinction.

3. This is a literal translation of Tolstoy's unusual adverb.

you mustn't be angry. It was all the result of a momentary fit of the warmest tenderness towards you.

Turgenev will be in Sinzig until the beginning of August (old style). Read Currer Bell's biography,[4] it's awfully interesting for its intimate picture of the literary view of the various leading circles of modern English writers and their relationships. Goodbye, dear friend, I press your hand warmly and cordially, and wish you the most important thing—a full recovery. Perhaps you can write to Turgenev as soon as you get this letter, saying when you'll be in Ostend. Perhaps I'll find a letter from you at his house, and find you in Ostend, where I promised the Tolstoys to call in.

62. To COUNTESS A. A. TOLSTAYA

The Countess Alexandra Andreyevna Tolstaya (1817–1904) was a relation of Tolstoy's (the daughter of his grandfather's brother). From 1846 until her death, she was attached to the Imperial Court in Petersburg. From 1846 to 1866, she was Maid of Honour to the daughter of Nicholas I, the Grand Duchess Marya Nikolayevna, and from 1866 she was entrusted with the education of the Grand Duchess Marya Alexandrovna, the only daughter of Alexander II. When her charge married Alfred, Duke of Edinburgh, in 1874, Alexandra Tolstaya remained at court as a Lady of the Order of St Catherine, living in the Winter Palace and fulfilling the duties of Lady-in-Waiting to the Empress. She never married. With her close connections at court, Alexandra Tolstaya held a position of great influence, and on a number of occasions was able to assist Tolstoy and even to protect him from persecution at the hands of both Church and State.

Tolstoy's life-long friendship with Alexandra Tolstaya dates from the spring and summer of 1857—although he had been acquainted with her previously in Petersburg—when Tolstoy fled from Paris after witnessing an execution, and went to join Alexandra and her sister in Switzerland where they were in attendance upon the Grand Duchess Marya. 'I have rushed headlong to you', Tolstoy said to her on his arrival, 'feeling sure you would save me from despair.' Tolstoy stayed in Switzerland from 9 April until about the end of July, and spent much of that time in her company. An entry in his diary for 22 July/3 August 1857 records: 'Priceless Sasha [i.e. Alexandra]. A marvel! A delight! I don't know a better woman.' There can be no doubt that there was more than a shade of poetic love in their relationship, at least during the early years. On 12/24 May 1857 Tolstoy confided to his diary: 'Love stifles me, both carnal and ideal love', and it is very probable that had Alexandra been younger, Tolstoy would have fallen in love with her. 'If only Alexandrine were ten years younger', he wrote in his diary on 29 April/11 May 1857—but although there was indeed scarcely more than ten years' difference in age between them, Tolstoy frequently addressed her in a jocular way as 'Granny'.

4. Elizabeth Gaskell's *Life of Charlotte Brontë*.

62. To Countess A. A. Tolstaya

For her part, Alexandra Tolstaya appears to have been very attracted to Tolstoy. In a letter to him of 29 August 1857 she wrote: 'I can't tell you how much joy our meetings—often unexpected—have given me, and how often I recall them. All that I love in life disappeared when I left Switzerland...' She continues: 'I never see you without wishing I were a better woman.' In her *Reminiscences*, Alexandra wrote of her relationship with Tolstoy:

Our pure simple friendship triumphantly refuted the generally accepted and false opinion about the impossibility of friendship between a man and a woman. We stood on some special ground, and, I can say completely sincerely, we concerned ourselves above all with what can ennoble life—each, of course, from his own point of view. Lev sometimes reproached me for not letting him into the innermost recesses of my heart and for not confiding to him what personally concerned me; but for my part I did this quite unwittingly and unintentionally. His nature was so much more forceful and interesting than mine, that quite involuntarily all attention was focused on him, and I was merely a secondary character donnant la réplique. As I've already said, religion was the main subject of our conversations.

From the beginning, Alexandra Tolstaya took a particular interest in Tolstoy's spiritual development: 'I do so delight in following your progress, and seeing you move step by step towards perfection, as I understand it', she wrote, while Tolstoy found it particularly valuable to be able to talk to her about his religious searchings, especially during the 1870s. However, their differing attitudes towards religion—Alexandra was very religious in an orthodox sense and adhered strictly to the laws of the Church—caused some strain and brought the relationship near to breaking point in 1880, and it was not until 1887 that their friendship was fully restored. Correspondence between them was interrupted once again following a serious quarrel in 1897 in Petersburg. This was their last meeting, but they soon began to write to each other again. Tolstoy said of his correspondence with Alexandra Tolstaya that their letters were 'one of the best source materials' for his biography. About 200 of their letters to each other have survived.

Baden-Baden, 16/28 July 1857

Dear Granny,

I've a strange and amusing thing to write to you about. Well, what must be must be. The devil himself trapped me into coming to Baden, and there's roulette in Baden, and I've lost everything down to the last copeck. But that wouldn't have mattered, as I'd arranged for money to be sent to me, and had got enough for living expenses; but en route I met a Frenchman who had also lost everything: I loaned him money, and he then gave me what he won back, and I ended up owing him 200 francs until he got to Paris; but he writes to say he needs the money in Geneva. Couldn't you give me a loan for a couple of weeks? If so, deposit 200 francs at the poste restante in Geneva, in the name of Pegot-Ogier. If you're going away, won't batyushka[1] loan the money to me? I'll return it punctually in 2 weeks'

[62] 1. A. Petrov, a priest at the Russian Church in Geneva.

time. Well, go on, scold me as you wish, only don't stop loving me, even though I don't deserve a hundredth part of it.

When I'm in a normal state I'll write at length; just now I'm ashamed to look people like you in the eye, even mentally.

Goodbye, and forgive me.

Address: Baden-Baden, Hôtel Holland.

I timidly press both Grannies' hands.[2]

Yours,
Count L. Tolstoy

28 July.

N.B.—the 28th.

If possible, reply by telegraph *franco*.

63. To COUNTESS A. A. TOLSTAYA

Yasnaya Polyana, 18 August 1857

Precious Granny!

I'm trusting to luck and sending this letter to Ostend, although I'm afraid it won't reach you; but sitting alone in the country and sifting involuntarily through my memories, I now see that of all my life abroad, it's the memory of you that is the sweetest, dearest and most serious one for me, and I long to write to you—to imagine you more vividly and intimately. Having written this, I sat and thought for a long time, not because I didn't know what to write—on the contrary, there's so much I would like to say to you that might offend your modesty. You say yourself that in the country all feelings grow to enormous proportions and my friendship for you has grown here into such a vast and unwieldy friendship that were I to speak of it, you would very likely say once again that I live for ever on paradoxes. Well, why speak about it? You're a wonderful Granny for not wanting to know about it; and you see in dear Alexandra Alexandrovna[1] a brilliant mind and erudition, and in me—kindness and all sorts of good qualities. And the astonishing thing is that this incredible modesty is to be found—in the *Court*[2] of all places! Really, it's far more astonishing than if a pickled cucumber were to grow on a rose-bush.

In Dresden, to my delight and astonishment, I met dearest Philemon in a grey wig and Baucis,[3] a graduate of the Smolny,[4] and I travelled with them to Petersburg. Of course, time and again these dear friends and I chided you a little, and Mikhail Ivanovich, picking at one nail after another, kept repeating with a puzzled look: yes, she's astonishing...and suddenly in his honest round eyes, beneath his grey brows, there were traces of tears. Also in Dresden I quite unexpectedly met

2. A. A. Tolstaya and her sister.

[63] 1. A. A. Voyeykova, a Lady-in-Waiting to the Grand Duchess Marya Nikolayevna.

2. The word literally means 'pipe'. A. A. Tolstaya says in her memoirs that she did not understand why Tolstoy used it to refer to the Imperial Court.

3. The Pushchins.   4. A school in Petersburg for the daughters of the aristocracy.

63. To Countess A. A. Tolstaya

Princess Lvova. I was just in the right mood for falling in love: I had lost money gambling, was dissatisfied with myself, and completely idle (according to my theory love consists in the desire to forget oneself, and so, like sleep, it most frequently comes over a man when he is dissatisfied with himself or unhappy). Princess Lvova is a beautiful, intelligent and honest person; with all my heart I wanted to fall in love, I saw a great deal of her—and all to no avail! For goodness sake, what does it mean? What sort of a freak am I? It's clear that there's something lacking in me. And it seems to me that this something is just the tiniest grain of fatuité. It seems to me that the majority of people falling in love with each other become close friends this way: they see each other often, they both flirt, and finally each is convinced that the other has fallen in love with him or her respectively; and only then, in gratitude for this imaginary love, do they begin to love each other. But how can I, who always carefully observe a woman I'm on friendly terms with, and the degree of aversion that my person inspires in her, how can I yield to this sweet illusion? But that's quite enought of that, of that dessert—it's time to stop worrying about sweet dishes when you've got grey hairs on your head. I thank God he has given me the essential thing, i.e. the ability to love, though this too might seem a paradox in your opinion; but that's my conviction.

Both my health and my literary affairs detained me in Petersburg for a whole week, but despite that I didn't go to see K.N.[5] because I completely forgot. In Russia things are bad, bad, bad. In Petersburg and Moscow people are continually shouting and being angry and waiting for something to happen, and in the backwoods too there is patriarchal barbarism, thieving and lawlessness. Believe me, on my return to Russia I struggled for a long time with a feeling of disgust for my country, and I'm only now beginning to get accustomed to all the horrors which make up the endless background to our life. I know you won't approve of this, but what's to be done—Plato is a great friend, but truth is a still greater one, as the saying goes.[6] If you had seen, as I did one week, how a lady in the street beat her girl with a stick, how the district police officer got me to say I would send him a cart-load of hay before he would provide my man with a legal permit, how, before my eyes, an official almost beat a sick old man of 70 to death because the official had got tangled up with him, how the village elder, wishing to be of service to me, punished a gardener who had been on a drinking spree not only by having him beaten, but by sending him barefoot over the stubble to watch over a herd, and was rejoiced to see that the gardener's feet were covered with cuts—if you had seen all this, and a whole lot more besides, you would believe me that life in Russia is continuous, unending toil and a struggle with one's feelings. Happily, there is one salvation—the moral world, the world of the arts, poetry and attachments. Here no one—neither the district police officer, nor the village elder—disturbs me; I sit alone, the wind howls, it's dirty and cold, and I play Beethoven badly, with unfeeling fingers, and shed tears of emotion, or I read *The Iliad*, or I invent people

---

5. Yekaterina N. Shostak (*née* Islenyeva), first cousin to the Islavins and for a time headmistress of a school.
6. The saying is Aristotle's.

myself, invent women, and live with them, and scribble over sheets of paper; or else I think, as now, of the people I love. You won't think so, but I see you now much more clearly and better than does some prince of Wurstemberg,[7] who has fastened his big horsey eyes on you. My sister is better and more cheerful than she was before. But if I start writing about her, the letter won't be finished. I kiss yours and Granny Liza's hands most cordially, and wish the wonderful Rebinder[8] every success and strength of mind, and I press his hand in friendship.

[In the margin:] I'll send the money to Petersburg, or wherever you say. My address is Tula. Drop me a line—you know, seriously, I'll rejoice with all my heart to get a letter from you.

64. To N. A. NEKRASOV

Yasnaya Polyana, 11 October 1857

I received September's *Contemporary* today. It's clear the effect your letter has had on me—I feel I want to talk to you. First of all, to take the points in order: what a commonplace and loathsome thing my article[1] turned out to be in print when I reread it. I made a complete fool of myself by it, and you too, it seems. I haven't yet read Avdotya Yakovlevna's story.[2] Now for your poems. Perhaps you don't even want to know my opinion, but for some reason I feel an inner compulsion to express it to you as frankly as I would wish people always to speak to me. The first part is superb. It's a gem, a wonderful gem, but *all* the others, in my opinion, are weak and *contrived*—at least that's the impression they made on me in comparison with the first.[3] *The Contemporary Review*,[4] although interesting, was different from what I expected. It's too Petersburgish, and not Russian. The issue generally is so-so, or even poor.

What will there be, or rather what is there in the October issue? Please don't count on me any more, I'm sick of writing trifles, and bad ones at that. I read yesterday how they tore me to pieces in *The Petersburg Gazette*, and rightly so. Please tell me frankly the opinion of Druzhinin and Annenkov. What did they say to you about the article?[5] I wrote all sorts of nonsense to Kolbasin[6] yesterday, and forgot the main thing. Be so kind as to tell him that I implore him to make an effort to get my discharge papers sent as soon as possible, otherwise I shan't have a residence permit. I'm hurrying to catch the post and I must confess I feel in low spirits at the moment, so I'll stop now.

   7. Prince Alexander of Wurtemberg, whom Tolstoy met in Frankfurt. Tolstoy often makes this pun on the German word for sausage, *wurst*.
   8. Tutor to the children of the Grand Duchess Marya Nikolayevna.
[64] 1. *Lucerne* was published in the September issue of *The Contemporary*. Tolstoy frequently referred to his stories as 'articles'.
   2. A. Y. Panayeva's *Domestic Hell*, published under the pseudonym N. Stanitsky.
   3. Nekrasov's poem *Silence*.
   4. The review section of *The Contemporary*.
   5. Annenkov, like Botkin and Panayev, thought *Lucerne* immature.
   6. The letter has not survived.

64. To N. A. Nekrasov

I hope to be in Petersburg in about a fortnight. Goodbye. Kindest regards to Ivan Ivanovich.[7]

Yours,
Count L. Tolstoy

And please tell Kolbasin too that if the translation of the article hasn't been done, not to do it.[8]

65. To COUNTESS A. A. TOLSTAYA

Moscow, 18–20(?) October 1857

Dear Granny,

Laziness, shameful laziness was the reason why you didn't receive an answer to your last letter at the time you wrote it. There would have been sympathy again.[1] I was still living in the country and was busy from morning till night with manure, horses and peasants, and the work was getting on, though not very well. I am partly indebted to you for my activity. You wrote and said you disliked empty windbags, and feared for your grandson, and I began to fear too, and tried to win the right to show off to you. Besides, I must say that your letter from Ostend made me not only glad but proud. You see—I said—even though the steward and Auntie consider me a trivial fellow, just look who's writing me a letter and, moreover, a friendly one, and moreover, a clever, nice and edifying one! On the very day that you wrote from Petersburg, I was riding round the estate. It was a good day, everything was going well and besides, all the peasants had suddenly become unusually intelligent and kind, and as I rode back home (it was a glorious, bright, cold autumn evening) I experienced a feeling of joy that Lev Nikolayevich was alive and breathing, and a feeling of gratitude for someone for allowing Lev Nikolayevich to breathe. This is a very pleasant feeling which I rarely experience, but one which you, I think, know. All my good thoughts and memories suddenly swarmed into my head and blocked up the whole corridor, so that the drawers containing my disagreeable thoughts and memories couldn't slide in and out. The head, you know, is arranged like this: the skull à vol d'oiseau:

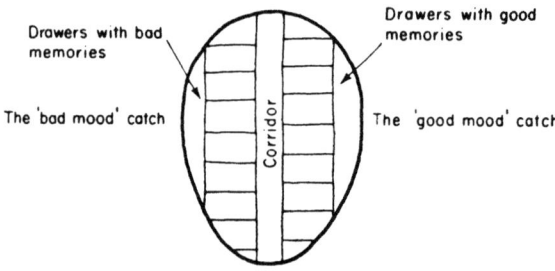

7. Panayev.
8. The translation of *Lucerne* into French. Kolbasin did not in fact translate it.

[65] 1. A reference to a sentence in A. A. Tolstaya's letter of 29–30 August: 'Je vous saute au cou mentalement—voila [un?] de ces coups de sympathie que j'adore comme si j'étais une *schoolgirl*.'

65. To Countess A. A. Tolstaya

All drawers slide in and out into the corridor.

The drawers can slide in and out several at a time from each side, while leaving a passageway through the corridor. When, owing to fine weather, flattery, good digestion, etc., the right-hand catch is pressed, all the drawers spring out immediately, and the right-hand drawers fill up the whole corridor, like this:

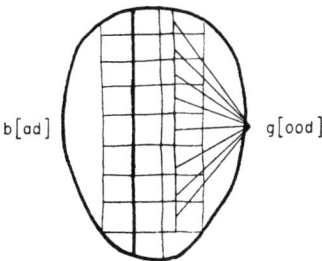

and conversely: when rain, a bad stomach, or truth press the left-hand catch, the whole corridor is also blocked up.

And here is a sketch of the normal state of affairs, when first some and then others slide in and out:

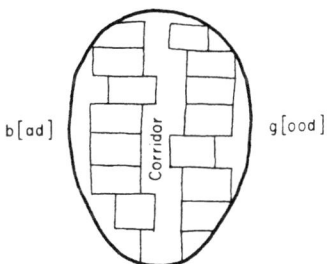

In addition, you must know that each drawer has a host of subdivisions. These subdivisions depend on the person. With one person it's a division into people in court circles and people not; with another, into beautiful and ugly people; with a third, into intelligent and stupid people, etc., etc. With me, there are divisions into memories of good, very good, and really very good people, and people who are mediocrities. Here it is in cross-section and on a large scale:

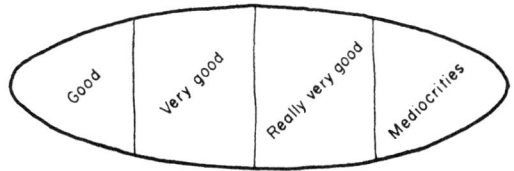

So I was riding along, and the 'good mood' catch was pressed, and all the drawers sprung out, your drawer included. Subsequently, they gradually began to go back

65. To Countess A. A. Tolstaya

in, but your drawer—goodness knows by what right—sprang out to its full extent and stuck right across the corridor, blocking the whole passageway. So I concentrated all my attention on it for quite a long time, and kept on riding, and mentally wrote you a very long letter. But when I arrived home, I had to let new things into the corridor, things like the problem of how to arbitrate in the case of a peasant who had come to blows with his wife, the problem of the purchase of a wood etc; and these problems pushed right into the corridor in a most rude manner. If I hadn't managed to return your drawer to its proper place, they would have broken it. In a word, I began writing you a letter that same day, but it wasn't finished, and I simply gave it up.

I didn't reply to your letter straightaway, as I thought I would be in Petersburg very soon, and I still think so, but things keep postponing my departure, and I'm already beginning to feel ashamed. My sister had to go to Moscow, and I went with her. She won't be going abroad this winter, nor to Petersburg; so I'll also spend the winter in Russia, but will come to Petersburg very soon. I've so much I want to talk to you about. You ask me for reassuring advice; but I'll go to *you* for that, and neither of us will find what we're looking for. Endless anxiety, toil, struggles and deprivations—these are the unavoidable conditions from which no man may dare think of escaping, even for a second. It's only honest anxiety, struggles and toil, all based on love, that constitute what we call happiness. And why happiness?—a silly word; not happiness, but *well-being*; and dishonest anxiety, based on love of oneself—that is unhappiness. And there you have in its most compact form the change in my attitude to life that has recently taken place in me. It makes me laugh to recall how I used to think—and as you still appear to think—that it's possible to create your own happy and honest little world, in which you can live in peace and quiet, without mistakes, repentance or confusion, doing only what is good in an unhurried and precise way. Ridiculous! *It's impossible*, Granny. Just as *it's impossible* to be healthy without movement and exercise. To live an honest life you have to strive hard, get involved, fight, make mistakes, begin something and give it up, begin again and give it up again, struggle endlessly, and suffer loss. As for tranquillity—it's spiritual baseness. That's why the bad side of our soul desires tranquillity, not being aware that its attainment entails the loss of everything in us that is beautiful, not of this world, but *of the world beyond*.

There's a sermon for you, Granny! But no, I wrote it in all seriousness. And the more I think about it, the more I see that it is so.

Goodbye, I cordially press your hand, and the hands of all your people, whom I hope to see in a day or two. Tell Katerina Nikolayevna[2] that V. Islavin[3] is getting married to a certain Kiryakova.

2. Shostak.
3. V. A. Islavin, a civil servant and eldest son of A. M. Islenyev.

66. To V. P. BOTKIN and I. S. TURGENEV

Moscow, 21 October–1 November 1857

Hello, dear Vasily Petrovich. I think you're angry with me, and rightly so. All the while I knew you were at Fécamps and Aix-les-Bains I could have written to you, but kept putting it off, either from laziness or pressure of work—in short I was to blame. But in the last couple of months which I spent in the country, not a day passed without my being cross with myself for losing sight of you and not thinking of you. I found out your address yesterday from dearest Fet and am writing now. What pleased me more than your address was the fact that you are better. Don't wear yourself out again in Rome by too much activity and excitement. I can imagine how Rome will make you excited and happy in the mood you were in when I last saw you and which you are in just now. I dare say you know about me up to the time I left *dear* Baden from Turgenev. I came home almost without stopping, and before I had recovered. Throughout the journey I couldn't help making plans for the future as a result of my sister's new situation and my brother Nikolenka's arrival.[1] And although I knew in advance that disappointment was in store for me I couldn't help devising for myself a beautiful life so remote from reality that reality has had a painful effect upon me. I've hardly seen my brothers—they've gone off hunting to Kursk—while my sister, with her provincial aunts, friends and habits, a sick woman, delicate and in the grip of this provincialism and of her illness, has had an awfully painful effect on me. It's terrible for me to tell you of the disgust Russia has aroused in me. Affairs on my estate where I started to emancipate the serfs last year had gone badly and—more important—had come to a halt, so that an effort was required on my part—either to go ahead the way I had begun or else to drop it all. My sister's health and the education of her children required a move to Moscow.

My views and those of my sister were very different and we antagonised each other; but we had to live together and now the result is that it's difficult for us to be apart. I made concessions, she made concessions; each of us is grateful for the concessions made and is prepared to make new ones. We only had to make a start and now things are going splendidly, so that when we are together we keep wanting to smile, and we feel an agreeable, though unspoken something between us. And this unspoken something is gratitude to one another and the fact that we love one another more than we expected. We've been living together in Moscow now for about a month and every day we expect the children and our aunt, who are evidently held up by the Oka. The day before yesterday I returned from Petersburg where I had been for about 4 days. Druzhinin has been ill, but is now on a diet and is recovering. Annenkov is well and happy, still as clever and evasive as ever, and clutching at the present even more fervently than before, for fear of lagging behind it. He will, indeed, feel sick if he does lag behind it. That's the one thing the infallibility of which he believes in. Druzhinin also is clever, composed and

---

[66] 1. Marya Tolstaya had separated from her husband, Valeryan, and Nikolay Tolstoy had retired from the army.

66. To V. P. Botkin and I. S. Turgenev

resolute in his convictions. He was always out when I called and I saw him the last of all our mutual friends. After the gloom of Nekrasov and Kovalevsky,[2] and Annenkov's nebulous volatility and various half-felt political effusions, I found Druzhinin refreshing. On the whole I must say that the new trend in literature has meant that all our old friends and your obedient servant don't know what sort of people they are, and look as though they've been spat upon. Nekrasov laments about our contract, so does Panayev;[3] they're no longer concerned about writing themselves, but are showering Melnikov and Saltykov with gold,[4] and all in vain. Annenkov spends his evenings at Saltykov's etc. Ostrovsky says he'll be understood in 700 years time, Pisemsky too;[5] Goncharov sits in a corner and furtively invites the elect to listen to his novel;[6] Maykov is awfully contemptuous of the multitude; Woolf buys shares, but not a share in *The Contemporary*; Shchedrin, Melnikov and Count N. S. Tolstoy[7] who used to write without rereading what they wrote have now taken to writing no more than a couple of words each and dictating them too, and that's not all. Saltykov even explained to me that the time for belles lettres has now passed (not only for Russia, but altogether) and that Homer and Goethe will no longer be read throughout Europe. All this is amusing, you know, but it can drive you mad when the whole world suddenly assures you that the sky is black when you can see that it's blue, and you're bound to wonder whether you can see properly. Druzhinin is inflexible. For myself I can say that I haven't changed my opinion either, but there is less merit in that. Thank God I didn't listen to Turgenev who tried to convince me that a man of letters must only be a man of letters. Such a thing wasn't in my nature. You can't make of literature a crutch, or a stick, I think, as Walter Scott said.[8] What would my position be if, as now, the crutch is knocked away? *Our* literature, i.e. poetry, is, if not an unlawful phenomenon, at least an abnormal one (you remember we argued about this), and therefore to build one's whole life on it is unlawful. I think Turgenev is with you, so read this letter to him. The news that you are staying on in Rome, dear Ivan

---

2. Nekrasov was ill at the time, and Kovalevsky was suffering from fits of depression.

3. With the departure of Druzhinin in 1856 to become editor of *Reader's Library*, Nekrasov had sought to bind writers such as Turgenev, Tolstoy and Ostrovsky to publish exclusively in *The Contemporary*. A general 'agreement' was reached on this at the time, but the writers' failure to fulfil their obligations towards *The Contemporary* led to the collapse of the agreement early in 1858.

4. M. Y. Saltykov-Shchedrin (see Letter 295) and P. I. Melnikov-Pechersky (1818–83), novelist, archaeologist and ethnographer. Tolstoy's remark seems to have been unfounded. Melnikov published nothing in *The Contemporary* during 1856–7, while Saltykov-Shchedrin received the same rate of payment as Tolstoy—the maximum rate of 100 roubles per printer's sheet.

5. A. F. Pisemsky. See Letter 165.

6. Goncharov was currently working on his novel, *Oblomov*.

7. N. S. Tolstoy (1812–75), a second cousin of Tolstoy and author of *Sketches from beyond the Volga*.

8. Tolstoy probably learned of this saying of Scott's from an article by Druzhinin, 'Count L. N. Tolstoy's Military Stories; M. Shchedrin's Provincial Sketches'. Druzhinin quoted Scott as offering the following advice to young writers: 'Remember, gentlemen...remember that literature must be for us a wanderer's staff and not a cripple's crutch. Love art, serve it—but don't lean on art alone, don't forget to have in life some practical activity other than literature.'

66. To V. P. Botkin and I. S. Turgenev

Sergeyevich, distressed your friends and gave your enemies a great pretext for censuring you for weakness and fickleness of character, while asserting that they love you very much. I haven't met a single person who hasn't asserted or hasn't considered it necessary to assert that he loves you very much, but at the same time hasn't censured you. Pisemsky said that he's written you an abusive letter. K. Aksakov says that I'm to write and tell you to come back at once, etc.[9] I'm sad that you're not here now, both for my sake and for the sake of literature which you could put in order by your influence, and for the sake of affairs on your estates which they say are in a bad way. If I remember rightly, I think I also allowed myself to censure you, but only a little. Only with my sister do I talk about you freely and at length. In essence, though, I can say, with my hand on my heart, what I usually say when the conversation is about you, and what I think in a calm frame of mind: you can't burrow into another person's soul. There's no life so strange that it doesn't have its own laws and its own explanation, which you can't discover until it's over. And there is an explanation for your life. Bring back from Rome the book which you still have to write and which is expected from you by those who understand you, and then all will be clear. If you believe in my friendship for you, write and tell me as frankly as possible what you are doing, what you are thinking, and why you have stayed on. These questions nag at me a lot. And indeed apropos of this, the hounds have put up an idea in my head which they've been chasing for a month.

Did you get my long letter at Fécamps? I would like to write a lot more to you both, but I have to go. I sometimes envy you for having settled down so well, I think, in Rome. My sister and I are leaving on the first boat in spring—to Italy, I think, first of all.

1 November

I tore out a sheet at the beginning which, on rereading, seemed to me to be quite inappropriate. I apologise for this muddle. It's still better than writing nothing, and I would hardly have time to copy it out again.

[The sheet that Tolstoy tore out and did not send read as follows.]

Several times in my life it has befallen me to come up against some painful reality and to have to choose whether to clamber on up the same dirty path, or to make a detour, and I have always chosen a detour: philosophy (not any one I have studied, but a foolish one of my own, stemming from genuine spiritual need), religion of a similar nature and, in recent times, art have been my detours. I tried and I still try to tell myself that I am a poet and that another reality exists for me, and to give all the rest up; only this time, either because I'm older or because the matters facing me were more serious or my powers of imagination had weakened, I wasn't able, as before, to rise above life, and I was horrified to see that all this painful, foolish and dishonest reality was not an accident, not an annoying thing happening to me alone, but a necessary law of life. It was sad for me to part with my dream of a tranquil and honest happiness without entanglements, hard work, mistakes, new undertakings, remorse and dissatisfaction with myself and others; but, thank God, I'm sincerely convinced that the tranquillity and purity which we seek in life are not for

9. K. S. Aksakov (1817–60), Slavophile publicist, critic and poet, son of S. T. Aksakov.

66. To V. P. Botkin and I. S. Turgenev

us; that the only legitimate happiness is honest hard work and the surmounting of obstacles. For a long time I found it very hard in the country—my youth is over!—but my state of affairs and my sister's situation were such that I felt myself to be the sort of support that if I didn't stand firm, then whatever rested on me would also collapse. This made me act and come to life; at first I was attracted by the activity, then I grew very enthusiastic, saw some results and foresaw others, and felt fine, although from time to time I regretted my lost youth. For about 3 months I busied myself in the country and now things are fine there, so that in short, if the emancipation were to come tomorrow, I wouldn't go back to the country and nothing would change there. The peasants pay me for their land and I farm my own with free labour. Moreover, I've devised a big afforestation scheme with the treasury which interests me very much. Moreover—and most important—relations with my sister were strained at first; my views and those of my sister...[continued above]

67. To N. A. NEKRASOV

Moscow, 18 December 1857

I'm very, very grateful to you, Nekrasov, for the frankness of your letter. I wrote to you that I was pleased with the thing;[1] I have only read it in its revised form to old Aksakov, who was very pleased with it; but now I believe you, although I don't agree, especially as I don't have it with me and as you don't say anything serious against it. It can't be published now, because, as I wrote to you, a great deal in it needs to be corrected and altered. On the 30th I again asked you to send it back to me. It was wrong of you not to have sent it. There is no doubt that it isn't a narrative tale, but an exceptional one, which ought for its purpose to rest entirely on its psychological and lyrical passages and for that reason ought not to, and cannot please the majority; but to what extent my task has been fulfilled is another matter. I know I fulfilled it as far as I could (except for the material finish of the style). The thing cost me a year of almost exclusive hard work but, as I can see, it won't seem so to others—and therefore it's better to consign it to oblivion, for which I'm very, very grateful to you. Only please send me the manuscript or the proofs, so that I can correct what is necessary while it's still fresh, and put the whole thing out of sight. Turgenev writes to say that he's sent you a story. Please tell me what it is[2] and in what number it will appear. Thank God he writes about it without his characteristic morbid modesty. If you should see Maykov, please ask him whether he received the poems from S. T. Aksakov. Aksakov is surprised that he hasn't had a reply.

Goodbye. Give my regards to Panayev and all our friends.

Yours,
Count L. Tolstoy

[67] 1. *Albert.* Nekrasov had criticised Tolstoy's choice of theme and had advised him not to publish it.

2. *Asya* (published in *The Contemporary*, 1858, No. 1). For Tolstoy's opinion of it, see Letter 69.

68. To V. P. BOTKIN

Moscow, 4 January 1858

Thank you for your wonderful, long letter, dear Vasily Petrovich. Why haven't you sent, and why won't you send me your earlier letters that were returned to you?[1] Your letters are a genuine help to me. When I think that you regard my writing so seriously, I pluck up courage myself. We—i.e. Russian society—are in an unprecedented muddle, brought on by the question of the emancipation.[2] Suddenly and unexpectedly everybody has been caught up in political life. However little prepared he may be for such a life, everybody feels the need for activity. And whatever they say and do, it's getting dreadful and disgusting. So far only one thing has emerged clearly: the gentry has sensed that it has had no other prerogatives quite like serfdom, and has clung hold of it bitterly. 90 out of a 100 are opposed to the emancipation, and those 90 include all sorts of people. Some are perplexed and embittered and don't know where to turn for support, since both the government and the people have disclaimed them. Others are hypocrites, hating the very idea of emancipation, but carping at its form. A third lot are self-centred schemers. They are the most disgusting. They simply don't wish to understand that they are citizens of a certain kind, with rights and obligations which are neither greater nor smaller than others'. They either want to do nothing, or to do everything in their own way and change the whole of Russia according to their own set, narrow, despotic design. The fourth and largest number are the stubborn and the submissive ones. They say: we don't want to, and we shan't judge the issue ourselves. If they want to, let them take everything away, or else leave everything as it was before. Then there are the aristocrats in the English manner. There are the Westerners, and there are the Slavophiles. But there aren't any people who can attract other people to themselves simply by the power of goodness, and reconcile them through goodness. As far as the public is concerned there's positively no place now for belles lettres. But don't think that this prevents me from loving it now more than ever before. I've grown tired of talk, arguments, speeches, etc. To prove it I'm enclosing the following little piece which I'd like to have your opinion about. I was impudent enough to consider it an independent, finished work, although I haven't the impudence to publish it.[3]

'I said in my sleep all that was in my soul and that I hadn't known before. My thoughts were clear and bold and were clothed in inspired words. The sound of my voice was beautiful. I wondered at what I said, and rejoiced to hear the sound of my voice. I stood alone on a swaying height. Around me jostled my unknown brothers. Close by I could distinguish faces; far off, endlessly, like the swelling sea, I could see heads. When I spoke, a thrill of rapture ran through the crowd, like a wind through leaves; when I stopped speaking, the crowd paused like one man and took

[68] 1. Botkin had addressed these two letters to Turgenev in Sinzig.
 2. Two government rescripts of 20 November and 7 December 1857 had openly declared for the first time the need to prepare for the emancipation of the serfs.
 3. Tolstoy sent Botkin a draft of his unfinished work, *A Dream*.

68. To V. P. Botkin

a deep breath. I felt the eyes of millions of people upon me, and the power of these eyes crushed me and made me glad. They moved me, as I moved them. The rapture burning within me gave me power over the maddened crowd, and this power, it seemed to me, had no limits. A distant, barely audible voice whispered within me "it's terrible!", but the swiftness of movement drowned the voice and drew me further on. The morbid stream of thoughts appeared inexhaustible. I surrendered entirely to this stream, and the white height on which I stood trembling rose higher and higher. But as well as the cramping force of the crowd, I had for a long time sensed behind me something separate that was importunately beckoning me towards it. I suddenly felt behind me another person's happiness, and I was forced to look round. It was a woman. I stopped and stared at her, without thinking and without moving. I felt ashamed at what I was doing. The dense crowd allowed no passage, but by some miracle the woman moved slowly and calmly in the midst of the crowd without merging with it. I don't remember whether this woman was young and beautiful; I don't remember her clothes or the colour of her hair; I don't remember whether it was a first vanished dream of love or a late memory of my mother's love—I only know that she had everything, and an irresistible force drew me sweetly and painfully towards her. She turned aside. I dimly saw the outlines of her half-turned face and just for a moment caught her gaze upon me, expressing gentle mockery and loving pity. She didn't understand what I said; but she wasn't sorry for that, she was sorry for me. She didn't despise me or the crowd or our rapture—she was charming and happy. She needed no one, and because of that I felt I couldn't live without her... With her appearance, my thoughts, the crowd and the rapture all vanished; but she didn't remain with me either. All that remained was a burning, pitiless memory. I wept in my sleep, and these tears were sweeter to me than my earlier rapture. I woke up and did not spurn my tears. There was happiness in those tears, even when I was awake.'

If Turgenev is still with you, read this to him and decide if it's impudent rubbish or not.[4] But enough of that. I've a serious matter to put to you. What would you say at the present time when the sordid stream of politics is seeking to engulf everything and, if not to destroy art, at least to sully it—what would you say about those people who, because of their belief in the independence and eternity of art, were to join forces and by word (criticism) and deed (i.e. the art of the written word) try to demonstrate this truth and save what is eternal and independent from fortuitous, one-sided and grasping political influence? Couldn't *we* be those people? i.e. Turgenev, you, Fet, myself and everyone who shared and *will continue* to share our convictions. The way to do this of course is through a journal or an anthology, as you wish. Such a journal should attract all that is purely artistic, now and in future. Everything Russian and foreign that is artistic should be discussed. The journal will have one aim: artistic enjoyment—tears and laughter. The journal won't try to prove anything or know anything. Its one criterion will be educated taste. The journal won't want to know about this or that trend, and obviously, therefore, will want to know still less about the requirements of the public. The

4. Turgenev apparently refrained from giving an opinion.

68. To V. P. Botkin

journal won't want quantitative success. It won't imitate the public's taste, but will stand out boldly as the public's teacher in matters of taste, and of taste alone. If I now began to depict the results I foresee for this enterprise, I'd never finish; and besides, I think, there would be no need to do it for you. You share this opinion yourself, and can see better than I can what I shall be striving to demonstrate. If so, then of course nobody but you should be the editor. You'll raise a monument to yourself, not built by human hands.[5] We'll all give money for the publication—Turgenev, you, Fet, and I, etc.

Please think about it and give me a definite answer.[6]

I haven't continued the Caucasian novel that you liked.[7] It seemed to me to be not quite right, and after [...][8] I twice began to think again. I've always noticed with me that the best time for activity is from January till spring, and I'm working now; but I don't know what will come of it. I can't complain about my life in Moscow. There are good people here, as there are everywhere. It's pleasant at home, if only my sister wasn't unwell. She's been suffering the whole winter. There's also good music, and now at last a music society is being formed under the leadership of Mortier.

I haven't been to Petersburg, and don't want to. Grigorovich has been here. He's written quite a good story, and intends to go to Rome shortly.[9] Dear Fet has been ill and hasn't quite recovered yet. How fretful and malicious he is when he's ill, and what a wonderful woman your sister Marya Petrovna is.[10]

There was a luncheon at the Merchants' Club here,[11] arranged by Kavelin, apropos of the emancipation. Katkov, Stankevich, Pogodin, Kavelin, Pavlov, Babst and Kokyrev all gave speeches. Only Pavlov's and Babst's speeches were worthy of note.[12] The luncheon caused bitterness among the gentry as a whole. The Slavophiles didn't want to attend it. The fact that I'm writing this to you is *vanitas vanitatum*, like decorations and ranks. Man is man everywhere—i.e. weak. I suppose the martyrs—only the martyrs—acted directly for the sake of the good, i.e. they did the particular good they wanted to do. But all these politicians are slaves of themselves, and of events. If they desire decorations or glory, and it turns out for the good of the state, the good of the state turns out to be bad for

5. An adaptation of a line from Pushkin's poem *Exegi Monumentum* (1836).
6. Botkin's reaction to Tolstoy's proposal was negative, as was Turgenev's. In a letter to Fet of 6 February 1858 Botkin advised against the idea of the journal, insisting that neither Tolstoy nor Fet was in a position to undertake such a task, particularly in view of the public's current lack of interest in fiction. He thought the completion and publication of Tolstoy's new novel, *The Cossacks*, would have a much more far-reaching influence on the public's taste than any journal.
7. *The Cossacks*.
8. One word is indecipherable.
9. Grigorovich's *Cat and Mouse* was published in *The Contemporary*, 1857, No. 12. Grigorovich's journey to Rome did not materialise.
10. Botkin's sister, Marya Petrovna, was married to Fet.
11. This dinner was arranged by some well-known liberal professors and writers to mark the occasion of the promulgation of the government's rescripts on the impending emancipation.
12. The writer N. F. Pavlov (1803–64) not only denounced serfdom, but placed the responsibility for carrying out the reforms on the gentry. I. K. Babst, a professor of political economy, defended the principle of free labour.

68. To V. P. Botkin

mankind. And if they desire the good of the state, someone gets a decoration and is content with that. *Glaubst zu schieben und wirst geschoben.*¹³ That's what's offensive about all this activity. And if you've grasped this law, grasped it properly with your whole being, then this sort of activity becomes impossible. It's far better to fell a wood, build a house, etc.

But I must say goodbye; I embrace you with all my heart, and Turgenev too. My address is Vargin's house, Pyatnitskaya St.

Yesterday Kokyrev's speech was published[14]—it had been prepared, but not delivered. Obolensky has sent it to Rome. You'll get it there. What happened to all my Olympian calm when I read this speech? Everyone likes the speech. What are we coming to? It's terrible. I'm convinced that we not only don't have a single talent, but we don't even have a single intelligent man. The people now to the fore and in the public eye are idiots and dishonest people. You should know that this speech is the only commentary on the rescript and circular which the censors have passed. The only person in Moscow I know who is indignant at the speech is my brother Nikolay.

69. To N. A. NEKRASOV

Moscow, 21 January 1858

It's a bad thing, dear Nikolay Alexeich, that you've let yourself go so much. It's a bad thing for those who love you, it's a bad thing for business, and especially for yourself. We'll die soon enough as it is and be completely forgotten, so it's not worth driving yourself to oblivion, and that without any happiness for yourself, and without any profit or happiness for others.

About the first number,¹ I would frankly report that it's very poor. Cavaignac,² a good political article, comes right at the beginning, as it would in *The Russian Herald*, and this makes an unfavourable impression. *The Contemporary* should have, and is entitled to have its own traditions. There are two awful misprints in Fet's poem...[1 line omitted] Turgenev's *Asya* is in my opinion the weakest thing he has ever written. I haven't read all Ostrovsky's thing, but I know it reads badly. The political pepper sprinkled everywhere even in the *Uncle Tom's Cabin* supplement,³ doesn't suit *The Contemporary* in my opinion, and can never compare with that of the Moscow journals owing to the conditions of the Moscow censorship.

13. A quotation from Goethe's *Faust*. It was one of Tolstoy's favourite dictums.
14. In this published speech, Kokorev called for a strengthening of the merchant class *vis à vis* the landed gentry. The censor was reprimanded by the government for allowing the speech to be published.

[69] 1. *The Contemporary*, 1858, No. 1.
2. Chernyshevsky's article *Cavaignac* was critical of moderate liberalism and insisted on the rights of the working class. General Eugène Cavaignac was responsible for crushing the Paris insurrection of 1848.
3. Mrs Beecher Stowe's *Uncle Tom's Cabin* appeared in a supplement to *The Contemporary*, 1858, Nos. 1 and 2.

As for myself, I can now report that I'm writing something short in terms of the number of pages, and on a very strange subject, which I'll perhaps send you at the end of the month.[4] I've put my story aside,[5] but I've thought up some more alterations to it which I'll tell you about some time when we're together. I keep revising the plan of my Caucasian novel[6] and make no progress.

Tell me, how are our accounts and the dividend? Send what you owe me to Moscow.

If Grigorovich hasn't left, tell him that I may perhaps go abroad soon and want to know when he's setting off. Perhaps we could travel together.

If my short trip to Italy for a month or two comes off, I'll see you soon, so goodbye; I cordially press you hand, and send my regards to all mutual friends.

Yours,
Count L. Tolstoy

[Postscript omitted]

70. To N. A. NEKRASOV

Yasnaya Polyana, 17 February 1858

After careful consideration I'm now convinced, dear Nikolay Alexeich, that our alliance serves no useful purpose at all. Everything that we said about it in Petersburg was right, but now two new reasons have cropped up as well: firstly the fact that I want to publish in other journals, and secondly the fact that you haven't sent me a dividend account now for six weeks.

As a result of all this I've taken the decision to sever the alliance. We can settle our accounts when we meet in Petersburg this spring.

I hope that the severance of our mutual agreement won't influence our personal relations. For my part I'll always try to publish all my best work in *The Contemporary* and in a few days I'll send you two things to choose from, one of which is the same unfortunate musician, rejected by everyone, which I can't give up and have revised again.[1]

Please reply as soon as possible to Moscow; although I'm in the country now, I'll be returning to Moscow in a few days.

I've forgotten Anichkov's name and address; do me a favour and tell him when you see him that I can't give him a definite answer before March. Please tell him this. It's very important to me.

Goodbye now; I cordially press your hand, and wish you all the best.

Yours,
Count L. Tolstoy

4. In January 1858 Tolstoy was working at his story *Three Deaths*.
5. *Albert*.
6. *The Cossacks*.

[70] 1. *Albert*. The other work sent was probably *Three Deaths*.

71. To COUNTESS A. A. TOLSTAYA

Yasnaya Polyana, 14 April 1858

Granny! It's spring!

Life on earth is a wonderful thing for good people, and it can sometimes be good even for people like me. Nature, the air, everything is filled with hope and a future —a delightful future.

At times you delude yourself into thinking that a happy future is in store not just for nature, but for yourself as well; and you feel good. I'm feeling in that state now, and with characteristic egoism I'm rushing to write to you about things which are only interesting to me. When I think about it sensibly, I know very well that I'm an old potato, frozen, rotten, and boiled in sauce moreover, but spring has such an effect on me that I sometimes catch myself in the full flush of dreaming that I'm a plant which is just bursting into leaf with other plants, and which will grow simply, peacefully and joyfully in God's world. On occasions like these, and at times like these, such an inner process of sorting out, cleansing and ordering goes on that anyone who hasn't experienced the feeling can't possibly imagine it. Away with all the old—with all worldly conditions, all idleness, all egoism, all vices, all involved and uncertain attachments, all regrets and even repentances—away with them all! Make way for the extraordinary flower which swells out its buds and grows with the spring! It's sad to recall how often I've vainly tried to do the same thing as a cook does on Saturdays, and yet I still rejoice in my delusion, and I sometimes seriously believe in the new blossom, and wait for its coming.

I've been alone here in the country for a week already, and I feel fine. I've settled accounts for my life in Moscow, and for everything, and I'm quits with everyone, income and expenditure alike.

It was a strange feeling I experienced when I left for the country in identical circumstances to those in which I came to town. My first feeling was one of a joyful awareness of freedom—the possibility of immediately stepping out of the carriage and walking to Astrakhan, or of turning the horses round and going to Paris, or of halting at the first station and living there forever. It's a glorious feeling, and women don't know it. But then, the nearer I got to the country, the sadder and sadder I felt at the prospect of my approaching solitude, so that when I arrived, I imagined that I was a widower and that a whole family I had lost had recently lived there. And indeed, this imaginary family of mine *had* lived there. And what a charming family! I was especially sorry for my eldest son! And my wife had been a marvellous woman, though a strange one too. There, Granny, teach me what to do with myself when memories and dreams combine to form an ideal of life to which nothing conforms, everything goes wrong, and you don't rejoice and don't thank God for the blessings He has given, but in your soul there is eternal discontent and sadness. Discard this ideal, you will say. It's impossible. Far from being a figment of the imagination, this ideal is for me the most precious thing in life. Without it I don't wish to live. Do you remember Pushkin's *Madonna?* Your

Madonna[1] hangs in my room and makes me glad, but those last lines torment me.[2] The idea sometimes occurs to me of saying a requiem over everything, but then my soul would be left with no other prayers to say. Goodbye, dear Granny; don't be angry with me for all this nonsense, but send me a sensible few words in reply, steeped in goodness and Christian wisdom.

For a long time I've wanted to tell you that you're more at ease writing in French; and to me, a woman's thoughts are far more comprehensible in French.

72. To COUNTESS A. A. TOLSTAYA

Yasnaya Polyana, 1 May 1858

Hello, Granny dear! Thank you for your letters, both of which I received, and congratulations on spring! Only please don't be sad and don't give vent to the sort of thoughts which crop up in one of your letters. Spring is a wonderful time for you; there is always spring in your soul, and you even radiate spring; and yet you seem to be distressed about something, and dissatisfied with something. Either say nothing to me, please, about feeling sad, or else tell me everything. You know, quite seriously, in my good moments (when I'm not being too horrible), I consider myself a true friend of yours, and for that reason I'm happy and proud when you talk to me as an equal who doesn't need helping all the time, but who can himself be of use to you in some way, even if only to sit silently and listen with joy and obedient attention. How are you at present? And where are you? Can you really be in town? Spring has arrived: it's been coming and going for some time, but now it's arrived! Miracles take place before one's very eyes. Every day there is a new miracle. There was a barren branch—and suddenly it's in leaf! Green things, yellow things, blue things come out from under the ground—goodness knows where from! Small creatures fly like things possessed from shrub to shrub, whistling at the top of their voices for some reason—and so splendidly! Even at this very moment two nightingales are performing beneath my windows. I'm experimenting with them, and can you imagine that by playing sixths on the piano I'm able to coax them up to the window? I discovered this quite by chance. The other day I was strumming away on the piano in my usual way, playing some Haydn sonatas with sixths in them, when suddenly, from the direction of the courtyard and Auntie's room (she has a canary), I heard the sound of whistling, chirping and warbling, in time to my sixths. I stopped, and they stopped. I started again, and they started (two nightingales and a canary). I spent about three hours doing this, and the balcony window was open, the night was warm, the frogs were going about their business, and the watchman his—it was splendid. Please forgive me if this letter is rather wild. I must confess, I'm a little intoxicated with the spring and

[71] 1. A. A. Tolstaya had presented a print of Raphael's *Sistine Madonna* to Tolstoy.
 2. The last lines of Pushkin's poem *Madonna*:
>My wishes have been fulfilled. The Creator
>Has granted you to me, you, my Madonna,
>The purest image of purest charm.

72. To Countess A. A. Tolstaya

my solitude. I wish you the same with all my heart. There may be moments of happiness stronger than these, but there is nothing to equal the fullness and harmony of such happiness.

> And plunge, cheerful and lordly,
> Into this life-giving ocean.

Tyutchev's *Spring*, which I always forget in winter, I recite spontaneously, line by line, in the spring.

Yesterday I rode into a wood which I've bought and am felling, and there on the birch trees the leaves were coming out and the nightingales nesting; and they've no wish to know that they don't belong to the crown now, but to me, and that they'll be felled. They will be felled, but they'll grow again, and they've no wish to know about anyone. I don't know how to convey this feeling—one becomes ashamed of one's human dignity and the arbitrariness one is so proud of—the arbitrariness of drawing imaginary lines and not having the right to make a single solitary alteration to anything—not even to oneself. There are laws governing all things, laws you don't understand, but you feel this curb everywhere—everywhere *He* exists. My disagreement with your opinion about my little piece[1] goes right back to this. You are wrong to look at it from a Christian point of view. My idea was this: three creatures died—a lady, a peasant and a tree. The lady is pitiful and loathsome because she has lied all her life, and lies when on the point of death. Christianity, as she understands it, doesn't solve the problem of life and death for her. Why die when you want to live? With her mind and her imagination she believes in the future promises of Christianity, but her whole being kicks against it, she has no consolation (except a pseudo-Christian one)—but her place is already reserved. She is loathsome and pitiful. The peasant dies peacefully just because he is not a Christian. His religion is different, even though by force of habit he has observed the Christian ritual: his religion is nature, which he has lived with. He himself felled trees, sowed rye and reaped it, and slaughtered sheep; sheep were born, and children were born, and old men died, and he knew this law perfectly well and never deviated from it as the lady did, but looked it fairly and squarely in the face. Une brute, you say; but how can une brute be bad? Une brute is happiness and beauty, and harmony with the whole world, and not discord as in the case of the lady. The tree dies peacefully, honestly and beautifully. Beautifully—because it doesn't lie, doesn't put on airs, isn't afraid, and has no regrets. There you have my idea, and of course you don't agree with it; but it can't be disputed—it is in my soul, and in yours too. That the idea is badly expressed I agree with you. Otherwise, you, with your fine sense, would have understood it, and I wouldn't have had to write this explanation which I'm afraid will anger you and make you give me up as a bad job. Don't give me up, Granny. I do have Christian feelings, and highly developed ones even; but I have something else too, that's very dear to me. It's a feeling of love and tranquillity. How these two are reconciled I don't know and can't explain; but dogs and cats do lie in the same shed—that's for certain. Goodbye, Granny dear;

---

[72] 1. *Three Deaths*. Tolstoy must have sent her a manuscript copy, as the story was not published until January 1859.

74. To Countess A. A. Tolstaya

please write to me about yourself. Give my very best regards, of course, to all your people and don't tell them what a godless fellow I am. You're quite different: it seems to me that you understand everything—you have a chord that responds to everything. Well, come what may: I'm expecting an explosive letter back from you, or even worse, one of gentle commiseration.² No, I'd rather you were angry. I'm expecting Mashenka, Auntie and all of them in a day or two.

Goodbye, Granny dear; I cordially press your hand.

Yours,
Count L. Tolstoy

73. To T. A. YERGOLSKAYA

[Original in French]

Moscow, 25 December 1858

⟨First of all, a happy Christmas! secondly, I'm afraid that news of my adventure will reach you in an exaggerated form and so I'm wasting no time in telling you about it.⟩

Nikolay and I were out bear-hunting; on the 21st I killed a bear; on the 22nd we went out again and a most extraordinary thing happened to me. A bear threw himself at me without seeing me; I fired at him at 6 paces and missed with the first shot; with the second shot, at 2 paces, I mortally wounded him, but he threw himself on me, flung me to the ground and while people were running to the rescue bit me twice on the forehead above and below the eye. Fortunately it only lasted 10 or 15 seconds; the bear took to flight and I got to my feet with only a small wound which has neither disfigured me nor caused me pain. Neither my skull bone nor my eye are damaged and the result is that I got away with a small scar on my forehead. At present I'm in Moscow and I'm feeling perfectly well. I'm telling you the absolute truth without hiding anything so that you shouldn't worry. It's all over now and I have only to thank God for saving me in such an extraordinary way...[6 lines omitted]

74. To COUNTESS A. A. TOLSTAYA

Moscow, 15 April 1859

Christ is risen, Granny dear!

I'm writing, not so much because another week is nearly up, or because I want to write—but there's a lie on my conscience which I must confess to. When I wrote to you on Tuesday, I was deeply moved, simply because the weather was fine, and I felt I wanted to prepare myself for communion and that I was very nearly as holy as your old woman. However, it turned out that I wasn't able to

---

2. She replied that his religious views in no way appalled her, that the seed was germinating in him and that God had planted it in too good a soil for it to be choked.

74. To Countess A. A. Tolstaya

prepare myself properly for communion on my own. There now, you must teach me! I can eat Lenten fare all my life, I can pray in my room every day of the year, I can read the Gospels and, for a time, think that it's all very important; but to go to church, to stand there and listen to unintelligible and incomprehensible prayers, and watch the priest and all that motley crowd around him—that I *absolutely cannot* do. That's why I've stopped going to communion for over a year now. On Thursday I went off to the country, and celebrated Easter and the spring with my own people; I kissed the peasants (their beards smelt wonderfully of the spring), drank birch wine, dirtied all the children's dresses put on especially for the holiday (nanny scolded me terribly for this), picked little yellow and lilac flowers, and went back to Moscow. Why?—I don't know. It's as though I'd forgotten something—but I don't know what...[62 lines omitted]

75. To A. V. DRUZHININ

Moscow, 16 April 1859

Are you really not coming to Yasnaya Polyana this spring, dear Alexander Vasilyevich? I still don't want to believe it, and I hope your Masha will get better.[1] In any case, write and say how things are. I want to see you so much and am sorry about your grief. I went to the country for Easter and welcomed spring and the Easter holiday with my family. The lilac was already out, the birch trees were covered in green, the nightingales were singing, there was a thunderstorm which settled the hot dust, there was a smell of freshness and dust in the air and the frogs were croaking. I would like to be with you this summer more than ever, because the estate doesn't require all my attention as it used to, and I intend to enjoy mysel in a simple way. Life is short. All the more reason for it to be good. I'm sure you'll become friends with, and grow fond of both my brothers. How glad I was that they were both genuinely delighted with *Sargin's Grave*.[2] How's Petrov? Incidentally, get a copy of each of my books from Davydov's and present them to him from me, and give me his address. A propos de literature. *Oblomov*[3] is an absolutely capital thing, the like of which hasn't been seen for a long, long time. Tell Goncharov that I'm delighted with *Oblomov* and am reading it through again. But what will please him more is the fact that *Oblomov*'s success with the real public is not fortuitous or sensational, but solid, substantial and enduring. This I was à même de savoir from talk in the country, from the young people and from the ladies of Tambov.[4] But since I became a writer I can't help looking for faults in all great and powerful works, and there's a lot I wish to say about *Oblomov*. Who is writing 'Country

---

[75] 1. Druzhinin's young niece, who died shortly afterwards.
2. M. A. Petrov's *Sargin's Grave* was published in *Reader's Library*, 1859, No. 2. He was a clerk in the War Office and a self-taught writer whose talent was much admired by Tolstoy.
3. Goncharov's novel *Oblomov* was published in *Notes of the Fatherland*, 1859, Nos. 1–4. It was published also as a separate volume in the same year.
4. A reference to the sister of Chicherin and the daughter of a Tambov landowner (Sytina) whom Tolstoy frequently met in Moscow in the late 1850s.

Letters' in *Notes of the Fatherland*?[5] He has in my opinion a remarkable talent, and it's an excellent thing and an underrated one, I fear. Anyway, congratulate Krayevsky[6] on his acquisition. I haven't seen Turgenev, but my brother Nikolay has been living with him all the time. He (i.e. Turgenev) goes hunting, visits the neighbours and is firmly convinced that he's establishing farms and doing *'what has to be done once and for all'*.[7] The fact that I sent money to you like that means nothing. Kokhanovskaya's new story is s... in my opinion,[8] although even so it does have a sweep and a boldness which is rare and valuable in our times; but on the other hand, alas, it has no sense of proportion, and she is no artist. I'm revising my story[9] for the 3rd time, and I keep thinking that something is emerging. Goodbye. For goodness sake don't let me down. Give my regards to your mother and all our friends.

Botkin has a carbuncle on his arse and he's in bed, but the poor fellow's a dear.

76. To COUNTESS A. A. TOLSTAYA

Yasnaya Polyana, end of April–3 May 1859

Good lord! How you do go on at me![1] Really and truly, I'm at my wits' end! But seriously, Granny dear, I'm bad and worthless, and I've hurt you, but do you have to punish me so cruelly? Everything you say is both true and untrue. A man's convictions—not the ones he talks about, but those he has culled from life's experience—are difficult for another person to understand, and you don't know mine. If you did, you wouldn't have come down on me so. Still, I'll try to make my profession de foi. As a child I believed passionately, sentimentally and unthinkingly; then, when I was 14 years old, I began to think about life in general, and ran up against a religion which didn't accord with my theories, and, of course, I thought I was doing a service in destroying it. Without it, I lived very peacefully for about 10 years. Everything began to reveal itself to me, clearly and logically, and fall into neat divisions, and there was no place for religion. Then there came a time when everything had been revealed, and there were no longer any mysteries in life, but life itself began to lose its meaning. At that time I was alone and unhappy, living in the Caucasus. I began to think in a way that people have the

5. 'Country Letters' were published in *Notes of the Fatherland*, 1858, No. 4 and 1859, No. 3. Written by A. P. Sumarokov, they were signed only with the initials P.S. These 'Letters' described the difficulties encountered by a landowner returning to his estates prior to the reform —a topical subject of especial interest to Tolstoy.

6. A. A. Krayevsky (1810–89), editor and publisher of *Notes of the Fatherland* from 1838–68.

7. Turgenev was transferring his serfs from the corvée to the quitrent system, whereby they paid him in cash or kind for the land they worked, and not in labour.

8. The pseudonym of N. S. Sokhanskaya; her work, *From a Provincial Gallery of Portraits*, was published in *The Russian Herald*, 1859, No. 3.

9. *Family Happiness*.

[76] 1. In answer to Tolstoy's previous letter, A. A. Tolstaya wrote to him, criticising him for his idleness, ignorance and pride in matters of religion, particularly in view of his failure to confess and take communion at Easter. She observed that he embodied all the idolatries of the pagan world, worshipping God in a sunbeam or in some manifestation of nature.

76. To Countess A. A. Tolstaya

strength to think only once in their lives. I have my notes from that time, and rereading them now, I couldn't understand how a man could attain to such a pitch of intellectual excitement as I did then. It was both an agonising time and a good one. Never again, either before or since, did I attain to such heights of thought, or peer into *the beyond*, as I did at that time, for a period of 2 years. And all that I discovered then I shall remain convinced of forever. I can't do otherwise. From 2 years of mental activity I discovered something old and simple, but something I now know in a way no one else does—I discovered that there is immortality, that there is love, and that one must live for others in order to be happy for all eternity. These discoveries amazed me by their resemblance to the Christian religion, but instead of discovering them for myself, I began to look for them in the Gospels, and found little. I didn't find God, or the Redeemer, or the *sacraments*, nothing; and I searched with all, absolutely all the powers of my soul, and wept, and tormented myself, and craved for nothing but the truth. For goodness sake, don't think you can even remotely understand from my words all the power and concentration that went into my searchings at the time. It's one of those mysteries of the soul that are in all of us, but I can say that I've rarely met in other people such a passion for truth as I had at that time. And so I've stayed with my religion, and it has been good to live with it. I ought to say more.

3 May. This was written immediately after I received your letter. I stopped, because I was convinced it was all idle chatter, which wouldn't give you any idea of even a hundredth part of what really happened, and that it was no good going on. But as I promised myself never to alter any letters to you, I'm sending you this one as well. The fact is that I love and respect religion, and consider that without it a man can be neither good nor happy; that I would like to have a religion more than anything else in the world; that without it I feel how my heart shrivels up with every passing year; that I still have hope, and for brief periods almost believe; but I don't have a religion and I don't believe. Furthermore, with me it isn't religion that makes life, but life that makes religion. When I lead a good life, I'm closer to it, and feel quite ready to enter this happy world; but when I lead a bad life, I feel there's no need for it. Just now, in the country, I feel so horrible, and my heart feels so arid, that it's dreadful and horrible, and the need for religion is all the more apparent. God willing, it will come. You laugh at nature and the nightingales. For me nature is religion's guide. Each soul has its own path, and this path is unknown, and is only sensed in the depths of the soul. Perhaps it's only for this reason that I love you. Ah, Granny, my dear friend! Write to me more often. I'm feeling so horrible and sad here in the country. My soul is so cold and arid that it's frightening. There's no point in living. These thoughts came home to me with such force yesterday, when I began to question myself in earnest: who do I do good to? Who do I love?—No one! And there isn't even any grief or tears for myself. Even repentance is cold. So is reasoning. Only work remains. But what is work?—Empty trifles!—you dawdle along and fuss about, while your heart contracts, shrivels up and dies. I'm not writing this to you so that you can tell me what it means and what I should do, and can console me. That's not possible at all. I'm

77. To V. P. Botkin

writing simply because I love you and because you'll understand me; open up a little window into your heart and let in all your grandson's nonsense, and shut the little window again, and—*all right!*[2] *Please don't even bother to reply about it.* The main thing is that I can't lie to myself. I've a sister who's ill and an old aunt, and there are peasants I could be useful to and show affection to, but the heart is silent, and to do good *deliberately* is shameful. The more so since I've experienced the happiness (however rarely) of doing it unconsciously, quite by accident, and straight from the heart. It shrivels up, grows numb, and contracts, and I can't do anything about it. You mustn't be angry with the likes of us, or scold us, but pity and caress us. It's all right for you. You always have somewhere to warm your soul, but with us it shrivels up, and you can feel it and are terrified—and there is no remède.

Goodbye; give my regards to your people and don't forget me. How silly your Courts and all that nonsense are, which prevent you from writing to me. I think your grandson who loves you, is much more important than all the *truby*[3] in the world.

My sister and Aunt send their love and ask to be remembered to you. There's another distressing thing. When I got back to the country and reread my Anna,[4] it seemed such horrible, disgraceful stuff, that I can't get over my shame, and I don't think I'll ever write anything again. But it's already in print. And don't try to console me about it either. I know what I know. And there's yet another distressing thing: my farming is going terribly badly, but I stick to it, and it seems that I'll soon be completely ruined. On top of everything else, the rye has failed this year. There!—now I feel like laughing and jumping up and down, and simply because 5 minutes ago I wanted to cry, and because I'm writing to you.

L. Tolstoy

It's the first day of fine weather here.

77. To V. P. BOTKIN

Yasnaya Polyana, 3 May 1859

Vasily Petrovich, Vasily Petrovich! What have I done with my *Family Happiness*! Only here and now, having come to my senses at leisure and having read the proofs yet sent me of the 2nd part, have I come to see what disgraceful s... this loathsome work is—a blemish on me, not only as an author, but as a man. You tricked me into handing it over; now you can be privy to my shame and remorse.[1] I'm now dead and buried as a writer and as a man! That's positive, especially as the 1st part is worse still. Please don't write me a single word of consolation, but if you

2. In English.   3. I.e. *Courts*. See Letter 63, note 2.
4. *Family Happiness*, published in *The Russian Herald*, 1859, No. 4. In his diary Tolstoy called it 'a shameful abomination'.

[77] 1. At first Botkin disliked Tolstoy's *Family Happiness*—he found it cold and boring—but he nevertheless advised him to publish it, recognising its obvious merit. However, in reading the proofs of the second part of the work, Botkin's attitude changed considerably; on 13 May he wrote to Tolstoy of its 'enormous inner dramatic interest', and he spoke of it as an 'excellent psychological study'.

77. To V. P. Botkin

sympathise with my sorrow and wish to be a friend, persuade Katkov not to publish this 2nd part but to take the money back from me, or consider me in his debt till autumn. I'm keeping my word and I've corrected the proofs with a disgust which I can't describe to you. There isn't a living word in the whole thing, and the ugliness of the language stemming from the ugliness of the idea is inconceivable. But if it's not possible to take away this cup from me, be a friend, look through the proofs and cross out and correct what you can. I can't. I feel like crossing everything out. If, however, you can manage to save me from the still greater shame of having the 2nd part published, burn it, and get the manuscript from Katkov and burn that too. I was right to want to publish it under a pseudonym. I can return the 350 roubles in a week. The end of the story hasn't been sent to me, and there's no need to send it. It's torture to see it, read it and be reminded of it.

Goodbye now; I press your hand and beg you seriously and sympathetically to try to understand what I am writing.

Yours,
L. Tolstoy

I'm sending the proofs to Katkov, but hope that you receive this letter before he does the proofs.

78. To COUNTESS A. A. TOLSTAYA

Yasnaya Polyana, 12 June 1859

How glad and grateful I was for your letter, my dear Granny; I haven't written for a couple of weeks just because I was glad and at peace with myself, nasty egoist that I am. What else do I need to say? That I'm aware of the fact that you are so far away now, and I'm feeling quite sad. Do you know what feelings your letters arouse in me (such as the last ones in which you try to convert me)? It's as though I'm a sick child, unable to speak—I'm ill, I've a pain in my chest, and you feel sorry for me, love me, and want to help me, and you rub me with balsam and stroke my hair. I'm grateful to you; I want to weep and kiss your hands in return for your love and tenderness and concern; but the pain isn't there and I can't and don't know how to tell you about it.

I'm still living in the country, and haven't been to the Troitsa Monastery because of all my affairs which, however unpleasant they are, have taken complete hold of me. You took what I told you about being ruined too much au pied de lettre. I can't be ruined, because I'm single, and I know how to earn my living (I'm proud to say). I'm amusing myself, or rather, I'm trying to dope myself, to forget myself in my preoccupation with my own affairs and agriculture, and although I like it, I'm not dry enough to be capable of making it profitable. If you were in Russia I would send you Eliot's *Scenes of Clerical Life*; but for the present I'll only ask you to read *Janet's Repentance*[1] in particular. Fortunate are the people who, like the English,

---

[78] 1. George Eliot's *Scenes of Clerical Life* include *Amos Barton, Mr Gilfil's Love-Story*, and *Janet's Repentance*. All three appeared in *Blackwood's Magazine* in 1857.

imbibe Christian teachings with their mother's milk, and in such an elevated, purified form as Evangelical Protestantism. It's a moral and religious book, but one which I liked very much and which made a deep impression—*deep*—that's a lie: nothing makes a deep impression on me now—I've shrivelled up. If you're free and it's not too boring, write and tell me about yourself. Where are you? How have you settled down? What new and deep impressions have you had? You are capable, and always will be capable, of experiencing them, only not for the reason you think, but because God has granted you the sort of nature which I, at least, have never met the like of. Goodbye, dear, kind helper and teacher; please go on stroking my head and rubbing me with balsam—even though the pain isn't there, I feel marvellous for it.

L. Tolstoy

As from today, the days get shorter. And yet so many days have already been shortened for me, uselessly and unhappily, and continue to get shorter and shorter all the time; and yet it still seems they could be used for some purpose.

79. To A. V. DRUZHININ

Yasnaya Polyana, 9 October 1859

I believe, my dear Alexander Vasilyevich, that you love me as a man, and not as an editor loves a hack writer who might be some good to him. As a writer I'm no longer good for anything. I'm not writing, and I haven't written since *Family Happiness*, and I don't think I shall write in future—at least I flatter myself with this hope. Why is this? It's a long and difficult story. The main reason is that life is short, and to waste it in my adult years writing the sort of stories I used to write makes me feel ashamed. I can and must and want to get down to business. It would be good if it could be the sort of thing which would tire me out, which urgently needed doing and would give me courage, pride and strength—that would be all right. But I really can't lift a finger to write stories which are very nice and pleasant to read, now that I'm 31. It's funny that I should even think about writing a story at all. And so I can't grant your wish, however disappointing it is for me to refuse you anything. To sell wheat, to manage your estate or anything else of the sort—that I can do. But most of all I can and want to kiss you, and to come to Petersburg to while away the time with you, and talk and have supper with you while your mother presides at table. And I shall do all this without fail. I've just read Petrov's new story.[1] I definitely didn't like it, although it obviously has great power. But his misfortune—the opposite of ours and a serious one—is a complete unawareness of his gifts. He doesn't know himself what is great in him, and Katerina[2] is only a hint and a shadow, when she should be everything. If he were younger this misfortune would be reparable, but now, I fear, he will always be 'a disappointment' rather than 'a hope'. To think what he might have been! Give my regards to

[79] 1. M. A. Petrov's *The Elections*, published in *Reader's Library* 1859, No. 9.
2. The heroine of *The Elections*.

79. To A. V. Druzhinin

Pisemsky, Goncharov and all the others; I wouldn't want my friends and former colleagues to forget me. I certainly shan't cease to value them. Is it true that dear old Polonsky is in a difficult position?³ Fet has gone to Moscow; he's in great distress, poor fellow; his sister is very ill.⁴ Yes, Fet gagne à être connu; the better I know him, the better I love and respect him. It's just the opposite with Turgenev; during his present visit I was finally convinced that he's both clever and gifted, but also one of the most insufferable people on earth. And ever since I've adopted this new point of view towards him I've felt at ease with him. I feel guilty about Petrov for not having replied to him; give him the enclosed, if I get it finished.⁵ Goodbye; I embrace you with all my heart.

Yours,
L. Tolstoy

80. To COUNTESS A. A. TOLSTAYA

Yasnaya Polyana, 12 October 1859

I learned of your sorrow,¹ Alexandrine, my dear friend, not from Katerina Nikolayevna,² but from an indifferent stranger, and I was afraid for you when I heard of it. I was out hunting, I didn't have your address, I didn't believe it was true, and moreover there wasn't any time. The day before yesterday, on my return home, I was thinking of you again, and meant to write, and then found Katerina Nikolayevna's letter here. Do you realise how apropos it all is? Recently I went hunting with a certain Mr Borisov,³ who's married to Fet's sister⁴—I think I've mentioned them to you before. Borisov is one of the nicest, most tender, loving and likeable creatures I've ever met in my life, and one who, for some reason, most arouses one's compassion at the same time. He's a small man with kind eyes, a timid smile and hesitant movements, but for all that a man who's firm and unshakeable when it comes to honesty and justice. His father was a scoundrel, hanged by his own peasants, and his mother a gentle, downtrodden woman. He was brought up at Pyotr Petrovich Novosiltsev's, and there led the life of a downtrodden ward. From childhood onwards he was in love with a pretty little girl of his own age who lived in the neighbourhood—Fet's sister—and never ceased to love her. He proposed, but was refused, and went away to serve in the Caucasus, and everywhere he went he was liked and respected, but nothing ever made him happy—he thought only of the chance of one day being accepted. 10 years later he returned. Her father was dead. He proposed again, but this time she refused him because she was in love with someone else. That very same day he put

---

3. Y. P. Polonsky, a deputy editor of *The Russian Word*, was at loggerheads with A. Grigoryev, the assistant to the editor.
4. See Letter 81.
5. Nothing survives of Tolstoy's correspondence with Petrov.

[80] 1. The death of her niece Pasha.   2. Shostak.
3. Ivan Petrovich Borisov, an army officer, and keen sportsman.
4. Nadezhda Afanasyevna Shenshina, a half-sister of the poet A. A. Fet.

80. To Countess A. A. Tolstaya

a pistol to his brains, but the pistol misfired, and he was saved and persuaded to go on living and hoping. He went away again to serve in the war. Everywhere he lived honourably, in the strict sense of the word, which is rare for someone with a military upbringing, and everywhere he was brave and modest. He's a religious man. 3 years later he tried again, and again was refused. But at this time something very unfortunate happened to the girl; she had a fit of madness, but recovered, and the doctors told her that she might have a relapse if she didn't get married. God knows whether it was due to the pleas of her relatives, her unhappy love affair or Borisov's persistence, but she consented coldly and unwillingly.[5] Borisov was sure of himself and married her. A year later a wonderful child was born to them. I saw them over a period of two years, and they are the only happily married couple I've seen in my life. She saw his true worth and loved him, and he, for the first time in his life, blossomed forth at the age of 35. A smile never left his face, he wanted to tell everyone about his happiness—his wife and child were the best in the world! It was a pleasure to look at him, and having seen him for a moment you would say: there's a happy man. And this was the same Borisov who two years previously was nice and pitiful, so pitiful! He's a huntsman. We arranged to go hunting together this autumn. His wife and child and her brother Fet went to Moscow. They were separating for the first time for a whole month. You should have seen all his concern, all his love down to the smallest trifle, and his self-satisfaction at being able to bear the separation. We hunted together for a fortnight, and during that time I grew to love, respect and admire him even more. On 3 October, we arrived with the hunt at Turgenev's village in the very best of spirits. He was gay, and charming, drank a little, and advised me to get married, assuring me that only then should I live and be happy, and that he himself couldn't be happier. We slept in 2 adjacent rooms. When all was quiet and I couldn't sleep on account of various agreeable thoughts about him, Turgenev came to me on tiptoe with a letter he had just received from Fet, in which Fet wrote and asked him to find Borisov and tell him that since her arrival in Moscow his wife had been in a terrible state of madness, a hopeless one, the doctors said. The next day Borisov came to me, waddling along on his short legs, smiling, rubbing his hands and pressing me to have the horses saddled quickly, as the weather was fine and the hunting would be perfect. And I had to carry out this ghastly operation on him, and I did so, and my flesh still creeps when I recall that moment. Of course, he rushed off straightaway; but I know that her condition is terrible; she's like the majority of mad women: the purer and more moral they have been, the more cynically immoral and brazen they become in their madness. It's awful! And Fet writes that there's no hope now.

Yes, my friend, there's your sorrow and there's his sorrow; what terrible and refined sorrow has God ordained man to live with! That's all I can say to you about your sorrow, which I sympathise with, as you know, with all my heart. I'm especially sorry for your poor mama. At our age one still retains an interest in oneself,

---

5. When abroad in 1856, N. A. Shenshina fell in love with a certain Erbel, and they planned to marry. However, Erbel broke off the engagement, and Shenshina suffered a nervous breakdown shortly afterwards.

80. To Countess A. A. Tolstaya

one still has happy delusions, and people of one's own age are still kind to one; but at her age one loves for the last time, and loves not adults, who are finished and done with, but hope, the germ of something that is to outlive us. She loved you, her daughters, in this way when you were little, but now I'm sure she loved Pasha more than any of you. So it seems to me.

What are you doing? How has this misfortune affected you? Who are your friends there? You've fallen in love with Rostovtsev.[6] I'm very glad of it. He's an excellent man. There's something about him that makes one afraid of a brusque approach. Something noble, delicate and tender. In my relations with him I've always felt an agreeable respect and wariness. I can't say anything good about myself. Pride, laziness and scepticism continue to govern me. But I go on struggling, and still hope to be better than I am. How I'd like to be with you and talk to you—to listen while you speak of your sorrow, sit silently gazing at you, and rejoice that I'm not yet completely good-for-nothing, as long as you love me. Goodbye; Christ be with you.

L. Tolstoy

81. To B. N. CHICHERIN

Boris Nikolayevich Chicherin (1828–1904) graduated from the Faculty of Law at the University of Moscow in 1849, and had a distinguished career as a lawyer, historian and liberal politician. In 1856 he published several articles, including 'The Eastern Question from the Russian Point of View' and 'The Holy Alliance and Austrian Policy' in Herzen's journal *Voices from Russia*. In the same year he became a regular contributor to *The Russian Herald*. From 1861 to 1868 he was Professor of Law at the University of Moscow and from 1881 to 1883 Mayor of Moscow. He travelled widely and wrote extensively on European history and philosophy. His friendship with Tolstoy probably dates back to the winter of 1856–7, and he later recalled his early meetings with him as follows: 'I was attracted by his sensitive, receptive, talented, affectionate, yet firm nature; his was a distinctive combination of gentleness and strength that lent him a special charm and originality. We saw each other almost every day; sometimes we went out to dine together and had long conversations.' Fourteen of Tolstoy's letters to Chicherin have survived, and thirty of his to Tolstoy.

Yasnaya Polyana, end of October–begining of November 1859

Thank you for your letter, my dear Chicherin. I was already afraid that you had *given up* writing to me because of my unpunctuality, the cause of which is nothing more nor less than my nature. All right, I know this sounds like an explanation to one's parents! We haven't seen each other for a long time, my friend, and it would

---

6. Nikolay Yakovlevich Rostovtsev (1831–97) served in the Artillery in 1854–5 and collaborated with Tolstoy and several other officers in the scheme to publish a military journal (see Letters 27 and 31).

82. To B. N. Chicherin

be good to take each other's measure; have we drifted apart a lot, and in what direction? I sometimes think that I've changed a very great deal since we used to watch each other eating quatre mendiants[1] at Chevalier's; I also think that it's the purblindness of egoism, which only sees the marks of time on oneself and doesn't sense them in others. And no doubt much has matured and much has crumbled away in your soul too during the last 18 months, and we shall get on well together again.

I was meaning to philosophise with you about the immortality of the soul and other things, but I was interrupted at this point the day before yesterday, and now I don't know how to finish what I was saying. I'll give you an account of my past and of my plans for the future. I spent the winter in Moscow and the summer in the country. In the country I'm busy with the estate, and although it's dull and hard work, some traces of my efforts can be seen this year both on the land and on the people. And you know that nothing makes you so fond of a job as the signs of your own participation in it. I can now definitely say that I'm not engaged in this job in a casual or temporary way, but that I've chosen this form of activity for life. Literature I think I've given up for good. Why? It's hard to say. The main thing is that everything I was doing and felt able to do was so remote from what I would have liked to do and ought to have done. As proof of the fact that I'm speaking sincerely and not posing (and few men can resist the temptation to pose when speaking about themselves, even to a very close friend), I confess that my abdication from literary activity (the best activity in the world) was, and sometimes still is hard to bear. Meanwhile, at times I've tried to write again; at times I've endeavoured to fill the void left by this abdication with something else: hunting, society, even science. I began to study the natural sciences, but now life is going smoothly and is full without them.

I definitely can't finish this; I've been interrupted twice and I must post it now. Send me a proper address; I want to write to you. Goodbye, dear soul; I love you very much. So does Auntie; she likes you best of all my friends. I'm spending this winter in the country, and the next one too, I think. Come and have a talk at Yasnaya. It's a good place to talk and sound each other out a bit. It's impossible to pose here.

Tolstoy

82. To B. N. CHICHERIN

Yasnaya Polyana, 30 January 1860

If your letter had the object of provoking me to reply, it has achieved its object.[1] It even made me angry. You give me advice in a nonchalant and kindly way about *how an artist should develop, what a beneficial effect Italy has on one with its*

---

[81] 1. A dry dessert made of figs, raisins, almonds and nuts.
[82] 1. In his previous letter, Chicherin had spoken ironically of Tolstoy's liking for country life, and advised him to go to Italy and study art.

82. To B. N. Chicherin

monuments and its sky, and other banal commonplaces—*how harmful inactivity in the country is*—*life in a dressing-gown*—and *how I should get married and write nice stories etc.* However petty and false your activity seems to me, I won't give you any advice. I know that *a man* (i.e. a creature who lives freely) sees in every thing and in every thought something special of his own which no one else sees, and that this alone can tie him down to his work to the point of self-sacrifice. I know that such a man knows after his own fashion his own place in the world and his own value and the value of his work; I know that he is sometimes unable to talk about all he knows, but he knows it for certain. Just in order to show you how mistaken you can be in not admitting this or in forgetting it, I will merely say in reply to your advice that at our age and with our means, roaming around away from home is, in my opinion, just as bad and just as unseemly as writing stories which are pleasant to read. At our age, when you have reached, not merely by the process of thought but with your whole being and your whole life, an awareness of the uselessness and impossibility of seeking enjoyment; when you feel that what seemed like torture has become the only true substance of life—work and toil—then searchings, anguish, dissatisfaction with yourself, remorse etc.—the attributes of youth—are inappropriate and impossible. I won't say that it is necessary to, but rather that it is impossible not to do the sort of work of which the fruits are the ability to see sufficiently far ahead to be able to give yourself up entirely to that work—one man to plough the land, another to teach young people to be honest etc. But the self-delusion of so-called artists which you tolerate (I flatter myself with the hope) only out of friendship for a friend you don't understand—this delusion is the meanest baseness and falsehood on the part of the person who yields to it. To do nothing all one's life and to exploit the labour and all the good things of other people in order to reproduce them, badly and perhaps worthlessly, later on, is a monstrous and foul act of which I have seen too many disgusting examples round about me for me not to be horrified by it, and which you, if you think about it carefully and if you love me, should not be able to tolerate. But what am I doing, you ask? Nothing special or artificial; I'm doing a job which is as natural for me as breathing the air, and at the same time a job from the heights of which, I confess, I often like to look down on vous autres with sinful pride. You'll like it and understand it, but I can't talk about it; come to Yasnaya Polyana when you've finished your travels, and tell me truthfully whether you don't envy me when you see what I've done, and the peace of mind with which I'm doing it. I'll leave you to guess what it is.[2] I haven't been away from the country this year and I won't go away, and I can't imagine how and why I should go away in future. My sister lives 40 versts away from me, she sends her kind regards. My Aunt loves you very much. My brother Nikolay has gone out shooting bears. Goodbye; write soon.

2. Tolstoy was particularly involved with farming and estate management over the winter of 1859–60, and he also devoted much time to his school and his teaching activities.

83. To A. A. FET

Afanasy Afanasyevich Fet (1820–92), a poet and landowner, and Tolstoy's closest friend from the late 1850s to the middle 1870s. Unusual circumstances surrounded Fet's birth. He was born of German parents, Johann and Charlotte Foeth, but the birth took place in Russia at the home of Afanasy Shenshin, a landowner, with whom his mother was then living. Fet was christened as Shenshin's son, even though the marriage between Shenshin and Charlotte Foeth had not yet taken place. When Fet was fourteen years old, the ecclesiastical authorities declared the christening illegal, and he was obliged to assume the name Fet and forfeit his inheritance and status. Later Fet wrote: 'If you ask me what all the sufferings, all the sorrows of my life are called, I will answer: they are called Fet.' The forfeiture of his heritage affected Fet deeply, and much of his energy and ambition was devoted to the attempt to prove himself, and secure what he considered to be rightfully his. In 1845, after a successful university career, Fet joined a cavalry regiment, and there can be little doubt that he was largely drawn by the lure of gentry status that was automatically conferred on all serving officers above a certain rank. Having served in the army for eleven years, he eventually retired and purchased a large property at Stepanovka, not far from Yasnaya Polyana, where he applied himself successfully to estate management.

As a poet Fet's name is frequently linked with that of Tyutchev, and like Tyutchev, he was a master of the short lyric poem. The two principal motifs dominating his poetry are love and nature. Many of his lyrics were inspired by his love for Marya Lazich. Fet fell in love with her during his army days, but he considered marriage to be impossible because they were both too poor. The ending of their relationship was soon followed by Marya's death (there were suggestions of suicide at the time). Fet's subsequent marriage to Botkin's sister did not prevent him from devoting much of his later poetry to the memory of Marya. As a poet Fet spanned the period of realism, but his poetry echoed the Romantics and foreshadowed the Symbolists, in vision as well as in form. He was a prolific translator from Latin and German, and his translations include Goethe's *Faust* as well as numerous poems of Horace, Virgil, Catullus and Propertius.

Fet's formal acquaintance with Tolstoy dates from the post-Crimean War period when Tolstoy was introduced to most of the Petersburg literary establishment. However, their friendship only really flourished when Tolstoy severed his connections with Petersburg circles as he became increasingly absorbed in his estate to the detriment of his own literary work, and the friendship was cemented by a mutual interest in literature which Tolstoy continued to pursue even when he temporarily gave up writing himself, a dislike of urban life and society, a concern for the responsibilities entailed by their estates and their peasants at a time of great social change and a mutual addiction to Schopenhauer (whose works Fet translated into Russian). They met frequently and kept up a lively correspondence, and indeed Fet was one of Tolstoy's few really close friends during the early

83. To A. A. Fet

years of his marriage. They also frequently sent their writings to each other for comment.

Tolstoy's religious crisis in the late 1870s put a great strain on their relationship. Fet had always been deeply conservative in his social and political opinions, and what he admired in Tolstoy's work was its artistry, not its polemicism. When Tolstoy became engrossed in religious and ethical questions, Fet followed him by reading Renan and Strauss, but came to conclusions diametrically opposed to Tolstoy's own. In the 1880s Fet sold his estate near Yasnaya Polyana and moved to the Province of Kursk, having been permitted by imperial decree to resume the name of Shenshin and its accompanying status, and from that time the two men saw very little of each other, and hardly ever corresponded. Nevertheless, their extant correspondence is considerable, and comprises 139 letters from Fet and 159 from Tolstoy. Fet's memoirs (*My Reminiscences*, Moscow, 1890) contain some useful and interesting material about Tolstoy.

Yasnaya Polyana, 23 February 1860

I was terribly pleased to get your letter, my dear Afanasy Afanasyevich. Our ranks will be swelled, and swelled by an excellent recruit. I'm sure you'll be an excellent landlord. But the point is—what are you to buy? The farm I spoke about near Mtsensk is a long way away from me, and as far as I remember it was being sold for 16,000. I know nothing more about it. But next door to me, with adjacent boundaries, there's an estate of 400 desyatins of good land and, unfortunately, 70 wretched serfs as well. But that's no problem: the peasants will willingly pay quitrent, as on my estate, of 30 roubles a household: on 23 households—660 roubles—and more rather than less when the emancipation comes, and that leaves you with 40 desyatins of arable—4 fields of fertile soil and about 20 desyatins of pasture, which should yield around 2,000 roubles in income: a sum total of 2,500, and the asking price for the estate is 24,000, not allowing for the debts, which should be about 5,000. The location, with its scenery and its proximity to the highway and to Tula, is very good; the soil is good—it's loam soil. The estate is dilapidated, i.e. the manor house is old and tumble-down, but there is a house and a garden. It will all need to be re-done. At all events, it would be to your advantage to buy this estate for 20,000. A particular advantage for you would be the fact that you have in me a perpetual overseer. I won't mention all the other things. If this isn't to your liking, I'll sell you some hundred desyatins of my own land, or ask my brother Nikolay if he'll sell Alexandrovka. But really, trying to leave personal advantages completely aside, the best thing for you would be to buy Telyatinki (that's the one for sale next door to me). The seller is a ruined old man who wants to sell as quickly as possible in order to get rid of his son-in-law, and he's approached me twice. The estimate I did at the beginning is an estimate of what this estate will yield if you put about 5,000 capital into it, and a couple of years' work; but even in its present condition it could still answer for 1,500 roubles, and therefore more than 7 per cent. There's also my farmstead, 10 versts from here, of 120 desyatins, but it's not a good place to live—there's no water and no woods. Let me know as soon as possible and

83. To A. A. Fet

as fully as possible how much money you intend to put towards the estate. That's the main thing.

I've read *On the Eve*. This is my opinion. Writing stories generally is a vain occupation, but even more so for people who are melancholy, and who don't rightly know what they want from life. However, *On the Eve* is much better than *A Nest of Gentlefolk*,[1] and it has some excellent negative characters—the artist and the father. But the other characters are not only not types; even the ideas behind them and their situations are not typical, or else they are completely commonplace. But then, that is Turgenev's habitual mistake. The girl is thoroughly bad—*ah, how I love you...she had long eyelashes...* Generally it always astonishes me how Turgenev, for all his intelligence and feel for poetry, can't refrain from banality, even in the matter of literary devices. Most of this banality is in the negative devices, which remind one of Gogol. There's no humanity or sympathy for the characters, but you're presented with monsters whom the author rails at instead of pitying. This somehow conflicts badly with the tone and the sense of liberalism of everything else. This was fine in the year dot and in Gogol's day (yes, and it must also be said that if one is not to have any sympathy for one's own worthless characters, one must abuse them till the sparks fly, or mock them till you're blue in the face) and not do as Turgenev does, obsessed as he is with spleen and dyspepsia. Generally speaking, no one should write a story like that now, quite apart from the fact that it won't have any success. Ostrovsky's *The Storm* in my opinion is also a deplorable work, but it will be successful. It's not Ostrovsky or Turgenev who are to blame, but the age. It will be a long time now before the man is born who can accomplish in the world of poetry what Bulgarin accomplished.[2] No one is preventing lovers of the classics, of whom I am one, from reading poems and stories seriously and discussing them seriously. But something else is needed now. We don't need to learn, but we do need to teach Marfa and Taras at least a little of what we know. Goodbye, dear friend. I've a million requests. I've forgotten the name of the German libraire on the Kuznetsky Bridge, on the left going up the street. He sends me books; drop in and ask him: (1) what I owe him, and (2) why he hasn't sent me anything new for so long. Take Pikulin's advice and select at the shop any good medical handbooks for ignoramuses, and also any veterinary handbooks (up to 10 silver roubles), and send them to me. Ask my brother Sergey whether he's ordered the ploughs for me; if not, call in at Wilson's the engineer's and ask whether he has 6 Starbuck ploughs, or when he can get them.

Ask in Meier's seed shop in the Lubyanka about the price of clover seed and timothy grass. I want to sell.

What's the cost of the best veterinary instrument?

What's the cost of a pair of lancets and a cupping-glass?

[83] 1. Both novels by Turgenev, published in 1860 and 1859 respectively.
    2. F. V. Bulgarin (1789–1859), writer and journalist. He was publisher and editor of the newspaper *The Northern Bee* in the reign of Nicholas I and acquired an unsavoury reputation as a police informer and sycophant. A prolific writer in many genres, he is perhaps best remembered today as a novelist. Presumably Tolstoy had in mind the edifying and didactic sides of Bulgarin's work.

83. To A. A. Fet

Perhaps dear Ivan Petrovich[3]—whom I embrace—will undertake to do some of this. I kiss Marya Petrovna's hand. Auntie thanks you for remembering her and sends her regards.

84. To Y. P. KOVALEVSKY

Yegor Petrovich Kovalevsky (1811–68), a writer, traveller and mining engineer. He travelled widely in Russia and abroad, conducting geological research, taking part in expeditions to Montenegro and Egypt, and assisting in the conclusion of a trade treaty with China in Peking. He met Tolstoy in Sevastopol during the Crimean War and again in Petersburg on many occasions. Subsequently Kovalevsky was promoted to the rank of Lieutenant-General and was made a Senator. It was a testimony to his versatility that he was an Assistant President of the Imperial Geographical Society and also the first President of the Literary Fund.

Yasnaya Polyana, 12 March 1860

Perhaps you recall, dear Yegor Petrovich, that I've been living in the country for more than 2 years now, and have been busy with my estate. This year (since the autumn) apart from the estate, I've also been busy with a school for boys and girls and for older people, which I've started for all who are interested. I've gathered together about 50 pupils, and the number is growing. The progress of the pupils and the success of the school in the eyes of the people have been quite unexpected. But it's impossible to tell you everything, the whys and wherefores; one either has to write a book or go and have a look for oneself. The point is this. It seems to me that wisdom in all everyday matters consists not in knowing what has to be done, but in knowing what to do first and what next. As far as Russia's progress is concerned, it seems to me that however useful telegraphs, roads, steamers, carbines, literature (Fund and all),[1] theatres, Academies of Arts etc. are, they are all premature and wasted until such time as it can be seen from the calendar that 1 per cent of the total population of Russia, including all so-called students, are receiving instruction. They are all useful (the academy etc.) but useful in the same way as dinner at the English Club would be useful if it were all eaten up by the steward and the cook. All these things are produced by all 70,000,000 Russians, but are used by several thousand. However ridiculous the Slavophiles are with their nationalism and isolationism et tout le tremblement, it's only that they can't call things by their proper name—instinctively they are right. Not only we Russians, but any foreigner who has travelled 20 versts in Russia is bound to be struck by the numerical disproportion of educated and uneducated, or rather of barbarous and literate people. And there's nothing to be said if you compare the figures for various European states. But then, if only 1 person in 100 in England was a barbarian, it is

3. Borisov.

[84] 1. The Literary Fund was established in 1860, for the purpose of providing state subsidies to writers and artists, and Yegor Kovalevsky was its first president.

84. To Y. P. Kovalevsky

probable even so that social evil would result from that percentage of barbarians. The social evil that we've grown accustomed to acknowledge and call by various names—mostly coercion and despotism—what is it but the coercion of prevailing ignorance? Coercion cannot be practised by one man over many, but only by the prevailing majority, single-minded in its ignorance. It only seems that Napoleon concluded the Peace of Villafranca, banned the newspapers and wanted to seize Savoy—in fact it is the Felixes and the Victors, who can't even read newspapers, who do all this. However, my pedagogic habits have run away with me—it's ridiculous for me to try to prove so seriously to *you* that $2 \times 2 = 4$, i.e. that the most vital need of the Russian people is public education. Such education doesn't exist. It hasn't yet begun, and it never will begin as long as the government is in charge of it. It's impossible to prove that this education doesn't exist, but if you were here, we could set off at once right round the village and watch and listen. To prove that it hasn't begun we could also go at once to the school, and I'd show you the literate pupils who have studied before with the priests and deacons. They are the only pupils who are completely hopeless. You shouldn't laugh at the controversy as to whether literacy is useful or not. It's a very serious and melancholy controversy, and I frankly take the negative side. *Literacy*, the actual process of reading and writing, is harmful. The first thing a pupil reads is the Slavonic Creed, the Psalter, and the Commandments (the Slavonic ones); the second is a fortune-telling book, and so on. Without seeing for oneself in practice, it's difficult to imagine the terrible devastation that this causes to the intellectual faculties, and the destruction of the moral fibre of the pupils. You have to visit the village schools and the seminaries (I've investigated this matter), the seminaries which supply teachers for the government schools, in order to understand why the pupils from some schools turn out to be more stupid and more immoral than those who have never been to school. For public education to get going, it must be transferred into the hands of society. I won't cite the example of England, the most educated country—the very essence of the matter speaks for itself. If the government were to stop all business, close all its departments and committees (and what a good thing that would be) and concern itself only with public education, even then it would hardly be successful, because the government's own machinery would obstruct it and, above all, because its interests seem remote (in effect, it only has one interest) from public education. But society must be successful because its interests are directly related to the level of education of the people; because societies deprived of all coercive means of action will adapt themselves only to the needs of the people, which will be expressed in the philanthropic or financial success of an undertaking and will continually have their actions checked against the degree of satisfaction of the public needs. But once again, it seems, I've been trying to prove twice two. The only question, perhaps, is whether there exists the need to organise and be organised. For me this question is settled. The six months that my school has been in existence have produced three similar schools in the neighbourhood, and everywhere the success has been the same. The point is: what will the government say if presented with the following project:

84. To Y. P. Kovalevsky

'The Society for Public Education (or a more modest title) has as its aim the dissemination of education among the people.

'The resources of the Society will include members' contributions at 100 roubles or a percentage, pupils' fees (where possible), receipts from the Society's publications, and donations.

'The activities of the Society will be as follows:

1. The publication of a journal consisting of a strictly pedagogic section (on the laws and methods of primary teaching), a section containing elementary primers for teachers and readings for pupils, and a section containing information on the activities of the Society.

2. The founding of schools in those areas where there are none and where a need is felt for them.

3. The drawing up of a teaching programme, the appointment of teachers, and the supervision of teaching, economic accounting generally, and the administration of such schools.

4. The supervision of teaching in those schools where the founders wish it.'

So far I am the only member of the Society. But I say to you quite genuinely that whether such a Society is possible or not, I'll put all I can and all my powers into carrying out this programme. It goes without saying that my ideas are probably one-sided and that the Society will alter them and add to them a lot once it has taken them up. But if only it could muster the energies of a lot of people towards one goal! And you can help me, my dear Yegor Petrovich. *I* am in the government's bad books. On no account must this come from me; but you can tell Yevgraf Petrovich[2] about it, or better still, draft a note about it and show it to him. (I'm setting you this task straightaway because I know in advance that you can't help sympathising with it with all your heart). If I knew for certain that the government would authorise this Society, I'd work more seriously at drawing up the project itself and would present it through another person.[3] In Tula there's the headmaster of the school, Gayarin (your brother knows him)—a remarkable man —and I told him today of my intention. I'm hoping that he won't refuse to present it in his own name. In any case, with you the matter is in good hands. Either present this note (about the Society) directly, after altering and rewriting it, or explore the ground where necessary, and write and tell me what I should do; just one thing: I won't swallow the government's usual line of making one set out the project, the teaching programme, etc., in great detail, and then saying—it's impossible. My time is precious to me (and I can say with pride that it's precious to 100 boys as well). Apart from the schools on my estate and on my brother's, I'm preparing a long article on pedagogy which won't be suitable for the project for the government. Whether they allow it or not, I'll form a secret society for public education, even if I'm the only one. No, but seriously, if the Society should

2. I.e. Yegor Kovalevsky's brother, the Minister of Public Education at the time.
3. There is no record that this project was ever presented to the government. Certainly no permission was given.

85. To A. A. Fet

prove impossible, I nevertheless intend to publish the journal which I've written about in the project for the Society.[4] Please explore the ground and write to me about it. Will they authorise a journal with my name as editor? And how, and in what form, and to whom should I apply, and so on? However much I need to be here now, I'd come to Petersburg if my presence might be necessary for the success of the matter. When I think that you'll almost certainly reply to me: 'It's clear, Lev Nikolayevich, that you're just sitting in the country, amusing yourself with these projects'—when I think that, I'm liable to despair. But what can the government be frightened of? Is it really possible in a free school to teach what shouldn't be known? I wouldn't have a single person in the school if I mentioned that relics are not as sacred as God himself. But this doesn't prevent them from knowing that the earth is round and that $2 \times 2 = 4$. Well, come what may; only let me know just as soon as you possibly can. Keep well; don't be sad, and God grant you all the very best. I cordially press your hand.

Yours,
L. Tolstoy

85. To A. A. FET

Hyères, 17/29 October 1860

I think you already know what has happened. On 20 September, our style, he died, literally in my arms.[1] Nothing in life has made such an impression on me. He was telling the truth when he said that there is nothing worse than death. And if you really think that death is after all the end of everything, then there's nothing worse than life either. What's the point of struggling and trying, if nothing remains of what used to be N. N. Tolstoy? He didn't say that he felt death approaching, but I know he followed its every step, and surely knew what still remained to him of life. A few minutes before he died, he dozed off, then suddenly came to and whispered with horror: 'What does it all mean?' He had seen it—this absorption of the self in nothingness. And if he found nothing to cling to, what shall I find? Even less. And then it's most unlikely that I or anyone else would struggle with it up to the last minute quite as he did. A couple of days before, I said to him: 'We'll have to put a chamber pot in your room.'—'No', he said, 'I'm weak, but not as weak as that yet: we'll struggle on a bit longer.'

Up to the last minute he didn't give in to it; he did everything himself, continually tried to occupy himself, wrote, asked me about my writing, gave me advice. But I felt that he was no longer doing all this from any inner desire, but on principle. One thing remained for him to the end—nature. The night before he died he went into his bedroom to [...] and fell exhausted on the bed by the open window. I came in. With tears in his eyes he said: 'How I've enjoyed this whole last hour.' From the earth you came and to the earth you will return. The one thing that remains is the vague hope that there, in nature, of which you will become a part in

---

4. In fact, Tolstoy started to publish his educational journal *Yasnaya Polyana* in 1862.
[85] 1. Nikolay Tolstoy died of consumption.

85. To A. A. Fet

the earth, something will remain and be discovered. All who knew and saw his last minutes say: 'How wonderfully calmly and peacefully he died', but I know how frightfully agonising it was, for not a single feeling escaped me. I said to myself a thousand times: 'Let the dead bury their dead'; you must put the powers you still have to some use, but you can't persuade a stone to fall upwards instead of down, the way it's attracted. You can't laugh at a joke you find boring, you can't eat when you don't want to. What's the point of everything, when tomorrow the torments of death will begin, with all the abomination of meanness, lies, and self-deceit, and end in nothingness, in the annihilation of the self. An amusing trick! Be useful, be virtuous, be happy while you're alive, people have said to each other for centuries —we as well—and happiness and virtue and usefulness are truth; but the truth that I've taken away from my 32 years is that the situation in which someone has placed us is the most terrible fraud and crime, for which words would have failed us (us liberals) had it been one man who had placed another man in that situation. Praise be to Allah, to God, to Brahma. What a benefactor! 'Take life as it is', 'It's not God who has placed you in this situation, but you yourselves'. Nothing of the sort! I do accept life as it is, as a most mean, detestable and false condition. And the proof that it was not I who placed myself in this situation is the fact that for centuries we have been trying to believe that it's very fine; but as soon as man reaches a higher stage of development and ceases to be stupid, it becomes clear to him that everything is rubbish and a fraud, and that the truth which he nevertheless loves more than anything else is a terrible truth. So that when you see it clearly and truly, you come to, and say with horror like my brother: 'What does it all mean?'.

Well, of course, while there is the desire to eat, you eat, to [s...], you [s...]; while there is the unconscious, stupid desire to know and speak the truth, you try to know and speak it. That's the one thing left to me from the world of morality, higher than which I've been unable to rise; it's the one thing that I'll go on doing, only not in the form of your art. Art is a lie, and I can no longer love a beautiful lie. I'm spending the winter here for the simple reason that I am here, and it makes no difference where I live.

Please write to me. I love you just as my brother loved you and remembered you up to the last minute.

86. To COUNT S. N. TOLSTOY

Brussels, 12/24 March 1861

Every day I write letters to everyone except you; the reason is that there's too much I have to say, and that I can't say what I'd like to in writing. There are millions of impressions of Rome, Paris, London and the people I've seen, but how can I write, and what's the point, when I expect to see you in 3 weeks time? I've been staying in Brussels for a week now, waiting for a reply to my letter from London and an 'enclosure', but I shan't wait longer than the 18/30th, and then I'll borrow the money and go; please reply therefore to Dresden (poste restante) and reply at least briefly to the following questions: (1) how is your health, and what are your thoughts about your health? (2) what about the Emancipation?[1] How did the peasants take it, and how is the land being allotted? I don't think I've told you yet that I'm coming back with plans to publish a journal at my Yasnaya Polyana school, and that I'm going to get permission in Petersburg and am going to start straight after my return.[2]

I suppose you've seen Dyakov, and he's told you how things are. My health is not too bad, i.e. short of a thunderbolt etc. it depends on myself, just like yours. I'm glad to say, I think, that Turgenev and I are friends again, and that he no longer makes me see red. I only spent 20 days all told in London,[3] and was in a fog literally and metaphorically owing to ill health and the mass of things which had to be done. Here, on the contrary, I'm living very quietly; it's a provincial town compared with London and my friends the Dundukovs are here—an old man and woman, two sick daughters, and one aged 15—so there's nothing doing as far as Hymen is concerned. Anyway there's not much hope for me as far as that's concerned, since my last teeth are broken. But I'm in good spirits, especially today. The window is open and it's like a warm summer's day. I correspond regularly with Mashenka, and all's well with her, I think, except for her plan to send Nikolenka[4] to Paris to her governess' brother—but this plan has come unstuck. In general she gets on so well with Princess Golitsyna who is there, that nothing more could be desired. That's what Nikolenka said too.[5] It would have been splendid if they had gone to take the waters together in summer. Goodbye; please write to Dresden and to Petersburg (to Davydov)...[6 lines to his aunt omitted]

87. To A. I. HERZEN

Alexander Ivanovich Herzen (1812–70) was born the illegitimate son of a Russian nobleman, Ivan Alexeyevich Yakovlev, and his German mistress, whom Yakovlev lived with but never married. Their son was christened Herzen at birth and was brought up in his father's home with all the privileges of a legitimate son and heir. Herzen entered the University of Moscow in 1829, where he studied natural sciences, philosophy and literature, and where his radical ideas continued to develop in the prevailing atmosphere of German idealism and utopian socialism. After

[86] 1. The Emancipation of the serfs was proclaimed on 19 February 1861.
2. Tolstoy only started to publish his educational journal *Yasnaya Polyana* in January 1862.
3. Tolstoy, who had been in Western Europe since July 1860, travelled to England for two to three weeks in March 1861. His main purpose was to investigate English educational theory and practice, and to this end he visited Matthew Arnold, then Professor of Poetry at Oxford, from whom he obtained a note of introduction to seven schools in London. He attended lessons there and bought a number of English textbooks and works on educational theory which he sent back to Yasnaya Polyana. He also attended a lecture by Dickens on education and a debate in the House of Commons in which Palmerston took part. In retrospect, however, the event which stood out most from his short visit to London was his meeting with Herzen.
4. Marya Tolstaya's son.
5. Tolstoy's deceased brother.

87. To A. I. Herzen

taking his degree, he entered the civil service where, as an ambitious and highly gifted young man, he hoped to make an outstanding career. However, his ideas and personality proved ill-suited to government service and he was twice sent into exile, where he employed his free time in writing stories, essays and novels, expressing his discontent with the social and political climate of the day. His best novel, *Who is to Blame?*, is an early variation on the theme of the 'superfluous man' in Russian society, and his growing literary reputation and his social connections brought him to the notice of most of the outstanding writers and thinkers of his generation.

When Herzen's father died in 1846, leaving his fortune to his illegitimate son, Herzen decided to emigrate, in the belief that Russian conditions offered him no scope for useful activity. In 1847 he and his wife and family left Russia for Western Europe, where they were to remain for the rest of their lives. They travelled first in Germany, Italy and France, where they were caught up in the momentum of the revolutions of 1848. Herzen's sympathies lay firmly with the republicans, but his support for their methods was by no means unqualified. Following the collapse of the revolutionary movements after 1848 and a series of bitter family tragedies—his mother and one of his sons were drowned in a shipwreck, and his wife had an adulterous relationship with his friend the German poet, Herwegh—Herzen and his family eventually moved to England in 1852. Here he established two émigré journals—*The Polar Star* (1855), and *The Bell* (1857). The latter was smuggled into Russia and exercised a considerable influence on Russian political and social thought. His influence declined, however, after 1861, when he began to oppose the more extreme of the Russian revolutionaries. In 1865 he moved to Geneva. His best-known works include the long autobiographical *My Past and Thoughts*, and the short political essays *From the Other Shore* and *The Russian People and Socialism*.

Tolstoy saw Herzen several times during his visit to England in March 1861. Only three of his letters to Herzen have survived.

Brussels, 14/26 March 1861

I was just about to write to you, dear Alexander Ivanych, when I got your letter. I was going to write to you about *The Polar Star*, which I've only just finished reading properly. The whole volume is splendid, and that's not just my opinion, but the opinion of everyone I've seen. You keep saying, 'Give me a polemic.' What sort of polemic? Your article about Owen is, alas, much too near to my heart.[1] It's true—quand-même, in our time it's only possible for an inhabitant of Saturn who has flown down to earth, or for a Russian. There are a lot of people and 99 Russians out of 100, who will be too afraid to trust your ideas (and let it be said in brackets that it's very easy for them, thanks to the tone of your article which is too flippant. You seem to be addressing yourself only to people who are clever and brave). These people, i.e. the ones who aren't clever and brave, will say that it's better to keep silent if you've reached these results—i.e. that such a result

[87] 1. To understand this passage, it is necessary to refer to Herzen's exposition of Robert Owen's utopian socialist ideas in Part VI, chapter 9 of *My Past and Thoughts*, and his criticism of Owen's belief in individuals as agents of progress and as the embodiment of ideas.

1. The four Tolstoy brothers, 1854. From left, Dmitry, Nikolay, Sergey and Lev Nikolayevich

2. Tolstoy's sister Marya as a girl

3. Valeriya Arsenyeva

4. Tolstoy with a group of writers, 1856. From left, back, L. N. Tolstoy, D. V. Grigorovich; front, I. A. Goncharov, I. S. Turgenev, A. V. Druzhinin, A. N. Ostrovsky

5. L. N. Tolstoy, self-photograph, 1862

6. S. A. Tolstaya, 1862

7. Tanya Behrs (Kuzminskaya)

8. A. A. Tolstaya ('Granny')

9. A. A. Fet

10. N. N. Strakhov

11. N. N. Gay

12. N. A. Nekrasov, 1861

13. V. P. Botkin

14. A. I. Herzen

15. L. N. and S. A. Tolstoy with eight of their children, Yasnaya Polyana, 1884

16. L. N. Tolstoy on the road from Moscow to Yasnaya Polyana, 1886

17. V. G. Chertkov

18. L. N. and S. A. Tolstoy with seven of their children, Yasnaya Polyana, 1892. The two youngest children in the foreground are Ivan (Vanechka), born 1888 died 1895, and Alexandra, born 1884 and now living in America

19. The Tolstoy family, Yasnaya Polyana, 1903. From left, standing, Ilya, Lev, Alexandra, Sergei; seated, Mikhail, Tatyana, Sofya Andreyevna, Lev Nikolayevich, Marya, Andrei

20. L. N. Tolstoy telling his grandchildren, S. A. and I. A. Tolstoy, a fairy tale about a cucumber, 1909

21. Aylmer Maude with Tolstoy's daughter Tatyana Sukhotina and her daughter Tanya

22. Tuckton House colonists, Christchurch, Hampshire, 1907. Chertkov is fifth from the right on the back row. Mrs Chertkova is in the middle of the front row, next to her sister, Olga Tolstaya, Andrei's former wife

23. Tolstoy's house at Yasnaya Polyana

87. To A. I. Herzen

indicates that the path was wrong. And you give them some right to say this by the fact that in place of their shattered idols you put life itself, arbitrariness, or the pattern of life as you say. In place of tremendous hopes of immortality, everlasting perfection, historical laws etc., this pattern is nothing at all—a button in place of a colossus. So it would have been better not to give them this right, to have put nothing in their place—nothing except the force which overthrew the colossi.

Moreover, these people—the timid ones—can't understand that the ice cracking and breaking under their feet proves that man is advancing and that the only way not to fall in is to go on without stopping.

You say I don't know Russia. No, I know my own subjective Russia[2] which I look at through my little prism. If the soap bubble of history has burst for you and me, this is also proof that we're blowing a new bubble which we can't yet see. And for me this bubble is the clear and sure knowledge of my Russia, as clear, perhaps, as Ryleyev's knowledge of Russia in 1825.[3] We practical people can't live without this.

How did you like the manifesto?[4] I read it today in Russian, and I don't understand who it was written for. The peasants won't understand a word, and we won't believe a word. I don't like the fact, either, that the tone of the manifesto is one of a great boon conferred on the people, while in effect it offers nothing except promises even to the educated serf.

Apart from its general interest, you can't imagine how interesting I found all the information about the Decembrists in *The Polar Star*.[5] About 4 months ago I began a novel, the hero of which is to be a Decembrist returning from exile. I wanted to have a talk with you about it, but I didn't manage to. My Decembrist is to be an enthusiast, a mystic, a Christian, returning to Russia in 1856 with his wife and his son and daughter, and applying his stern and somewhat idealised views to the new Russia.[6] Please tell what you think about the propriety and the opportuneness of such a subject. Turgenev, to whom I read the beginning, liked the first chapters.

My regards to all your dear Orsett House folk (dear both by Tessié's standards[7] and my own judgment) and I enclose the promised photographs for you and Ogaryov[8] and look forward to yours in return.

L. Tolstoy.

[Postscript omitted]

2. Tolstoy used the expression 'my subjective Russia' to refer to the Russian people.
3. K. F. Ryleyev (1795–1826), a poet and one of the leading figures of the Decembrist uprising in 1825.
4. The Manifesto proclaiming the Emancipation of the serfs in February 1861.
5. This issue of *The Polar Star* published Bestuzhev's *Reminiscences of Kondratin Fyodorovich Ryleyev*, and other materials relating to the Decembrists.
6. Tolstoy abandoned *The Decembrists* after writing only three chapters, in order to turn his attention to the theme of Napoleon's invasion of Russia.
7. Marie-Edmond Tessié du Motay, a French chemist who lived in exile in London and was a friend of Herzen. Tolstoy met him and disliked his excessive addiction to flattery.
8. N. P. Ogaryov (1813–77) was, like Herzen, a political exile. He cooperated with Herzen in the publication of *The Bell* and *The Polar Star*.

88. To A. I. HERZEN

Frankfurt-on-Main, 28 March/9 April 1861

On the same day as I got your letter, dear Alexander Ivanych, I got a letter from Turgenev promising to come to Brussels in two days' time. *Tremendous light, sir* etc. so attracted me that I was intending to suggest to Turgenev when he arrived that we should come to your banquet.[1] But he didn't arrive, unfortunately, because of a cough and a plaster he had stuck on him, and I won't laugh because I had plasters stuck all over me myself at the time. Then for some reason I tore up two or three letters in which I wrote to you about Lelewel[2] and the impression he made on me. I won't write about that in case the same thing should happen again. I am only writing to thank you for *The Bell* and your kind advice about the novel. I won't thank you for your too flattering opinion about me. It does harm. I was delighted to read Ogaryov's memoirs[3] and was very proud of the fact that without knowing a single Decembrist, I instinctively divined the Christian mysticism peculiar to these people. Yesterday I tore myself away from Brabant lace and am spending tonight in Eisenach, a day in Jena, 2 days in Dresden and then on to Warsaw which interests me more and more. If I get the chance, I'll write to you from Warsaw. Have you read the detailed statutes on the Emancipation? I find it all completely idle chatter. I've received letters from two quarters in Russia which say that the peasants are positively discontented. Previously they had the hope that tomorrow would be fine, but now they know for certain that things will be bad for another two years, and it's clear to them that there will be more delay after that, and that it's 'the masters' who are doing it all. I send my regards to your daughter and to Nikolay Platonych[4] and his wife, and I press your hand in friendship, and hope to see you one way or another.

If you want to send me anything in the near future, send it to Dresden poste restante, otherwise via Klassen.[5]

L. Tolstoy

89. To COUNTESS A. A. TOLSTAYA

Yasnaya Polyana, 14 May 1861

I feel awfully guilty, my dear Alexandrine, for not having replied for so long to your wonderful, wonderful letter. In Moscow I was ill, while here in the country I've been so happy and so busy that I'm only now beginning to come to my senses.

---

[88] 1. The banquet organised by Herzen to mark the occasion of the Emancipation. The English phrase 'Tremendous light, sir', is clearly taken from Herzen's letter.

2. When in Brussels, Tolstoy visited the Polish revolutionary Joachim Lelewel, on the recommendation of Herzen.

3. Ogaryov's *Caucasian Waters* (*a Fragment from my Confession*) was published in *The Polar Star* in 1861.

4. Ogaryov.   5. A bookseller.

89. To Countess A. A. Tolstaya

I've been happy because, after being frightened by the tragedy,[1] I came back home in alarm—I kept thinking that some further sorrow was in store for me—and it turned out to be quite the contrary. Both Auntie and my brother are well, particularly my brother—he's even much better. And everybody loves me—my friends at the school in Tula and my school children—and even my peasants were so good at pretending to be glad, that I was quite prepared to believe them. Not to mention the whole host of memories which assailed me, as always, on my return. I've been busy firstly with business, secondly with the school, which had to be placed on a new and better footing right from the start, and thirdly—I've been nominated an arbiter of the peace[2] and I didn't consider I had the right to refuse. So now after a year's freedom, I'm not sorry to feel some collars round my neck—(1) the estate, (2) the school, (3) journalism, and (4) arbitration—which, whether for good or bad, I intend to wear with patience and perseverance as long as I have life and strength. So I hope I shan't feel the need to put on a fifth collar—that of marriage. In this respect I got through Moscow successfully. The beautiful young K.[3] is too much a hothouse plant, reared for too long on 'pleasure without obligation' for her to—I won't say share—but even sympathise with my labours. She's been accustomed to baking moral sweetmeats, while I have to do with earth and manure. She finds this coarse and alien to her, in the same way as moral sweetmeats have become alien and worthless as far as I'm concerned. And why you want me to become completely independent of you one day, I really don't know. Firstly, my inner secretary appears to have dried up or to have forgotten how to speak through lack of practice, and secondly it's difficult for me to conceive of a pleasant life without the knowledge that there, in nasty Petersburg, in an even nastier palace, there is a creature who surely loves me and whom I love, and so I can walk on more happily, just as it's easier to walk over a cross-beam when you know that there's a hand you can catch hold of. Only I'd like to feel more certain that my outstretched hand is as necessary to you as yours is to me. For this I must get to know you better and better. I'm learning all the time, and all is well and getting better still. And I hope it will continue to be so until we turn into nitrogen and oxygen as the clever people say. Goodbye, I kiss your hand and Lizaveta Andreyevna's.

Auntie was delighted to hear from me of your mother's promise to come and see us. On behalf of us all, beg her not to make us sad by passing us by. Do you know anything about my journal, and mightn't it be possible to ask Countess Bludova to speed things up?[4] Press Boris Alexeyevich's[5] hand for me. I can't visualise you without seeing his marvellous face as well. Don't forget his photo. How's your

---

[89] 1. The death of his brother Nikolay.

2. One of the Arbiters of the Peace, who were concerned with the allotment of land between the gentry and the peasantry after the Emancipation.

3. Yekaterina Fyodorovna Tyutcheva, the daughter of the poet.

4. Tolstoy was unaware that permission had already been granted for publication of his journal *Yasnaya Polyana*. Countess Bludova was acquainted with the Minister of Public Education.

5. Boris Alexeyevich Perovsky (1815–81) was also in attendance at court, and was a close friend of A. A. Tolstaya. He was the youngest of Count Razumovsky's illegitimate sons.

89. To Countess A. A. Tolstaya

establishment?⁶ My school is going marvellously, and if you're interested I'll write to you in greater detail in my next letter. And most important—what about our trip to Lubyanka?⁷ At present, the later on in summer the better as far as I'm concerned.

This letter was already written when I received your two from Moscow. It's sad that I didn't wait for you in Moscow, but clearly we'll have to wait till Lubyanka. The photos are both charming and I couldn't admire them enough yesterday.

Goodbye.

90. To I. S. TURGENEV

Novoselki, 27 May 1861

I hope that your conscience has already told you how wrongly you behaved towards me, especially in front of Fet and his wife.¹ Therefore write me a letter which I can send to the Fets. If you find my demand unjust, let me know. I shall wait at Bogoslov.²

L. Tolstoy

91. To A. A. FET

Bogoslov, 28 May 1861

I couldn't resist opening another letter from Mr Turgenev in reply to mine. I wish you well in your dealings with this man, but I despise him, as I wrote to him, thereby breaking off all relations with him except for satisfaction, if he should desire it. In spite of all my apparent calm I was uneasy at heart, and I felt I needed to demand a more positive apology from Mr Turgenev, which I did in a letter from Novoselki. Here is his reply¹ which I was satisfied with, and I merely replied myself that my reasons for forgiving him were not our contradictory natures, but ones which he could well understand himself. Owing to a delay² I sent him a second,

---

6. Tolstoy is probably referring to a charitable home for prostitutes, of which A. A. Tolstaya was a guardian. 7. A. A. Tolstaya's estate.

[90] 1. On 25 May Tolstoy arrived at Turgenev's house at Spasskoye. The same day Turgenev gave Tolstoy the manuscript of his new novel, *Fathers and Sons*, to read. He was angry when Tolstoy, bored by the novel, promptly fell asleep. On 26 May both writers went to visit Fet, at whose house their famous quarrel took place. The cause of the quarrel was a trivial disagreement over the nature of the education of Turgenev's natural daughter. Turgenev was stung by Tolstoy's caustic remarks, and apparently threatened to punch him in the face. Both writers left Fet's house in a rage.

2. After leaving Fet, Tolstoy went to the estate of I. P. Borisov at Novoselki, from where he wrote this letter to Turgenev. Bogoslov was a posting station not far from Spasskoye.

[91] 1. Tolstoy wrote this letter to Fet on the back of Turgenev's reply to his first letter. In his letter Turgenev expressed his regret at the incident and accepted responsibility for it, while assuming that relations with Tolstoy would now be at an end.

2. Turgenev's reply to Tolstoy's first letter was sent by mistake to Novoselki instead of Bogoslov. Before it eventually reached him, Tolstoy sent a second letter to Turgenev, challenging him to a duel. All Fet's attempts to reconcile the two men were unsuccessful.

rather harsh letter as well, containing a challenge, to which I haven't yet received a reply, but if I do I shall send it back unopened. So that's the end of this sad story which, if it should ever go any further than your doorstep, should do so with this addendum.

92. To COUNTESS A. A. TOLSTAYA

Yasnaya Polyana, beginning of August 1861

The she-ass of Balaam and the hay-cock have begun to talk.[1] No, you mustn't be cross with me—never be cross. Don't you think it makes some difference that every time I get a line from you I scribble down volumes of replies in my heart? You ought to know that. Besides, why do you need any letters from me? You have Maltseva, you have Perovsky, you have Vyazemskaya—you've got everything. Why do you need my drop in your ocean? As for me, that's quite another matter. I come back from the police station after explaining to the peasants that so far from not drawing each other's blood fighting, they simply mustn't fight at all, or that the landowners aren't supposed to marry off their serf-girls against their will any longer, etc.—and then I get your letter. Not that I should complain. I also have a charming and poetic occupation which I can't tear myself away from, and that's the school. When I break away from my office and the peasants who pursue me from every wing of the house, I go to the school; but as it's undergoing alterations the classes are held alongside, in the garden under the apple trees, and it's so overgrown that you can only get there by stooping down. The teacher sits there with the school children all round him, nibbling blades of grass and making the lime and maple leaves crackle. The teacher teaches according to my advice, but even so, not too well, and the children feel it. They are fonder of me. And we begin to chat for 3 or 4 hours, and nobody is bored. It's impossible to describe these children—they have to be seen. I've never seen the like among children of our own dear class. Just imagine that in two years, in the complete absence of discipline, not a single boy or girl has been punished. There's never any laziness, coarseness, stupid jokes or unseemly language. The school-house is now almost completed. The school occupies three large rooms—one pink, and two blue. One room moreover is a museum. On the shelves round the wall, stones, butterflies, skeletons, grasses, flowers, physics instruments, etc. are laid out. On Sundays the museum is open to everyone, and a German from Jena[2] (who's turned out to be an excellent young fellow) does experiments. Once a week there's a botany class, and we all go off to the woods to look for flowers, grasses and mushrooms. 4 singing classes a week, and 6 of drawing (the German again), and it's all going very well. The surveying is going so well that the peasants are already engaging the boys. Excluding myself

[92] 1. In June 1861 A. A. Tolstaya had written to Tolstoy complaining that 'corresponding with you is just like playing ball and throwing it into a haycock', i.e. her letters receive no reply.
2. Gustav Keller; Tolstoy had met him in Weimar, and invited him to Yasnaya Polyana.

92. To Countess A. A. Tolstaya

there are three teachers in all. In addition the priest comes twice a week. And you still think I'm a godless fellow! Moreover I teach the priest how to teach. This is how we teach: on St Peter's day we tell the story of Peter and Paul and explain the service. Then Feofan from the village dies—and we tell them all about the last unction etc. And in this way, without any obvious connection, we work through all the sacraments, the liturgy and the Old and New Testament festivals. The classes are supposed to be from 8 to 12 and from 3 to 6, but they always go on till 2 o'clock because it's impossible to get the children to leave the school—they ask for more. In the evening it often happens that more than half of them stay and spend the night in the garden, in a hut. At lunch and supper and after supper we—the teachers—confer together. On Saturdays we read our notes to each other and prepare for the following week.

I'm thinking of starting the journal in September. My work as an Arbiter of the Peace is interesting and fascinating, but the bad thing is that all the gentry have come to hate me heart and soul and are sticking des batons dans les roues from every side.

Goodbye, dear friend—do go on writing to me, though I'll always be unpunctual.

L. Tolstoy

93. To I. S. TURGENEV

Yasnaya Polyana, 8 October 1861

Dear Sir,

In your letter you call my conduct *dishonourable*, and furthermore you said to me personally that you would *punch me in the face*, but I ask your pardon, acknowledge myself to blame and decline the challenge.[1]

Count L. Tolstoy

94. To B. N. CHICHERIN

Yasnaya Polyana, 28 October 1861

The matter on which I'm asking your help is of the utmost importance to me. I want to impress this upon you before explaining the matter itself, so that if you're disposed to do anything for me and for the common good, you might do everything in your power to fulfil my request.

In the district where I'm an arbiter, the schools statute proposed by me was very quickly approved.[1] The statute is based on a lease I take out on the schools, and a

[93] 1. On 23 September Tolstoy had written a conciliatory letter to Turgenev, which he addressed to him via Davydov, the bookseller in Petersburg. During the long delay before this letter reached him, Turgenev himself wrote to Tolstoy bitterly condemning him as the instigator of rumours about him circulating in Moscow, and challenging him to a duel. The present letter is Tolstoy's reply.

[94] 1. There is no record of this statute surviving. However, there is extant an application

94. To B. N. Chicherin

payment of 50 copecks per pupil per month, regardless of canton, class and rural district. Three schools are already open because I have 3 educated and honest people, two of whom I brought from Moscow. Another 10 schools are due to be opened. 3 are ready now, and I have nobody to appoint to them. The teachers' position is as follows: I am responsible for a *minimum* salary of 150 roubles, but if the teacher wishes to take on the upkeep of the school the conditions are more favourable—it depends on him. Particularly since success depends on him, his very success and popularity can mean a decent remuneration, since in each district where there are up to 30 pupils, there could be 50 and more, which would amount to 25 roubles a month. Besides, there may be other favourable conditions as well. Yesterday I fixed up a teacher who will live all found and get 100 roubles as a *resident tutor* and 220 from the school. Moreover, all the teachers congregate on Sundays at Yasnaya Polyana for discussions about the common cause—the schools and the journal. Needless to say almost all my journals and my library are at their disposal. But the main thing—if you have skimmed through my programme—is that the work of any decent teacher is sure to provide material for articles in our journal *Yasnaya Polyana*. And articles earn a minimum of 50 roubles a printer's sheet. For goodness sake do all you can to help, talk to people yourself if you know any, and tell the Rachinskys and Dmitriyev[2] who have already made promises to me. You won't find perfection and I'm not too demanding. A semi-educated, second or third year student who isn't a scoundrel is all I want. I know there will only be 2 capable people out of 10, but you have to start with 10. If there aren't any students, I'll just have to risk taking seminarists, but then the risk will be 10 times as great. If you find any, send them to me. The fare costs 10 roubles. I'll pay for it. Give them the money, or if you haven't any, write to me and I'll send some. Please, my dear soul, say you're willing to do this and I'm sure you'll succeed.

About Turgenev [...][3] I've done all I can to pacify him. But to fight with anyone, especially him, in a year's time, when he's 2,000 versts away,[4] is just about as impossible for me as dancing in Tverskaya Street dressed up as a savage. Goodbye; I embrace you and look forward to your reply. What news of the student riots[5] and the Mikhaylov affair?[6] Tell me the latest facts, if only briefly. I don't know anything, and I don't trust Tula gossip.

L. Tolstoy

[Postscript omitted]

addressed by Tolstoy to the Tula Provincial Bureau of Peasant Affairs, on 12 November 1861, to which Tolstoy appended *A Statute on Village Schools* drawn up by himself and suggesting conditions of admission and curricula for these schools.

2. S. A. and K. A. Rachinsky were both lecturers at the University of Moscow; Varvara Rachinskaya had recently opened a school for peasant children. F. M. Dmitriyev was a professor of History at the University of Moscow.

3. Some words here are indecipherable.

4. Turgenev was in France at this time.

5. Student agitation had been provoked by the unpopular measures of E. V. Putyatin, the new Minister of Public Education.

6. On 14 September 1861 the poet M. I. Mikhaylov (1829–65) was arrested for writing and distributing the proclamation *To the Young Generation*.

95. To B. N. CHICHERIN

Yasnaya Polyana, 16/20(?) November 1861

I'm very grateful to you, dear friend, for the students. They haven't arrived yet, but I'm sure that 2 of the 3 recommended by you will be good. I'm sending you the 30 roubles which you gave them. About your first lecture[1]—I would say it's an excellent one; but as for your articles against Kostomarov[2] I would say frankly that not only do I not agree with them, but that I don't like them either. There is a conservatism at all costs about them, obviously provoked by Kostomarov's extreme views. You who live in the midst of action need to guard against the strong temptation to boast about your own independence. I can't express the reasons for my disagreement with you in a letter, but you'll find them in the first number of *Yasnaya Polyana*.[3] To put it briefly, you can't in my opinion reorganise a university or leave it as it is without reference to the whole educational hierarchy (not the external, administrative hierarchy, but the one that has grown up naturally among the people), and above all, the lowest rung and therefore the cornerstone of this hierarchy—the state school.[4] And so the question for me is simply: does the university answer the needs of this lowest rung or not? I say no. To the other question whether the state school now indicates what universities should be like, I also say no. And therefore whether you change them or leave them as they are has absolutely no interest or importance for me or for the people. However, we'll have time to argue about this again if my article seems to deserve it. Object as strongly as you like, and I'll gladly publish your objections in *Yasnaya Polyana*. Goodbye; I press your hand and send my regards to all our mutual friends. If any more students turn up, send them to me; I need another three.

Count L. Tolstoy

96. To A. A. FET

Moscow, December 1861

Turgenev is a *scoundrel who needs thrashing*; please pass that on to him as diligently as you pass on to me his precious utterances,[1] in spite of my repeated requests not to mention him.

Count L. Tolstoy

And please don't write to me any more, since I shan't open your letters any more than Turgenev's.

[95] 1. Chicherin's inaugural lecture on public law was published in *The Moscow Gazette*, 1861.
2. In his articles, Chicherin attacked Professor Kostomarov of the University of Petersburg, and his views that radical reform was needed in the universities, and that they should be transformed into open educational establishments for all-comers, including women.
3. In *Yasnaya Polyana*, 1862, No. 1, Tolstoy published his article *On Public Education*.
4. Tolstoy uses the expression *narodnaya shkola* here, the adjective meaning 'of the people'; I have translated this as 'state school' because of the ambiguity of 'public school' in English. The word 'public' has been retained for 'public education'.

[96] 1. Fet had sent Tolstoy an extract from a letter he had received from Turgenev. Tolstoy

97. To V. P. BOTKIN

Moscow, 26 January 1862

You write on a scrap of paper, and so do I, but you do so with bitterness apparently, while I do so with my customary sympathy. It's true, it looks as if I'm doing you out of 600 francs, but I'm in no wise to blame. I got your letter at a time when I thought for certain I would die. I was like that the whole of the last terrible and painful summer. I did nothing and wrote to no one, and for that reason I replied to your letter merely by a letter to my sister and the Marseilles banker whose address I've now forgotten. I thought you had received your money, but it turns out that the banker stole it. I'll send you the wretched 600 francs this week.

I'm now publishing the first issue of my journal, and am having terrible trouble. It's impossible to describe in writing how much I love and *know* my job, and I wouldn't be able to tell you either. I hope that they kick up a terrible fuss about me in the press, and I hope that as a result of it I shan't cease to think and feel just the same. Life here is in full swing. In Petersburg, Moscow and Tula there are elections, like your parliamentary ones,[1] but from my point of view, I must admit, its all of very little interest. Until there is greater equality of education there won't be a better system of government. I look out of my den and think—well now, who'll win? And really it's completely immaterial who wins. I became an Arbiter of the Peace quite unexpectedly, and despite the fact that I did my job in the coolest and most conscientious manner, I earned the dire wrath of the gentry. They want to thrash me and to bring me to trial, but they won't succeed in doing either.[2] I'm only waiting for them to calm down and then I'll resign. I've done what is most important for me. In my district of 9,000 people, 21 schools have sprung up this autumn—sprung up quite freely—and are holding their own despite all vicissitudes. Goodbye; I press your hand and beg you not to be angry with me. I'm not sending the money to you just now because I haven't any, but, as I said, I'll send it this week. Please write and tell me the address of this Marseilles banker, and what excuses he's offered.

Tell me about yourself in general; I know about your health from Fet who, having ceased to be a poet, has not ceased to be a most excellent man and enormously clever. You come to Moscow and think you're behind the times—Katkov, Longinov or Chicherin will tell you all that's new; but they only know the news, and are just as stupid as a year or two ago; many people are growing stupid, but Fet sits there and ploughs and goes on living and uses such strong language—it's delightful!

I can't speak about our mutual friends; I'm so out of touch with everything from sticking closely to my job that nothing else even enters my head. My teeth are

---

was incensed by Turgenev's interpretation of his last letter to him, and their relations were finally broken off. Tolstoy's anger with Fet, however, was short-lived.

[97] 1. Elections to the assemblies of the gentry.
2. Tolstoy had antagonised the landowners by defending the interests of the peasantry.

97. To V. P. Botkin

falling out and I still haven't got married, and I suppose I'll simply remain single.[3] I'm no longer afraid of being single. What are you doing and when shall we see you in Russia?—for you won't see me abroad.

98. To N. G. CHERNYSHEVSKY

Nikolay Gavrilovich Chernyshevsky (1829–89), an influential member of the new plebeian, radical intelligentsia of the early years of Alexander II's reign, and a puritanical and uncompromising advocate of utilitarianism. His anti-aesthetic stance made him unpopular with Turgenev (who called him a snake) and with Tolstoy, who was even ruder. In 1854 he began to work for *The Contemporary*, and in the following year he published his doctoral dissertation *The Aesthetic Relationship of Art to Reality*. As a journalist and critic he wrote numerous studies of Russian authors including Tolstoy, Turgenev and Gogol, and a tendentious and influential novel *What is to be done?* (1863), which Dostoyevsky parodied in *Notes from Underground*. He also wrote extensively on social and economic problems. In 1862 he was arrested for printing revolutionary proclamations, and imprisoned for two years in the Peter and Paul Fortress. After his release he was exiled to Siberia where he spent almost twenty years.

In the course of 1856 Tolstoy frequently met Chernyshevsky in Petersburg and often referred to him and his views in his diaries and letters, but the following letter is all that survives of their very slight correspondence.

Moscow, 6 February 1862

Dear Nikolay Gavrilovich

The first number of my journal came out yesterday. I earnestly beg you to read it through carefully and to express your opinion about it frankly and seriously in *The Contemporary*.[1] I had the misfortune to write stories, and the public will say without reading it: 'Yes, *Childhood* is very nice, but a journal...?'

But the journal and the whole cause mean everything to me.

Please reply to Tula.

L. Tolstoy

99. To V. P. BOTKIN

Moscow, 7 February 1862

I'm sending you a note from your brother in which he promised to send you some

---

3. Tolstoy here uses the word *bobyl*, meaning a 'landless peasant', rather than *kholostyak*, the usual word for a bachelor.

[98] 1. Chernyshevsky reviewed *Yasnaya Polyana*, in *The Contemporary*, 1862, No. 3. He viewed Tolstoy's practical methods of instruction favourably, but was critical of some of his educational theories.

101. To M. N. Katkov

money. Please help me to find the 600 francs. If you write, address your letter to Tula. I received news today of one of the most important events in my opinion of recent times, although it is likely to remain unnoticed. The gentry of Tver have resolved: to renounce their rights; not to hold any more elections—just like that!—and not to serve as mediators in the elections for the assemblies of the gentry and for the Government.[1] Bravo!

Here in Moscow I paid my customary due to my passion for gambling and lost so much that I found myself embarrassed, as a consequence of which I borrowed 1,000 roubles from Katkov to punish myself and to put things right, and promised to let him have my novel—the Caucasian one[2]—this year. On thinking it over properly, I'm very glad about it, for otherwise this novel which is much more than half written would lie about indefinitely and be used for pasting over the windows. You can tell me in April if that would have been better. Goodbye; I press your hand and wish you the very best.

L. Tolstoy

100. To COUNTESS A. A. TOLSTAYA

Yasnaya Polyana, 22 February 1862

Thank you for your letter—I haven't time to write, but please do one thing: get hold of *Notes from the House of the Dead*[1] and read it. *It's essential.*

I kiss your hand—goodbye.

L. Tolstoy

101. To M. N. KATKOV

Mikhail Nikiforovich Katkov (1818–87), the son of a provincial official, was a student at the University of Moscow where he studied philosophy and was associated with the liberal, westernising circle of students, especially Belinsky and Stankevich. After graduating, he lived for awhile abroad, but returned to Russia to become professor of philosophy at his old University in 1845. When philosophy was abolished from the curriculum five years later in a revision of educational policy ('philosophy provokes students to think dangerous thoughts' was the official view), Katkov turned to journalism where he soon achieved a wide reputation, first as a liberal publicist of English constitutional persuasion, then, after the

[99] 1. In December 1861 a group of thirty liberal landowners in the province of Tver, attending a congress of Arbiters of the Peace, protested against the inadequacies of the Emancipation charter; they claimed it did not satisfy the needs of the people either in terms of material well-being or in terms of civil liberty. Thirteen of the protestors were sentenced to two years' imprisonment.
2. *The Cossacks*. It was published in *The Russian Herald*, 1863, No. 1.

[100] 1. Tolstoy retained his admiration for this work of Dostoyevsky's throughout his life, and included it in *What is Art?* as an example of the highest form of art.

101. To M. N. Katkov

1863 Polish uprising, as an increasingly conservative chauvinistic and imperialistic journalist. His name is most frequently connected with *The Russian Herald*, a journal which he owned after 1856.

From 1859 to 1877 Tolstoy published several of his major works in *The Russian Herald*, including *The Cossacks, 1805* (i.e. *War and Peace*), and *Anna Karenina*. The latter work gave rise to difficulties between Katkov and Tolstoy, however, when Katkov refused to publish the last part of it which seemed to him to ridicule Russian popular sentiment towards fellow Slavs in the continuing series of Balkan wars, particularly the Serbo-Turkish War for which Vronsky enlists after Anna's death. Tolstoy never published in *The Russian Herald* again.

Yasnaya Polyana, 11 April 1862

Dear Mikhail Nikiforovich,

I only started work a few days ago on the novel I agreed to sell to you, and wasn't able to begin earlier.[1] Please write and tell me when you wish to have it. The most convenient time for me is November, but I can produce it much earlier. If that isn't convenient, tell me frankly and I'll return the money to you (I'm now able to do so) and I'll let *The Russian Herald* have the novel just the same. If you've completely changed your mind, I would be glad to give it up completely. Please write to me in detail, and *absolutely frankly*. The main thing is that I want you to be satisfied.[2] My journal is not going at all well, and so far there hasn't been a single word about it in the press.[3] No cookery book is received with such silence. I suppose problems of centralisation and decentralisation and the national spirit in science and Bezrylov's feuilletons are what matter.[4] I have material ready in advance for the 3rd number, especially for the supplement section,[5] and I'm more dedicated to this work than ever before. I look forward to your reply.

Yours,
L. Tolstoy

102. To P. A. PLETNYOV

Pyotr Alexandrovich Pletnyov (1792–1862), Professor of Russian Literature and Rector of the University of Petersburg. He was a close friend of Pushkin, and took over the publication of Pushkin's journal *The Contemporary* after his death. In 1847 he sold the publishing rights of the journal to Nekrasov and Panayev. Pushkin dedicated *Yevgeny Onegin* to him. Tolstoy first met Pletnyov in 1857 in Paris.

[101] 1. *The Cossacks*. Katkov had already bought the rights to the novel from Tolstoy.
2. Katkov agreed to wait for the novel.
3. In fact Chernyshevsky had already reviewed the journal and in the course of 1862 other reviews appeared.
4. These were the themes preoccupying many of the journals at the time. Bezrylov was the pseudonym of A. F. Pisemsky (see Letter 165); his 'feuilletons' in *Reader's Library* were directed against the democratic movement of the 1860s.
5. This section of Tolstoy's journal was devoted exclusively to materials for children's reading.

103. To Countess A. A. Tolstaya

Yasnaya Polyana, 1 May 1862

For goodness sake forgive me, dear Pyotr Alexandrovich, for not having replied sooner. I am all the more to blame because I seldom get such pleasant letters as yours. The sympathy you expressed is very dear to me, and you praised *Robinson*[1] in a way which was most flattering to me.

Turgenev's novel[2] interested me very much, but I liked it much less than I expected. My main reproach is that it is cold...cold—something which doesn't suit Turgenev's talent. Everything is clever, everything is refined, everything is artistic—I agree with you—and much of it is edifying and just, but there isn't a single page which is written with a stroke of the pen and with a palpitating heart, and therefore there isn't a single page which grips the soul. I very much regret that I don't agree with you and F. I. Tyutchev, but I don't. Incidentally, to avoid misunderstanding, I consider it necessary to tell you that all personal relations between myself and Mr Turgenev have been broken off...[5 lines omitted]

103. To COUNTESS A. A. TOLSTAYA

Moscow, 22–3(?) July 1862

I received your letter, dear friend, just before my departure from Samara,[1] and decided to answer it from Moscow. Thank you for your love; I'm not quite as ill as all that—in fact I'm not ill at all. But poor Kutler! I saw him, and had the impression that he was dead already. However, they say he's better. What are these misgivings you had on my account? I was quite intrigued all the while, and it's only now that I've heard the news from Yasnaya Polyana that I understand everything. What nice friends you have! For all these Potapovs, Dolgorukys, Arakcheyevs[2] and ravelins[3]—they're all your friends. They write to me from Yasnaya: on 7 July, 3 troikas full of gendarmes arrived; nobody was allowed to go out, not even Auntie, I suppose, and a search was begun.[4] What they were looking for I still don't know. A friend of yours, a slovenly colonel, read all my letters and diaries which I had intended to entrust just before I die to whoever is my closest friend at the time; he read two batches of correspondence that I would have given

---

[102] 1. An adaptation of Defoe's *Robinson Crusoe*, by a teacher at the school at Yasnaya Polyana, was published in Tolstoy's journal in February 1862.

2. Turgenev's *Fathers and Sons* was published in *The Russian Herald*, 1862, No. 2.

[103] 1. Tolstoy set off for Samara, via Moscow, on 14 May 1862. He felt in need of a respite from his work, and was worried by symptoms of consumption that he thought he detected in himself. Doctor Behrs had recommended him to take a kumys cure (fermented mare's milk) in Samara.

2. Potapov and Prince Dolgorukov were both at different times in charge of the Third Department, the Tsarist 'secret police'. Count Arakcheyev had been Alexander I's most influential adviser on internal affairs, and had the reputation of being a brutal martinet.

3. The ravelin of the Peter and Paul Fortress in Petersburg, where the most dangerous political prisoners were incarcerated.

4. The search lasted two days—6 and 7 July—and it followed a report on Tolstoy and his activities in connection with his school and the students who assisted him, submitted by an agent of the Third Department.

103. To Countess A. A. Tolstaya

anything in the world to keep secret—and then went away after declaring that he had found nothing *suspicious*. It was fortunate for me and for that friend of yours that I wasn't there—I'd have killed him! Charming! Marvellous! That's how the government makes its friends. If you remember me and my political views, you'll know that I've always—particularly since my love for the school—been completely indifferent to the government and even more indifferent to the present-day liberals, whom I heartily despise. I can't say that now. I feel malice and disgust, almost hatred, for that dear government which searches my house for lithographic and typographical machines for printing Herzen's proclamations which I despise, and which I haven't the patience to get through because of boredom. It's a fact—I once had all these charming proclamations and *The Bell* as well in my possession for a week, and I simply returned them without reading them. I find it boring, I know it all, and I quite genuinely despise it with all my heart.[5]

And suddenly they subject me and my students to a search, just as they might search you to try and find a murdered child. True, it's not quite as offensive. But if they know of my existence and are concerned about it, they could have enquired in a better way. What charming friends you have! I haven't seen Auntie yet, but I can just imagine her. I once wrote to you that one shouldn't look for a peaceful refuge in life, but that one should toil, work and suffer. That may be so, but I only wish it were possible to go off somewhere away from these brigands with their cheeks and hands washed with scented soap, and their affable smiles. And indeed, if I've a long life ahead of me still, I'll go off into a monastery, only not to pray to God—that's unnecessary in my view—but so as not to see all the abomination of worldly depravity—pompous, self-satisfied, and wearing epaulettes and crinolines. Foo! How can you, who are such an excellent person, live in Petersburg? That I shall never understand; or perhaps you've already got cataracts on your eyes, and can see nothing.

L. Tolstoy

104. To S. A. RACHINSKY

Sergey Alexandrovich Rachinsky (1833–1902), a botanist and Professor of Plant Physiology at the University of Moscow. He studied in Germany, where he met Lassalle and Liszt, and translated Aksakov's *Family Chronicle* into German. As one of the editors of *The Russian Herald* he published numerous popular articles on botany, music and educational theory. On his premature retirement from the university he devoted himself to school activities and to writing on educational matters.

Yasnaya Polyana, 7 August 1862

Your letter, my dear Sergey Alexandrovich, is one of those which I consider a

---

5. During the search a maid succeeded in concealing Herzen's books, and Marya Tolstaya hid some letters of Herzen that were in Tolstoy's possession.

104. To S. A. Rachinsky

reward for my thankless activity (thankless in terms of public sympathy).[1] I don't count on such rewards, and it's all the more pleasant to receive them. You have read and understood and to some extent agreed with what I wrote, but the *majority* say: 'Which Tolstoy is this? Alexey?[2] The Chief Procurator?[3] Oh yes, *Childhood*. He writes nicely', and leave it at that. I'll send my supplements to Stoy[4] in a few days time. I don't know him personally, but I know his institution, and it is the most interesting of all the German schools and, most important, the only one which is almost alive. The rest are dead, you know, quite dead.

I wish you or your sister would write about the life and progress of your school for *Yasnaya Polyana*.[5] The distinctive colouring of a school run by a woman is very interesting, particularly in your family. The teachers in my schools are all students. All the ex-seminarists (of whom I had six) gave up before the end of a year, took to drink, or started playing the dandy. The main condition necessary in my opinion for a village teacher is respect for the environment from which his pupils come; another condition is an awareness of the full importance of the responsibility which a tutor bears. You won't find either condition existing outside our educational system (in universities etc.). However many failings there may be in our system, this fact redeems them; but if it isn't there, it's best to have a teacher who is a peasant or a sacristan etc., a person who is so identified in his outlook on life, his beliefs and his habits with the children he is dealing with, that despite himself he doesn't educate them, but simply teaches. Either the teacher is completely free and respects the freedom of others, or he is a machine by means of which people learn what they have to. I have 11 students and all are excellent teachers. Of course our conferences and the journal make their contribution, but although I've known many students, these are really such splendid young people that whoever else you might accuse of student disorders, you could never accuse *them*. Of course everything depends on direction. To give a definite direction and to suggest a more serious outlook is the purpose of my journal. Recently we had with us some village school teachers—students not from our own circle—and these gentlemen tried to persuade us that the Bible was a hotch-potch of absurdities which shouldn't be passed on to pupils, and that the purpose of school was to destroy superstitions. I wasn't there myself, but all our people argued against them. You say—not students. But I advise you to take students, as long as they have a leader. Students in my view don't have, and cannot have directions; they are only people capable of receiving directions. I can't recommend one to you—I could myself take on and place another 10 I'm looking for. But I advise you to take on a student, and you'll see how all this quasi-liberal nonsense will melt away like wax before a flame from contact with the people.

[104] 1. Rachinsky had written to express his agreement with Tolstoy's views on education.
2. Count A. K. Tolstoy, a writer, and second cousin to Tolstoy.
3. Count A. P. Tolstoy, first cousin once removed to Tolstoy. He was Chief Procurator of the Holy Synod from 1856 to 1862.
4. Karl Stoy, a professor at the University of Jena, who founded several educational establishments in Germany. He had asked to have *Yasnaya Polyana* sent to him.
5. Rachinsky's sister, Varvara, had founded a school for peasant children.

104. To S. A. Rachinsky

I send my cordial regards to all your family and press your hand.

L. Tolstoy

I think I've got your patronymic wrong—please excuse me and correct it.[6] How are you?

105. To COUNTESS A. A. TOLSTAYA

Yasnaya Polyana, 7 August 1862

I wrote to you from Moscow; then I only knew about it all from a letter; but now the longer I'm at Yasnaya the more and more painful the outrage becomes, and the more unbearable my whole ruined life. I'm writing this letter after careful consideration, trying to forget nothing and to add nothing, so that you can show it to the various brigands, the Potapovs and Dolgorukys, who deliberately sow hatred of the government and discredit the Emperor in the eyes of his subjects. I *cannot* and will not let this matter pass. All my activities in which I found happiness and solace have been ruined. Auntie is so ill that she can't get up. The peasants no longer look on me as an honest man—an opinion I've earned over the years—but as a criminal, an incendiary or a forger, who's only got away with it by trickery. 'Well, my friend! You've come a cropper! Don't you go talking to us about honesty and justice; you've hardly escaped the handcuffs yourself.' As for the landlords, it goes without saying they gave a cry of rapture. Please write to me as soon as possible, after consulting Perovsky or A. Tolstoy or anyone you like, about how I can write a letter and get it to the Emperor. There's no other way out for me except to receive satisfaction as public as was the insult (it's impossible to undo what has been done), or to expatriate myself, and this I've firmly resolved to do. I won't go to Herzen. Herzen has his way and I have mine. Nor shall I hide. I shall loudly proclaim that I'm selling my estate in order to leave Russia, where it's impossible to know a minute in advance that they won't chain you up or flog you together with your sister and your wife and your mother—I'm going away.

Well, that's how it is, and it's laughable and loathsome and evil. You know what the school has meant to me ever since I opened it: it has been my whole life, it has been my monastery, my church, in which I sought and found refuge from all the anxieties, doubts and temptations of life. I tore myself away from it for the sake of a sick brother and returned home even more tired and anxious for work and love, to receive unexpectedly the appointment as an arbiter of the peace. I had my journal, I had my school, but my conscience wouldn't let me refuse just because of the terrible, uncouth and cruel gentry who had promised to devour me if I became an arbiter. The howls against my arbitration reached even you; but I twice went to court and both times the court declared that I was not only in the right, but that there was no case to bring; but I know, before my own conscience, not their court,

---

6. Tolstoy had at first written 'Sergey Alexeyevich', but he himself corrected it to 'Alexandrovich'.

105. To Countess A. A. Tolstaya

that I've relaxed the law, relaxed it too much, for the benefit of the gentry, particularly recently. That same year schools were opened in my district. I took on some students, and, despite all my other occupations, spent a lot of time with them. All 12 of them with one exception proved to be excellent people; I was so happy that they all agreed with me, and succumbed not so much to my influence, as to the influence of the environment and the work. Everyone arrived with manuscripts of Herzen in his trunk and revolutionary ideas in his head, and *everyone* without exception burned his manuscripts within a week, discarded revolutionary ideas, and taught the peasant children Bible history and prayers, and handed round the Gospels for reading at home. These are facts—and 11 men without exception did this, and not by compulsion but by conviction. I'll stake my life that in the year 1862 you couldn't find 12 such students in all Russia.

All this went on for a year—the arbitration, the schools, the journal, the students and their schools, in addition to all my domestic and family affairs. And it all went not just well, but splendidly. I was often amazed at myself and at my happiness, and thanked God that I'd found a quiet, inconspicuous pursuit that entirely engrossed me. Towards spring I grew weak and the doctor ordered me to go on a *kumys* cure. I resigned my post, my only wish being to conserve my strength for the continuation of my work with the schools and their reflection—the journal. Throughout my absence the students behaved themselves just as well as when I was there; they closed the schools for the working season and lived at Yasnaya with Auntie. My sister arrived from abroad to see us, and moved into my study. I was expected any day. On 6 July, 3 troikas came galloping up to the house at Yasnaya, with bells ringing and full of armed gendarmes. My overlords and judges, on whom my fate and the fates of a 75-year-old auntie, a sister and ten young people depended, consisted of a certain Colonel Durnovo of the gendarmerie, the Krapiva district police officer, and the regional and local police inspector, Kobelyatsky, who'd been dismissed from some post for being punched in the face, and now occupies the office of governor's Mercury in Tula. This same gentleman read all the letters which only I have read and the woman who wrote them,[1] and my diary which no one has read. They drove up and immediately arrested all the students. Auntie ran out to meet me—she thought it was me arriving—and it was then that she caught the illness from which she's suffering even now. They subjected the students to a complete search and found nothing. If there could possibly have been anything amusing about it, it was that the students concealed in the nettles innocent papers which they thought might be dangerous, and burned them right in front of the gendarmes. Everything seems dangerous when you're being punished without a trial and without the possibility of vindication. So even if there had been anything dangerous or harmful, it could all have been hidden and destroyed. So, in our view, the whole operation had no other purpose but to insult us, and to demonstrate that Damocles' sword of tyranny, violence and injustice is always hanging over everyone. The local police inspector and the gendarme didn't fail to let everyone in the house feel this: they lectured them, threatened arrest and demanded food for

[105] 1. V. V. Arsenyeva.

105. To Countess A. A. Tolstaya

themselves and fodder for their horses without payment. The armed gendarmes walked about, shouted and cursed under my sister's windows, as though they were in occupied territory. They wouldn't allow the students to move from one house to another to drink tea or have a meal. They went into the cellars, the w.c., the photographic room, the store-rooms, the school and the physics laboratory, demanded all the keys, wanted to break in, and produced no document entitling them to do all this. But that's not all: they went into my study, which was my sister's bedroom at the time, and rummaged through everything; the local police inspector read everything I was writing and had written since the age of 16. I don't know how interesting he found it all, but he gave my sister *permission* to move out into the sitting room and gave her *permission* to go to bed in the evening, and then only after a request had been made. Here again there occurred the same stupid and outrageous scenes. They read and set aside suspicious letters and papers, while my sister and auntie, frightened out of their wits, tried to conceal the most innocent of papers. The local police inspector thought *old* Prince Dundukov-Korsakov's letter suspicious, and my secretary pulled it out from the forage cap where it had been put. Of course they found nothing in it either. I'm sure they thought the most suspicious thing of all was the fact that they found nothing prohibited. I'm absolutely sure that no Petersburg palace would have turned out to be 1/100 part as innocent, if searched, as Yasnaya Polyana did. That's not all: they went to Chernskaya, another of my villages, and read my late brother's papers—papers which I hold as something sacred—and then they went away after *completely* reassuring us that they'd found nothing suspicious, and after lecturing everyone and demanding food for themselves.

I frequently tell myself how extraordinarily lucky it was that I wasn't there. If I had been, I should probably be on trial for murder by now.

Now just imagine the rumours that have begun to circulate among the peasants and the gentry in the district and the province as a result of all this. Since that day Auntie has been ailing more and more. When I arrived she burst into tears and collapsed: she can hardly stand even now. The rumours that I was in prison or had fled the country were so insistent that even those who knew me, and knew that I despised all secret activities, plots, flights etc., began to believe them.

Now they've left, and we're allowed to move from house to house; however, they've taken away the students' permits and won't give them back; but our lives, especially mine and Auntie's, have been completely ruined. There'll be no school, the people are laughing up their sleeves, the gentry are gloating, while we think willy-nilly, at the sound of every bell, that they've come to take us away. I have loaded pistols in my room, and I'm waiting for the minute when all this will be decided one way or another. Mr gendarme tried to reassure us that if anything had been concealed we should know that he would appear again, perhaps tomorrow, as our judge and master, together with the local police inspector. One thing: if this is done without the knowledge of the Emperor, then it's necessary to campaign and fight to the last against such a state of affairs. We can't live like this. But if all this has to be so, and it seems to the Emperor to be essential, then I'll have to go away somewhere where I can know that if I'm not a criminal, I can hold my head high, or else try to dissuade the Emperor from believing it to be essential.

Please forgive me: perhaps I'm compromising you with these letters, but I hope that your friendship is stronger than such considerations and that you, in any case, will tell me frankly your opinion about it all and give me your advice. If you don't agree with me, perhaps I'll be convinced by your arguments; or, if not, then at least I'll leave you in peace.

Goodbye; I press your hand; my regards to all your people, who, I confess, all appear to me in rather a bad light; it seems to me you are all to blame.

L. Tolstoy

106. To THE EMPEROR ALEXANDER II

Moscow, 22 August 1862

Your Majesty,[1]

On 6 July a field-officer of the gendarmerie visited my estate during my absence, accompanied by the zemstvo authorities. Some student school teachers in the district where I was an arbiter, who were my guests over the vacation, were living in my house with my aunt and my sister. The gendarme officer announced to the teachers that they were under arrest, and demanded to see their belongings and their papers. The search lasted two days; the school, the cellars and the store-rooms were all searched. In the words of the gendarme officer, nothing suspicious was found.

In addition to the insult to my guests, it was also deemed necessary to insult myself, my aunt and my sister. The gendarme officer entered and searched my study, which was my sister's bedroom at the time. In answer to the question what grounds he had for behaving in this manner, he declared that he was acting on the highest authority. The presence of the accompanying soldiers of the gendarmerie and officials corroborated his statement. The officials entered my sister's bedroom, read through all my correspondence and all my diaries and left, after announcing to my guests and my family that they were at liberty, and that nothing suspicious had been found. Consequently they were both our judges and our accusers with the power to detain us on suspicion. The gendarme officer added, however, that his departure should not finally set our minds at rest: we might come back any day, he said.

I consider it beneath my dignity to assure Your Majesty of the undeserved nature of this insult to me. All my past, my connections, my activities in the service and in public education, which are open for all to see, and, finally, the journal, in which all my most sincere convictions are expressed, could have proved to anyone

[106] 1. This letter was given to Alexander II through an aide-de-camp, S. A. Sheremetev. However, the Chief of Police, V. A. Dolgorukov, appended a note justifying his action in ordering the search of Yasnaya Polyana on the technical grounds that the student-teachers were living there without residence permits. This explanation appears to have satisfied Alexander, but the Governor of Tula was instructed in a subsequent letter from Dolgorukov on behalf of the Emperor that Tolstoy was not to be disturbed again for the same reason.

106. To the Emperor Alexander II

interested in me, without recourse to measures disruptive of people's happiness and tranquillity, that I could not be a conspirator, an author of proclamations, a murderer or an incendiary. In addition to the insult and the suspicion of having committed a crime, in addition to the disgrace in the eyes of society and the feeling of perpetual menace under which I am obliged to live and to work, this visit has altogether ruined the people's opinion of me, which I value, which I have earned over the years, and which is essential to me in my chosen occupation—the founding of schools for the people.[2]

With a feeling natural to any man, I am looking for someone to blame for all that has happened to me. I cannot blame myself: I feel that I am more in the right than I have ever been; I do not know of a false informer; nor can I blame the officials who passed judgment and insulted me: several times they repeated that they were doing it not of their own accord, but on the highest authority.

To be equally just to my government and the Person of Your Majesty, I will not and cannot believe this. I do not think that it can be Your Majesty's will that innocent people should be punished, and that people who are in the right should continually live under the fear of insult and punishment.

In order to know whom to reproach for all that has happened to me, I have decided to appeal directly to Your Majesty. I only ask that Your Majesty's name be free of any possible reproach of injustice, and that those who are guilty of the misuse of this name be, if not punished, at least exposed.

I remain Your Majesty's loyal subject,
Count Lev Tolstoy

107. To COUNTESS A. A. TOLSTAYA

Moscow, 7 September 1862

My dear Alexandrine,

What a happy man I am to have such friends as you! I was so cheered and comforted by your letter![1] I've been afflicted by every misfortune lately: the gendarmes, such censorship of my journal that I'm only publishing the June issue tomorrow, and that without my article which has been sent to Petersburg for some reason,[2] and the 3rd and chief misfortune or good fortune, depending on which way you choose to look at it: toothless old fool that I am, I've fallen in love.[3] Yes. I've written the word, and I don't know whether I've told the truth and whether it really is so. I shouldn't have written to you, because very likely in a day or two I shall somehow or other get out of that confused, painful and at the same time happy situation in which I find myself. You know yourself that nothing ever happens

---

2. In this particular context *narodnye shkoly* is translated 'schools for the people' and not 'state schools' as elsewhere.

[107] 1. A. A. Tolstaya had expressed sympathy over the police search and advised Tolstoy to write to the Tsar.
2. *Upbringing and Education*, eventually published in the July issue.
3. With Sofya Andreyevna Behrs, his future wife.

108. To S. A. Behrs later Countess S. A. Tolstaya

quite in the way that you talk or write about it—it's always so complicated and confused, and there's so much that you can't tell. Some day I'll tell you all about it either with joy or with the sadness of recollection. However, one's afraid of being to blame towards oneself. There aren't any rules, and there can't be any—there's only feeling; and one's afraid of that too...[23 lines omitted]

108. To S. A. BEHRS later COUNTESS S. A. TOLSTAYA

Sofya Andreyevna Tolstaya, *née* Behrs (1844–1919), was born at Pokrovskoye, her parents' estate near Moscow, on 22 August 1844; she was the second of three daughters in a family of eight children. Her mother's family had known the Tolstoys for a long time, as her grandfather, A. M. Islenyev, a Tula landowner, had been a friend of Tolstoy's father. Tolstoy himself as a young boy had known all the Islenyev children (the Islenyev marriage was not legal, so the children who where technically illegitimate went by the name of Islavin) and the story of how he pushed his future mother-in-law (still a little girl) off a low balcony in a fit of 'jealousy' was often jokingly referred to in later years. Lyubov Alexandrovna Islavina married a Moscow doctor, A. E. Behrs, and Tolstoy visited the Behrs family at Pokrovskoye from time to time, becoming something of a familiar figure in the family circle while Sofya Andreyevna was growing up. Sofya Andreyevna and her sisters were gay, high-spirited and intelligent girls. The poet Fet, who also knew the family, remarked that they were impeccably brought-up young ladies with an air of *du chien* about them. Both Sofya Andreyevna and her elder sister, Liza, had obtained certificates which entitled them to teach in private homes, and the younger sister, Tatyana, was a talented singer. Sofya and Tatyana were especially close as children and remained so throughout their lives.

Sofya Andreyevna always enjoyed writing. Before her marriage she had written a short story, *Natasha*, and an account of a family visit to the Troitse-Sergiyev Monastery. In the late summer of 1862 when Tolstoy began to visit the Behrs so frequently that it was assumed he had marital intentions, Sofya Andreyevna—who alone felt that he was interested in *her*, not in her elder sister whom custom required to be married off first, or her mother as Dr Behrs sometimes wondered—wrote a short story setting out the whole family entanglement which was troubling her, and in which she included her suitor under the name of Dublitsky. Tolstoy read it, and from then on their engagement progressed fitfully, but at a rapid pace. Tolstoy proposed on 16 September 1862, the day before Sofya Andreyevna's name-day, and they were married on 23 September in Moscow after a courtship of only a few weeks. They left that same day for Yasnaya Polyana.

Before their wedding Sofya Andreyevna's fiancé gave her his diaries, with the intention of beginning married life with no secrets to hide, but the frank record of her future husband's bachelor life was an enormous shock to the sheltered girl of eighteen—a shock from which, perhaps, she never fully recovered. The jealousy

108. To S. A. Behrs later Countess S. A. Tolstaya

to which it gave rise was particularly acute just after their marriage when the new wife found that a peasant woman with whom her husband had had a liaison before marriage and who had borne him an illegitimate child still worked every day in their house at Yasnaya Polyana. Her unfounded jealousy later extended momentarily to her sister Tanya, with whom Tolstoy was very friendly in a fatherly way, and to the 'nihilist' wife of a new estate factor in 1866. These jealousies might well have occurred without the revelations of the diaries, but the latter undoubtedly made the early days of marriage more difficult than they would otherwise have been, and in later years the diaries figure constantly in Sofya Andreyevna's reproaches against her husband. For the rest of her life, moreover, she took for granted that she had unqualified access to her husband's diaries and private papers of all kinds, and this made it particularly difficult for her when in later years an outsider, Chertkov, moved into the privileged role of confidant which she had always occupied *vis-à-vis* her husband.

Sergey Tolstoy, her eldest son, has said in his memoirs that in the early years of their marriage his parents were an exceptionally united couple, and this would appear to be true. They were very much in love, they shared a high ideal of family life, and they wanted many children. (They had eight in the first eleven years of marriage, and five more during the next fifteen years.) Tolstoy was happy in his work, and his wife who idolised him as a writer was more than eager to assist him in every way: by copying out and discussing what he was writing, by protecting him from distractions while working, and, above all, by her prodigious energy in running the house—looking after the growing number of children, engaging tutors, doing some teaching herself, keeping accounts, making clothes, toys and jam, doing embroidery, putting on puppet shows, or just cooking. In addition to all this, she read quite widely (her reading included Taine, the Roman philosophers and Spinoza) and kept a diary, which in the first fifteen years of marriage was relatively happy. Only in the late 1870s do dark clouds begin to appear when she complains of her husband's frequently abstracted air and lack of demonstrative affection for her or for the children.

Sofya Andreyevna's diaries show a perceptive and intelligent mind, strength of character and will, and at least some attempt to follow her husband in his changing ideas, for all her hysterical outbursts and frenzied attempts to justify herself. She clearly recognised the contrast between the luxurious way of life led by her family and that of the peasants, but her sense of guilt was not profound enough to make her wish to jeopardise her children's future. Her religious beliefs were strictly conventional, and she was quite unable to follow the development of her husband's unorthodox Christianity. To her he was hypocritical in that he professed love for mankind, but seemed to deny it to his own family and especially his wife who sorely needed it. She complained bitterly of the gulf between his theory and practice of sex, and she resented his vegetarianism because it caused her the extra effort and expense of cooking two menus daily. With the introduction of her husband's 'disciples' into the home, Sofya Andreyevna felt increasingly beleaguered, and her strong sense of duty came under great strain. Her later diaries take on a defensive

108. To S. A. Behrs later Countess S. A. Tolstaya

and acrimonious tone: her life as a whole seems to be filled with the need to justify her behaviour—not only to posterity, but to herself.

In the period when her relations with her husband were deteriorating, her daily activities continued as usual, although her responsibilities were doubled in 1881 when her husband transferred all his property to her name. Her diary periodically expresses her wish to live a life of her own in which she would not be bound by all the innumerable obligations to her husband, home and children. She continued, however, to protect his literary activities and reputation in every way, handing over his manuscripts and letters to the Rumyantsev Museum in Moscow for preservation, publishing new works of his, agitating for the lifting of censorship restrictions on those of his works which were banned (in this connection she actually visited the Tsar to plead successfully for permission to publish the hated *Kreutzer Sonata*), writing to the press in her husband's defence and continually copying out even those of his works which she found utterly alien and repugnant. Her editions of her husband's works, which were a bone of contention between them during his lifetime when he wished to renounce his copyright entirely, were later acknowledged by his English biographer, Aylmer Maude, to have been of better quality and value than the posthumous edition of Chertkov. She participated in the famine relief of 1891–2. As she grew older she acquired new hobbies—photography and painting—and devoted more and more time to playing the piano. She translated Tolstoy's *On Life* into French, and at his request made translations for him from English and German. In 1895 she published a story, *Grandmother's Treasure*, in a children's journal, and in 1904, under a pseudonym, a group of nine poems in prose. She also published an anthology of children's stories and wrote two other unpublished stories, one on the subject of *The Kreutzer Sonata*. On the basis of her diaries and letters she wrote her autobiography, *My Life*, over the years 1904–16, and she was also the author of the first printed biographical essay on her husband, as well as of several letters to the press.

The death of her young son Vanya in 1895, coupled with the generally unhappy home atmosphere, was the prelude to an intense but platonic infatuation with the composer and family friend, Sergey Taneyev. It would appear from her diary that his music brought out in her an almost hysterical emotional response to the loss of her son and her own need for moral support.

After 1900 the story of Sofya Andreyevna's relationship with her husband and family is a constant tug-of-war over questions concerning Tolstoy's diaries and manuscripts which she felt—justifiably—were being taken away from her protection. Towards the end of her life there were increasing signs of neurotic instability, culminating in attempts at suicide, and her condition required frequent medical attention as the stresses and strains of her life became almost intolerable.

She outlived her husband by nine years, and although, despite the revolution, she was allowed to continue living at Yasnaya Polyana, she was not buried as she would have wished by her husband's side on the family estate, but in the village graveyard two miles away where her children were interred.

108. To S. A. Behrs later Countess S. A. Tolstaya

Moscow, 14 September 1862

Sofya Andrevna,[1]

It's getting more than I can bear. For three weeks I've been saying every day: today I'll tell her everything; and I go away with the same anguish, remorse, fear and happiness in my soul. And every night, as now, I go over the past, torment myself and say: why didn't I speak? What should I have said, and how? I'm taking this letter with me in order to hand it to you, in case, once again, I'm unable to, or haven't the courage to tell you all.

Your family's false attitude towards me consists in the fact, as it seems to me, that I'm in love with your sister Liza. *This is unjust. Your story stuck in my head*,[2] because when I read it through I felt certain that I, Dublitsky, oughtn't to dream of happiness, that your *excellent*, poetic requirements of love [...],[3] that I neither did nor would envy the person you loved. It seemed to me that I could rejoice for you, as one can for a child.

At Ivitsy I wrote: *your presence reminds me too vividly of my old age and the impossibility of happiness...*[4]

But both then and afterwards I lied to myself. Even then I could have broken everything off and gone back to my monastery of solitary work and enthusiasm for my job. Now I can do nothing, and I feel that I've spread confusion in your family, and that the simple, precious relations I had with you as a friend and honest woman have been destroyed. I can't go away and I daren't stay. Tell me, as an honest woman, your hand on your heart—*without hurrying, for the love of God, without hurrying*—tell me what I must do. This is no joke, but a serious matter. I would have died of laughter if I'd been told a month ago that it was possible to be tormented as I've been tormented, and joyfully tormented, all this time. Tell me as an *honest woman*—do you wish to be my wife? Only say *yes* if you can do so *fearlessly*, with all your heart; otherwise better say no, if there's a shadow of doubt in your mind.

For the love of God, question yourself carefully.

It will be terrible for me to hear 'no', but I foresee it and I'll find the strength to

[108] 1. Tolstoy uses the abbreviated form Andrevna.

2. S. A. Tolstaya's story was written in 1860, well bfeore her marriage. According to T. A. Kuzminskaya (Behrs) (*My Life at Home and at Yasnaya Polyana*), it described a family situation exactly parallel to that of the Behrs family, and included two characters—Dublitsky and Smirnov. The portrait of Dublitsky was modelled on Tolstoy, while S. A. Tolstaya portrayed herself in the heroine of the story, Yelena. Yelena feels drawn to the younger Smirnov as well as to the older man, Dublitsky, described as intelligent, energetic, but of 'unattractive external appearance'; however, Yelena's elder sister, Zinaida, is also attracted to him. S. A. Tolstaya destroyed the story, along with her diaries, before her marriage. T. A. Kuzminskaya regretted the loss of the manuscript, since 'it vividly portrayed the Rostov family in embryo: the mother, Vera and Natasha'. S. A. Tolstaya in fact called Yelena's younger sister Natasha. She gave Tolstoy the manuscript to read at his request, and he commented on it in his diary on 26 August: 'What energy, truth and beauty!' He did not fail to recognise himself in the portrait of Dublitsky.

3. The text of the letter is defective here.

4. Ivitsy, the estate of A. M. Islenyev, S. A. Tolstaya's grandfather, in the province of Tula, where Tolstoy unexpectedly turned up and wrote this message for Sofya Andreyevna, using only the initial letters of each word and leaving her to guess the meaning.

bear it; but if I should never be loved as a husband as much as I love, that would be even more terrible.

109. To COUNTESS A. A. TOLSTAYA

Yasnaya Polyana, 28 September 1862

My dear and beloved friend and Granny,

I'm writing from the country; as I write I can hear upstairs the voice of my wife, whom I love more than anything in the world, talking to my brother. I've lived to the age of 34 and I didn't know it was possible to be so much in love and so happy. When I'm calmer, I'll write you a long letter—no, not when I'm calmer—I'm calm now and serene, as never before in my life, but when I'm more accustomed to it. Just now I feel continually as though I've stolen an undeserved, illicit happiness that wasn't meant for me. There she is walking about and I can hear her, and it's so good. Thanks for your last letter. And why am I loved by such good people as you, and most surprising of all, by such a creature as my wife?

Auntie is still unwell. Ever since the scare she's been afflicted with some woman's disease, and she can only walk and stand with difficulty. Now joy appears to have raised her up and fortified her. What a pity Liza[1] won't be with us—we'd already started day-dreaming, and my wife had even started being apprehensive: you are Court people, you know. She doesn't understand yet, and it's impossible to explain to her the sort of person *you* are. Goodbye; I kiss you hand.

L. Tolstoy

110. To T. A. and Y. A. BEHRS

Tatyana Andreyevna Behrs (1846–1925) and Yelizaveta Andreyevna Behrs (1843–1919), Tolstoy's wife's sisters. Tatyana, after an unhappy love affair with Tolstoy's brother Sergey which led to an attempt to poison herself, eventually married her cousin A. M. Kuzminsky in 1867. Impetuous, high-spirited and artistically gifted, she served Tolstoy as the prototype of Natasha Rostova in *War and Peace*. She always remained on intimate terms with her sister Sonya, and was a great favourite of Tolstoy's. For many years she and her growing family spent the summers at Yasnaya Polyana, and she wrote many articles about Tolstoy and the people close to him, as well as several short stories. Her memoirs *My Life at Home and at Yasnaya Polyana* were first published in 1925–6.

Yelizaveta (Liza) was the most scholarly and withdrawn of the three sisters, and several features of her character were incorporated in Vera Rostova. She collaborated with Tolstoy on his journal *Yasnaya Polyana*, and sometimes acted as his amanuensis. In later life she published some articles on economic problems. She was twice married.

[109] 1. A. A. Tolstaya's sister.

110. To T. A. and Y. A. Behrs

Yasnaya Polyana, 1(?) October 1862

My dear Tatyana,

Have pity on me, I have a stupid wife (I pronounce *stupid* the same way as you do). [*S. A. Tolstaya's hand:* He's the stupid one, Tanya.] The news that we're both stupid is bound to distress you very much, but after grief comes consolation; we're both very pleased that we're stupid and don't want to be different.

[*S. A. Tolstaya's hand:* I want him to be more intelligent.]

There's a problem for you. Do you feel how we're rocking with laughter at it? I'm sorry they've cut out your lump;[1] send me a piece. Or have they already taken it to Vagankovo and erected a cross with the inscription:

> Passer-by, undo your shirt
> And breathe the air more freely;
> And look at Tanya's little lump
> And don't sit down to rest here.

Sonya says that it's offensive to write to you in this tone. That's true. So listen and I'll talk seriously. The passage in your letter where you write about seeming to see Vasinka, Polinka[2] and me in the darkness and Sonya without her rouleau and in her going away clothes, is charming. I detected in it your wonderfully sweet nature with its laughter and its background of poetic seriousness. Such another Tanya would take a lot of finding, it's true, and such another admirer as L. Tolstoy.

I kiss Mama's hand and embrace Papa and the Pandigashki[3] and Sasha.[4]

How grateful I am to you, dear Liza, for sending *Luther*.[5] But why don't I address you in the familiar way?[6] Let's start, at least in writing, so that it will be quite natural when we meet—if you agree and allow it, of course. Better still is the fact that you promise to do some more work for my journal. I don't want to write about this now, so as not to spoil the disinterested nature of the purely friendly feeling which dictates this letter. To tell the truth, my journal is beginning to weigh heavy on me, particularly the students and the proofs etc. which are necessary conditions of it. I am now very drawn to writing a free work de longue haleine—a novel or the like. Life is very, very good for me, and I flatter myself with the hope that it is for Sonya too. How is your life progressing? Before we left, you were en train of undertaking all sorts of jobs and duties. That's splendid, and so appropriate to you. God grant you success (the familiar 'you', if you agree). I kiss your hand. Do abandon your habit of not writing letters.

Your brother,
L. Tolstoy

[110] 1. She had had her tonsils removed.
2. The Perfilyevs.
3. S. A. Tolstaya's younger brothers.
4. Her elder brother.
5. Y. A. Behrs' article, written for *Yasnaya Polyana* and published in September 1862.
6. The Russian language, like the French, distinguishes between the more formal *vy* (*vous*) and the familiar *ty* (*tu*) in forms of address.

111. To Y. N. AKHMATOVA

Yelizaveta Nikolayevna Akhmatova (1820–1904), writer and translator, was a regular contributor to the *Reader's Library*. From 1864 to 1866 she published a children's journal, and subsequently spent some thirty years publishing 'A Collection of Foreign Novels'.

Yasnaya Polyana, 1 October 1862

Dear Lizaveta Nikolayevna,

Ever since I've been occupied with the schools and the journal, I haven't heard a word of sympathy from anyone which was as welcome and precious to me as your letter was[1] (I received the letter the day before yesterday and am hastening to reply. I don't understand why there has been such a long delay.) What I value is the fact that, simply because you love your Seryozha and look on the world clearly and without prejudice, you have reached precisely those same convictions that I appear to have reached by another path.

I don't feel able to answer your questions briefly, clearly and convincingly. I'll only say one thing: I cannot approve of your plan to make an architect or anything else of Seryozha. To prepare a child for some occupation is one of the oldest and most dangerous forms of despotism. You want to give him an assured slice of bread, but perhaps he's preparing himself to spend all his life as a poverty-stricken but great poet or thinker.

Another thing—at his age (indeed at all times) there are only two sciences that you can be firmly convinced will be of use—they are language or languages, the art of expressing and understanding any ideas in whatever form, and mathematics. I, at least, would try to interest a child only in these two sciences.

Your letter touched me deeply. It seems to me that as a result of it I have understood and recognised in you an old friend. But apart from that, your letter is of great significance to me as a living, rather than logical, confirmation—confirmation, that is, that my ideas are not only correct as ideas, but as life, as feeling. I would be very glad if this letter could be published, after omitting, of course, the names and everything personal. What would you say to that?[2] At all events, I beg you to write to me again and in greater detail and for publication. You yourself can't be aware of all the importance that your words have in my eyes and in the eyes of the public—words which stem from a source completely opposite to the one from which most literature comes—the heart.

I'll write to you another time in greater detail. I hope to be in Moscow, and perhaps in Petersburg, around the New Year. I hope that we shall correspond again before then.

With sincere respect,
Count L. Tolstoy

[111] 1. Akhmatova wrote a letter to Tolstoy in three parts between 6 July and 19 August, expressing her agreement with his educational views.

2. Akhmatova agreed to the publication of her letter, but owing to the discontinuation of Tolstoy's journal it was not in fact published.

112. To COUNTESS A. A. TOLSTAYA

Yasnaya Polyana, 8 October 1862

[The first part of the letter is written by Tolstoy's wife, S. A. Tolstaya—in French:]

My dear, new Auntie, your kind letter was a delightful surprise for me. I have not been able as yet to earn your favour, and I know that you are so good and kind to me only on Lev's account. He has told me so much about you that I have already grown to love you and to value your love for my husband. I already know you slightly from your letters to him which he has shown to me, and also from your portrait which I have stolen from him. I am doing everything possible to make him happy, and I know that only in this way can I earn your love. I have never had any doubts as to my own happiness. I have known Lev from childhood, and have always loved him with all my heart.

I hope we shall soon come to Petersburg, and then at last I shall have the happiness of meeting you. If you should happen to be in Moscow sometime, maman would be very glad to see you: you see, she also knows you from Lev's stories. Please give my respects to your mother and to my other two aunties.

Your respectful niece,
Countess Sofya Tolstaya

[Tolstoy continues the letter:]

I find this letter of Sonya's to you rather annoying, my dear Alexandrine; I sense that direct relations between you will be quite different—but probably, however, it has to be like this. You understand that I can't speak the truth about her at present—I'm afraid of myself and afraid of the disbelief of others. One thing—she immediately strikes one as being an honest person, that is both *honest* and a *person*. Well, you'll see her for yourself, God willing.

How dear and delightful your letter was; and how well it tones in with that happy, that new and happy state in which I've been living now for two months. Where is it all leading? I don't know, only I feel calmer and better every day. I was getting tired of keeping accounts with myself, of starting new lives (you remember); I was becoming reconciled to my nastiness, I was beginning to consider myself, if not absolutely, then at least relatively good; now I've renounced my past as I've never renounced it before; I'm aware of all my vileness every second when I compare myself with her, with Sonya, but 'I cannot wash away the sorrowful lines.'[1] It's 2 weeks now, and I still feel clean as it were, and I tremble for myself every second, in case I should stumble. Living two together is such a frightening responsibility. I'm writing all this to you because I love you with all my soul. That's the sacred truth. I find it terribly frightening to live now: one feels life so intensely, one feels that every second of life is in earnest, and not as it was before—or so it seems now.

[112] 1. A line from Pushkin's poem *Recollection*.

112. To Countess A. A. Tolstaya

The main question which interests you about me[2] hasn't been touched upon as yet, but I'm feeling mellow and receptive to everything. Write to me please, just as you used to. Goodbye.

She's reading this letter and doesn't understand a thing and doesn't want to understand, and there's no need for her to understand; that very thing which the likes of us arrive at by a whole laborious, sickly round of doubt and suffering, is bound to be so for fortunate people like her.

[At this point S. A. Tolstaya takes up the letter:]

I cannot leave it at that, dear Auntie. He's mistaken; I understand everything, absolutely everything that concerns him, but his letter is so gloomy because he's got a headache and is in low spirits.

[Tolstoy adds:]

There! you see!

2. Religion?

IV
1863–1869

The years 1863–9 were, in Tolstoy's literary biography, occupied entirely with the writing and publication of *War and Peace*, and if in one sense this was a momentous period of his life marked by almost continuous hard work, in another sense it was uneventful: there was only *one* literary event. Tolstoy's biographer, Aylmer Maude, has written, 'These years follow one another with so little change that the story of a decade and a half [i.e. 1863–78] can almost be compressed into a sentence.' In 1864 the first collected edition of Tolstoy's works appeared in four volumes. Tolstoy now felt himself to be at the height of his powers as a writer, as he wrote to Fet in January 1865. In November 1866 he was still so single-mindedly committed to literature that he wrote to Fet again, belittling all other activity except creative work. This attitude is in marked contrast to the predominant tone of the previous period in Tolstoy's life when 'useful' activity was the keynote, and writing was subordinated to teaching and farming. In September 1867 Tolstoy visited the battle site at Borodino and questioned survivors of the battle; he also paid several visits from time to time to the Rumyantsev Library in Moscow to consult archive material in connection with his novel.

On the home front during these years four children were born to the Tolstoy family (Sergey, Tanya, Ilya, and Lev), and Yasnaya Polyana was a hive of productive activity. Notwithstanding his literary endeavours, Tolstoy became an ardent bee-keeper, planted a birch wood which later became very valuable, and had a brief burst of enthusiasm for sculpture (he modelled a bust of his wife in 1866). Nor did he neglect the ordinary affairs of the estate: pig-farming, horse-breeding and agriculture. His closest friends at this time were Fet, Ivan Aksakov, Prince D. Obolensky and Prince S. S. Urusov, who, along with the historian M. P. Pogodin, may have contributed to the passages in *War and Peace* which concern the philosophy of history.

One event which stands out in this period is Tolstoy's defence before a military court of a private who had been charged with striking an officer and who faced the death penalty if found guilty. The man was of subnormal intelligence and had evidently been provoked by the officer, and Tolstoy based his defence on diminished responsibility. The man was found guilty and executed, and the episode served to strengthen Tolstoy's growing hostility to the state's military and judicial organs and institutions, which reached its climax many years later in *Resurrection*.

113. To T. A. BEHRS

Yasnaya Polyana, 20–3 March 1863

Mademoiselle![1]

Aimer ou avoir aimé cela suffit!... Ne demandez rien ensuite. On n'a pas d'autre perle à trouver dans les plis ténébreux de la vie. Aimer est un accomplissement.

> Make a glad sound on the psaltery,
> I will sing you a song.[2]

La jeune fille n'est qu'une lueur de rêve et n'est pas encore une statue.

[...][3]

In the centre of the earth is the alatyr stone and in the centre of man is the navel. How inscrutable are the ways of Providence! Oh, younger sister of the wife of her husband! In *his* centre, other objects are sometimes found as well. All objects are subject to the law of gravity in inverse proportion to the square of the distance. But let us assume the contrary. Natalya Petrovna[4] can't eat cold beet soup.[5] The horse returns to its stall. The son of dust is the victim of the sport of chance. Take him and raise him up.

I had a dream:[6] two doves were riding in a carriage; one dove was singing, the other was wearing Polish dress; a third—more like an officer than a dove—was smoking cigarettes. Oil, not smoke, was issuing from the cigarette, and this oil was love. Two other birds lived in a house; they had no wings, but they had a crop; attached to the crop was only one gizzard, and in the gizzard was a fish from Okhotny Ryad.[7] In Okhotny Ryad Kupferschmidt[8] was playing the horn, and Katerina Yegorovna[9] tried to embrace him and couldn't. She had 500 roubles salary on her head and a hairnet made of calves' feet. They couldn't get out and this made me very sad. Tanya, my dear friend, you are young, beautiful, gifted and lovable. Guard yourself and your heart. Once your heart has been given away you can't get it back again, and the mark on a tormented heart remains for ever. Remember Katerina Yegorovna's words: *never add sour cream to a fancy pastry*. I know that the artistic demands of your rich nature are not the same as the demands of ordinary girls of your age; but Tanya, as an experienced man who loves you not

---

[113] 1. I have translated this jocular and, in places, nonsensical letter as literally as possible. Little light is thrown on it by Tanya Behrs in her memoirs, or by the Tolstoy specialists whom I consulted in the U.S.S.R.
2. The words of a popular song.
3. Three indecipherable Russian words in the original.
4. N. P. Okhotnitskaya.
5. A cold soup of beet, leaves, pot-herbs and fish.
6. Tolstoy's dream apparently refers to a projected trip to Yasnaya Polyana of T. A. Behrs, her brother Alexander, and A. M. Kuzminsky who later became her husband. The 'two other birds' are presumably Tolstoy and his wife.
7. A street in the centre of Moscow.
8. A violinist in the Bolshoy Theatre orchestra, and a hunting companion of A. Y. Behrs, Tolstoy's father-in-law.
9. A teacher of German in the Behrs household.

just because we are relations, I'm telling you the whole truth. Tanya, remember Mme Laborde;[10] her legs are too fat for her body—a fact which you can always observe with a little care when she comes on to the stage in pantaloons. Life alters many things. Forgive me, Tanya dear, for giving you advice and trying to develop your mind and your higher faculties. If I permit myself to do so, it's only because I love you sincerely.

Your brother,
Lev

114. To T. A. BEHRS

Yasnaya Polyana, 23 March 1863

[*S. A. Tolstaya's hand (21 March 1863)*: What's the matter, are you unhappy, Tanya... You don't write at all, and I so love to get your letters, and Lyovochka has had no answer to his scatter-brained epistle. I didn't understand a single word of it.]

23 March

You see she started writing and suddenly stopped because she couldn't go on. And do you know why, Tanya dear? A strange thing happened to her, and an even stranger one to me. You know yourself that she was always made of flesh and blood like the rest of us, and enjoyed all the advantages and disadvantages of that state: she breathed, she was warm, sometimes hot; she breathed and blew her nose (loudly at that) etc.; above all she possessed all the limbs, such as arms and legs, which could take up various positions; in a word, she was corporeal, like the rest of us. Suddenly at 10.00 p.m. on 21 March 1863, this extraordinary thing happened to her and to me. Tanya, I know you always loved her (I don't know what sort of feeling she will arouse in you now); I know you are sympathetic towards me, I know your good sense, your correct outlook on the important things in life and your love for your parents (do prepare them and tell them), and I am writing to tell you everything that has happened.

On that day I got up early, and did a lot of walking and riding. We had dinner and supper and read together (she could still read), and I was happy and at peace. At 10.00 o'clock I said goodnight to Auntie (Sonya was there as usual, and promised to come up later) and went to bed on my own. I heard her opening the door, breathing and getting undressed, all in my sleep...I heard her coming out from behind the screen and walking towards the bed. I opened my eyes...and saw Sonya —but not the Sonya that you and I knew—a Sonya made of *china*!—of the same china your parents used to argue about. Do you know those little china dolls with cold, bare shoulders and neck, and arms folded in front but made of the same piece of china as the body, with hair painted black and big artificial waves, with the black paint faded on top, and with protruding china eyes also painted black at

---

10. A French singer with the Italian opera in Moscow who for a time gave singing lessons to T. A. Behrs.

114. To T. A. Behrs

the edges and set too widely apart, and a bodice with firm pleats, also of china and made out of one piece? Sonya was just like that—I touched her hand—it was smooth, pleasant to touch, cold and made of china. I thought I was asleep and shook myself, but she remained the same and stood motionless in front of me. I said: 'Are you made of china?' She replied without opening her mouth (her mouth remained folded at the corners and daubed with bright crimson): 'Yes, I am.' A chill ran down my spine, and I looked at her legs: they too were china, and (you can imagine my horror) they stood on a china base made from the same piece as she was, representing the ground and painted green like the grass. Near her left leg a little above the back of the knee was a china support painted brown and probably representing a tree stump. It too was made from the same piece of china as she was. I realised that without this support she wouldn't have been able to stand up, and I became so sad, as you can imagine—you who loved her. I still couldn't believe my eyes and began to call her; she couldn't move without the support and the base beneath her, and she could only rock a little bit on her base so as to fall towards me. I heard the china bottom bumping against the floor. I began to touch her—she was all smooth china, pleasant to touch and cold. I tried to raise her arm—I couldn't. I tried to put my finger, or at least my nail, between her elbow and her side—I couldn't either. There was some china paste in the way—the sort of thing they use at Auerbach's for making gravy boats. It was all done just for show. I began to examine her bodice—all of one piece with her body, top and bottom. I began to look more closely and noticed that one piece of a pleat of her bodice had been broken off at the bottom, and you could see something brown. The paint on the top of her head had peeled off a bit, and the white was showing. The paint had come off her lips in one place, and a piece of her shoulder had broken away. But everything was so true to life that you could tell it was the same Sonya of ours. The bodice I knew, embroidered with lace, and the black bun of hair at the back—only made of china—and the lovely delicate hands and the big eyes and the lips—they were all exactly alike, only they were china—even the dimple on the chin and the shoulder bones in front. I was in a terrible state; I didn't know what to say or do or think; she would have been glad to help me, but what could a china creature do? The half-closed eyes, and the eyelashes and the eyebrows—from a distance they all looked real. She didn't look at me, but through me, at her bed. She obviously wanted to go to bed, and she kept rocking back and forth. I was at my wit's end, and took hold of her and tried to carry her over to the bed. My fingers made no impression on her cold, china body and, what surprised me even more, she had become as light as a glass phial. And suddenly she seemed to shrink away, and she grew tiny, tinier than the palm of my hand, although she still looked exactly the same. I took hold of a pillow, stood her up in one corner, pummelled another corner with my fist and laid her down there; then I took her nightcap, folded it into four and covered her with it up to the chin. She lay there, looking exactly the same. I put out the candle and laid her down to sleep under my beard. Suddenly I heard her voice from the corner of the pillow: 'Lyova, why have I become china?' I didn't know what to reply. Again she said: 'Does it matter that I'm china?' I didn't

114. To T. A. Behrs

want to upset her, and said that it didn't. I felt her again in the darkness—she was still cold, still china. Yet her belly was the same as when she was alive, protruding upwards like a cone, and rather unnatural for a china doll. I had a strange feeling. I suddenly felt glad that she was like that, and I ceased to be surprised—it all seemed natural to me. I took her out, transferred her from one hand to the other and put her down again by my head. She was quite happy. We went to sleep. In the morning I got up and went out without looking at her. I was so afraid of all that happened the previous night. When I came back for lunch she was just the same again as she had always been. I didn't remind her of the previous night, being afraid to upset her and Auntie. I haven't told anyone about it except you. I thought it was all over, but during these past days, whenever we are alone, the same thing has happened again. She suddenly becomes a little china doll. When she is with others, everything is normal. She isn't dismayed by this, nor am I. To be frank, however strange it is, I'm glad about it, and despite the fact that she is made of china, we're very happy.

I'm only writing to you about all this, Tanya dear, so that you can prepare your parents for the news and find out from the doctors via papa what it all means and whether it is bad for the future child. We're alone just now, and she is sitting by my necktie, and I can feel her sharp little nose digging into my neck. Yesterday she was left alone. I went into the room and saw Dora (the dog) dragging her into a corner and playing with her, and almost breaking her. I gave Dora a thrashing and put Sonya into my waistcoat pocket and took her off to the study. However, I've now ordered a wooden box with a clasp (it was delivered today from Tula), covered on the outside with morocco and on the inside with crimson velvet, with a place made for her so that her elbows, head and back can fit exactly into it, and she can't get broken. I'm covering it on top with suede as well.

As I was writing this letter a dreadful accident happened; she was standing on the table, Natalya Petrovna knocked against her as she was passing, and she fell and broke off her leg above the knee, together with the tree stump. Alexey says that it can be glued on again with a white of egg substance. Do they know the recipe in Moscow? If so, please send it.[1]

[114] 1. This 'dream' may have its origin in an earlier dream which Sofya Andreyevna had in which she saw herself destroying a 'doll' which was in fact the natural son of Tolstoy and the peasant woman with whom he had had a prolonged affair before his marriage and who continued to work at Yasnaya Polyana after his marriage. Tolstoy's 'dream' makes use of the same symbol, a doll, (Sofya Andreyevna's diary and letters of the period indicate that he used the term to refer to her in a derogatory sense) but uses it in a different way. As the dream reveals, Sofya Andreyevna was pregnant with their first child at the time, and was evidently unresponsive to her husband's amorous attentions (hence, the various references to the coldness of the doll). Boris Eichenbaum suggests in his biography of Tolstoy that the letter was written primarily for Sofya Andreyevna to read, and that it was an attempt to smooth over difficulties which had taken place between Tolstoy and his wife over their marital relations. In the Behrs family, where it was read aloud *en famille*, it was taken only as a sophisticated work of literature and was much admired.

115. To A. A. FET

Yasnaya Polyana, 1–3 May 1863

Both your letters were equally important, significant and welcome, dear Afanasy Afanasyevich.[1] I live in a world so remote from literature and its criticism that when I get a letter like yours, my first feeling is one of astonishment. Who is this person who wrote *The Cossacks* and *Polikushka*? And what's the use of discussing them? Paper can stand anything, and editors pay for and print anything. But that's only a first impression; later on one enters into the meaning of your words, rummages about in one's head and finds in some corner of it, among old, forgotten rubbish, something undefined, labelled *art*. And comparing it with what you say, one agrees that you are right, and even gets pleasure from rummaging about in that old rubbish, and that once favourite old smell. One even feels like writing. You are right, of course. But then there are not many readers like you. *Polikushka* is drivel on the first subject that comes into the head of a man who 'wields a good pen'; but *The Cossacks* has some *pith* in it, though it's bad. It's badly discussed, though, by poor Polonsky in *Time*.[2] I'm now writing the story of a piebald gelding,[3] and I expect to publish it by the autumn. But how can I write now? Invisible efforts— even visible ones[4]—are being made now, and moreover I'm up to my ears again Yufanising.[5] Sonya is working with me too. We have no steward; I have people to help with the field-work and the building, but she manages the office and the cash by herself. I have bees, sheep, a new orchard and a distillery. Everything progresses little by little, although of course poorly compared with the ideal. What do you think of the Polish business?[6] It looks bad! Will you and I and Borisov have to take our swords down again from their rusty nails? What if we come to Nikolskoye;[7] shall we see you? When will you be at the Borisovs? Can't we arrange things so that we can meet? Goodbye. Give my cordial greetings to Marya Petrovna. Sonya and Auntie send their regards.

116. To COUNTESS S. A. TOLSTAYA

Yasnaya Polyana, 3–16 August 1863

Sonya, forgive me; I only realise now that I'm to blame, and how much I'm to blame. There are days when you live, as it were, not by your own will but are subjected to some external, irresistible law. I've been like that recently with regard

[115] 1. Fet had expressed his enthusiasm for *The Cossacks*, but was critical of *Polikushka*.
2. Polonsky was critical of Tolstoy's eulogistic portrayal of the way of life of the Cossacks in contrast to the civilised world of the Russian capitals.
3. The original title of *Strider. The Story of a Horse*, which was not published until 1886.
4. A reference to a line from Fet's poem 'Again invisible efforts...' He probably also had in mind his wife's pregnancy.
5. A common expression in Tolstoy's correspondence with Fet, referring to a peasant ploughman, Yufan, who epitomised rustic strength.
6. The Polish uprising of 1863.
7. An estate of the Tolstoys, not far from Borisov's estate.

118. To Countess A. A. Tolstaya

to you and who [...] I always thought that I had many failings, but also a tithe of feeling and generosity. I was rude and callous—and to whom? To the one creature who has given me the best happiness in life and who alone loves me. Sonya, I know that these things are not forgiven and forgotten, and I know and understand better than you all my baseness. I'm to blame, Sonya darling, and I'm loathsome [...], but there is an excellent man inside me who is sometimes asleep. Love him and don't reproach him, Sonya.[1]

117. To COUNTESS M. N. TOLSTAYA

Yasnaya Polyana, 10(?)–15(?) October 1863

My dear, dear, thousand times beloved Mashenka, I can't tell you what I felt as I read your letter.[1] I wept, and am still weeping as I write. You say: let my brothers judge me as they will. In my heart there is nothing, and never will be anything but love for you—all that love which used to be somewhere remote—pity and love. No honest man will ever lift a finger to reproach you. But why didn't you write to me, my dear? As it was, I was the first to read the letter, but if you had sent it to *me*, nobody else would have known about it. What's to be done now? First of all marry him; secondly, don't on any account keep the child yourself, but give it to me. Thirdly—and most important of all—keep it secret from the children and from society, especially from the children. Perhaps I'll come myself and bring some money, or perhaps Seryozha will (he's away hunting). It's not a question of me, but of the money—I hope to collect 1,000 roubles or so in a week. I'm writing to you immediately after getting your letter, and before I've decided anything. Be sure of one thing, that Auntie T.A. and I will not pass judgement on you, and will do everything we possibly can for you.

118. To COUNTESS A. A. TOLSTAYA

Yasnaya Polyana, 17–31(?) October 1863

My dear Alexandrine,

I have here 4 pages of a letter I began writing to you, but I won't send it. I've so lost sight of you and am feeling so guilty towards you that I'm frightened of you.

[116] 1. Tolstoy wrote this note to his wife in her diary sometime between 3 August and 16 August. The birth of their first child, Sergey, on 28 June 1863, was followed by family quarrels and differences of opinion. Tolstoy had obstinate ideas on the rearing of children, ideas that were originally suggested to him by his reading of Rousseau, and he frequently found himself at variance with the Behrs family and the medical diagnoses of Dr Behrs. Tolstoy was angered by his wife's inability to nurse her child, due to mastitis, and by the engagement of a wet nurse. He wrote this note to his wife in a fit of penitence, but subsequently crossed it out in a renewed burst of anger, leaving some of the text indecipherable.

[117] 1. M. N. Tolstaya had written to inform her family of the birth of a daughter, on 8 September 1863. In the summer of 1861 she had met a Swede, Viscount Victor-Hector de Kleen, who subsequently became her common-law husband, and she spent the winters of 1861–2 and 1862–3 with him in Algiers.

118. To Countess A. A. Tolstaya

But the threat of losing you as a friend is too terrible for me.[1] You'll recognise my handwriting and my signature; but you're probably wondering who I am and what sort of a person I am now. I am a husband and a father,[2] who is fully satisfied with his situation, and I'm getting so used to it, that in order to be aware of my happiness, I have to think what it would be like without it. I don't analyse my situation (I've given up grübeln) or my feelings—I only *feel* my family circumstances, and don't think about them. This condition gives me an awful lot of intellectual scope. I've never felt my intellectual powers, and even all my moral powers, so free and so capable of work. And I *have* work to do. This work is a novel of the 1810s and 1820s, which has been occupying me fully since the autumn.[3] Does this prove weakness of character or strength? I sometimes think both— but I must confess that my views on life, on the *people* and on *society* are now quite different from what they were the last time I saw you. They can be pitied, but it's difficult for me to understand how I could have loved them so deeply. Nevertheless, I'm glad that I passed through this school; this last mistress of mine was a great formative influence on me. I love children and teaching, but it's difficult for me to understand myself as I was a year ago. The children come to me in the evenings and bring with them memories for me of the teacher that used to be in me and is there no longer. Now I am a writer with *all* the strength of my soul, and I write and I think as I have never thought or written before. I am a happy and tranquil husband and father who has no secrets from anyone and no desires, except that everything should go on as before. You, I love less than before, but still sufficiently for you not to abandon me, and still more than all other people (and how many there have been!) whom I have met in my life. I have always reproached you with one thing, and I still have that reproach in my heart, and my feelings and thoughts are sufficiently clear for me to be able to express it. In our relations you have always shown me only the *general* side (you'll understand me) of your mind and heart, you have never spoken to me of the details of your life, of the simple, tangible, private incidents of your life. I'm now writing to you about myself, but I don't know about you—what to ask, what to think, what to want for you. I don't even know what is most intimate and precious to you in your life, other than your general love of what is good and what is refined in it, which is your principal feature. I would like you to lead me, not into your sanctuaire, but into the everyday interests of your life. I'm afraid you won't understand me. I express myself stupidly. I have a weak character and submit easily to the influence of people I love, and so I've submitted and am submitting to yours. As soon as I come into contact with you, I put on white gloves and a tail-coat (a moral one, to be sure); after an evening with you, I remember, I always used to have an arrière-goût of something delicate, fresh and fragrant, but I always wanted something more substantial.

[118] 1. A. A. Tolstaya had written to Tolstoy on 1 May 1863, complaining about his long silence: 'You are exactly like the novels that usually come to an end with the chapter on marriage—i.e. just at the moment when life becomes most interesting.'

2. Tolstoy's first son, Sergey, was born on 28 June 1863.

3. When Tolstoy abandoned his novel *The Decembrists* he turned to work on the novel *1805*, which subsequently became the first part of *War and Peace*.

There was nothing to grasp hold of. Perhaps it had to be like that and it was a good thing, but I should have liked something different. Do you remember, you once wanted to write a novel for me? It seems to me that we could then have entered into these more essential relations. Can this really have been lost for ever?...[4] I haven't written at all what I wanted to, but it would be dangerous to leave this letter unsent as well; in that case I couldn't bring myself to write again. Where are you? What are you doing? What are your plans? Our plans are as follows: in the winter, Seryozha's health permitting, (Seryozha means a good, sweet smile with bright eyes—there's nothing else to him), we'll go to Moscow for two weeks. The summer we'll spend in the country, and the following winter we'll go to live somewhere in town. Goodbye. Like girls at school do, I beg you not to show this letter to anyone and to tear it up.

Sonya loves you very much (that's the truth) and has been intending to write to you. I don't know what she will write, but I would like to know.

119. To T. A. BEHRS

Yasnaya Polyana, 1–3 January 1864

Yesterday when there was a new moon I looked in Auntie's almanac and found: aujourd'hui Léon et sa femme sont partis pour Moscou accompagnés de la chère Tanya. You always were chère to me, but then you became even *chèrer* for no apparent reason, as always happens. Yet you say that I'm your enemy. Your enemy is the 20 extra years which I've lived on earth. I know that whatever happens to you, you mustn't lose control of yourself, but must be your sweet, wild, energetic nature when fortune smiles and the same indomitable nature in misfortune. You can be, if you don't lose a grip on yourself. Say to yourself: keep a tight rein on yourself; and do so. Well, supposing he were to die?[1] Well, supposing for me Sonya were to die, or I for her? You know it's easy to say I would cease to live. The main thing is that it's easy to say it, but foolish and base and false, and you have to keep a tight rein on yourself. You have your sorrows, but besides them you also have so many friends who love you (think of me), and you won't stop living, and you'll be ashamed to remember your lapse at this time, however it may turn out. Really, don't be angry with me. You'll be convinced that it's a bad thing to lose control of yourself, and all will be well.

And how do I see your future? You want to know, and I'll tell you. Seryozha promised to come and see us in a couple of days time, but he hasn't come so far. We've heard that Masha is in labour, but even before that I began to get very worried. The thought tormented me that he once said: 'I must end all this one way or another by marrying Masha or Tanya.' Rationally speaking, I'm more sorry for Masha than for you, but when it occurred to me that he might make his mind up without us I was afraid. We wrote him a letter to say we had something important

4. Two and a half lines have been carefully erased here.
[119] 1. S. N. Tolstoy, whom Tanya Behrs was in love with at the time.

119. To T. A. Behrs

to tell him. Now she's in labour and he's present for the first time, and I'm afraid. In my heart of hearts—*I say this to you with God as my witness*—I want it to be *yes*, but I'm afraid it will be *no*. Everything may appear to him in a different light in the face of her sufferings, which may be coupled with moral sufferings too. Dyakov was here and then at his house, and spoke to him a lot about you, without suspecting anything of course, and his words could have greatly influenced him against you. He praised Masha, spoke generally about his situation, and spoke about you—how young you are, how soon it is for you to get married, and, of course, how charming you are.

For my part I'm convinced that if he marries Masha he will very likely ruin himself and her. I told him that if he didn't marry her, he would instinctively be leaving himself une porte du salut. He said: 'Yes, yes, yes.' But now, if he gets married, this porte du salut will be sealed off, and he will hate her. He can go on living with her like this, but if he marries her he will come to grief. But it's difficult to read another person's soul, Tanya, and the better you know him, the more difficult it is. I know nothing, and I have no definite wishes for you, although I love you both with all my heart and soul. God knows what will be best for you both, and you must pray to Him. Yes. I know one thing, that the more difficult a choice becomes in life for a person and the harder it is to live, the more he needs to take command of himself (at least to make every effort to take command of himself, and not to lose control), because at such a moment a mistake can cost himself and others dear. Every step, every word at such moments, at the moment through which you are living, is more important than years of life afterwards. Tanya darling, perhaps this seems like the mirror of virtue;[2] but what can I do if my most intimate thoughts and wishes are like the mirror of virtue. Every word has been carefully thought out and heart-felt; perhaps it won't seem the truth to you, but I've said everything I think and feel about it, except for one little thing which I'll tell you some other time later.[3] Goodbye. Pray to God; that is the best thing of all.

120. To A. A. BEHRS

Alexander Andreyevich Behrs (1845–1918), Sofya Andreyevna's elder brother, served in the Preobrazhensky Guards regiment and was later governor of Batum, vice-governor of Oryol Province and a member of the council of the Moscow Land Bank.

Yasnaya Polyana, 28 October 1864

My arm is still bad,[1] but I can't resist adding a postscript to you.[2] Sonya is talking

2. *Le miroir de la vertu*...containing edifying children's stories.
3. The fear that Tanya would be unhappy, whatever the outcome of her relationship with Tolstoy's brother.
[120] 1. Tolstoy had shortly before broken his arm when out riding. The bone was set incorrectly, and it had to be reset later by surgeons in Moscow.
2. This postscript was added to a letter from S. A. Tolstaya to her brother, who was then serving with his battery near Warsaw.

nonsense when she says she's ashamed. It's not she, but I who am ashamed. I came in and said: you know we're pigs, not writing to Sasha. She said: I thought so too. That's how it was. We're well and happy. Sonya has moved downstairs into my old study with both children, and we stay there for days at a time, we—that is my sister Masha's girls who are living with us. They are sweet and wonderful girls. Everything is fine, especially since we got the news that Andrey Yevstafyevich[3] is better. You describe your life in a small Jewish town and, believe it or not, I envy you. How good it is at your age to be face to face with yourself, and actually in a group of artillery officers. There aren't many of them, as there are in a regiment, and there are no riff-raff; and you aren't alone, but with people whom you can get to know thoroughly and make good friends with. It's both agreeable and good for you. Do you play chess? I can't imagine such a life without chess, books and hunting. If there was a war on as well, it would be absolutely fine. I'm very happy, but when one imagines your life, it seems that happiness proper consists in being 19, riding on horseback past an artillery platoon, lighting a cigarette, fumbling with a linstock which some Zakharchenko[4] or other at No.4 hands to you, and thinking: if only everyone knew what a brave fellow I am! Goodbye, my dear. Please write more often.

121. To M. N. KATKOV

Yasnaya Polyana, 28–9 October 1864

I'm sending you, dear Mikhail Nikiforovich, a translation of Karl Vogt's article on bees[1] which was done on my advice. The article in the original is ruined by political illusions. The translation retains only the unusually vivid exposition of the natural history of the bee, remarkable both from an artistic and a scientific point of view. I've become an ardent bee-keeper, and so I can judge. If you should wish to publish this article, send the fee you pay to the translator, care of me. The person who adapted the article[2] would like to have some work—translations and adaptations from French, German or English. If you could give her some work, you would very much oblige me and acquire an educated and *conscientious* translator. In a few days' time I shall finish the first part of a novel about the period of the first wars between Napoleon and Alexander,[3] and I am in doubt where and how to publish it. Of all the journals, I would most like to publish it in *The Russian Herald*, because it is the one journal which I take and read. The point is that I want to get as much money as possible for this work which I'm particularly fond of and which has cost me a great effort. I want to get 300 roubles a printer's sheet for publishing it in

---

3. S. A. Tolstaya's father A. Y. Behrs.
4. In *War and Peace* Tolstoy gave the name 'Zakharchenko' to Captain Tushin's sergeant-major.

[121] 1. Karl Christoph Vogt (1817–95), a German naturalist. The article sent by Tolstoy was a translation of a chapter, entitled 'Bienenstaat', from Vogt's book *Altes und neues aus Thier- und Menschenleben*.
2. Tolstoy's sister-in-law, Y. A. Behrs. The article was not published.
3. The novel *1805*, which ultimately became the first part of *War and Peace*.

121. To M. N. Katkov

a journal (you are the first person, and probably the last, to whom I am making this offer), otherwise I shall publish it in separate volumes. Please send me a few words in reply, both about the fate of Vogt's translation, and about this proposal of mine, and don't hesitate to give me a straight refusal, since your refusal or consent obviously depend on financial considerations, and not on taste or personal sympathies.[4] When out hunting I damaged and dislocated my right arm, so much so that this is the first time for 5 weeks that I've written at such length with it.

Yours very truly and respectfully,
Count L. Tolstoy

P.S. There should be about 10 printer's sheets in the first part which I intend to publish this winter.

122. To COUNTESS S. A. TOLSTAYA

Moscow,[1] 27 November 1864

For the first time yesterday I didn't manage to write to you the same evening, and I'm writing now in the morning, when everyone is still asleep, in order to catch the post before 9.00. Please send Kondraty or Seryozha[2] to Tula every day. I didn't manage to write yesterday because I was engrossed in reading *Roslavlev*.[3] You can understand how necessary and interesting it is for me. I didn't go out anywhere yesterday, as I was expecting Foss, the man from the gymnasium, and I tried writing, but there was no place to write, people kept interrupting, and besides I wasn't in the mood, I suppose. It's sad, quite sad in the Kremlin. Andrey Yevstafyevich talks about nothing but the illness he imagines he has in his intestines. Liza sits there quietly and gets on with her own affairs, but Tanya cries day after day, as she did yesterday morning. You can't get her to tell you what about, whether it's the same old thing[4] or the fact that she's bored. It's true, 2 or 3 years ago there was your whole world, yours and hers, with various amours and ribbons, and with all the poetry and folly of youth; but now she has suddenly come back home after our world which was so attractive to her and after all the commotion—i.e. the feelings she experienced—and she can no longer find the world she shared with you, but is left with the virtuous, but dull Liza, and is confronted at close quarters with her parents who have become difficult as a result of illness. We've

---

4. Eventually Tolstoy's conditions were met, and the sum of 300 roubles a printer's sheet was agreed.

[122] 1. Tolstoy was in Moscow from 21 November to 12 December in order to have his arm reset following his riding accident. He lived with the Behrs family.

2. Kondraty was the coachman at Yasnaya Polyana; Seryozha was an errand boy employed by Tolstoy.

3. A historical novel by M. N. Zagoskin (1789–1852) dealing with the year 1812.

4. T. A. Behrs' unhappy relationship with S. N. Tolstoy.

booked for skating, we've made a lambskin hat, we've booked for a concert—but it's not enough for her.

Besides that, she was crying her heart out yesterday because she had apparently learned from Alexey that Seryozha was going to marry Masha. I had a talk with her, but talking was sad and wearisome. Then Lyubimov came from Katkov's. He's in charge of *The Russian Herald*. You should have heard how he bargained with me, for 2 hours, I should think, over 50 roubles a printer's sheet, and though foaming at the mouth, smiled his professorial smile withal. I stood firm, and am expecting his answer today. He's very keen, and will probably agree to 300 roubles, while I, I must admit, am afraid to publish on my own, afraid of the bother with the printers and especially with the censorship. After he had gone I walked round to Foss's. Unfortunately, now that I want to begin, he's away for a couple of days. During dinner the bell rang—it was the papers. Tanya ran to fetch them, and the bell rang again—it was your letter. They all asked me if they could read it, but I grudged giving it to them. It's too good, and they wouldn't and couldn't understand it. But on me it had the same effect as good music—it was gay and sad and pleasant, and I wanted to cry. What a clever woman you are, telling me not to give the novel to anyone to read; but even if it wasn't clever, I would have done so because you wanted me to. Your parents have had no tiffs over the corned beef etc. and Tanya cheered up after dinner (youth will assert itself), and it was nice and pleasant. Petya, Volodya[5] and I went off together to the baths, and Tanya and mama to Kuznetsky Bridge. After the baths I was given *Roslavlev*, and over a cup of tea I went on reading with a delight which no one but an author can understand, as I listened and talked, and listened to Tanya singing. Andrey Yevstafyevich made cocoa and kept stubbornly urging me to drink it. Goodbye. My arm aches, but I'm hopeful about it. I've rubbed it with iodine, and I'll track down Foss today at all costs. Goodbye, dear; write to me, and send someone to Tula every day.

Oh yes, think about this and try to explain it. The day before yesterday Sasha Kupferschmidt and I talked for a couple of hours about hunting, and yesterday I went round to nanny's and talked to her about the children and various odd things, and would you believe it?—these two conversations were more pleasant than any I've had during my stay in Moscow, including those with Lyubimov, Sukhotin[6] and Tyutcheva.[7] The more I come into contact now with people as an adult, the more convinced I am that I'm an altogether special person, and that I differ from others simply because I don't have the vanity and childishness which I used to have, and which very few people grow out of.

5. S. A. Tolstaya's brothers.
6. S. M. Sukhotin, a civil servant and an acquaintance of Tolstoy, who was married to the sister of Tolstoy's friend, Dyakov. Sukhotin and his wife were divorced in 1868, and the history of this divorce gave Tolstoy some material for his novel *Anna Karenina*. Sukhotin was, in some respects, the prototype of Karenin.
7. Y. F. Tyutcheva, the third daughter of the poet. In 1858 it had been rumoured in literary circles that Tolstoy was intending to marry her. See Letter 89.

123. To P. I. BARTENEV

Pyotr Ivanovich Bartenev (1829–1912), an eminent historian, and founder of the journal *Russian Archives*, which he edited from 1863 until his death. He was head of the Chertkov Library where Tolstoy worked in November and December 1864. He supplied Tolstoy with numerous materials necessary for his work on *War and Peace*, and assisted with the proof-reading of the novel.

Moscow, 7 December 1864

Pyotr Ivanovich,

I've been to Uvarov's.[1] He's in Petersburg. I'm quite sure he won't refuse me his consent to read the letters you spoke about. Can you give them to me to look through if I don't take them away from your flat? If you can, fix a time when I can come round and work on them. I'm pestering you like this because I have to go away at the end of the week. They haven't had time yet to dig *Yasnaya Polyana* out of the storeroom where it's lying in piles, but it will be brought round to you tomorrow. Please send me *Russian Archives*[2] and de Maistre.[3]

Truly respectfully and gratefully yours,
Count L. Tolstoy

How many parts are there altogether of *The Gallery of the Winter Palace*?[4]

124. To COUNTESS S. A. TOLSTAYA

Moscow, 7 December 1864

I got your good letter yesterday, my dear. For the 4th day running the postman has rung regularly during dinner and brought your letters.

Remember, darling, that I count on you to let me know at once if Seryozha isn't well. He evidently has catarrh of the stomach. The remedies for it are hygiene, warmth and easily digestible food—milk and soup—and Andrey Yevstafyevich strongly advises calves' feet and sago. I'll bring some sago for you. I wrote to you yesterday about my plans, my arm and my boredom here. It's all exactly the same

---

[123] 1. A. S. Uvarov (1828–84), President of the Moscow Archaeological Society. Tolstoy wished to get Uvarov's permission to have access to the letters of F. P. Uvarov, a general during the campaign of 1812.

2. A variety of materials relating to the campaign of 1812 were published in this journal in 1864.

3. Joseph de Maistre (1754–1821), French historical and political writer, and the representative of the King of Sardinia at the Court of Alexander I for many years. Tolstoy was particularly interested in de Maistre's *Correspondance diplomatique* and *Les soirées de Saint-Petersbourg ou Entretiens sur le gouvernement temporel de la Providence*. De Maistre himself appears in *War and Peace*, and Tolstoy made extensive use of his letters, aphorisms and historical ideas.

4. A. I. Mikhaylovsky-Danilevsky's *The Emperor Alexander I and his Associates in 1812, 1813, 1814 and 1815. The Military Gallery of the Winter Palace*, published in 1845–9 in five volumes.

124. To Countess S. A. Tolstaya

today. I expect to be with you on Sunday; I make Alexey[1] move my arm a couple of times a day and I wear a bandage which makes it much easier for me. I can't get down to any work. Yesterday morning I read an English novel by the author of *Aurora Floyd*.[2] I've bought 10 instalments of those English novels I haven't yet read, and I dream of reading them with you. You and Liza ought to study English. Then that awful Alexander Mikhaylovich[3] came again, then Katerina Yegorovna, and Liza. I couldn't even read, there wasn't a corner to sit. I went for a walk before dinner, but I couldn't do anything in the libraries or in the shops because it was Sunday. After dinner it was *'I have squandered my youth'*[4] again, and at 7 o'clock *'A Life for the Tsar'*.[5] Very good, but monotonous. There was only the Sunday public at the theatre and so I was deprived of half the interest of watching. But when we came back we were on our own: Lyubov Alexandrovna,[6] who was very very sweet and nice, Liza, Tanya and Petya, and for some reason everything was very jolly. We reminisced and argued. Tanya assured us that the only thing she wanted was to live very high up in a tower with a guitar. Lyubov Alexandrovna contended that even in a tower you have to eat and go to the lavatory, and Tanya burst out crying in a nervous but hilarious manner, as she did that time over the priest's daughter, and we went off to bed. Apart from that, Petya slept and talked nonsense, and I told them how I had to confess, despite my wife's jealous nature, to disgraceful behaviour with Annochka,[7] in order to clear my conscience. As I was taking off my jacket, I swung my arm just as she was walking past, and I caught her right on the chest. I can see you putting on that familiar squeamish expression... Oh, Sonya, won't these 5 days hurry up and pass. To clear my conscience I want to show my tender arm to Nechayev.[8] I haven't received an answer or the manuscript from Katkov and Lyubimov, and I'm annoyed, but at the same time I don't want to go to Katkov's. There's practically nothing of any use to me in the archives. Today I shall go to the Chertkov and Rumyantsev libraries. I've felt loathsome and bored, especially these last two days. You tell me to go out. I don't want to go anywhere. My only thought is not to forget to do what I need to do. But if I have to choose between two empty occupations—contriving to talk about what is clever and affected or loafing about the Kremlin rooms with nothing to do, the latter is always preferable, especially in the absence of Alexander Mikhaylovich, who has become so loathsome to me—I could tell you why—that I can't look at him impassively, and I deliberately treated him so coldly in the end that he won't call to see us. He left yesterday at 5 o'clock. All the black people in your family are nice and sympathetic. Lyubov Alexandrovna is awfully like you. The other day she was

[124] 1. Tolstoy's valet, A. S. Orekhov.
    2. Mary Elizabeth Braddon (Mrs Maxwell) (1837–1915). Tolstoy had two of her novels in his library—*Lady Audley's Secret* and *John Marchmont's Legacy*.
    3. A. M. Islenyev, S. A. Tolstaya's grandfather.
    4. A romance.
    5. An opera by Glinka, now known in the Soviet Union as *Ivan Susanin*.
    6. S. A. Tolstaya's mother, the daughter of A. M. Islenyev.
    7. S. A. Tolstaya herself wrote an explanatory note on the letter: 'My sisters' aged maid'.
    8. An eminent Moscow surgeon.

124. To Countess S. A. Tolstaya

making a lampshade, just like you—once you set to work, nothing will distract you. Even your bad features are identical. I sometimes hear her confidently starting to say something she doesn't know and to make positive assertions and to exaggerate, and then I recognise you. But you are dear to me whatever you are like. I'm writing in the study, and in front of me are pictures of you at 4 different ages. Sonya, my darling. What a clever woman you are in everything you want to think about. For *that* reason I say that you are indifferent to intellectual interests, but so far from being narrow-minded, you are intelligent, very intelligent. And the same is true of all you black Behrs who are especially sympathetic to me. There are black Behrs: Lyubov Alexandrovna, you and Tanya; and white Behrs: all the others. The mind of the black Behrs is asleep; they can, but they don't want to; hence their self-confidence, sometimes inopportune, and their tact. But their mind is asleep because they love passionately, and because, moreover, the mother of the black Behrs, i.e. Lyubov Alexandrovna, was intellectually immature. The white Behrs show a great concern for intellectual interests, but their mind is feeble and shallow. Sasha is motley coloured, half-white. Slavochka is like you and I love him. I don't altogether like his upbringing with its entertainments and over-indulgence, but he'll probably turn out a splendid fellow. Only Styopa, I'm afraid, will cause us all a lot more sorrow. He's bad in himself for some reason, and his upbringing is still worse. Yesterday, on account of an argument about a tutor in which Tanya, Petya, and Volodya took part and attacked the tutor, Lyubov Alexandrovna decided to send all of them except Petya to school. And I said: splendid; at least your conscience will be at rest. It's true, though, that their father is away. I said: if I die, I'll leave a legacy to Sonya so that she can send Seryozha away to school. But I didn't say why you're a clever woman. As a good wife, you think about your husband as you do about yourself, and I remember your saying to me that all the military and historical side over which I'm taking such pains will turn out badly, but the rest—the family life, the characters, the psychology—will be good.[9] That couldn't be more true. I remember how you said that to me, and I remember you just like that. And like Tanya, I feel like crying out: mama, I want to go to Yasnaya, I want Sonya. I started writing to you in low spirits, but I'm finishing as quite a different person. My dear heart. Only love me as I love you, and nothing else counts for me, and everything is fine. Goodbye; it's time to get on with my work.

125. To M. N. KATKOV

Yasnaya Polyana, 3 January 1865

Dear Mikhail Nikiforovich,

I am sending you the remaining part of the manuscript which I brought to you that time in Moscow[1] and which you still have. What you now have, including

---

9. *1805* (*War and Peace*).

[125] 1. When in Moscow, Tolstoy had given to Katkov thirty-eight chapters of the novel *1805*. He enclosed the remaining chapters of the first part with this letter.

126. To Countess A. A. Tolstaya

what is now being sent, comprises the first part, in my opinion, and it would gain, I think, if it were published in a single issue.

The second part contains a description of the battles of Schöngraben and Austerlitz, and will, I think, be the same length as the first. I have it written, and it will be ready by the end of this month (if nothing untoward happens to me). I would like to, and would find it better—not for me personally, but in order to display the work to better effect—to publish all the first part in the January issue and all the second part in the February one.[2] But of course you have your own considerations, and if you find it better to divide the first part, it can't be helped. But in that case, write and tell me whether you wish to have the 2nd part this year, i.e. this winter. It would be a nuisance for me to leave it until next autumn, since I can't hold on to what I have written without correcting and revising it endlessly. Please tell me, if you wish to publish the second part, what months will it be? If it's March and April, that would be very convenient for me.

The manuscript is full of crossings out, and I do apologise, but as long as it's in my hands I revise it so much that it can't look any different.

I have translated the French letters,[3] and in my opinion the translation need not be printed, but the French text must be printed. I couldn't write the introduction the way I wanted, however much I tried. The gist of what I wanted to say is that the work is not a novel and is not a story, and cannot have the sort of plot whose interest ends with the dénouement. I am writing this in order to ask you *not to call my work a novel* in the table of contents, or perhaps in the advertisement either. This is very important to me, and I particularly request it of you.[4] If possible, send the proofs to me. They can be returned in a fortnight.

And now goodbye; I press your hand and wish you success in the cause which is nearest of all to your heart.

Yours truly and respectfully,
Count L. Tolstoy

126. To COUNTESS A. A. TOLSTAYA

Yasnaya Polyana 18–23 January 1865

My dear Alexandrine,

A lot of water has flowed under the bridge since we last saw each other and wrote to each other—very good and happy water for me, and I'm swimming in it now—but I still need to know, as before, that you sometimes remember me and love me, as I do you. You aren't really angry with me, are you? All inclination to write vanishes at the thought. And the thought does occur to me because you told old Islenyev that I'd written to you to say that I'd apparently ceased to love you.

---

2. The first part of the novel was published in *The Russian Herald*, Nos. 1 and 2. Tolstoy only completed the second part of the work in the autumn.
3. The letters of Julie Karagina and Marya Bolkonskaya. Only the French text of the letters was published initially. In succeeding publications the translation was also given.
4. Katkov ignored this request.

126. To Countess A. A. Tolstaya

Why did you say that? And why to that old man? I don't like him. What are your people doing? And what are you doing? Are you still the same as you used to be in the old days in Switzerland, when—do you remember?—on account of the fine weather, we loved everyone so much and found them such good people, from Stroganov[1] to Ketterer?[2] Even now I sometimes have fine Swiss weather at Yasnaya Polyana, in the nursery and in my study; do you have it too? Do you remember I once wrote to you that people are mistaken if they expect the kind of happiness where there are no labours, no deceptions, no sorrow, but where all goes smoothly and happily. I was mistaken myself then. There is such a happiness, and I've been living with it for over 2 years now. And each day it becomes smoother and deeper. And the materials that make up this happiness are of the very plainest: the children who (excuse me) soil themselves and scream, my wife who nurses one child and leads the other along and reproaches me every minute for not seeing that they are both on the edge of the grave, and paper and ink, by means of which I describe events and the feelings of people who have never existed. In a day or two the first half of my novel *1805* is coming out. Tell me your frank opinion. I should like you to love these children of mine. There are marvellous people in it. I love them very much. Life's been particularly good to us this winter. Back in the summer my sister arrived with her two little girls, one aged 15, the other 13. They spend the greater part of their time with us. How charming little girls are at that age, both good and pretty, like ours. Boys are necessary, things are expected of them, and for that reason they are nasty, but little girls (feeding them is like throwing money out of the window, as the peasant said) are not at all necessary, particularly up to the age of 15. For that reason, they are pure poetry. I think I love my *dimpled*[3] Tanichka for that reason too. However, I'm not praising my nieces because I'm having a spell of fine Swiss weather, but because they are charming: what love they have for the little children, what interest in everything good! Their diaries are a chef d'oeuvre. There's no sense in mine as yet. Seryozha has only just started walking by himself, and only now am I beginning to understand and take an interest in that game of life, which hitherto has been invisible to my coarse male eyes. How are your Magdalens? I've changed terribly since I got married, and much of what I didn't acknowledge before has become intelligible to me; and vice versa. Goodbye.

I meant to write and forgot: a few days ago we received news of the death of my sister's husband, Valeryan. He died alone, somewhere in Lipetsk. It's terribly pathetic. The worst thing about death is the fact that when a man is dead it's impossible any longer to undo the harm you have done him, or to do the good you haven't done him. They say: live in such a way as to be always ready to die. I would say: live in such a way that anyone can die without you having anything to regret.

[126] 1. Count G. A. Stroganov, a court equerry.
2. Tolstoy's former landlord at Clarens, in Switzerland.
3. In English in the original.

127. To A. A. FET

Yasnaya Polyana, 23 January 1865

You ought to be ashamed, my dear Fet, to treat me as though you didn't love me, or as though we are all going to live to be as old as Methuselah. Why don't you ever come to see me? Why don't you come and spend two or three days and have a quiet time? That's the proper way to behave towards other people. Perhaps if we don't see each other at Yasnaya, we'll meet somewhere on the Novinsky Boulevard? No, you won't see me on the Novinsky. I'm lucky enough to be fettered by chains of rich liquid green and yellow children's s... to Yasnaya Polyana. But you're a free man. And look out, one of us will die, as Valeryan Petrovich, my sister's husband, died the other day, and then you'll say: 'what a fool I was to fuss all the time about the mill, and not go to see Tolstoy. We could have had a talk together.' Really, it's no laughing matter. You were writing 'And the gun misfired', and have probably finished it by now.[1] I terribly want to read it, but I'm terribly afraid that you have disregarded much that is *significant*, and been attracted to much that is insignificant. I'm very interested.

You know, I have a surprise to tell you about myself. When I came to after a horse had thrown me to the ground and broken my arm, I said to myself: 'I'm a writer.' And I am a writer, but a solitary one, a writer on the quiet. In a few days the first half of the first part of *1805* will be out. Please write and tell me your opinion in detail. I value your opinion and that of a man whom I dislike all the more, the older I get—Turgenev. He *will understand*.[2]

What I have published in the past I consider a mere trial of the pen, a rough draft;[3] what I am publishing now, although I like it more than my previous work, still seems weak—as an introduction is bound to be. But what's to follow will be—tremendous!!! Write and tell me what they say about it in the various places you know, and particularly its effect on the masses. Probably it will pass unnoticed. I expect it to, and want it to, as long as they don't abuse me, for abuse upsets the passage of this long sausage which for us who are not lyric poets is so hard and tough. Goodbye. Come and stay with us. We all love you with all our hearts. My regards to Marya Petrovna.

I'm very glad that you love my wife; although I love her less than my novel, still, you know, she is my wife. Someone's coming. Who is it? My wife!

Do come and see me. If you don't call in from Moscow with Marya Petrovna, it really will be very stupid, no joking.

[127] 1. Fet was continuing work on his essays *From the Country*.
2. The Russian word *poymyot'* has an unusual soft sign ending: an allusion, perhaps, to a speech mannerism of Turgenev's. At first Turgenev was critical of *1805* (he called it 'poor, tedious and unsuccessful'), but when the whole novel was eventually published in book form, he responded to it very favourably.
3. I have chosen the more likely of two alternative readings.

128. To PRINCESS L. I. VOLKONSKAYA

Princess Louisa Ivanovna Volkonskaya (1825–90), the wife of Tolstoy's second cousin, Prince A. A. Volkonsky. Tolstoy portrayed her as the heroine of his story *A History of Yesterday*, written in 1851, and she was largely the prototype for the character of the 'little princess', Liza Bolkonskaya, in *War and Peace*.

Yasnaya Polyana, 3 May 1865

I am very glad, dear princess, of the occasion which made you think of me, and as proof of it I hasten to do the impossible for you—i.e. answer your question. Andrey Bolkonsky is nobody, like any character by a novelist, as opposed to a writer of personalities or memoirs. I would be ashamed to be published if all my work consisted of copying a portrait, trying to find things out, and memorising things. Mr Akhsharumov[1] comme un homme de métier and a man of talent ought to know that. But as I said, as proof of the fact that I want to do the impossible for you, I will try to tell you what sort of a man my Andrey is.

I needed a brilliant young man to be killed at the battle of Austerlitz, which will be described later,[2] but with which I began my novel. In the further course of the novel I only needed the old Bolkonsky and his daughter, but since it was awkward to describe a character not connected with the novel in any way, I decided to make this brilliant young man the son of the old Bolkonsky. Then he began to interest me; I imagined a part for him to play in the further course of the novel and I took pity on him, merely wounding him seriously instead of killing him. So there you have, dear princess, a completely truthful, although for that very reason unclear, explanation of who Bolkonsky is. But he is all the more agreeable to me now for providing me with the occasion for writing to you and reminding you of myself and my unwavering friendship for you and your family. I am very sorry that you have not told me much about your former *pindigashki*.[3] They are sweet and dear to me, both because of family ties which I value more and more as I get older, and because they remind me of poor Sasha[4] and yourself.

Please encourage them to look on me as a friend and relation. I kiss your hand and wish you all the very best.

Yours,
Count L. Tolstoy

[128] 1. A novelist and critic, he was one of the first writers to comment on *1805*. Of the character of Prince Andrey he wrote: 'This character is not invented...it's a truly Russian, a fundamentally Russian native type.'

2. The Battle of Austerlitz and the wounding of Andrey Bolkonsky were described in the closing chapters of *1805*. Tolstoy completed these chapters in November 1865.

3. Her children.

4. Her husband, who died the previous month.

129. To A. A. FET

Yasnaya Polyana, 16 May 1865

Forgive me, my dear Afanasy Afanasyevich, for not replying to you for so long. I don't know how it happened. It's true that one of the children has been ill recently, and I myself narrowly escaped a heavy fever and spent 3 days in bed. We're all well now, in very good spirits in fact. Tanya is with us and my sister and her children, and our own children are well and out of doors all day. I'm still writing on and off, and am pleased with my work. The woodcock still attract me, and every evening I shoot *at them*, i.e. generally past them. My farming is going well, i.e. it doesn't worry me much—which is all I demand of it. So much for myself. Your question whether to mention the Yasnaya Polyana school I must answer in the negative. Although your arguments are just, people have nevertheless forgotten about it (the *Yasnaya Polyana* journal), and I don't want to remind them about it, not because I've repudiated what I expressed in it, but on the contrary because I never cease to think about it; and, if I live long enough, I still hope to write some books on the basis of it all with the conclusions which emerged for me from my 3 years' ardent dedication to the cause.[1] I didn't fully understand what you wanted to say in the article you are writing; all the more interesting to hear it from you when we meet. Our affairs as landowners are like the affairs of a shareholder who owns shares which have lost their value and are not in demand on the stock market. It's a very bad business. For myself I'm simply determined that it shouldn't require from me so much attention and involvement as to deprive me of my peace of mind. I've been satisfied with my own affairs recently, but the general trend of affairs, i.e. the impending national famine disaster, worries me more and more each day.[2] It's so strange, and terrible, yet good too. We have pink radishes on our table, yellow butter, and soft, well-baked bread on a clean table-cloth; the garden is green and our young ladies in muslin dresses are glad it is hot and shady; but elsewhere the evil devil famine is already at work, covering the fields with goose-foot, causing cracks to appear in the dried-up earth, chafing the calloused heels of the peasants and their women, cracking the hooves of the cattle and penetrating everywhere and causing such havoc to everyone that even our people under their shady lime trees in their muslin dresses and with their yellow creamy butter on a painted dish will feel the effects, I think. Our weather and the corn and the fields are really terrible.

How are things with you? Write as truly and fully as possible. If Botkin is with you, press his hand for me. Why hasn't he been to see me? In a few days I'm going to Nikolskoye on my own without the family and so I shan't be visiting you for a long time, but it would be splendid if fate were to take you to Borisov's just now.

Regards to Marya Petrovna from my wife and me. In June we intend to move to Nikolskoye with the whole family—we shall see each other then, and I shall visit you for sure.

[129] 1. In the early 1870s Tolstoy wrote and published his *Primer* (1872), an article *On Public Education* (1874) and *A New Primer* (1875).
2. In 1865 there was a disastrous crop failure in the Province of Tula.

129. To A. A. Fet

What an evil fate has befallen you! From your talks I always realised that there was only one aspect of farming which you liked very much and which gave you pleasure, namely stud farming, and this is precisely where the trouble has descended. You'll have to reharness your carriage and transfer your Yufanising from the shafts to the outrunner; your thought and art have long since moved over to the shaft-horse. I've changed horses and have begun to travel far more peacefully.

130. To P. D. BOBORYKIN

Pyotr Dmitriyevich Boborykin (1836–1921), author of more than a hundred novels, plays, stories and critical studies from the 1860s onwards. His autobiographical novel, *Setting Forth*, published in 1862–4, brought him a renown which was reinforced by his untiring literary and journalistic work over the next three decades. He was for some time considered 'the doyen of Russian letters'. From 1863 to 1865, Boborykin was publisher and editor of the journal the *Reader's Library*. In 1871 he was sent to Paris after the fall of the Commune by Nekrasov as a correspondent for *Notes of the Fatherland*. In the early 1890s he emigrated to Western Europe, where he was to remain until his death in Switzerland several years after the Bolshevik Revolution.

Boborykin's major work of literary criticism is *The European Novel in the Nineteenth Century*, and his best-known novel is probably *Chinatown* (1882).

Tolstoy met Boborykin for the first time in the early 1880s in Moscow; they saw each other on only three occasions in all. Boborykin described these meetings in an article *At Tolstoy's House in Moscow*. Tolstoy supported his candidature for election to the Academy of Sciences in 1900.

[Not sent]   Nikolskoye-Vyazemskoye, July–August 1865

Dear Pyotr Dmitriyevich,

I never answered your last letter.[1] Excuse me. But thanks to your kindness in sending me the *Reader's Library* which I did not deserve, since I am so occupied simply with my own writing that I can hardly write anything else—thanks to your sending the *Reader's Library* I got your letter to the public, *The Forces of the Zemstvo*,[2] to which I very much want to reply. I used to live in the world in which you now live, and I know the pernicious influence under which your remarkable artistic talent is perishing. Having read both your novels,[3] especially the two parts

[130] 1. Two years previously Boborykin had twice written to Tolstoy, asking him to contribute to the journal *Reader's Library*; only the second of these letters has survived. Nothing is known of the letter that Tolstoy is replying to here, and his own letter can only be approximately dated by the date of publication of the issue of *Reader's Library* (18 June 1865) sent by Boborykin.

2. Tolstoy frequently referred to his own works and the works of other writers as 'letters to the public' or quite simply 'letters'. The work in question is in fact a novel.

3. *Setting Forth*, published in *Reader's Library* in 1862, 1863 and 1864, and *The Forces of the Zemstvo*, published in the same journal in 1865, Nos. 1–8.

of the last one, I feel that I have come to like your talent very much. I say this so that you might forgive me the reproaches which I consider myself entitled to make on the basis of that feeling. I am not writing in order to declare my sympathy for you, nor in order to make friends with you—though both things would be very desirable—but I have the naive conviction that my remarks may perhaps have some influence and rid you of the pernicious Petersburg literary excrescences which have affected your talent:

1. You write too carelessly and hurriedly; you do not discard enough of what you have written (there are prolixities), and you do not make sufficient use of that device which constitutes the whole wisdom of art for the epic prose writer—you do not sift the sand sufficiently to separate out the pure gold.

2. Your language is careless, but with all your refined taste which can be felt throughout, you have adopted the ugly mannerism recently introduced, I don't know by whom, of saying: ' "Hello", he greeted him', and you use trivial, albeit pointed expressions which do not offend in Pisemsky,[4] but do in you.

3. And this is the main thing. Both your novels are written on contemporary themes. Problems of the zemstvo, literature and the emancipation of women etc. obtrude with you in a polemical manner, but these problems are not only not interesting in the world of art; they have no place there at all. Problems of the emancipation of women and of literary parties inevitably appear to you important in your literary Petersburg milieu, but all these problems splash about in a little puddle of dirty water which only seems like an ocean to those whom fate has set down in the middle of the puddle. The aims of art are incommensurate (as the mathematicians say) with social aims. The aim of an artist is not to solve a problem irrefutably, but to make people love life in all its countless inexhaustible manifestations. If I were to be told that I could write a novel whereby I might irrefutably establish what seemed to me the correct point of view on all social problems, I would not even devote two hours' work to such a novel; but if I were to be told that what I should write would be read in about 20 years' time by those who are now children, and that they would laugh and cry over it and love life, I would devote all my own life and all my energies to it.

It is a couple of weeks since I wrote this and I have not sent it to you, thinking that you might be offended by advice which I am in no way entitled to give.[5]

131. To COUNTESS A. A. TOLSTAYA

Yasnaya Polyana, 14 November 1865

Thank you very much, dear friend, for your last letter and your talk with Dolgoruky.

I've sent your letter, and the draft of the letter to Dolgoruky, to Mashenka. It seems to me that the case can be won. The people who have possession of the notes

---

4. The author of the novel *A Thousand Souls* (1858). Tolstoy generally thought very highly of his works. See Letter 165.   5. Despite this postscript Tolstoy did not send this letter.

131. To Countess A. A. Tolstaya

of hand are very timid, feeling guilty as they do. They'll give in at the first threatening remonstration. But Mashenka is much to be pitied, with her inability to conduct business matters, and her debt-encumbered estates.[1] Your soul will then have another nice good deed to its credit.

Your last letter was written in a hurry. I have no right to expect another; but all the same I'm afraid you're displeased with me about something. God willing, I'll be with you this winter, and talk to you and listen to you late into the night behind the screens in Liza's room[2] and in the morning in your room upstairs, with which I always connect one of my most precious memories—rather like this—energy, 107 steps, a lot to look forward to, friendship, 107 steps. So I can say that after seeing you, I know I shall be provided for a long time with renewed confidence, which will remove the fear of being unnecessary to others which I have with the majority of people—and even with you. This must be because I have little need of people. Write more to me about yourself; as it was, you always seemed rather incomprehensible to me—a stranger—but now I'm afraid you will seem even more so, and it will spoil our meeting, from which I expect so much joy. You can't say the same about me. I think I have always been comprehensible, and even more so now that I've entered the rut of family life which leads along the beaten track of moderation, duty, and moral tranquillity, in spite of all pride and the need for originality. And a good thing too! I have never been so keenly aware of myself and of my soul as now, when impulses and passions know their limit. I now know that I have a soul, and an immortal one (at least I often think I know it), and I know that there's a God. I'm telling you this because you used to be interested in my inner education.

I admit to you that formerly, a long time ago now, I didn't even believe in this. Recently, and more and more often, I've been seeing proof and confirmation of it in everything. And I'm glad of it. I'm not a Christian, and am still far from being one; but experience has taught me not to believe in the infallibility of my judgements and that anything can happen! Don't write or say anything to me about this. All knowledge comes to people by irrational paths. I teach Seryozha to say 'Tanya'; he can't, but says 'sponge', which is much more difficult.

Why do you say that I've quarrelled with Katkov? I didn't think so. Firstly because there was no reason for it, and secondly because there is as much in common between him and me as there is between you and your water-carrier. I don't sympathise with the fact that the Poles are forbidden to speak Polish, but I don't get angry about it, and I don't accuse the Muravyovs[3] and Cherkasskys,[4] and

---

[131] 1. On the death of Marya Tolstaya's estranged husband, V. P. Tolstoy, his estates were sequestrated. Before his death he had given a note of hand involving a considerable sum to a certain Likharyov, an arbiter of the peace, and left two letters in acknowledgement of debt to his mistress Goltseva. Furthermore, he had drawn up his will in favour of Goltseva and her illegitimate children. Marya Tolstaya was contesting this will. Her rights of inheritance were not legally established until 1872.

2. A. A. Tolstaya's sister.

3. Governor of Vilnius and an extreme reactionary, notorious for his harsh suppression of the Polish uprising.

4. A liberal landowner of Tula, and an acquaintance of Tolstoy. He served in Poland after the uprising.

131. To Countess A. A. Tolstaya

it's a matter of complete indifference to me who suppresses the Poles,[5] or captures Schleswig-Holstein, or delivers a speech at a zemstvo meeting.

Butchers kill the oxen we eat, but I'm not obliged to accuse them or sympathise with them.

Only the 3rd part of my novel is written, and I won't publish it until I've written a further 6 parts, and then—in about five years time—I'll publish the whole lot as a separate work.[6] The writer Ostrovsky whom I like very much once said a very wise thing to me. Two years ago I wrote a comedy[7] (which I didn't have published) and asked Ostrovsky what to do to have it staged in the Moscow Theatre before Lent. He said: 'What's the hurry? Better stage it next year.' I said: 'No, I'd like to do it now, because the comedy is very topical, and it won't have the same success next year.'

—'*Are you afraid that people will soon be much cleverer?*'

I've no fears like that about my novel. And to work without regard for an applauding or whistling public (shall I be alive myself, or will that audience be alive in 5 years' time?) is much more pleasant and the work more worthy of (dignité).[8]

It's now late autumn; the hunting which takes up a lot of my time has finished, and I'm writing a lot and thinking over in advance many of my future works which will probably never come to be written, and I'm doing all this with faith in myself and the conviction that I'm doing a serious job of work. That's the main thing. We writers have many tedious sides to our work, but to make up for it we have this volupté of thought (which is probably unknown to you)—of reading something, and understanding it with one side of the mind while thinking with the other, and conjuring up for ourselves in very general outlines whole poems, novels, and philosophical theories. I still think a lot about education, and am impatiently awaiting the time when I begin to teach my own children; I intend to open a new school then, and to write a résumé of everything that I know about education and that no one else knows, or that no one agrees with.

See with what touching naiveté and with what pleasure I write to you about myself. It's either egoism or confidence, or both. Take me as an example. You'll say: what do I want to know about you?—What I'd like to know about myself, and what I've just written—i.e. all my innermost thoughts and plans—what goes on inside me.

I'm writing this letter at Auntie's table. You would have been touched to see with what loving pleasure she gave me writing materials in order to write to you. She loves you very much, in a very special way. She loves all your family, but especially you. What a wonderful creature: but however many times I've spoken to you about her, I know I can't have given you a clear idea of her. There's nothing one can say—you have to know this simple and beautiful soul as I have these 35

5. Tolstoy's attitude towards the Polish rising altered considerably in later years.
6. *War and Peace* was published in book form in 1868–9.
7. *An Infected Family*, a satire on nihilism and feminism. The play was rejected by the Moscow Maly Theatre.
8. *Sic.*

131. To Countess A. A. Tolstaya

years. She was so ill this summer that we thought it was the end. Now she's better; but we have realised how precious she is to us. We wanted to go to Moscow before the holidays, but now it turns out we'll be going later. That's always the case with us when we decide to go somewhere. It's good where we are. If only it could always be like that! However, we'll still go, so that Sonya can see her family and show them the grandchildren. I understand what a pride and joy this must be. We'll leave the children with her parents, and come on to Petersburg for a few days, where I'll have the honour of introducing my wife to you, not without some trepidation and pride. If I weren't today in a mood of absolute sincerity (sometimes—always even—one wants to be sincere, but can't be), I'd tell you that she loves you, but now I'll (simply) say that she's prepared to love you, but feels a little perplexed about you; as she herself says, you interest her greatly, as no other woman has ever interested her, but at the same time, I'm sure, she feels in her soul—and only La Rochefoucauld would have noticed it—a feeling of slight hostility such as we always have towards people whom we don't know, and whom everyone, beginning with one's husband, praises beyond measure. She can't see with her husband's eyes, since a good wife sees everything with her husband's eyes except women.

What are all your people doing, and where are they?

Goodbye—till we meet again. Do you still have that terrible hall-porter whom I frightened at midnight?

Where's Alexey Tolstoy?[9] Give him my regards if he's in Petersburg.

132. To COUNTESS A. A. TOLSTAYA

Yasnaya Polyana, 26–7 November 1865

I've just received your nice, kind, bright letter and said to myself: I'll answer it tomorrow; but I can't restrain myself—all the thoughts prompted by your letter give me no peace, and I'm writing straightaway. The day before yesterday I was in Tula and saw Mr Longinov, and among other items of news he told me casually about Tyutcheva's marriage[1] and your appointment. Although he doesn't know you, I think, you'll be interested to know the expressions he used to tell me this: 'Anna Tyutcheva so bored them all that they were glad to get rid of her, and they were unable to find, i.e. it was impossible to find—anyone better than Tolstaya to take her place.' I was terribly struck by the news. For me it was a shot from a double-barrelled gun. Firstly the marriage (not marriage—it should be called something else, a new word should be found or invented), but for the moment—the marriage of A. Tyutcheva to Aksakov struck me as one of the strangest of psychological phenomena. I think if they have male offspring, it will

---

9. Count A. K. Tolstoy.

[132] 1. The poet's daughter. She was tutor to Alexander II's daughter, the Grand Duchess Marya. When she married I. S. Aksakov of the well-known Slavophile family, A. A. Tolstaya was appointed in her place.

132. To Countess A. A. Tolstaya

be a troparion or a kontakion,² and if the offspring is female, it will be a Russian idea, but perhaps the offspring will be neuter—a proclamation or the like.

How are they to be married? And where? In a monastery? In the Faceted Palace or in the Cathedral of St Sophia in Tsargrad?³ Before the wedding they will have to don the murmolka⁴ three times and, reaching out their hands to the works of Khomyakov,⁵ pronounce their vow in the Slavonic language before all the representatives of the Slavonic lands. No seriously, I find there is something unpleasant, unnatural and pathetic about this alliance. I like Aksakov. His vice and misfortune is pride—pride (as is always the case) founded on the renunciation of life, on intellectual speculation. But still he was alive. Last year, I remember, he came to see me and unexpectedly found us at the tea table with my belles-soeurs. He blushed. I was very glad about that. A man who blushes can love, and a man who can love can do anything. After this I had a long tête-à-tête with him. He was complaining about his awareness of the futility and emptiness of his work as a journalist.⁶ I said to him: 'Get married. No offence meant—experience has convinced me that an unmarried man remains a little boy till the end of his days. A new world opens up for the married man.' And now he's got married. And now I'm ready to run after him and shout: that's not what I meant, not what I meant at all. Flesh and blood are necessary for happiness and a moral life. One mind is good, but two are better, says the proverb; but I say: one soul in a crinoline is bad, but two, one in a crinoline and the other in trousers, are even worse. Wait and see what a frightful moral monstruosité comes of this marriage. I know you'll be angry with me for speaking like this of your predecessor whom you're trying to love now even more than before, but I couldn't help it. Ever since I heard the news I've thought about it several times a day—it's not a marriage, but a fusion of two—not souls, but trends⁷—and I can't calm down and talk to you about *you*, until I've told you everything. Forgive me if I've distressed you.

Sonya was astonished that you're so afraid of what's in store for you, but I didn't expect any different. It's frightening—I understand that very well. I used to educate my Yasnaya Polyana boys fearlessly. I knew that whatever I might be like myself, my influence was probably better for them than any they might be subjected to without me. But in your case I understand that the Empress wanted and was able to have just about the very best tutor in the whole world. And lo and behold this very best tutor is me—Alexandra Andreyevna Tolstaya! I understand that it's frightening, But there's nothing for you to be afraid of—in as much as I know you, and try to look at you in the most dispassionate way. And this is why, as it seems to me. Others know that you are an intelligent, educated and good

---

2. Slavonic service books. Tolstoy is alluding to the Slavophile Orthodoxy of both Tyutcheva and Aksakov.
3. The Faceted Palace in the Moscow Kremlin; Tsargrad—the Slavonic name for Constantinople.
4. A tall boyar hat—another allusion to the Slavophile nostalgia for pre-Petrine Russia.
5. A. S. Khomyakov (1804–60), a leading Slavophile writer and thinker.
6. A reference to his short-lived newspaper *The Day*.
7. The word often means political or religious beliefs.

woman; I know that in addition to all this, and contrary to your predecessor, you are not just a soul in a cage,[8] but are flesh and blood—you have had, do have, and will continue to have human passions. You will prepare yourself, you will reason and ponder, and you will pray, but you will act only on instinct, without hesitation, without choice, and because you will be incapable of acting in any other way. And such passionate, human influence has a beneficial, educational effect on human children, while rational, logical influence has a harmful effect. This conviction of mine is not the fruit of invention but of experience. Everyone, always and everywhere, has made and does make one mistake over education: they want to educate by reason, and by reason alone, as though a child possessed only reason. And they educate the reason alone, and everything else—i.e. everything essential—is left to get along as it likes. They think up a system of education by reason again, and want to conduct everything according to it, without taking into account that tutors are themselves people and incessantly recoil from reason. In the schools the teachers sit on a rostrum and *cannot* make mistakes. Tutors too stand in front of their pupils on the rostrum and try to be infallible.

But you can't deceive children—they are wiser than us. We want to prove to them that we're intelligent, but they aren't at all interested in this, but want to know whether we're honest, truthful, good, and compassionate, whether we have a conscience, and unfortunately they see that beyond our efforts to appear infallibly intelligent, there's nothing else at all.

To make a mistake in front of a child, to be carried away, to do something stupid, humanly stupid, even to behave badly and blush in front of a child and admit it, has far more educational value than to make a child blush 100 times in front of you, and to be infallible. A child knows that we are more resolute, more experienced than he is, and are always able to retain this halo of infallibility in front of him, but he knows that this doesn't require much, and he doesn't value such cleverness, but values the flush of shame appearing on my face against my will, telling him about all that is most secret and best in my soul. I remember how Karl Ivanych[9] once blushed in front of me. If, in fact, there could be a soul, or rather, reason in a crinoline, then all would have been well; but unhappily there was so much earthy clay (limon) in this soul that she married Aksakov. And children look on their tutor not as something rational, but as a person. The tutor is the first person very close to them on whom they make observations and draw conclusions which they then apply to all mankind. And the more this person is endowed with human passions, the richer and more fruitful these observations. And you are such a person. You possess that Tolstoyan wildness that's common to us all. Not for nothing did Fyodor Ivanovich[10] have himself tattooed. I expect your pupil will love you as all your friends love you, and then all will be well. Women have only one moral weapon in place of all our male arsenal—and that is love. And only with this

8. The French for 'crinoline'.
9. Tolstoy's former tutor (the Karl Ivanovich of *Childhood* and *Boyhood*).
10. F. I. Tolstoy, the 'American': an original and eccentric character, portrayed by Tolstoy in *Two Hussars*.

one weapon can women's education be conducted successfully. If you have it, you won't need to study, to think or to prepare yourself; if you haven't, then you'll resign from the post.

You're fond of my nonsense; here are four whole pages for you. Auntie and Sonya kiss you; I love you such a lot and wish you happiness and success. I don't even wish it—I rejoice in advance for your happiness in the knowledge of the real task—one of the best in life—to which you have devoted yourself entirely.

Goodbye. Till we meet again, God willing.

133. To M. S. BASHILOV

Mikhail Sergeyevich Bashilov (1821–70), an artist and sculptor, and a second cousin of S. A. Tolstaya. He acquired a reputation with his illustrations for Griboyedov's *The Misfortune of Being Clever* and for Saltykov-Shchedrin's *Provincial Sketches*. From 1855 to 1870 he was inspector at the College of Art, Sculpture and Architecture, and a cartoonist for *The Spectator* and other journals In 1866 he agreed to Tolstoy's request to provide illustrations for a separate edition of *War and Peace*. Originally Tolstoy hoped to have seventy such illustrations, but he became somewhat disillusioned with Bashilov both as an artist and as a man, and eventually wrote to him on 31 May 1867, asking him to stop work for the time being. Bashilov never resumed work on the illustrations. In all he provided twenty-one drawings for the first two parts of the first volume of the novel. Five of Tolstoy's letters to Bashilov have survived.

Yasnaya Polyana, 4 April 1866

I was just going to write and ask you about our affairs, dear Mikhail Sergeich, when I got your letter, and now, after due notice, the drawings.

1. *Anna Mikhaylovna asking Prince Vasily a favour on behalf of her son*[1] is splendid. She—and he—are charming. Can't Hélène be made fuller in the chest? (plastic beauty of form is her most characteristic feature). Generally speaking, I only want this drawing to be as good on wood as it is at present.

2. *The wager.*[2] Pierre is not good, but Anatole is excellent, and

3. *Pierre*—his face is good (only you need to add to his forehead something to suggest a greater disposition towards philosophising—a wrinkle or some bulges above the eyebrows), but his body is too small—it should be broader, larger and stouter.

4. *The soirée at the Scherers.*[3] The group is good, but Prince Andrey is too tall, and he should be more superciliously languid and gracefully supine.

5. The portrait of Prince Vasily is charming.

6. *Idem* the portrait of Princess Bolkonskaya. This portrait is exceptionally good. You can't imagine the pleasure it gave me. I don't know whether you need to make

[133] 1. Part 1, ch. 4.   2. Part 1, ch. 6.   3. Part 1, chs. 1–5.

133. To M. S. Bashilov

it smaller in dimension, but the limbs need to be more diminutive, i.e. her bras is too long; still, it's so good that it would be awful to touch it.

7. The portrait of Hippolyte, whom you mistakenly called Anatole, is excellent, but couldn't you make him more of an idiot, more of a caricature, by raising his upper lip and lifting his leg a bit higher?

I wonder if you can do a portrait of Pierre lying on a sofa reading a book, or pensively and absent-mindedly gazing into space over the top of his spectacles, his attention distracted from his book—leaning on one elbow, with his other arm thrust in between his legs? It would probably be even better than if he were standing up, but you know best.

I entirely approve the choice of scenes and portraits, except for Hippolyte (whom you mistakenly call Anatole), but you have done him so well that you ought to leave him.

In general I can't enthuse too much over our undertaking. For goodness sake don't put off your intention of exhibiting your drawings. As long as Richau[4] doesn't spoil them, they will be remarkable, masterly works. I'm writing by the same post to Andrey Yevstafyevich[5] about the money; I hope, however, that Richau has already received it. Oh yes, one more thing: Anatole is very good in the *wager* scene, but can't you make him bigger and also fuller-chested? He's going to play in future the important role of a handsome, sensuous and coarse stallion.

From what you have sent me, I see you are in the right mood for working. I was not mistaken either when I told you that I felt very pregnant. Since I left Moscow, I have finished a whole new part, equal in length to the one I read to you, i.e. I have finished what I intended to publish in autumn, but things have gone so well that I am going on writing, and I flatter myself with the hope that I shall write another 3 similar parts by autumn, i.e. finish the year 1812 and one whole section of the novel. If my dreams were to come true, I would ask you to do another 30 drawings. And I would publish a huge novel of 30 printer's sheets with 30 drawings in October, and 30 sheets and 30 drawings by the New Year. The one thing that makes me fear and tremble is that some circumstance or other might prevent you from finishing the job. May the god Phoebus help you and give you strength for your sake and the sake of your family, and for my sake.

My wife sends her regards to you and Marya Ivanovna[6] and so do I. Our children are well, and I hope and wish that yours are too.

Since we came back I have been doing a bust of my wife, but so far nothing has come of it.

Count L. Tolstoy

I have looked through all the drawings again and couldn't tear myself away from them. They are extraordinarily good, especially the portraits and the scene between Prince Vasily and Anna Mikhaylovna. I have reread my letter, and I'm afraid that

---

4. An engraver. He eventually refused to do the engraving of the illustrations.
5. Behrs.
6. Bashilov's wife.

you'll think that I'm making carping and irrelevant observations. Take no notice of them, but write and tell me whether observations of that sort might be any use to you or are merely a nuisance. In the first case I will boldly write whatever comes into my head. But in any case I will say that I expected a lot from you, but that what you have done has exceeded my expectations.

I'm writing to Andrey Yevstafyevich, who has my money, to ask him to pay it out at your request. If he hasn't give any to Richau yet, write him a note to do so.

I press your hand in friendship, and wish you all the very best.

134. To A. A. FET

Yasnaya Polyana, 10–20 May 1866

I'm very ashamed, my dear Afanasy Afanasich, that I haven't written to you for so long, and especially that I haven't replied to your last, wonderful letter. I particularly liked the uvula! It's so true, and that's just how I understand it.

Sonya thanks you for the poems, with blushes of pleasure.[1] The main reason why I haven't written is that I can't write simply; and not to write simply is disagreeable. The closer people are to one another (and you are one of the closest to my heart), the more disagreeable it is to write, the more one feels the discrepancy between the tone of a letter and the tone of one's actual relations. You already understand me, but for my own satisfaction I can't help giving an example.

To judge from his letters Borisov is a great big jolly fellow weighing 7 poods, a sanguine man ready to risk his last copeck.[2]

My real letters to you are my novel, of which I have written a great deal. As some Frenchman said: 'une composition est une lettre, qu'on écrit à tous ses amis inconnus.' Please write and tell me your opinion—frankly. I value your opinion very much, but as I told you, I've put in so much work, time and foolish author's effort (something you know), and I'm so fond of my writing, especially the part still to come—the year 1812—on which I'm working now, that I'm not afraid of the censure even of those whom I value; I'm actually glad of censure. For example, Turgenev's opinion that you can't take 10 pages to describe how NN placed her arm helped me very much, and I hope to avoid this fault in future. Please tell me as truthfully, i.e. as bluntly, as possible. What do you think of 4 April?[3] For me it was the coup de grâce. The last shred of respect and reticence on the part of the conscience of the crowd has vanished. It's all over the country; all Russia within earshot, with great solemnity and to the sound of bells, is doing stupid things with a sort of pride and joy, and what stupid things! Things which I would be ashamed of in my 3-year-old Seryozha. Osip Ivanovich Komissarov a member of various

[134] 1. Poems dedicated 'To the Countess S. A. Tolstaya' that Fet had forwarded with his letter.

2. Borisov was, in fact, a sickly man of small stature.

3. On 4 April 1866 a young man, D. V. Karakozov, fired on Alexander II as he was entering his carriage after a stroll in the Summer Garden. Although Karakozov was a member of a small group of communist students, he appears to have acted entirely on his own initiative.

134. To A. A. Fet

societies;[4] public prayers about them shooting at the Tsar; students at the Iverskaya Chapel—it's all a lot of stuff and nonsense.

And your friend Katkov is ruined.[5] And do you know what ruined him? The fact that he got angry: 'Il n'y a pas de bonne cause qui ne soit perdue dès qu'on se fâche.'

And this is particularly true in literature, even in the newspapers, not to speak of our newspapers. Pushkin knew how to be angry in a special way. But to be angry in a novel or a long article as you have sometimes attempted is no use.

How did you welcome the spring this year? It's the most delightful I ever remember. You've probably written a spring poem. Send it to me.[6]

When spring began, I read all your old letters to unknown friends about it in all its various phases a thousand times over. I, who don't remember poetry, read through several times 'the sun encircled...' and 'the pussy willow is all fluffy...' and 'the invisible efforts...'

You are reading Aristophanes. I understand that very well, and I am reading something of the same kind, only more recent—*Don Quixote*—and Goethe, and recently the whole of Victor Hugo. You know nobody talks about V. Hugo, and everyone has forgotten him for the very reason that he will always be with us all, unlike the Byrons and the Walter Scotts. Have you read his critical articles in his complete works? Everything that we were debating about art 10 years ago, and I suppose are still debating à tort et à travers, was said by him 30 years ago, and in such a way that not a word can be added or subtracted.

I'm pleased with my farming, very pleased with my family life and enormously pleased with my work (particularly before the blazing heat). I wish you the same and I'm sure you already have it, because you deserve it.

Do you know that during my recent stay in Moscow I began to study sculpture? I shan't be an artist, but this occupation has already afforded me much pleasure and edification.

I hope to finish my novel by 1867 and to publish it all as a separate work with pictures commissioned by me, and partly drawn by Bashilov (I'm very pleased with them), under the title *All's Well That Ends Well*.[7]

Please tell me your opinion about the title and the pictures.

Now the most important thing. I can't visit you this year. My wife is expecting a baby in June. But do please come and visit us, you and Marya Petrovna (Sonya and I both press her hand in friendship)—come and stay with us between the

---

4. O. I. Komissarov, a hatter by profession, who happened to be standing near the Tsar when the assassination attempt was made. Komissarov's shout and his involuntary movement when the shot rang out were subsequently claimed to have distracted the assassin's aim. He was proclaimed a hero, ennobled, and elected a member of several learned societies.

5. Following the assassination attempt, Katkov wrote a series of articles in his paper, *The Moscow Gazette*, calling for greater repression of the 'nihilists', and criticising the government for its liberalism, and its ineffectual action following the attempt. The paper was cautioned by the authorities for its outspokenness, and publication was suspended for two weeks.

6. Fet published a poem, *Spring*, in *The Russian Herald*, 1866, No. 6; it was dated '20 May'.

7. This is the only extant reference to this title. Tolstoy first called his novel *War and Peace* in March 1867.

beginning of July and September. You will probably be in Mtsensk then after all. And it's only 100 versts. Please.

Goodbye, dear friend.

135. To M. S. BASHILOV

Yasnaya Polyana, 4 June 1866

Dear Mikhail Sergeich,

When I first began writing *1805*, I discovered somewhere that powder had been done away with at the beginning of Alexander's reign, and I wrote on that basis; later I came across evidence, as you did, that it was still used in 1805. I didn't know what to do, and I made the same decision as in the well-known anecdote about the clerk and his superior who didn't know whether a comma was needed or not, and decided to put in a small one. I put in a *small one*, i.e. I avoided talking about uniform; but *you* can't get round it with a *small one*; you must make a decision.

Decide for yourself, whatever is most agreeable and convenient for you. In favour of drawing people wearing powder, is the reason that if there is positive proof that powder was in use in 1805, I can correct the new edition and allude to powder and uniform. In fact it's probably necessary to draw people wearing powder and in historically accurate uniform, to which I shall try to be faithful in the new edition.

I look forward to your drawings and the feeling of excitement which they produce in me; otherwise my work has come to a standstill this summer. How is your work—the picture—going? God grant you success and pleasure in your labours—that is the best form of happiness.

My wife gave birth to a son on 22 May.[1] She kisses your wife and children and sends you her regards.

You did well to take the money from Andrey Yevstafyevich. I now have some money to spare, and so am at your service.

Yours,
Count L. Tolstoy

136. To A. A. FET

Yasnaya Polyana, 7 November 1866

My dear Afanasy Afanasich,

I didn't answer your last letter of 100 years ago,[1] and I'm all the more to blame because I remember you wrote some very interesting things about my novel in it,

[135] 1. Tolstoy's second son, Ilya.

[136] 1. Fet had written on 16 July 1866 giving his opinion of Part 1 of *1805*. He wrote: 'I understand that the main task of the novel is to turn a historical event inside out and examine it, not in its official, gold-embroidered dress uniform, but in its shirt-sleeves...' He commented particularly on Tolstoy's apparent failure to develop the character of Prince Andrey.

136. To A. A. Fet

and you also wrote *irritabilis poetarum gens*.² Well, I'm not one. I remember on the contrary that I was very glad of your opinion about one of my heroes, Prince Andrey, and I derived some instruction from your criticism. He is tedious, monotonous, merely un homme comme il faut throughout the first part, it's true, but it's not his fault, it's mine. Apart from my conception of the characters and their movement, apart from my conception of the conflict of characters, I have another, historical, conception which complicates my work in an extraordinary way, and which I'm evidently not coping with. As a result I was concerned in the first part with the historical side, and the character stood still and didn't move. And this was a fault which I clearly understood as a result of your letter, and I hope I've corrected it. Please write and tell me, dear friend, all the bad things you think about me, i.e. about my writing. It's always a great help to me, and I have nobody except you. It's 4 months since I wrote to you and the danger is that you'll pass through Moscow without calling to see me, and yet you are the person I value more than all my other friends for your intelligence, not to mention anything else, and who alone provides me, through your personal contact, with that other sort of bread than *bread alone*, by which man lives. I'm writing to you chiefly in order to implore you to come and see us when you're 'going the family rounds'. It's a disgrace that we haven't seen each other for so long! My wife and I, with tears in our eyes, beg Marya Petrovna to come and see us. In a few days I'm going to Moscow for a short time on my own, i.e. with my sister-in-law, Tanya. I'm taking her to her parents, and I'm going myself to get the 2nd part of my novel published. What are you doing? I don't mean your zemstvo work or your farming—those are a man's involuntary activities. You and I do them as spontaneously and involuntarily as ants dig an anthill, and there is nothing either good or bad about activities of that sort; but what are you doing with your thoughts, your very own Fetish main-spring which was, is and will be unique in the world? Is the spring active? Is it on the point of release? How is it operating? It hasn't forgotten how to operate, has it? That's the important thing. Goodbye, dear friend; I embrace you and beg you on behalf of myself and my wife to give our cordial greetings to Marya Petrovna whom we hope to see at our house—this I do earnestly beg of you.

137. To M. S. BASHILOV

Yasnaya Polyana, 8 December 1866

Dear Mikhail Sergeyevich,

I got your letter and the drawings. The old prince is very good, especially where he is with his son.¹ That's exactly what I wanted, but I don't like Prince Andrey at all. He's too tall, his features are too big and coarse, his mouth has an unpleasant sour expression and his whole attitude and dress are not dignified enough. He should be listening to his father with a gentle and indulgent smile. Apropos of this picture, I've

2. A quotation from Horace.
[137] 1. Part 1, ch. 25.

137. To M. S. Bashilov

thought a lot about the previous ones and the ones to follow, and I hasten to pass on to you my ideas:

Can't you soften Count Rostov and Marya Dmitriyevna in the Daniel Cooper by reducing the caricature and adding a touch of tenderness and kindness?[2]

In the kiss[3] can't you model Natasha on Tanichka Behrs—there's a picture of her at 13—and make Boris not so raid?

Pierre needs to be given larger features.

From what you want to do in the 2nd part, I would only cut out Prince Andrey with Bilibin, replacing it by a picture of Bilibin by himself, cutting or filing his nails.[4]

In general, I would ask you to do these drawings and engrave them as quickly as possible, so that as soon as you have finished them I can send you the text for the next ones.

I'm now quite certain that the whole novel will be finished by next autumn, and you know that the sales success depends on it being out by the beginning of winter i.e. in November *au plus tard*.[5]

There should be at least twice as many drawings as there are now, including those which you intended for the 2nd part, i.e. a *minimum* of 65.

Can you and the engravers manage to get them done by November? Please write and tell me. This is a *conditio sine qua non*. I'm giving instructions for the money both for the engravers and yourself to be handed over to you by Andrey Yevstafyevich before Christmas. With regard to payment, may I ask you to give me credit of 10 roubles a drawing until the book comes out?

Is that possible? Write and tell me.

You would also need to come to definite terms with the engravers over what part of the payment they can wait for from me until the book comes out—a half or even a third. Would you be so kind as to answer all these questions.

Please send me your drawings in their roughest form; I feel I might be some use to you with my comments. After all, I know *them all* better than you, and sometimes an idle comment may give you an idea. And I will write down everything that occurs to me about your rough drawings, and you can choose what you need.

I feel ashamed to speak to you now about Natasha, when you've already done a charming drawing of her, but of course you can disregard my words. But I'm sure that you, as an artist, having seen a daguerrotype of Tanya when she was 12, then her picture in a white blouse when she was 16 and then her big portrait last year, won't fail to make use of this model and its stages of development which are so very close to those of my model.

Goodbye, dear Mikhail Sergeich; I anxiously await your reply. Kindest regards to Marya Ivanovna and a kiss for your children.

L. Tolstoy

2. Part I, ch. 17.   3. Part I, ch. 10.   4. Part II, chs. 10 and 11.
5. The novel was not completed until 1868/9.

138. To Y. F. SAMARIN

Yury Fyodorovich Samarin (1819–76), an eminent public figure, writer and leading Slavophile. He entered public service in 1840, serving in the Senate and later in the Ministry of Internal Affairs. In 1849, following his work as clerk to a committee set up to inquire into the administration of Riga, he published *Letters from Riga*, a work which earned him a short spell of imprisonment on a charge of divulging confidential information. In 1856 he began to contribute to the Slavophile journal *Russian Conversation*. In 1858 he was appointed to serve on the committee set up to improve the conditions of the peasantry in the Province of Samara, and took an active role in carrying out reforms. From 1866 until his death he was a member of the Moscow Duma and of the Moscow Provincial Zemstvo, and was widely acclaimed for his speeches. Tolstoy first met Samarin in Moscow in 1856, and was struck by his 'cold, supple and educated mind'. He is reported to have referred to Samarin as '...one of the pleasantest people I've known'. He frequently conferred with Samarin, as well as with Prince S. S. Urusov, when working on the sections of *War and Peace* to do with the philosophy of history.

[Not sent]   Yasnaya Polyana, 10 January 1867

Yury Fyodorovich,

I don't know how and why it is, but you are closer to me in the moral and intellectual world than any other person. I haven't been friendly with you or spoken to you much, but for some reason it seems to me that you are the very person I need (and if I'm not mistaken, you need me), the very man I lack—a person of independent mind, loving many things, but above all the truth, and seeking it. I'm the same sort of person. I have my partialities and habits, my vanities and ties of the heart, but up to now—I shall soon be 40—I have loved the truth above all else, and have never despaired of finding it, and I go on seeking it. Sometimes, and never more so than this year, I have managed to raise a corner of the curtain and look in that direction, but it's difficult and frightening on one's own, and it seems I'm losing my way. I'm seeking help and for some reason you alone always involuntarily come to mind. Since the beginning of autumn I've been meaning to see you and to write, but I've kept putting it off—but now it's reached the stage where I'm writing my novel, writing something else...and I must write to Samarin, I must. So here I am writing. But what do I want to say to you? It's this. If I'm not mistaken, and you really are the person I imagine you to be, seeking an explanation for all this muddle that surrounds us, and if I am at least one hundredth part as interesting and necessary to you as you are to me, then let us be friends, let us help each other, work together and love each other, if that's possible. I know you well enough for there to be no need for me to say: when you answer me, be absolutely frank and truthful, i.e. write to me, answer my questions or, of course, tear up my letter and don't mention it to anyone if it should seem to you—well—

138. To Y. F. Samarin

the strange manifestation of a crank. Leaving aside the questions which interest me and about which I can't even begin to speak now, but which, if we become friends, we will explore in writing and in conversation, answer me some questions which concern you personally. I learned about your presence in Moscow from the meetings of the zemstvo something or other. I read your speeches and was horrified. In order to speak *there*, you have to trim your thoughts (as recently about the gentry), which stem from broad and fundamental thinking, to such an extent that they become respectable, and once they have become respectable they carry exactly the same weight for everybody (except the few who can see you behind them, as I can) as the sensible but commonplace word of some well-born member of the gentry, or that vile old man Smirnov.[1] I can't understand it. How can you vous commettre with the zemstvo etc? I associate these speeches of yours with what you said to me when I saw you in passing—that I'm a has-been...That's not so, I feel sure. The zemstvo, the courts, war or the absence of war etc. are all manifestations of the social organism—the swarm organism (as with bees); any bee can manifest it, and in fact the best ones are those who don't know themselves what they are doing and why—and the result of their common labour is always a uniform activity and one that is familiar to the laws of zoology. This zoological activity of the soldier, the emperor, the marshal of the gentry or the ploughman is the lowest level of activity, an activity in which—the materialists are right—there is no arbitrariness. Bismarck thinks that he has outwitted all Europe, but he has only contributed with 1,000 other causes to the blood-letting of Germany necessary in 1866.[2] Let old jades walk around in this tread-wheel if they want, but you are walking in the wheel deliberately, you—a good racehorse who could gallop freely across the fields—have stepped on to the wheel and walk in step with the old jades, saying to yourself: 'I'll walk this way so that we shall get the very finest flour.' But the flour will be just the same as it would be with horses which naively think they will get a long way by treading the wheel. Can you explain this to me? The other thing I don't understand about you is your religious convictions. However, I have never heard your convictions *from* you, I have only heard *about* you. Is it true? Is this an open question for you, or one that is closed to discussion? Please tear up my letter or else write to me; but the way I regard you, I don't see any conventional obstacles between us, and frankly I feel myself at once completely open with respect to you. I don't want to pose in any way before you, nor do I want to hide from you the most intimate or the most shameful thing about myself, if you should need to know it. I shall be very happy if I receive the same sort of letter from you. I don't

[138] 1. The occasion that prompted this letter to Samarin was the publication in *The Moscow Gazette* (No. 274, 29 December 1866) of an account of a session of the Moscow Provincial Zemstvo, during which a clash of views occurred between a senator, N. M. Smirnov, and Samarin. Smirnov attacked the declining moral standards of the peasantry, and blamed this on too rapid a transition from serfdom to emancipation. Samarin responded by attacking Smirnov's speech as inappropriate to the occasion, and by maintaining that the argument might equally well apply to the landowning classes.

2. The Austro-Prussian War of 1866, started by the Prussian government of Bismarck in an attempt to gain the dominant role in German affairs and to bring about unification of the German states.

138. To Y. F. Samarin

know how and why, but I expect a lot from this sort of intellectual friendship with you, and not only for ourselves. But if you don't wish it, simply write and tell me that you have received my letter—then I shall simply be rather ashamed to meet you.

Count L. Tolstoy

139. To M. S. BASHILOV

Yasnaya Polyana, 28 February 1867

Here are my remarks on the rough drawings you sent, dear Mikhail Sergeich:

1. Kutuzov and Dolokhov—splendid; but can't you give Dolokhov a more dashing appearance—more of a military bearing—shoulders higher, chest out?[1]

2. Rostov and Telyanin—splendid;[2] but the more pleasant, handsome and attractive Rostov is, the better.

3. Bilibin—a chef d'oeuvre.

4. The Emperor Francis—charming; but Prince Andrey is a bit too affecté.[3] Still, he's good all the same. If you can't get a better expression in pencil, don't spoil it.

5. On the bridge[4]—it's all very good except Denisov (I apologise in advance if I'm talking nonsense), but he's holding his sword very badly, and he's certainly sitting badly, with his legs bent and too long—the knees too far back, the foot extended and almost propped against the stirrup, and his arse tucked up.

6. Tushin and the artillerymen are very good,[5] although I'd imagined Tushin as younger, but you've expressed the respectable, but comic side of him splendidly. Bagration is not at all good. His features should be much coarser, and then he should have an *astrakhan cap*, not a fur hat—that's the dress of the time. The cloak is always worn on one side—there should be a vent above the right shoulder. His seat, as a Georgian, should be relaxed—slightly to one side, with his feet not propped against the stirrup. The horse should be more natural and more placid. However, I don't know about the horse, but what I say about the man I do insist on.

7. The camp-fire—all three figures are charming.[6]

The manuscript is being copied out for you, a part almost as long as the part that has been published—and I'll send it to you in a few days. Since you are probably now drawing on wood, you won't be held up at all.

The engraving of the scene of the mathematics lesson is magnificent,[7] the others not so good.

I entirely agree to all your suggestions about the time and place of printing. Only I think it wouldn't do any harm to publish sooner.

[139] 1. Part II, ch. 2.   2. Part II, ch. 4.   3. Part II, ch. 12.
4. Part II, ch. 7.   5. Part II, ch. 17.   6. Part II, ch. 21.
7. Part I, ch. 22.

141. To A. A. Fet

Goodbye. I press your hand and your wife's in friendship, and I beg you to give her a kiss from me.

Yours ever,
Count L. Tolstoy

140. To P. I. BARTENEV

Yasnaya Polyana, 31 March 1867

Dear Pyotr Ivanovich,

I'm sending you a letter from Paul to my grandfather, Nikolay Sergeyevich Volkonsky,[1] which I've had lying about here for a long time. It might possibly be of some interest to you.

I shall certainly write an article for *The Archives*, only not now. I can't do anything now except finish my novel. But because of my intention, or simply because you're a kind person, do me a favour. Write to me with material for a history of the Emperor Paul, if it won't present too much difficulty for you. Don't be embarrassed by the fact that you don't know everything. I know nothing except what is in *The Archives*. But what is in *The Archives* delighted me.[2] I've found my historical hero. And if God gives me life, leisure and strength, I'll attempt to write his history. I wish you all the very best.

Your collaborator,
Count L. Tolstoy

I'm not sending Paul's letter, as the seal on it is very heavy, but I'll send it in a day or two with people who are going to Moscow.

141. To A. A. FET

Yasnaya Polyana, 28 June 1867

If I wrote to you, my dear Afanasy Afanasich, every time I thought about you, you would get two letters a day from me. But I still couldn't tell you everything, and besides, I'm either lazy or else too busy, as at present. I came back the other day from Moscow, and am undergoing a strict course of treatment under the direction of Zakharin, but the main thing is, I'm publishing my novel at Rees' printing press, working on the manuscript and the proofs and sending them off, and I have to do so day after day for fear of a fine and the book not coming out on time. It's both agreeable and irksome, as you know.

[140] 1. Nikolay Sergeyevich Volkonsky (1753–1821), Tolstoy's maternal grandfather, the prototype of the old prince Nikolay Andreyevich Bolkonsky in *War and Peace*. Two letters from the Emperor Paul to Volkonsky, dated 18 and 19 May 1799, were preserved in Tolstoy's papers, and so were probably never sent to Bartenev. The letters relate to the time Volkonsky spent as military governor in Archangel.

2. From 1864 onwards a series of materials on the reign of Paul I was published in *The Russian Archives*, including official documents, memoirs, and Paul's correspondence. In 1867 six articles on the reign were published.

141. To A. A. Fet

I meant to write to you long ago about *Smoke*,[1] and of course just the very thing that you wrote to me. We love each other precisely because we think alike with the *heart's mind*, as you call it. (Very many thanks again for that letter. *The mind's mind and the heart's mind*—that explained a lot to me.) What I think about *Smoke* is that the force of poetry lies in love—and the direction of this force depends on character. Without the force of love there is no poetry, and a misdirected force—a poet's disagreeable and weak character—sickens one. In *Smoke* there is practically no love for anything, and practically no poetry. There is only love for fickle and wanton adultery, and so the poetry of the tale is repulsive. You see, that's just the same as what you wrote. I'm only afraid to express this opinion because I can't take a sober view of an author whose personality I don't like, but it seems that my impression is shared by everyone. One more person is finished. I wish and hope that my turn never comes. And I think the same about you. I keep expecting things from you, as though you were a 20-year-old poet, and I don't believe that you are finished. I don't know any man fresher and stronger than you. Your stream keeps on flowing, providing a certain number of buckets of water-power. The wheel on which it used to fall is broken, out of order, dismantled, but the stream keeps on flowing, and if it disappeared into the ground, it would spring up again somewhere and turn other wheels. For goodness sake don't think that I say this to you because one good turn deserves another, and because you always say encouraging things to me—no, I've always thought this about you and only about you. I meant to write more, but guests have come and interrupted me. Goodbye. I embrace you, dear friend, and kiss Marya Petrovna's hand and beg you to press Borisov's hand for me; I hope to stay with him in autumn. I'm addressing this to Mtsensk because you'll be there for the elections.

I so much want to and need to see you, that I would have come to you had it been possible. My benefactor, my dearest one, do come and see me for a day.

L. Tolstoy

142. To P. I. BARTENEV

Yasnaya Polyana, 16–18 August 1867

I haven't received any proofs for a very long time (5 days). Please give them a prod.[1]

I can't help scribbling the way I do, and I know for certain that this scribbling serves a very useful purpose.[2] And so I'm not afraid of the bills from the printers, who I hope won't be very captious.

The very thing that you like would have been much worse if it hadn't been scribbled over about 5 times.

[141] 1. Turgenev's novel *Smoke* was first published in *The Russian Herald* in 1867.

[142] 1. Tolstoy had enlisted Bartenev to supervise the publication of a separate edition of *War and Peace*.

2. Bartenev was unhappy about Tolstoy's prodigious proof-correcting, and said so in a letter of 12 August.

143. To Countess S. A. Tolstaya

I read about Nikolev and Alexander Balashov[3] in Zhikharyov's *Memoirs of a Contemporary*,[4] and so I doubt whether your correction is justified. I'm very grateful about the birch copse.[5]

I didn't manage to finish reading *Memoirs of a Sevastopol Veteran*[6]—it was boring. I don't like that playful—and untruthful—tone.

A. Y. Behrs promised to give you some powder if and when you need it.

I would like the last proofs I sent about Pierre's admittance to the masonic lodge to be returned to me when they have been corrected. If it's not possible, then it can't be helped, but it would be better.

Now the most important thing:

I think that to publish the first two volumes in September would be disadvantageous to the whole editon. The whole lot ought to be published together.

Besides, with the publication of 2 volumes, I lose the margin of time allowed me by the first part which I've not corrected. I need this margin for the 4th volume in particular, which I'm afraid will hold up the printing, as it's not quite ready. I hope to send the whole of the 3rd volume or bring it with me at the beginning of September.

So I would ask you to speed up the printing of the 2nd volume and to devote all the print and all your energy to it exclusively, but to reserve the 1st for the time when there is a delay with my manuscript.

Yours ever,
L. Tolstoy

143. To COUNTESS S. A. TOLSTAYA

Moscow, 27 September 1867

I've just returned from Borodino.[1] I'm very pleased with my trip, very, and even with the way I stood up to it in spite of the lack of sleep and decent food. If God gives me health and peace and quiet, I'll write a battle of Borodino, the like of which there has never been before. Still boasting! I dreamed about you as I lay in the monastery, and so clearly that I can recall the dream as though it were reality and it frightens me to think about you.

---

3. In his letter, Bartenev had pointed to some corrections that he had made to the proofs. He had removed the name of the poet Nikolev, since, as he pointed out, Nikolev could not have read his poems in the club due to his blindness; and he had replaced the name of Alexander Uvarov with that of Fyodor Petrovich Uvarov who, in fact, accompanied Bagration to Moscow. Tolstoy mistakenly here refers to Uvarov as 'Balashov'.

4. S. P. Zhikharyov's *Memoirs of a Contemporary from 1805 to 1814. The Diary of a Student*. Tolstoy made extensive use of this work as source material for the novel.

5. Bartenev had pointed out that the copse at Sokolniki where the duel of Pierre and Dolokhov took place was a pine wood, not a birch wood.

6. By F. N. Berg (*The Russian Archives*, 1867, No. 12).

[143] 1. Tolstoy visited the site of the battle of Borodino with his brother-in-law, drove round the battlefield and talked to peasants who still remembered 1812. After two days he was able to draw up the plan of the battle which he used in *War and Peace*.

143. To Countess S. A. Tolstaya

I won't write to you about the details of the trip—I'll tell you about it. The first night I travelled 100 versts to Mozhaisk and had a sleep in the morning at the station, and the second night we spent in the monastery hotel. I got up at dawn and drove round the battlefield once more, and we spent the whole day getting back to Moscow.

I got your two letters. I was sad about big Tanya and frightened, very frightened for little Tanya (I know, I see and I love her, and I fear for her with her high temperature). But the main thing is that your letters made me feel good at heart, because there is *you* in them. And you put all the best of you into your letters and your thoughts about me. But in daily life this is often stifled by sickness and quarrelsome feelings. I know it.

I'm borrowing 1,000 roubles from Perfilyev, so I'll be rich, and I'll buy a fur hat and boots and everything you say. I know you'll be angry with me for borrowing. Don't be angry; I'm borrowing in order to be free, unconstrained and untroubled by money matters during this early part of winter, and with this purpose in view I intend to save the money as much as possible and to keep it simply in order to know that there is money there to pay off an unprofitable and redundant person etc. You'll understand and will help me. Your letters are an enormous pleasure to me, darling, and don't talk nonsense about me giving them to people to read.

I enjoyed being in Borodino, and I was conscious of the fact that I was doing a job of work; but I can't stand being in town, yet you say that I love loafing about. I could only wish that you loved the country and hated the empty vanity of the town $\frac{1}{10}$ as much as I do. Tomorrow I shall go to the Perfilyevs to thank them, and I'll see Rees and do some shopping, and if I finish everything and Dyakov is ready, I'll leave on Friday morning. Goodbye, darling; I kiss you and the children.

144. To P. I. BARTENEV

Yasnaya Polyana, 1 November 1867

I'm sending the proofs. The manuscript of the third volume is ready at last. I say 'at last' because the end of the 3rd volume was the most difficult part, and the keypoint of the whole novel.[1] Besides, I only got up the other day after a chest infection and am still ill now. I'm sending the manuscript tomorrow with Dyakov. I waited for him before sending it off. I'll deliver the fourth volume to you at the beginning of November—the 4th volume can't hold things up.

I'm thinking of selling 3 volumes together with a subscription for the 4th, which is at the printers. What do you think?[2]

In the latest proofs I've sent you, in the passage where Nikolay Rostov returns

---

[144] 1. The story of Natasha's infatuation with Anatole Kuragin.
2. Bartenev endorsed this plan, and the first three volumes were offered for sale along with a subscription for the fourth volume. The whole edition was to extend to six volumes.

from the army, it says that at the next to last station he thrashed the driver, but that at the last one he gave him 3 roubles for vodka. Cross this out.[3]

L. Tolstoy

145. To P. I. BARTENEV

Yasnaya Polyana, 6 December 1867

I'm sending you everything I have in print, dear Pyotr Ivanych. I'm not sending the next part of the manuscript today only because it's more convenient for me to send a bit more at the same time. I still haven't received the page proofs of the 3rd volume.

I've been slightly delayed in my work by the foreword, which I'll send in a day or two.

How and where should it be included?

Shouldn't it be called an afterword?[1]

What do you think about it?

In vol. 4 Rostov makes an attack,[2] and there's a word *pace*[3] there which they are sure to misinterpret.

In vol. 4 there are rather a lot of French and German phrases. They must be translated, especially the German ones.

In vol. 4 there is frequent mention of the Tsar and the Grand Duke. There's a passage there where Napoleon says to Balashev: 'Bennigsen ought to awaken terrible memories in the Emperor Alexander.'[4] Cross out this passage and ones like it, if you find them dangerous as far as the censorship is concerned. I give you carte blanche to cross out everything that seems dangerous. You know better than me what is allowed, and what isn't.

I'm sending you the foreword, and before it's set up, read it in manuscript and write and tell me your opinion.

Yours,
L. Tolstoy

146. To M. P. POGODIN

Mikhail Petrovich Pogodin (1800–75), a professor at the University of Moscow, a historian and archaeologist, and a Slavophile. Tolstoy met him in Moscow in January 1863, and saw him frequently during the course of the year. They

---

3. The scene of the thrashing was excluded from the final text; Rostov's promise to give 'three roubles for vodka' was retained.

[145] 1. There was no published foreword or afterword to *War and Peace*. However, Tolstoy developed some of his ideas in the article 'A Few Words About the Book *War and Peace*' (*The Russian Archives*, 1868, No. 3).
2. Vol. IV, Part I, ch. 15 (first edn); (Vol. III, Part I, ch. 15—definitive edn).
3. The Russian word is 'allure'.
4. Vol. IV, Part I, ch. 6 (first edn); (Vol. III, Part I, ch. 6—definitive edn).

146. To M. P. Pogodin

discussed historical topics together, and Pogodin provided Tolstoy with manuscripts and other historical material for his work on *War and Peace*.

Moscow, 21–3 March 1868

I was delighted to get your letter,[1] dear Mikhail Petrovich. My ideas on the limits of freedom and dependence, and my views on history, are not a casual paradox which engaged my attention for a moment. These ideas are the fruit of a whole lifetime's intellectual activity and constitute an inseparable part of that outlook on life which was formed in me—God alone knows by what toil and suffering—and which has given me complete tranquillity and happiness. But at the same time I know, and always knew, that in my book people would praise the sentimental scene with the young lady, the gibes at Speransky, and other such rubbish which they are equal to, and that no one would notice the chief thing. You will notice it, and please read it and make notes in the margin. And please let's discuss it. Fix a time when we can see each other.[2]

Yours,
L. Tolstoy

The 5th part, the beginning of it, is in proof form, and is at your disposal, but my manuscript is impossible to read.

Thank you for the book.[3] I shall read it and I'm sure I shall find confirmation of my views.

147. To THE EDITOR OF 'THE RUSSIAN INVALID'

Moscow, 11 April 1868

Dear Sir,

I have just read in issue No. 96 of your newspaper an article by Mr N.L.[1] about the 4th volume of my work.

May I ask you to convey to the author of this article my profound gratitude for the feeling of joy which his article gave me, and to ask him to reveal his name to me and, as a special honour, to allow me to enter into correspondence with him.

I must confess I never dared to hope for such indulgent criticism on the part of military men (the author no doubt is a military specialist).

With many of his arguments (where he takes a contrary view to mine, of course) I am in complete agreement, with many I am not. If I could have availed myself of the advice of such a man during my work, I would have avoided many mistakes.

---

[146] 1. In his letter of 21 March, Pogodin commented on Tolstoy's interest in the question of 'predestination and free will, freedom and necessity...' He asked Tolstoy to send him the manuscript of the fifth volume of *War and Peace*.

2. Tolstoy visited Pogodin on 15 April 1868. In his diaries and his letters to Tolstoy, Pogodin expressed great enthusiasm for the novel.

3. Pogodin had sent Tolstoy his book *Historical Aphorisms* (1836), in which were set forth his views on history, including the problem of freedom and necessity.

[147] 1. N. Lachinov, a military historian.

The author of this article would oblige me very much, if he were to inform me of his name and address.

> With the utmost respect,
> I have the honour to be,
> Your obedient servant,
> Count L. Tolstoy

148. To M. P. POGODIN

Yasnaya Polyana, 7 November 1868

I can only answer your flattering and tempting proposal[1] in the negative, dear Mikhail Petrovich, for several reasons, of which one will suffice: I am not free and am still held enthralled by my as yet unfinished work[2] (which has recently progressed near to its conclusion). I say 'flattering proposal', because however indifferent one tries to be towards success, your proposal (although probably overstated by you) sets a high value on my literary name.

Your proposal is tempting because at times, and quiet often recently, I have had ideas about a permanent publication devoted to the philosophy of history, with a trend that is familiar to you more than anyone through your book *Historical Aphorisms* which you sent to me in Moscow. I could imagine calling this publication *The Non-Contemporary*, so as to define its trend by a nickname.

Everything that could count on failure in the 19th century, and if not on success, then at least on having readers in the 20th and succeeding centuries, would have a place in this publication.

History, the philosophy of history and the raw materials of history.

The philosophy of natural sciences and the raw materials of those sciences which could serve a practical purpose, but also of those which could serve to elucidate philosophical problems.

Mathematics and its applied sciences—astronomy, mechanics. Art which is not contemporary.

And that's all.

Only what now keeps 99 out of 100 of the world's printing-presses busy would be excluded—i.e. criticism, polemics, compilations, i.e. unproductive fervour and cheap, rotten merchandise for consumers of low intelligence.

There you have my dreams, vividly recalled to mind by your proposal.

I have told you about them because you're the same Pogodin who wrote *Historical Aphorisms*, and however distant your paper and such a publication might seem, I can foresee the possibility of a deal.

Have you read Urusov's book *A Survey of 1812 and 1813*?[3] If you have, you would greatly oblige me by dropping me a line and giving me your opinion about it.

[148] 1. Pogodin had invited Tolstoy to contribute to his newspaper, *Russia*, which from 1868 was to be published daily instead of weekly.   2. *War and Peace*.
3. Prince S. S. Urusov's *A Survey of the Campaigns of 1812 and 1813; Military–Mathematical Problems and the Railways*, an attempt to ascertain the 'laws of war'.

148. To M. P. Pogodin

My fifth volume is progressing rapidly, but I daren't think of completing it in less than a month, and until then I daren't think of anything else.[4]

With sincere respect,
Count L. Tolstoy

149. To COUNTESS S. A. TOLSTAYA

Moscow, 18 January 1869

My dear,

I had an excellent journey to Moscow. I slept almost all the way. I called in to see Rees. All is well with him. I sent word to Urusov. He came round to see me. I talked with him all morning and went with him to see Yuryev and Samarin. Both of them were invited to Urusov's in the evening. I had dinner with Urusov. From there I went to the theatre to give my head a rest and to see a new play by Ostrovsky.[1] I didn't sit through the whole play and went back to Urusov's, where the four of us talked until after 2. My ideas about history made a great impression on Yuryev[2] and Urusov and were greatly appreciated by them, but we didn't manage to talk about them with Samarin, as we got involved in another philosophical argument. I'm a bit disappointed in him. I came home last night at 2.30 with a headache, and mainly because there was no paper and envelopes I couldn't write to you. I woke up today at 12, refreshed and well, sent for tea (I'm sensible, really) and have just been talking with Rees. The wool hasn't been sold yet, and he's just going to the railway station to fetch it, and I'm entrusting this letter to him to give to the conductor, so that it can be posted to Tula...[13 lines omitted]

...Goodbye, darling, until we meet. Except for the needs of the mind there is nothing on earth which could interest me even the slightest, or could distract me from the thought of you and of home. The theatre showed me that yesterday. I walked out because I was bored, without staying to the end of a new play and one that was splendidly acted. I was bored.

150. To A. A. FET

Yasnaya Polyana, 10 May 1869

Dear friend,

I received your books and the letter, and I thank you for them both. About Tretyakov—I don't know, I don't want anyone.[1] I was touched by your sympathetic interest in my epilogue. I read it to Yurkevich[2] and he said nothing in

---

4. Volume v of *War and Peace* was published in February 1869.
[149] 1. *A Warm Heart*.
2. S. A. Yuryev (1821–88), mathematics teacher and friend of Urusov, translator of Lope de Vega, Goethe and Shakespeare, and for some years editor of *Russian Thought*.
[150] 1. A reference to P. M. Tretyakov's request, via Fet, for Tolstoy to allow his portrait to be painted by Kramskoy. Tolstoy refused more than once, but finally consented in 1873. For Tretyakov, see Letter 349.   2. A professor of Philosophy at the University of Moscow.

reply except to read an extract from a lecture of his. The main reason why I'm not afraid is that what I've written, especially in the epilogue, wasn't invented by me, but painfully torn from my inside. There is further support in the fact that Schopenhauer in his *Wille*[3] says the same thing as I do, approaching it from the other side. I'm waiting any moment for my wife to give birth. If, God willing, all is well, I'll certainly come and see you, since you don't wish to know me.

Yours,
L. Tolstoy

151. To A. A. FET

Yasnaya Polyana, 30 August 1869

I received your letter, and I'm not so much answering it as answering my own thoughts about you. I grieve no less than you, no doubt, over the fact that we see so little of each other. I've made plans to visit you and still do, but so far I haven't been. The 6th volume which I thought I would finish 4 months ago is still not finished, although the type has been set up long ago.

Do you know what this summer has meant for me? Constant raptures over Schopenhauer and a whole series of spiritual delights which I've never experienced before. I've sent for all his works and I'm reading them (I've also read Kant), and probably no student ever studied so much in his course, and learned so much, as I did this summer.

I don't know if I'll ever change my opinion,[1] but at present I'm certain that Schopenhauer is the most brilliant of men.

You said that he wrote something or other on philosophical subjects, not too badly. What do you mean, something or other? It's the whole world in an incredibly clear and beautiful reflection.

I've begun to translate him. Won't you also take it on?[2]

We could publish it jointly. As I read him, it's inconceivable to me how his name can remain unknown. There's only one explanation—the one that he rejects so often, that there is hardly anybody on earth except idiots.

I await a visit from you with impatience. I'm sometimes overwhelmed by the unsatisfied need for a kindred nature like yours, in order to express all that has accumulated in me. Cordial regards to Marya Petrovna.

Yours,
L. Tolstoy

[Postscript omitted]

3. *Die Welt als Wille und Vorstellung.*

[151] 1. Tolstoy's attitude towards Schopenhauer did change somewhat in later life and he made some adverse comments about his pessimism. Nevertheless Schopenhauer's influence remained a very powerful one.

2. Nothing is known of a translation by Tolstoy, but Fet later translated *Die Welt als Wille und Vorstellung*, which was published in 1881.

152. To COUNTESS S. A. TOLSTAYA

Saransk, 4 September 1869

I'm writing to you from Saransk, my dear. I've almost reached the place.[1] It's 46 versts from here. I'm hiring private horses, and going straight on to the place.

How are you and the children? Has anything happened? For two days now I've been tormented with anxiety. The day before yesterday I spent the night at Arzamas, and something extraordinary happened to me. It was 2 o'clock in the morning, I was terribly tired, I wanted to go to sleep and I felt perfectly well. But suddenly I was overcome by despair, fear and terror, the like of which I have never experienced before. I'll tell you the details of this feeling later: but I've never experienced such an agonising feeling before and may God preserve anyone else from experiencing it.[2] I jumped up and ordered the horses to be harnessed. While they were being harnessed, I fell asleep, and woke up perfectly well. Yesterday the feeling returned to a far lesser extent during the drive, but I was prepared for it and didn't succumb, more particularly as it was weaker. Today I feel well and happy, in so far as I can be, away from the family.

During this journey I felt for the first time how much I have grown together with you and the children. I can remain alone doing a regular job, as I do in Moscow, but when I have nothing to do, as now, I definitely feel I can't be alone.

It seems according to all I've learned here that I'll go back to Morshansk, which is much nearer. I'll write to the post office at Saransk and Nizhny enclosing a stamp, so that they can send me your letters to Tula.

I've been travelling all the time alone, as though in a desert, without meeting a single civilised person.

From Nizhny for $\frac{2}{3}$ of the way the country has the same character: sandy soil and fine peasant buildings like the ones near Moscow. I don't like this character. Towards Saransk the black earth begins, quite like Tula and very picturesque.

I hope to cut short my holiday, but I can't say anything definite until I've been to the place. The main thing is, the weather is awful. The mere thought of travelling back these 300 versts through the mud makes my flesh creep.

I left two things behind: my leather coat and the jam. I intend to replace the leather coat by a caftan which I'll buy, and I'm replacing the jam by sugar.

Goodbye, darling. One good thing is that I'm not thinking at all about the novel or about philosophy.

[152] 1. Tolstoy was travelling to a small place in the province of Penza in the hope of buying an estate he had seen advertised in the papers.

2. The incident is described in Tolstoy's *Memoirs of a Madman*, written in the middle 1880s and published posthumously.

V
1870-1879

The years immediately following the publication of *War and Peace* were years of deep and extensive reading and a rediscovered vocation to teach children and to write for them. Tolstoy now began to study in earnest the language and literature of classical Greece, particularly Homer, Xenophon and Herodotus. He reread the plays of Molière, Goethe and Shakespeare and the classics of the Russian stage. He applied himself to Schopenhauer, Kant and Pascal with enthusiastic dedication. Despite a temporary revulsion from fiction, especially his own, he returned to work on *The Decembrists* and began a historical novel on the life and times of Peter the Great—only to abandon it as a result, no doubt, of his antipathy towards its hero. His list of books which made the deepest impression on him during the years 1863 to 1878 included not only the *Iliad*, the *Odyssey*, the *Anabasis* and the Russian *byliny*, but also *Les Misérables* and the novels of Trollope, George Eliot and Mrs Ward. His main efforts, however, in 1871 and 1872 were concentrated on writing his *Primer* for peasant children. Not only did he write many stories himself, whose narrative interest, brevity and simplicity were calculated to make a direct moral appeal; he also translated and adapted fables and folk-tales from Greek, Jewish, Oriental and Arabic sources, compiled a section on arithmetic and provided passages for reading from the natural sciences, the Russian chronicles and the Lives of the Saints. Among his own compositions for the *Primer* were *A Captive in the Caucasus* and *God Sees the Truth but Waits*, which he was later to value more highly than all the rest of his fiction. In 1873 he returned to belles-lettres and began work on what he insisted on calling his first 'novel'—*Anna Karenina*. The first instalments were published in 1875 and the final one in the spring of 1877.

Apart from his literary and pedagogical activities, the main events in Tolstoy's life during the 1870s were his visits to the Bashkir province of Samara, first to convalesce from illness, and later to spend summer holidays with his family on an estate he purchased there. In the summer of 1873 he witnessed a serious famine in the Samara province, to which he gave wide publicity by writing to the papers and setting up a Famine Relief Fund. In 1874 he lectured on his educational theories in Moscow and wrote an article on the subject. As his work on *Anna Karenina* neared completion he became increasingly preoccupied with the Christian religion, and for a while he resumed regular church-going—a practical result of his 'change of heart' was his reconciliation with Turgenev. In 1879 he visited the monasteries of Kiev and the Troitse-Sergiyev Monastery near Moscow, and had numerous conversations on religious matters with monks and laymen. In the same year he began his *A Confession* and several religious articles.

In the course of the 1870s six more children were born to the Tolstoys of whom two died in infancy. Their tenth child was born in 1879, but by then their marriage was already showing signs of strain which were to be seriously aggravated in the next decade.

153. To A. A. FET

Yasnaya Polyana, 4 February 1870

I received your letter, dear Afanasy Afanasyevich, on 1 February. But even if I'd received it a little earlier, I couldn't have come.

You write: *'I'm alone, alone!!!'* But I read it and think: lucky man to be *alone*. I have a wife, three children, a fourth at the breast, two old aunts, a nanny and two maids, and the whole lot are suffering from fever, a temperature, debility, a headache or a cough. This is the state your letter found me in. They are beginning to get better now, but I still dine at table with only old N.P. present out of 10. Besides I've been ill myself for two days now—chest and side. As soon as we get better I'll come and visit you. There's a very great deal I want to tell you. I've read a lot of Shakespeare, Goethe, Pushkin, Gogol and Molière, and there's a great deal I want to say to you. This year I haven't been taking a single journal or newspaper, and I find it very beneficial.[1] Please write to me occasionally so that I shall know whether I can find you at home.

Yours,
Tolstoy

154. To A. A. FET

Yasnaya Polyana, 16(?) February 1870

I didn't write to you immediately, because I hoped to visit you on the night of the 14th, but I wasn't able to. As I wrote to you, we have all been ill—myself last of all—and I only went out yesterday for the first time. I had to stop, though, because of a pain in the eyes which is aggravated by the wind and by insomnia. With great sorrow I must now postpone my visit to you until Lent.[1] I have to go to Moscow now to take Auntie to my sister's and to see my sister myself and do something about her health, and to let an oculist see my eyes. Please write more often so that I may know whether you are at home and what you are doing, and so that I can come just the same if my eyes are better. I so much want to. The trouble is that I can't do so except after a sleepless, cigarette-smoky, hot and stuffy railway carriage night of petty vulgar talk. You want to read me your story about cavalry life.[2] I expect well of it as long as it's simple, without any contriving of situations and characters.

[153] 1. According to his wife, a subscription was still taken out for *Revue des deux mondes* in 1870, while two other periodicals were sent free of charge.

[154] 1. In fact Tolstoy visited Fet from 18 to 20 February and went to Moscow in early March.
2. *The Goltz Family*, published in *The Russian Herald* later the same year.

But I don't want to read you anything, and I haven't anything to read, because I'm not writing anything; but I want to talk about Shakespeare, Goethe and the drama in general. All this winter I've been occupied solely with drama in general and, as is always the case with people who have never thought about a subject until they are 40 and have no conception about it, but suddenly turn their attention to this unsavoured subject with 40-year-old clarity of vision—they always think they see much that is new in it.

All winter I've been enjoying myself lying down, going to sleep, playing bezique, skiing, skating, and most of all lying in bed (ill), and the characters in a drama or comedy begin to act. And they perform very well.

That's what I want to talk to you about. You are a classic in this, as in everything, and you understand the essence of the matter very profoundly. I would also like to read a bit of Sophocles and Euripides.

Goodbye; our regards to Marya Petrovna. If my letter is very odd, it's because I'm writing on an empty stomach. Auntie is just off to Tula.

Yours,
L. Tolstoy

155. To N. N. STRAKHOV

Nikolay Nikolayevich Strakhov (1828–96), journalist, literary critic and philosopher. A scientist by education, Strakhov's range of interests was unusually wide. Following his studies at the University of Petersburg, he spent several years as a teacher of mathematics, physics and natural sciences, first in Odessa and later in Petersburg. He gave up teaching to become a librarian at the Public Library in Petersburg, where he remained until 1885.

In 1858 he published *Letters on Organic Life*, a work which attracted the attention of the public and the friendship of Apollon Grigoryev, who was attempting to synthesise the ideas of Slavophiles and Westerners. From 1861 to 1863 Strakhov worked with Grigoryev on the staff of Dostoyevsky's journal *Time*, which he co-edited. The journal was banned in 1863 as a result of an article by Strakhov, 'A Fatal Question', which was alleged by Katkov and others on flimsy evidence to be sympathetic to the Polish insurrection of that year.

Dostoyevsky, who was much influenced by Grigoryev's ideas, termed Grigoryev and his followers '*pochvenniki*' (from the word *pochva*, meaning 'soil') because they believed a work of art to be an 'organic product' of its age and its national milieu, deeply rooted in the 'soil' of national life. While on the staff of *Time*, Strakhov had enthusiastically embraced Grigoryev's ideas, and following the latter's early death in 1864 he was instrumental in popularising them in his many articles and books. In his best-known work, *The Struggle with the West in our Literature* (3 vols., 1882–95), subtitled 'Historical and Critical Essays' and analysing the ideas of such men as Herzen, Taine, Renan, Strauss, Darwin and Mill, Strakhov again took up Grigoryev's central theme that the concepts of Slavophilism and Westernism were

155. To N. N. Strakhov

too narrow to provide a solution to the problems of Russian literature and philosophy. His short book *The Poverty of our Literature* (1868) is a criticism of Gogol's work and of the 'naturalist' school of writers which followed Gogol (again Strakhov took his lead from Apollon Grigoryev); Strakhov considered Ostrovsky and Tolstoy—especially the latter—to have 'corrected' the mistakes of Gogol and to have offered a positive national ideal (in Tolstoy's work, Platon Karatayev embodies this ideal) in opposition to Gogol's essentially negative and ironical view of Russian life.

As a philosopher, Strakhov lacked any distinctive or original ideas. He was particularly influenced by Hegel and German idealist philosophy, and by the theories of Taine. Strakhov translated into Russian a large number of French and German philosophical works, including Kuno Fischer's *Geschichte der neuern Philosophie* and Lange's *Geschichte des Materialismus*. Religion played an important part in his philosophical thinking, but he never expounded his religious ideas systematically or in depth. He saw the limitations of rationalism, but could also defend rationalist principles on occasion. There is an eclecticism about his thought that led to frequent inconsistencies, and he found himself able to accept very different ideas of Tolstoy, Dostoyevsky, Danilevsky and Grigoryev, as well as retaining a great admiration for Renan.

In the 1880s, as an eminent conservative, Strakhov was the principal link between the late Slavophile movement and the mystical revival that took place in the late 1880s and 1890s. Strakhov acted as literary mentor to V. V. Rozanov, who considered himself a follower of Dostoyevsky; one of Rozanov's publications was an edition of Strakhov's letters to him, *Literary Exiles* (1913).

Strakhov's other works on Russian literature include *Notes on Pushkin and Other Writers*, several articles on Dostoyevsky, the first biographical sketch of Dostoyevsky, and *Critical Articles on I. S. Turgenev and L. N. Tolstoy, 1862–85*. It was Strakhov's very favourable review of *War and Peace* which served as the basis of his later friendship with Tolstoy (although an earlier article by Strakhov on women's rights had also attracted Tolstoy's attention, prompting him to write the following letter to the young journalist, which was never sent). Strakhov wrote to Tolstoy in 1870 asking him to contribute to a Slavophile journal with which he was then associated, and although Tolstoy declined, he invited Strakhov to visit him at Yasnaya Polyana. Strakhov came the following year and continued to visit Tolstoy almost every summer for the rest of his life. (Tolstoy's favourite path at Yasnaya Polyana where he liked to walk while meditating was dubbed 'Strakhov's Walk' by the Tolstoy children.)

Tolstoy valued Strakhov's philosophical knowledge and literary judgement highly. He asked him to proof-read *Anna Karenina* and was grateful for the various important corrections of detail which he made, as well as his general appraisal of the work. Strakhov was also associated with Tolstoy's favourite work, the *Primer*, and he edited a collection of Tolstoy's works which was published in 1873. In the late 1870s Tolstoy frequently drew on Strakhov's knowledge for compiling reading lists on philosophical and religious subjects, solicited his help in obtaining the books

155. To N. N. Strakhov

he needed, and discussed the ideas which were exercising him at the time. Subsequently Tolstoy revised his opinion of Strakhov as the latter became more reactionary with the years; he came to consider Strakhov lacking in both intellectual firmness and originality, as well as liveliness of character. In fact Strakhov lived the life of a bachelor-scholar and was only really at home among his literary friends. Rozanov once remarked that Strakhov's Petersburg flat was like a tomb, filled entirely with books and papers. Tolstoy did not share Strakhov's later enthusiasm for Rozanov either. Nevertheless, they continued to correspond until Strakhov's death in 1896.

Strakhov was Tolstoy's main correspondent in the 1870s and 1880s, in succession to Fet who had dominated the 1860s. Well over 300 letters between Tolstoy and Strakhov have survived. Tolstoy once singled out Strakhov and Prince Urusov, together with Alexandra Tolstaya, as the three people to whom he wrote the most letters of interest 'to those who may be interested in my personality'.

[Not sent][1]   Yasnaya Polyana, 19 March 1870

Dear Sir,

I read your article on women[2] with great pleasure and wholeheartedly subscribe to its conclusions; but the one concession that you make on sexless women[3] seems to me to spoil it all. There are no such women, just as there are no four-legged people. The woman who can no longer bear children and the woman who hasn't found a husband are still women, and if we have in mind not the human society that Mill and co. promise to build for us, but the one which exists and always has existed through the fault of *someone* unacknowledged by them, then we shall see that there is no necessity for devising a way out for women who can no longer bear children and women who haven't found a husband: there always has been and always will be a demand for such women, exceeding the supply, without offices, university departments and telegraph offices. There are midwives, nannies, housekeepers, dissolute women. No one can doubt the necessity for midwives, and the shortage of them, and the woman without a family who doesn't wish to lead a dissolute life in body and soul won't look for a job in a department, but will go and help mothers in so far as she is able. Again, *nannies*—in the very broadest, popular sense. Aunts, grandmothers, sisters—they are nannies, finding for themselves in the family a vocation of the very highest worth. Where is the family in which there is no such nanny, in addition to the one that is hired? And the family and the children who

[155] 1. Tolstoy ultimately decided not to send this letter. He eventually revised his opinions, and in the 1880s, in his book *What Then Must We Do?*, he condemned prostitution as a social evil.

2. *The Woman Question*, prompted by the publication of John Stuart Mill's *The Subjection of Women*. Strakhov opposed Mill's argument that women should be allowed to enjoy the same rights and privileges as men. To Strakhov, woman was God's most perfect creation, but he insisted that her natural calling was to be a wife and mother, and that any involvement in male activities was detrimental to her femininity—something she should value above all else. (Strakhov never married.)

3. Strakhov conceded that there was some justification for granting equal social and political rights to unmarried and middle-aged women.

155. To N. N. Strakhov

have such a nanny are fortunate indeed. And the woman who doesn't wish to lead a dissolute life in body and soul will always choose this vocation rather than a telegraph office—she won't choose it even, but will of herself unwittingly settle into this groove and follow it until her death, conscious of her usefulness and love. I'm not speaking of the hired nannies that we import from Switzerland, England, and Germany.

By housekeepers, other than hired ones, I again mean mothers-in-law, mothers, sisters, aunts, childless women. Again, this is a female vocation, in the highest degree useful and worthy. I don't know why for the sake of the dignity of a woman as a human being, it should generally be considered superior for a person to deliver other people's telegrams or to write reports than to preserve the state of the family and the health of its members.

Perhaps you will be astonished that I include in the number of these honourable vocations that of unfortunate whores. I am bound to do so because my arguments are based not on what I would like to see, but on what exists and always has existed. These unfortunates have always existed and do exist and, in my opinion, it would be an act of godlessness and senselessness to suppose that God made a mistake in arranging things in this way, and that Christ made an even greater mistake in declaring forgiveness for one of them. I only look at what exists and try to understand why it exists. That women of this kind are necessary is demonstrated by the fact that we imported them from Europe; again it is not difficult to understand why they are necessary if we will only admit what has always been the case —that mankind only progresses within the family. Only in the most primitive and simple kind of life can the family hold its ground without the help of the Magdalens, as we see in the backwoods and in small villages; but as soon as there occurs an accumulation of people in centres—large villages, small towns, large towns, capital cities—so they appear, and always in proportion to the size of the centre. Only the man who works on the land who is never away from home, can, if he has married young, remain faithful to his wife and she to him, but in complex forms of life, it seems obvious to me that this is impossible (in the mass, of course). What on earth can the laws which govern the world do? Stop the accumulation of centres and progress? That would contradict other aims. Allow the free interchange of wives and husbands (as the liberal windbags want)? That wouldn't enter into the designs of Providence either, for reasons clear to you—it would destroy the family. And so by the law of economy of effort there arose a middle course—the appearance of the Magdalens—in proportion to the complexity of life. Imagine London without its 80,000 Magdalens! What would become of families? How many wives and daughters would remain chaste? What would become of the laws of morality which people so love to observe? It seems to me that this class of women is *essential* to the family under the present complex forms of life. And so, as long as we don't think of the social order as the product of the will of some fools and evil people, as the Mills do, but as the product of a will incomprehensible to us, then the place occupied in it by women who have no family will be clear to us.

They see things from the point of view of pride, i.e. the desire to show that they can organise the world better than it is organised, and so they see nothing; but one only needs to see things from the point of view of what exists and everything will become clear. They speak well of women. But women's main vocation is the bearing, nursing and upbringing of children. Michelet puts it very well, that there is only woman, and that man is le mâle de la femme.[4] Now have a look at this woman fulfilling her real duty. The man who has lived with a woman and loved her knows that for this woman, bearing children over a period of 10 or 15 years, there comes a time when she is overwhelmed by work. She is bearing or nursing; the older children must be taught, clothed and fed; there are illnesses, the upbringing of children, her husband, and at the same time there are her spirits to be kept up, for she has to give birth. During this period the woman is, as it were, dazed by the effort, she has to display a resilience of energy that would be incomprehensible if we couldn't actually see it. It's like the way our northern peasants harvest the fields in the 3 months of summer. Imagine a woman during this period subjected to the temptations of a whole pack of unmarried hounds, who have no Magdalens; and, above all, imagine a woman without the help of other women with no family—sisters, mothers, aunts, nannies. And where is the woman who has managed on her own during such a period? So what other mission need women with no family have? They can all go off as helpers to those who bear children, and still there will be too few of them, and children will still die from lack of supervision, and from lack of supervision will be badly fed and brought up.

156. To A. A. FET

Yasnaya Polyana, 11 May 1870

I received your letter, my dear Afanasy Afanasyevich, on my return from work, covered in sweat, with axe and spade, and consequently 1,000 versts removed from everything artificial, especially our occupation. The first thing I read when I opened the letter was your poem,[1] and I felt a tickling in my nose; I went to my wife and tried to read it, but couldn't do so for tears of emotion. The poem is one of those rare ones where you can't add or subtract or alter a single word; it's a living *thing in itself* and charming. It's so good that it seems to me that it's not a random poem, but the first jet of a long arrested stream. It's sad to think, after the impression the poem made on me, that it will be printed on paper in some *Herald* or other, and the Sukhotins will criticise it and say: 'But still, Fet writes nicely.'

'Oh, tender one!'[2]...but the whole thing is charming. I don't know anything better by you. It's all charming.

I'm writing to Ivan Ivanovich at Nikolskoye by the same post to ask him to send for the mare, and I'm delighted, and I thank you and Pyotr Afanasich.[3] Do write

---

4. Jules Michelet (1798–1874), a French historian and sociologist, the author of *L'Amour* (1858), a work devoted to the defence of marriage and the family.

[156] 1. *May Night*.   2. The beginning of a line in *May Night*.
3. Fet's brother.

156. To A. A. Fet

and tell me about the price. I've just finished a week's jury service, and found it very, very interesting and instructive.

I'm going to Kharkov on 15 May,[4] and after that I'll arrange to stay with you. Don't leave us without news of yourself. Please give Marya Petrovna regards from us both.

I only wish you a visit from the muse. You ask my opinion about the poem; but really I know the happiness it gave you from the knowledge that it's excellent, and that it actually came out of you, that it *is* you.

Goodbye, till we meet.

Yours,
L. Tolstoy

157. To A. A. FET

Yasnaya Polyana, 17 November 1870

My wife and I expect you and Marya Petrovna on the 20th. We foresee no inconvenience on the 20th; we only foresee the great pleasure of your visit. My wife tells me to say the same to Marya Petrovna.

The Hare[1] interests me very much. Let's see whether it can *all* be understood not just by my Seryozha, but by an 11-year-old boy.

The bicycle interests me even more. I see from your letter that you are well and happily occupied. I envy you. I am depressed and am writing nothing, but am working painfully. You can't imagine how difficult I find this preparatory work of ploughing deeply the field which I'm *compelled* to sow.[2] It's terribly difficult to think over and rethink everything that might happen to all the future people in a work to come, and a very big one, and to think over millions of possible combinations in order to choose 1/1,000,000 of them. And that's what I'm busy doing. The last volume of Béranger reached me the other day. I discovered *Le bonheur* in it, which was new to me.[3] I hope you will translate it.

I'm also depressed by the weather. But everything is fine at home—all are well. Goodbye.

Yours,
L. Tolstoy

158. To A. A. FET

Yasnaya Polyana, 1–6(?) January 1871

I received your letter a week ago, but I haven't answered it before because I've been learning Greek from morning till night[1]—your letter with the poems, which

---

4. As far as is known, Tolstoy did not go to Kharkov.

[157] 1. A story Fet wrote and dedicated to Tolstoy's son, Seryozha, which was later adapted by Tolstoy and published in his *First Russian Reader* under the title *How I first killed a hare.*
  2. Possibly the preliminary work on his projected novel about the times of Peter the Great.
  3. Not apparently new to him, as he had written about it in a letter to Botkin in 1857.

[158] 1. According to his wife he learned the language in three months.

were good but not first-rate, because the motif is too fortuitous, and the picture of the thing imagined is not sufficiently clear.² But I'm glad that you write with vigour and ease, and I look forward to more.

I'm not writing anything, only learning. And to judge from information which has reached me from Borisov, your skin, to be used as parchment for my Greek diploma, is in danger. Improbable and unlikely as it may seem, I've read Xenophon, and can now read him à livre ouvert. For Homer, though, I still need a dictionary and some effort.

I eagerly await the chance to show somebody this trick. And how glad I am that God inflicted this madness upon me! Firstly, I enjoy it, and secondly I'm convinced that until now I knew nothing of all that the human language has produced that is truly and simply beautiful (like everyone else except the professors, who might know it, but don't understand it), and thirdly because I've stopped writing, and will never again write verbose nonsense like *War and Peace*. I'm guilty, but I swear I'll never do it again.

Explain to me, for goodness sake, why nobody knows Aesop's fables or even the charming Xenophon, not to mention Plato and Homer who are still in store for me. So far as I can judge at present, Homer has simply been ruined by our translations based on German models. I can't help making a banal comparison between boiled and distilled warm water, and water from a spring which sets the teeth on edge, with its sparkle and sunshine and even its bits of debris and specks of dirt which make it cleaner and fresher. All these Fosses³ and Zhukovskys⁴ sing in a honeyed and syrupy, or mean, guttural and ingratiating voice, but this man, damn it, sings and roars with all his lungs, and it never occurred to him that anybody would listen to him.

You may crow about it—without a knowledge of Greek there is no education. But what sort of knowledge? How should it be acquired? For what purpose? I have arguments as clear as daylight in reply.

You don't mention Marya Petrovna, from which we are glad to conclude that her convalescence is making good progress. We are all well and send our regards.

Yours,
L. Tolstoy

159. To PRINCE S. S. URUSOV

Prince Sergey Semyonovich Urusov (1827–97), the son of a Senator, a mathematician, writer and well-known chess-player, was one of Tolstoy's closest friends from the days of the Crimean War, where Urusov had commanded a regiment and been decorated with the St George Cross for outstanding bravery. Tolstoy valued him for his intellectual independence and sincerity, and their friendship was

2. It is not known which poems are referred to.
3. J. F. Foss (1751–1826), German poet and translator.
4. V. A. Zhukovsky (1783–1852) translated *The Odyssey* from German into Russian.

159. To Prince S. S. Urusov

cemented by their mutual interest in chess (Urusov considered Tolstoy his pupil).

Two anecdotes about Urusov from the Crimean campaign illustrate certain traits of his character. After repeated battles for a certain trench which had changed hands many times at great loss of life, Urusov seriously proposed to his commanding officer that the matter be decided by a game of chess in which he would be pitted against any player from the English side. Again, during an inspection of Urusov's regiment by a particularly unpleasant inspector-general who slapped the face of one of his N.C.O.s, Urusov ordered his men to 'fix bayonets', which they did, whereupon the terrified inspector quickly left. Urusov supposedly only escaped court-martial because of his decoration, and because his action was so extraordinary that the publicity would have been embarrassing to the army.

The eccentricity displayed in both these episodes was a permanent feature of Urusov's character and, although he was extremely amiable, he also had a very high opinion of himself which was not always merited. He liked to say that all great men were born in August, (this included both himself and Tolstoy, as well as Napoleon and Goethe, by his reckoning); he considered it unjust that he was not acknowledged to be the best Russian chess-player, that his many mathematical works (which he published at his own expense) were ignored, and that his army career had not taken him as far as he expected. In fact, his chess-games were published as models of their kind and he played chess against the best players in the world; his army career was cut short by the bayonet incident (he resigned after an audience with Alexander II in which the Tsar offended him by making no mention of the incident!); and his mathematical publications (which extended to probability theories and formulae for making strategic calculations) attracted attention, but more for their controversial nature than for their excellence.

It is in connection with Urusov's mathematical theories that his friendship with Tolstoy is of particular interest to literary scholars. Boris Eichenbaum suggested that the sections of *War and Peace* to do with the philosophy of history and war were to some extent influenced by these theories. In 1866 Urusov had published *Studies of the Eastern War*, in which he made many comparisons between the Crimean War and that of 1812–13; in 1868 he published *A Survey of the Campaigns of 1812–13, Military-Mathematical Problems and the Railways*. This work begins with a reference to *War and Peace*, which, the author says, prompted him to write his mathematical study of the war, and the book abounds in references to Tolstoy's novel and ideas. Urusov was also a confirmed Slavophile, and the book expresses opinions about the characteristics of the Russian people which could only have met with Tolstoy's approval at the time. Eichenbaum also suggests that a circle consisting of Urusov, Yury Samarin (the Slavophile), S. A. Yuryev and Tolstoy, which met at this time (1866–8), contributed greatly to Tolstoy's own developing theories about war and causality. Letters from this period show that Urusov and Tolstoy frequently discussed the subject they were both working on. Urusov's particular approach to the campaigns was to reduce them to systems of mathematical probabilities. (He liked to turn everything into a mathematical problem even to the

159. To Prince S. S. Urusov

extent of working out a law for the mortality rate of tsars, and predicting the date of his friends' deaths—although he did not tell them!) Urusov's mathematical theories and examples, Eichenbaum claims, help to account for the frequent recourse in *War and Peace* to mathematical parallels and the many references to the existence of certain immutable laws governing human activity.

Tolstoy considered his correspondence with Urusov to be very important as he could be entirely frank with him, and he put it on a par with his correspondence with Alexandra Tolstaya and Nikolay Strakhov as revealing most about his personality. Unfortunately only a handful of his letters survive, because Urusov burned nearly all of them after Tolstoy's rejection of official Orthodoxy (Urusov himself became extremely devout in the 1880s and 1890s). In his old age, he became impoverished and was reduced to living in one wing of his former house, selling all the timber on his land, and living without any servants. Tolstoy continued to visit him until his death in 1897, and to value him as an old friend whose simplicity and kindness he never ceased to admire.

Yasnaya Polyana, April–May (?) 1871

Thank goodness, all is well with us. My wife is up and is feeding the baby a little, between the wet nurse's feeds—in the hope that she can discharge the nurse as her own milk increases. I thank you, dear friend, for your friendship which I see in everything. I'm very upset that I shan't see you yourself. I so much wanted to have a heart-to-heart talk with you in private. I'm afraid this letter won't find you in Moscow. If for some reason you did stay longer, write and tell me, and I'll come to see you. My health is still bad. I've never experienced such depression in my life. I don't want to go on living.

So I particularly want to see you. I'm not doing anything except reading Greek, and I don't want to do anything. I once read an article by Yelagin, and wrote a whole article about military reform.[1] And then I grew ashamed that I was bothering with such stupid things, as though our thoughts were needed for nothing else except our own amusement. How is the problem of the knight? You write in passing about the law of the mortality rate of tsars. This is very interesting to me. I believe in it. For tsars this law must be more apparent than for any others, although even for them the matter must be veiled in obscurity, so that it is possible to guess, but impossible to know. If everything were known, there would be no interest for God in watching our comedy. And we would cease to act our parts so seriously.

If you can, write and tell me how it is. It interests me very much. You've sold your geometry too cheaply.[2] I once began reading it, starting at the second part, and was happy for three hours or so because I understood it all. The article I tore up on military reform was partly mathematical. This is what I said:

[159] 1. Tolstoy destroyed his article, which may have been prompted by the publication in 1870 of a plan to introduce universal military conscription.
2. *A Guide to the Study of Geometry* (*Elementary and Advanced*), *Algebra and Trigonometry*, Parts II and III, published in December 1870.

159. To Prince S. S. Urusov

1. The army is a force composed of a quantity of people and a length of time for which a man trains as a soldier. Hence:

2. The longer the time, the fewer the people, and vice versa, so that the force does not vary. And the force is increased both by length of time and by quantity.

3. In Russia the monetary interests of the state and the people are identical. A proof of that is the fact that the state can compel all men to become soldiers. If it can compel all men to become soldiers, then it can levy on them all an extra money tax in place of conscription.

4. The strength of the army is not increased or decreased simply according to the length of time which people spend in military training, but is increased or decreased in a particular progression: i.e. 1,200 soldiers each of whom will spend three days in the service will not equal one soldier of 10 years' service, but will be 1,000 times weaker than him. Or 100 old soldiers of five years' service will not equal 1,000 soldiers of 6 months' service, but will be much stronger, etc. And therefore if the strength of the army is increased in a temporal progression, the longer the period of service, the more advantageous it will be.

If these 4 propositions are correct, then the problem of military reform, the essence of which is the problem of how to have the strongest army with the least expenditure, is solved simply and in a manner directly opposite to the Prussian solution. The advantage of this solution is that one need do nothing at all, need not destroy the type of old Russian soldier who brought so much glory to the Russian army, nor try anything new or unknown.

Otherwise it turns out that the eternally glorious defence of Sevastopol really showed that the old Russian soldier was no good, and that we need to devise a new and *better* one on Prussian lines. It would turn out to be like the case of the foolish host who, having once made his guests drunk on good old wine, diluted the wine with kvass the next time he invited guests, so that there might appear to be more wine.

Goodbye, I embrace you. Write more often.

160. To COUNTESS S. A. TOLSTAYA

Karalyk, 18 June 1871

I'm writing my fourth letter to you, my dear; I haven't received one from you yet, nor could I have done. I look forward to Monday when the courier brings the letters from Samara. I can't give you any pleasant news. My health is still not good. Since I came here,[1] I've begun to get a feeling of depression like a fever at 6 o'clock every evening, a physical depression, the sensation of which I can't convey better than by saying that soul and body part company. I don't allow my spiritual longing for you to well up in me. I never think about you and the children, and I

---

[160] 1. Tolstoy spent six weeks in the Samara steppes in June and July 1871 taking a kumys cure for his health, and looking for a small estate to buy. His brother-in-law, the sixteen-year-old Stepan Andreyevich Behrs (Styopa), accompanied him.

don't allow myself to think because I'm tempted to do so every moment, and if I were to think hard I should go away at once. I don't understand my condition: either I caught a cold in the tent during the first cold night or else the kumys is bad for me, but I've been worse in the three days I've been here. The main thing is weakness, depression and wanting to play the woman and weep, and it's embarrassing, whether with the Bashkirs or with Styopa.

We're living in a tent and drinking kumys (Styopa as well, everybody treats him); the discomforts of life would strike terror in your Kremlin heart: no beds, no crockery, no white bread, no spoons. As for you, you would find it easier to endure the misfortune of underdone turkey or undersalted Easter cake. But these discomforts aren't at all unpleasant, and it would be good fun if only I were well. As it is, I make Styopa depressed, and I can see that he's bored. The hunting is quite decent. I went out once and killed two ducks.

Apart from us there are about 10 kumys drinkers of various sorts living here: an assistant prosecutor, a lawyer, a landowner, some priests and merchants, and I've also come across a professor of Greek from a seminary and have been reading with him. For myself, I've decided to wait till Sunday week, the 27th, and if the depression and fever haven't passed, I'll go home.

It's been cold at night, but yesterday, the 17th, a terrible heatwave began and I said to Styopa today, when he was moaning, that unless you take care you could be driven to desperation by the heat, and especially by the thought that you literally can't find a single tree for hundreds of versts round about, and that you can only shelter from the sun in the tent which is completely sun-baked, and where we're sitting with nothing on and still sweating.

The most painful thing for me is that because of my poor health, I only feel $\frac{1}{10}$ of what exists. There are no intellectual pleasures, especially poetic ones. I look at everything as though I were dead—the very thing for which I used to dislike many people. And now I myself can only see what exists; I understand and grasp it; but I can't see through it, as I used to, with love. And if I'm sometimes in a poetic mood, it's only a very sour and tearful one—I just want to cry.

Perhaps the illness has reached the crisis. Write and tell me in detail about everyone at home. I don't allow myself to think about you when I'm awake, but I've dreamed about you for two nights now. Yesterday you were going off somewhere very jauntily, and I was trying to stop you by all sorts of cunning means and was in despair. And today your sister Tanya was going somewhere in a velvet dress and we were both trying to stop her.

Goodbye, darling. Write more. Kiss everyone.

161. To COUNTESS S. A. TOLSTAYA

Karalyk, 23 June 1871

I'm glad to write to you, my dear, with good news about myself, i.e. that two days after my last letter to you where I complained about depression and ill health, I

161. To Countess S. A. Tolstaya

began to feel fine, and ashamed that I had alarmed you. I can't, from habit, either write or say to you what I don't think. What worries me only is the fact that it will be two weeks tomorrow since I left home, and I still haven't received a word from you. I'm seized with fear when I think about it, and vividly imagine you and the children and all that might happen to you.

Nobody is to blame for the fact that I've received no letters, except the locality—130 versts without a postal service. It will be a week tomorrow since the Bashkir messenger left; he was due back on Sunday, but it's Wednesday today and he's not here.

I've now learned my new address which I'll add at the end. Take it in turns to write—first to Samara, then to the new address. When I get the letters, I'll tell you which address is better.

The depression and indifference which I complained about have passed; I feel myself approaching the Scythian state, and everything is interesting and new. I don't feel boredom, only constant fear and the lack of you, and so I'm counting the days until my divorced and incomplete existence comes to an end. I'll hold out day after day for 6 weeks and then I intend—I daren't say it or think it—I intend to be home by 5 August. But how will things be at home? Are you all safe and sound, are you all as I left you? Particularly you! There is much that is new and interesting: the Bashkirs who reek of Herodotus, and Russian peasants, and villages which are especially charming for the simplicity and kindness of the people. I bought a horse for 60 roubles and Styopa and I go riding. Styopa is fine. Sometimes he's in high spirits and keeps abusing Petersburg with an important air, sometimes he hangs around me and I'm sorry for him because he's bored, and sorry he's not at Yasnaya. I'll have a lot to tell you about generally, and I'll be angry with you for listening to Masha whining, and not to what I'm saying. Will it be like that? And when? I shoot ducks and we have them to eat. We've just been riding after bustards and only scared them away as usual, then we came on a wolf's litter and a Bashkir caught a cub there. I'm reading Greek, but very little. I don't feel like it. Nobody has ever described kumys better than the peasant who said to me the other day that *we are out at grass*—like horses. I don't feel like anything which might harm me: vigorous exercise or smoking (Styopa is trying to cure me of the habit of smoking, and now gives me 12 cigarettes a day, reducing the number all the time)—or tea or sitting up late.

I get up at 6, drink kumys at 7, go to the village where the kumys drinkers live, have a talk to them, walk back, drink tea with Styopa, then read a bit, walk about the steppe in my shirtsleeves, go on drinking kumys, eat a piece of roast mutton, and either go hunting or riding, and in the evening go to bed almost as soon as it's dark.

You told me to see what the comforts of life and travel are like. I've kept asking about land here, and I've been offered it at 15 roubles a desyatina, which brings in 6 per cent without any trouble, and today a priest wrote me a letter about a piece of land 2,500 desyatinas in area at 7 roubles a desyatina, which seems very profitable. I'll go and see it tomorrow.

162. To Prince V. P. Meshchersky

Since it's very possible in general that I'll buy this land or another piece, please send me a credit note from the Merchants' Bank, which may be needed for a deposit (by transfer via the Samara bank)...[40 lines omitted]

162. To PRINCE V. P. MESHCHERSKY

Vladimir Petrovich Meshchersky (1839–1914), a publicist and author of satirical stories and novels; publisher of *The Citizen*, a journal with a distinct upper-class bias, which also flirted with Slavophile ideas. From 1870 until his death Meshchersky worked in the Ministry of Public Education.

[Not sent]   Yasnaya Polyana, 22 August 1871

Even before I received your welcome letter, dear Prince, I had replied to Prince Dmitry Obolensky that I regretted very much that I couldn't be of use to you and your publication;[1] your letter only increased this regret. I am not writing anything, and I hope and wish not to write anything, and particularly not to publish anything; but even if through human weakness I were to give way again to the evil passion to write and publish, I would in every respect prefer to publish in book form. And even if I took it into my head to publish anything in a journal, I have promised it first to *The Dawn*,[2] and then to *Conversation*.[3] From this you will see that I can't be of use to you, and you will probably agree that your publication will lose nothing by it.

And if you think—why can't he write something just for the sake of it for our paper as well as for *The Dawn* and *Conversation*, then I'm certain, to judge from the flattering opinion you expressed about my writing, that you will guess that I can't write *just for the sake of it*—i.e. for any other purpose except the satisfaction of an inner need.

To tell the truth, I hate newspapers and journals—I haven't read any for a long time now and consider them harmful institutions for producing double blooms which never bear fruit, institutions which exhaust intellectual and even artistic soil unproductively. The idea of a newspaper or a journal having a trend also seems very false to me. Intellectual and artistic work is the highest manifestation of man's spiritual strength, and so it directs all human activity, and no one can direct it. But if a newspaper or a journal chooses for its goal the interest of the moment—and a

[162] 1. Meshchersky was planning to publish *The Citizen*, a journal 'of politics and literature'. It was published from 1872 to 1914. (Dostoyevsky was editor of the journal from 1873 to 1874.)
2. N. N. Strakhov had written in the autumn of 1870, requesting Tolstoy to contribute to *The Dawn*. Tolstoy wrote to Strakhov on 25 November 1870, declining to do so, but promising any short work which he might write in future to *The Dawn*. He published *A Captive in the Caucasus* in *The Dawn*, 1872, No. 2.
3. Tolstoy published his story *God Sees the Truth but Waits* in *Russian Conversation*, 1872, No. 3.

162. To Prince V. P. Meshchersky

practical one at that—then such activity in my opinion is millions of miles away from genuine artistic and intellectual activity, and has as much to do with the business of poetry and thought as the painting of signboards has to do with art.

I wouldn't write all this to you if I didn't find your personality highly sympathetic to judge from your letter, your article in *The Russian Herald* which I skimmed through,[4] and particularly the stock you come from.[5] For this reason I will add one more thing—advice to you personally; don't be angered by it, and please think about it. All newspaper and journalistic activity is an intellectual brothel from which there is no retreat. In my lifetime I have seen many people who have perished irretrievably—ardent, noble and intellectually clever people, such as I consider you to be.

Just as your letter came from the heart, so too does mine, so don't reprimand me if it goes against the grain. I press your hand and would very much like to meet you.

Yours,
L. Tolstoy

163. To N. N. STRAKHOV

Yasnaya Polyana, 13 September 1871

I'm replying to you, dear Nikolay Nikolayevich, in the same order as you wrote to me, i.e. first of all so-called business matters, i.e. trifles, and then what is not business, i.e. what is essential. When I read the first part of your letter,[1] I meant to reply that I agreed to Perog's[2] proposal, and would agree to such a proposal now, mainly because I would otherwise have to publish it myself, and it's a lot of bother, and I'm not up to it. That's all about business matters. There's just one thing—I didn't expect you to trouble yourself with the business of mine, and if I had expected it, I wouldn't have dared ask you. I'm very grateful to you for everything you've done in this matter, and I beg you not to concern yourself further with these trifles. I value a different kind of conversation with you. You are wrong to praise me as you do. Firstly (and more especially had it been a couple of years ago) I should have to put on airs in front of you and be unnatural if I were to try to maintain in your eyes the image you have of me; secondly, praise has a harmful effect on me (I'm too inclined to believe it to be justified), and I've only recently, and with a great effort, succeeded in eradicating from myself all that nonsense caused by the success of my book.[3] You yourself have such a fine understanding of this—like A. Grigoryev, who promoted everyone to the rank of genius, so as to bathe in an atmosphere of praise. And it isn't difficult to deceive me about the importance of

---

4. Meshchersky's 'Russia from the Pen of a Remarkable Man. Contemporary Letters', published in *The Russian Herald*, 1871, No. 4.

5. Meshchersky was the grandson of N. M. Karamzin (1766–1826), the writer and historian.

[163] 1. Strakhov referred to his attempts to find a publisher for a proposed new edition of Tolstoy's collected works.

2. It is not known to whom this refers.

3. *War and Peace*.

163. To N. N. Strakhov

my work—I'm only too pleased to be deceived.[4] To your expression of sympathy, I will only reply that I am simply overjoyed by it, since in meeting you, I felt the joy that you felt when you met the same views on life in me as you have yourself. In one thing only are we at odds with each other: I can't get rid of the thought that I have been won over by your praise. Soon after you left I met Tyutchev on the railway, and we talked for 4 hours. I did most of the listening. Do you know him? He's a brilliant, imposing and childlike old man. I know no one alive, except you and him, whom I am so alike in what I feel and think. But on a certain high spiritual level, identity of views on life does not unite people in pursuit of earthly objectives in the same way as it does in lower spheres of activity, but leaves each person independent and free. I felt this with you and with him. We are alike in our view of what is below and beside us; but we don't know who we are and why and how we live and where we are going, and we are unable to tell each other, and we are more alien to each other than my children are to me or even to you. But it's a joy to meet these alien travellers along this desert road. And I felt just such a joy in meeting you and Tyutchev. Do you know what struck me most of all about you? —it was the expression on your face when you once came in from the garden through the balcony door, not knowing that I was in the study. This alien, preoccupied and severe expression explained you to me (with the help, of course, of what you have written and said). I am sure you are destined for purely philosophical activity. I say *purely* in the sense of the renunciation of what is contemporary; but I don't say *purely* in the sense of renouncing the poetic and religious interpretation of things. For purely intellectual philosophy is an ugly Western product; and neither the Greeks—Plato—nor Schopenhauer, nor the Russian thinkers understood it in this way. You have one quality which I haven't met in any single Russian: with all your clarity and conciseness of exposition, you have softness combined with strength: you don't tear with your teeth, but with soft, strong paws. I don't know the content of your proposed work, but I like the title very much,[5] if it defines the content in a general sense. But then, of course, it won't be an *article*, I suppose, but a book. But do give up depraved journalistic activity. I'll tell you something about myself: you're probably experiencing what I experienced when I lived like you (in a turmoil)—namely that occasionally over the months some hours of leisure and silence occur, when little by little your own atmosphere is created around you, undisturbed, and in this atmosphere all the phenomena of life begin to occupy the place they should have and do have for you, and you are conscious of yourself and your powers, like an exhausted man after a bath. And at such moments you really want to work for yourself (not for others), and are happy, simply in the consciousness of yourself and your powers, and sometimes your work too. You are experiencing this feeling, I think, as I occasionally did previously:

4. A slight variation of the last two lines of Pushkin's poem, *A Confession* (1826):
    Ah, it is not difficult to deceive me!
    For I am only too pleased to be deceived!
5. Strakhov had started work on his book: *The World as a Whole*. In a letter to Tolstoy he referred to it as *A Book on the Origin of Things*. It is not known which title Tolstoy is referring to here.

163. To N. N. Strakhov

but now it's my normal condition, and only occasionally do I experience the turmoil in which you found me, and which only occasionally interrupts this state. This is what I would wish for you. As for myself, I'll say that either because I give way too much to this feeling, or because of ill-health (I've been unwell all this time), I am writing nothing and have no wish in my heart to write.

I wanted to write a lot more, but my mood has been interrupted, and I'm sending the letter just as it is.

Once again, thank you for your letter and for the trouble you've gone to over the business of mine.

Yours,
L. Tolstoy

164. To COUNTESS A. A. TOLSTAYA

Moscow, 12 January 1872

My dear Alexandrine;

I've been asked to make a request to you, and I couldn't refuse. Do as you please with my request; I'm glad of this opportunity of writing to you. The request is from my friend Bessonov,[1] an excellent man and a well-known connoisseur and collector of Russian antiques. *In Moscow a society has been formed of lovers of Russian folk songs* (I am one of the founder-members). *The statutes of the society have been submitted to the Minister of Internal Affairs, approved by him and sent on to the Minister for the Court, and there they have been held up; and it is very much hoped to have the authorisation in time for the Polytechnical Exhibition in Moscow, so as to be able to give a series of popular performances in honour of Peter I.*

I've been dreaming all the time that on one or other of your journeys you'll whistle to me, and in my imagination I've prepared a whole series of conversations with you; but evidently there's no need yet—these berries haven't ripened. And there's nothing to write about: my outward life remains the same—i.e. in accordance with the saying: les peuples heureux n'ont pas d'histoire. Everything is just as good at home; I've five children, and so much work that there's never any time. These last years I've been writing a *Primer*,[2] and now I'm having it published. It's very difficult to explain what this labour of many years, this *Primer*, means to me. I hope to send it to you this winter, and then, perhaps, you'll read it out of friendship for me. My proud dreams about this *Primer* are: that two generations of *all* Russian children, from tsars' to peasants', will study with the aid of this *Primer* alone, and

---

[164] 1. P. A. Bessonov (1828–98), a Slavonic scholar, Slavophile, and an expert on Russian folk art. From 1867 to 1879, he was librarian of the University of Moscow. Tolstoy included a story by Bessonov, *Peter I and the Peasant*, in his *Primer*.

2. This *Primer* was published in 1872. It contained a complete course for beginners, and was the fruit of Tolstoy's own educational theories and his experience of teaching in his school at Yasnaya Polyana. There were sections on reading and writing, natural sciences and arithmetic, with accompanying exercises and examples, some of them entirely Tolstoy's own, others drawn from various folk sources. The *Primer* was not well received.

165. To A. F. Pisemsky

will receive their first poetic impressions from it, and that having written this *Primer* I'll be able to die peacefully.

Goodbye; I kiss your hand; don't forget me and don't miss any opportunity for us to see each other. My sister, for whose sake I'm glad that you've grown to love her, is in Nice, and her daughter Varya, my favourite, is getting married to Nagorny, and for the first time I've experienced the feeling of the *cruel father* they have in comedies. Although there's nothing bad in the young man, I'd have killed him if he had come my way out hunting. And I ruined their childlike, so-called happiness by my gloominess; but I can't help it. God forbid I should live to see my daughter a bride. It's a feeling of sacrifice, of immolation on the altar of some terrible and cynical deity. I'm writing this letter from the Perfilyevs', with whom I'm staying in Moscow, and they send you their cordial greetings.

Yours,
L. Tolstoy

165. To A. F. PISEMSKY

Alexey Feofilaktovich Pisemsky (1820–81), journalist, novelist, short-story writer and dramatist. He gained a high literary reputation in the 1850s with his novels and plays, the best-known today being the novel *A Thousand Souls* (1858) and the realistic drama of peasant life *A Hard Lot* (1859), which has been ranked with Tolstoy's *The Power of Darkness* as the best Russian example of this *genre*. Pisemsky, who came from a gentry family so impoverished that he is usually thought of as coming from plebeian stock, is credited with the introduction of a new, more genuine peasant type into Russian literature (*Sketches of Peasant Life*), a departure from the somewhat 'condescending' portraits of the pre-Emancipation peasantry by Turgenev and Grigorovich. His later anti-nihilist stance (the younger, radical generation is satirised in several of his novels, e.g. *Troubled Seas*, 1863) lost him some friends. On the whole, however, he had very little concern with social ideals in literature, and his work presents a fairly bleak, frequently satirical, portrait of Russian life in the years just before and after the Emancipation.

Tolstoy first met Pisemsky in 1855 in Petersburg, when Pisemsky was at the height of his literary and journalistic popularity and they saw each other frequently in 1856 and 1857. The following letter is all that survives of the correspondence between the two men.

Yasnaya Polyana, 3 March 1872

Dear Alexey Feofilaktovich,

I thank you with all my heart for your letter and for sending the book. Apart from the pleasure of your letter, it meant that I read your novel[1] a second time, and

[165] 1. *In the Whirlpool*, first published in 1871, an anti-nihilist novel which harks back to some of the themes of his earlier *Troubled Seas*. It had few admirers apart from Tolstoy and Leskov.

165. To A. F. Pisemsky

the second reading only confirmed the impression I told you about. The third part which I had not read at the time is as excellent as the first chapters which I was delighted with on first reading. The only disagreeable impression your letter made on me was that I felt ashamed that I had not been to see you.

The first time I come, I will arrange to spend an evening with you. Perfilyev, however, knows how mad I always am in Moscow.

Yours most truly and sincerely,
Count L. Tolstoy

166. To N. N. STRAKHOV

Yasnaya Polyana, 3 March 1872

How sorry I am, dear Nikolay Nikolayevich, that there's been such a long silence between us. It seems I'm to blame for this. When I received your letter I so much wanted to talk to you. And there have been no articles from you until the splendid one on Darwin which has just appeared.[1] What are you doing? I can't write about myself and what I'm doing—it would take too long. The *Primer* has been occupying me and still is, but not entirely. And it's this 'residue'[2] that I can't write about, but would like to talk to you about. My *Primer* is finished and is being printed very slowly and badly at Rees', but in my usual way I'm scribbling over everything and altering everything 20 times over. Because of this I didn't send it to *The Dawn*. Between ourselves let it be said that this promise embarrasses me; and *The Dawn* won't derive any benefit from it. It's so worthless, and the stipulation that it should be something out of the *Primer* will destroy everything that my name might have meant. If it's at all possible for you to obtain my release, you would greatly oblige me.[3]

If there is any merit in the *Primer* articles, it will lie in the simplicity and clarity of stroke and line, i.e. of the language; and in a journal this would be strange and disagreeable—as if it were something unfinished. Rather like pencil drawings without any shading in some picture gallery.

Our life in the country is the same as ever. The only new addition has been a new school for peasant children, which came into being of its own accord. And it fully occupies all of us, including my children.

The other day a certain Alexandrov, a contributor to *The Family and the School*,[4] came to see me, read me his articles and asked for advice and instruction; and he left me with an ill-defined impression that he's either a very good and talented man,

[166] 1. 'The Revolution in Science', an article published by Strakhov following the publication in 1871 of a Russian translation of Darwin's *The Descent of Man*. Strakhov opposed Darwin's theory vehemently.

2. He is alluding to his work on a novel of the age of Peter the Great.

3. Tolstoy had promised to send one of the stories from the *Primer* to *The Dawn* for publication. On 10 March Strakhov replied that it was not possible to release Tolstoy from his obligation since it had already been announced in the journal that one such story was due to be published there.

4. A pedagogical journal published in Petersburg from 1871 to 1888.

or else he's absolutely worthless. When you write to me, tell me whether you've heard what sort of man he is.

Have you noticed in our time in the world of Russian poetry a connection between two phenomena which are in inverse relation to each other: the decline of every kind of poetic work of art—music, painting, poetry—and the urge to study Russian folk poetry of every kind—music, painting and poetry? It seems to me that this is not actually a decline, but a death, with the pledge of a rebirth to folk art. The last poetic wave—parabola—was at its zenith in Pushkin's time, then there was Lermontov, Gogol, and we sinners, and it then went underground. Another line moved in the direction of the study of the people and will come to the surface, God willing,

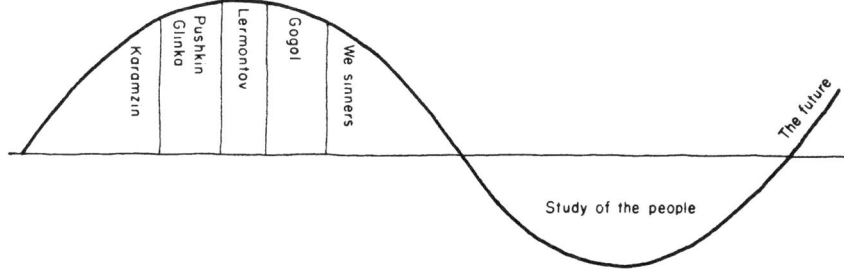

but the age of Pushkin is completely dead and buried.

You surely understand what I want to say.

Happy are those who will take part in this surfacing. I hope to.

Goodbye; I press your hand firmly and look forward to a good long letter. I'm very glad that A. N. Maykov[5] remembers me. I find him a very sympathetic person.

Count L. Tolstoy

167. To N. N. STRAKHOV

Moscow, 22/25 March 1872

You've touched me on the raw, dear Nikolay Nikolayevich. I felt sad after reading your letter. As always, you came directly to the nub of the question and indicated what it was.

You are right that we have no freedom for science and literature, but you see this as a misfortune, and I don't. True, it wouldn't enter the head of a Frenchman, a German, or an Englishman, unless he's a madman, to pause in my place and ponder whether his methods are false, or whether the language we write in and I have written in is false; but the Russian, unless he is insane, must ponder and ask himself: should he go on writing, or rather dictating his precious thoughts, or should he recall

5. A poet whom Tolstoy had met in Petersburg in 1855.

167. To N. N. Strakhov

that even *Poor Liza*[1] was read with enthusiasm and praised by somebody, and look for different methods and a different language? And not just because his reason tells him so, but because our present language and methods are repulsive, and *involuntary dreams attract one*[2] to a different language which happens to be the popular one, and to different methods. Danilevsky's observation is very true, especially with regard to science and literature, so-called, but the poet, if he is a poet, cannot be unfree, whether he is under fire or not. Every man is just as free to get up or stay in bed safely in his own room, as he is to be under fire. It's possible to remain under fire, it's possible to go away, it's possible to defend oneself, or to attack. But it's impossible to build under fire: one must go to where it *is* possible to build.

Notice one thing: we are under fire, but not altogether. If we were, life too would be as insecure and worthless as science and literature, but life is resolute and majestic, and goes its own way without bothering about anyone. I mean that the shots only strike the tower of our idiotic literature. And so we must climb to somewhere lower down—and there we shall be free. And once again *this somewhere lower down* happens to be among the people. *Poor Liza* squeezed out tears, and people praised it, but surely no one will ever read it any more; but songs, folk tales, and byliny—everything simple—will be read as long as there is a Russian language.

I have changed my writing methods and my language, but, I repeat, not because my reason told me it was necessary to do so, but because even Pushkin seems funny to me, not to mention our own lucubrations; while the language which the people speak and which has sounds to express everything a poet might want to say, is dear to me. This language moreover—and this is the main thing—is the best poetic regulator. If you try to say anything superfluous, bombastic or morbid, the language won't permit it; but our literary language is spineless; so spoilt that whatever nonsense you write looks like literature. The nationalism[3] of the Slavophiles and true nationalism are two things as different as sulphuric ether and universal ether, the source of warmth and light. I hate all these *choral principles* and *systems of life* and *communes* and fictitious *Slav brethren*;[4] but I simply love what is definite, clear, beautiful and unpretentious, and I find all this in popular poetry and language and life, and just the opposite in our own.

I've scarcely started writing, and will hardly do so before the winter. All my time and energies are taken up with the *Primer*. I've written an entirely new article in the *Primer* for *The Dawn—A Captive in the Caucasus*[5]—and will send it in no later than a week's time. Thank you for the suggestion, and please do correct the proofs.

Please write what you think about this article. It's a model of the methods and the language that I'm writing in, and will write in, for adults.

I know that I shall be abused, and I'm afraid that you will abuse me too. Please

[167] 1. Karamzin's sentimental tale (1792).
2. A quotation from Pushkin's poem *The Genealogy of My Hero.*
3. *Narodnost* in Russian.
4. References to Slavophile concepts and terminology.
5. Published in *The Dawn*, 1872, No. 2.

abuse me as boldly as you like. I trust you, and so your abuse will be useful to me. I don't say that I'll heed it, but it will weigh heavy on the scales.

>Yours,
>Count L. Tolstoy

This letter has been lying about for three days. I've finished the article and am sending it tomorrow.
25 March

168. To COUNTESS A. A. TOLSTAYA

>Yasnaya Polyana, 31 March 1872

When I wrote you a letter, my dear *Alexandrine*, and didn't receive an answer for a long time, I didn't doubt for a minute that there was some reason preventing you from writing; but when I received your letter, I suddenly understood that in your place I wouldn't have written at all. And I felt ashamed, particularly because you had been ill. Years can pass without my corresponding with people I love, as long as I know that these people are not unhappy—not ill—even if they aren't happy. But to think that I know nothing while a person dear to me is suffering physically or morally is very unpleasant; and so, as from today, I've turned over a new leaf and am beginning, if you wish, a regular correspondence. Don't be alarmed—if I receive three letters a year from you, it's enough. There's one bad thing, and that's the fact that you and I are not on a par—I don't know how it is with your other friends—in the sense that our interest in each other has always been composed of a large part of me and a small part of you, i.e. that you have always interested yourself more in me than you have allowed me to be interested in you. And I find this embarrassing. As far as my mental activity is concerned, I am an egoist, i.e. it seems to me that my thoughts must always be of interest to everyone, and I'm prepared to thrust them on everyone; but I consider my person of very little worth, and of no interest to myself, let alone to anyone else.

How's your health? Be sure to write to me about this; and if you add to it even the briefest of *bulletins* on your moral and spiritual state, it will be a surprise for me—a gift. When I was young and looked at grey, toothless old men like myself, how firmly convinced I was that if there was any interesting spiritual life or movement, it must be looked for in the young, and that these old men were withered up like relics, both inside and out, and were always the same; but now I see that the further one advances, the bigger and steeper are the steps—and you stumble on them quite unexpectedly. I'm saying this for the reason that even a brief *bulletin* on your spiritual state is interesting to me. My life is just the same, i.e. I couldn't wish for anything better. There are a few great and intellectual joys—just as many as I have the strength to experience—and a solid background of *foolish joys*, as for instance: teaching the peasant children to read and write, breaking in a young horse, admiring a large room newly built on to the house, calculating the future income from a newly purchased estate, a well done version of a fable by Aesop, rattling off a

168. To Countess A. A. Tolstaya

symphony for 4 hands with my niece, fine calves—all heifers—and so on. The great joys are a family which is *terribly* fortunate, children who are all fit and well, and, I'm almost certain, intelligent and unspoiled, and work. Last year it was the Greek language, this year it's been the *Primer* so far, and now I'm beginning a big, new work,[1] in which there will be something of what I told you, although the whole thing is quite different, which is something I never expected. I feel altogether rested now from my previous work, and entirely freed from the influence my writing had on me, and, most important, free of pride and praise. I'm starting work joyfully, timidly and apprehensively, as I did the first time.

Not only have I no thought of going to the exhibition in Moscow, but yesterday I returned from Moscow—where I was ill—with such a feeling of disgust for all that idleness and luxury, that wealth dishonestly acquired by men and women alike, that debauchery seeping into every stratum of society, that lack of firm social principles, that I've decided never to go to Moscow again. I think with dread of the future, when my daughters are grown up.

I kiss your hand. Sonya thanks you for remembering her, and kisses you.

Your old and faithful friend,
L. Tolstoy

If you see your people, give them my cordial greetings. I know nothing of them—drop me a line about them.

169. To A. A. FET

Yasnaya Polyana, 8–10(?) June 1872

[This 'letter' is written in doggerel iambic verse, with an irregular rhyming scheme, and is in reply to a letter in verse by Fet which has not survived.]

> As shamed the onion before the rose
> Although it has no cause for shame,
> So shamed am I in prose to answer
> Your latest challenge, my dear Fet.
> And so I pen my first reply
> In verse, though not without misgivings.
> When? Where? You must decide yourself,
> But come and see us, do, O Fet!
> Although our house is being painted,
> And full of folk as are the cells
> When Fet is serving on the bench—
> The more there are, the merrier,
> As the old Russian saying goes,
> And so we shall be glad to see you,

---

[168] 1. An historical novel on the life and times of Peter the Great. The work was later abandoned.

170. To Countess A. A. Tolstaya

> And my wife bids me say so, Fet.
> At an appointed hour a carriage
> Will meet your train at Yasenki.
> I'll search the carriages for Fet,
> Examine every hole and corner...
> Wise men are few upon this earth
> And fools there are in any number,
> So when I even think of Fet
> The very thought makes my mouth water.
> I'll be content with a dry summer,
> The rye and barley can all rot
> As long as I can somehow manage
> To talk my fill all day to Fet.
> We both are too solicitous;
> Let there be many cares to come;
> Sufficient to the day its evil,
> Far better live, my dearest Fet...

Joking apart, write as soon as possible so that we shall know when to meet you. My wife is expecting a baby any day now. But if I can't meet you myself because of the confinement, I'll send news to the station in any case. I terribly want to see you.

Yours,
Tolstoy

170. To COUNTESS A. A. TOLSTAYA

Yasnaya Polyana, 15 September 1872

My dear Alexandrine,

You are one of those people whose whole being says to their friends: '*I will share with thee thy sorrows, and thou thy joys with me*',[1] and here am I, forever telling you about my happiness, now seeking for your sympathy in my sorrow.

Unforeseeably and unexpectedly an event has befallen me which has changed my whole life.

A young bull at Yasnaya Polyana has killed a herdsman, and I'm under investigation, under arrest—I can't leave the house (all this because of the whim of a boy called an investigator), and in a few days I'm due to be charged and to defend myself in court—before whom? It's dreadful to think of, dreadful to recall all the vile things that they have done, are doing, and will do to me.

It's intolerable for a man like me with a grey beard and 6 children, with the consciousness of a useful, industrious life, with the firm conviction that I can't be guilty, with the contempt that I can't help feeling for the new courts from what I've seen of them, with the sole desire to be left in peace as I leave everyone in peace,

---

[170] 1. This quotation is in English in the original.

170. To Countess A. A. Tolstaya

—it's intolerable to live in Russia with the fear that any boy who doesn't like my face can make me sit on a bench before a court, and then in jail; but I'll stop being furious. You'll read the whole story in the press. I'll die of fury if I don't give vent to it; and let them try me for telling the truth as well. I'll tell you what I intend to do and what I'm asking of you.

If I don't die of fury and anguish in jail, where they'll no doubt send me (I'm convinced that they hate me), I've decided to emigrate to England for ever, or until such time as the freedom and dignity of every man is assured in our country. My wife views the prospect with pleasure—she loves everything English; it will be good for the children; I'll have sufficient means (I'll collect 200,000 roubles from the sale of everything); and for myself, notwithstanding my aversion to European life, I hope that over there I'll stop being furious and will be able to spend the few years of life remaining to me peacefully, working on what I still have to write. Our plan is to settle at first near London, and then to select a beautiful and healthy spot by the sea, wherever there are good schools, and buy a house and some land. For life in England to be pleasant, we'll need to know some good aristocratic families. This is where you can help me, and this is what I'm asking of you. Please do this for me. If you don't know any such families, you can doubtless arrange something through your friends: two or three letters which would open the doors of a good English circle to us. This is essential for the children who'll have to grow up there. I can't say anything yet about when we are going, since they can torment me as long as they like. You can't imagine what it means. They say that laws provide securité. With us it's just the opposite. I've organised my life with the utmost securité. I'm satisfied with little; I seek and desire nothing but peace and quiet: I'm loved and respected by the people; even thieves pass me by; I enjoy complete securité, only not from the laws. The hardest thing of all for me is my fury. I so love loving, but now I can't help being furious. I read the Lord's Prayer and the 37th Psalm, and the Lord's Prayer in particular calms me for a moment, and then I start seething again and can't do anything or think; I've abandoned my work out of a silly desire to get revenge, when there's no one to take revenge on. Only now that I've begun preparing for the departure and have firmly made up my mind have I calmed down, and I hope to be myself again soon. Goodbye; I kiss your hand.

171. To COUNTESS A. A. TOLSTAYA

Yasnaya Polyana, 19 September 1872

I hasten to write to you, my dear, about the new turn that my affair has taken quite unexpectedly, and as a result of which my plans have changed. Forgive me if I've alarmed you, but I'm not to blame: I've been tormented this month as never before in my life, and with my male egoism I wanted everyone to suffer with me, if only a little. I felt better as soon as I had told you about it and had made up my mind to leave. Today—just now—I received a letter from the president of the court—he writes that all the vile things done to me were a mistake, and that I shall be left in

171. To Countess A. A. Tolstaya

peace. If that is so, then I shan't go anywhere, and only ask you to forgive me if I've alarmed you. But to justify myself I must tell you the whole story.

While I was away in Samara,[1] a bull killed a man—a herdsman. Even when I was back at home, months passed without my seeing the steward and without my having anything to do with the estate. Then some youth arrives, says he is the investigator, asks me whether I'm the son of lawfully wedded parents etc., and announces to me that I'm charged with illegal activity, which resulted in a death, and demands that I sign a paper stating that I won't leave Yasnaya Polyana before the investigation is completed. I ask whether I have to sign or not. The procurator tells me that if I don't sign I'll be put in prison. I sign, and inquire whether the investigation can be completed soon. I'm told: the assistant procurator is obliged by law to complete the investigation within the space of a week—i.e. to drop it or to bring a formal charge. But I know that a peasant in my village has been waiting for this week for more than 3 years now. And I know it can drag on for one year, two years—as long as they like. Three weeks go by; consoling myself with the thought that in my case a decision will be made if not in one week, then in 3, I make inquiries. Well, not only has a decision not been made, but the case hasn't even been heard of 15 versts away. I inquire who is responsible either for dropping it or bringing a charge. It's a certain assistant procurator, little more than a boy, about 20 years old. If the assistant procurator is anything like the investigator, then that's that—I'll be in jail for 4 months. What hope is there of reprieve? The court. As ill luck would have it, I'm on jury service at this very time and have to go to court. The question is: should I go or shouldn't I? Who should I ask? I ask the president of the court. He writes and says that I'd be entitled not to go.

I write a note to the court saying that I can't come because I'm under investigation. In court the assistant procurator publicly states that I can't be a juror because I'm charged with a crime under article 1466, i.e. with murder (you understand how pleasant that is). The court imposes a fine of 225 roubles on me and demands that I appear, otherwise I shall be brought to trial.

There's nothing to be done. Carrying the letter from the president of the court saying that I'm legally entitled not to go to court, I arrive, and afford these gentlemen the pleasure of amusing themselves at my expense.

So that's the court which is going to try me! Furthermore, don't forget that in the affair of the bull which they've now foisted on to my steward, out of fausse honte, there's no possibility of charging anyone whatsoever; and since I was living in Samara and had had nothing to do with the estate, they could no more charge me than they could you. Furthermore, don't forget that I know no one in Tula and don't wish to know anyone; I don't interfere with anyone in any way, I only ask God and men for peace and quiet; I'm occupied from morning till night with a work that demands all my attention—the final revision of my book which is now being published.[2] I often wondered, in fact, whether I hadn't committed some crime or gone out of my mind. One gets furious, and feels the humiliation of fury,

[171] 1. Tolstoy spent the last two weeks of July at his newly acquired estate in the Province of Samara.   2. The *Primer*, published in 1872.

171. To Countess A. A. Tolstaya

and gets even more furious. And now they write to me that the investigator made a mistake, that the assistant procurator was in too much of a hurry, and that the court might also have taken a different view, and that all is well, and that everything has its little imperfections. A little imperfection—the fact that I've been under arrest for a whole month (and still am), that by some good fortune the assistant procurator surmised that it was impossible to charge me, otherwise I would have been tried—i.e. they would have enjoyed themselves to the full. Besides, I've not heard anything officially even now. Perhaps they'll think up something else. So I'll only say that I've changed my intention of leaving, and that it's more than likely that there won't be a trial. I made up my mind right from the start of the affair that if there was to be a trial I should leave. And when I wrote to you, it was obvious that there was going to be a trial. If an obliging commandant, wishing to be of service to the inhabitants of a town, were to post sentries for the protection of the householders, and these sentries, through human imperfection, were to kill all the householders they had been posted to guard, it would not be unlike these little imperfections of my month under arrest and the 3 years my peasant has been in prison.

So there you have my story. Although nothing is over and done with as yet, and my signed statement hasn't been returned, and although they can still do a lot of nasty things, I see from the president's letter that they want to leave me in peace now, and I'm sorry that I wrote to you and have now had to write all these explanations.

Today something happened to quell my annoyance before I even received the letter. In the morning my wife fell ill with a violent fever and pains in the chest, threatening mastitis (she's nursing), and I suddenly felt that a man has no right to dispose of his life, and particularly of his family, as he wishes. And my annoyance and this outrage appeared to me so petty, that I was doubtful whether I would go away at all. She's feeling better now, and I hope she'll escape mastitis. My sister Masha left us a few days ago. She spoke of you with tenderness every day and reproached herself with not having written to you, while I reproach myself for writing. Please forgive me; I kiss your hand.

L. Tolstoy

172. To COUNTESS A. A. TOLSTAYA

Yasnaya Polyana, 20–1(?) September 1872

My dear Alexandrine,

You write: 'si j'ai dit quelque chose qui vous irrite...'[1] Your whole letter had this effect on me, and I thank God that I got it when I'd already calmed down somehow.

It's impossible to understand another's situation with one's reason, and I didn't expect you to; but it is possible to understand with one's heart, and this I did expect

---
[172] 1. Her letter has not survived.

and was mistaken. I have always found that if you fall onto an anthill you have to get off it before you can stop squealing and struggling; but you don't find it so, but say that it's necessary to take courage, not to be an egoist, and to be a Christian. It's possible to take courage where there's an enemy, where there's danger; but where the struggle is with falsehood and pretence, you have to resign yourself to it in my view. In order not to be an egoist and to be of use to others, it's necessary first of all to stop suffering and struggling; it's necessary first of all to get off the anthill. In order to accept in a Christian way everything sent by God, it's necessary first of all to be aware of your own self, but when ants are crawling all over you and biting you, it's impossible to think of anything but how to escape. And it's impossible to accept as a trial sent from above the itch caused throughout your whole body by insects clinging to you. The whole point is not how the mind, but how the heart will regard a person (a child or an old man) struggling on an anthill. To many it will seem amusing, to others stupid, and to some pitiful and humiliating. I quite understand that many people of lofty refinement can be flogged, and they will only glance round to see if anyone has seen, and become even more agreeable than before, and you don't feel sorry for them; and I quite understand too, that there are other people who sacrifice everything to preserving their own dignity, for whom the slightest humiliation is physical pain, and these you are sorry for. The whole point is that you haven't understood that the fury which I experienced and which I suffered from was not the product of my will, but just as much an undoubted consequence of what I experienced, as swelling and pain are a consequence of a bee sting. One thing you don't tell me, but which I tell myself, is the reason why I wrote to you. When I recall that I wrote to you with the ulterior motive (clear to me now) that you should divulge what happened to me in the circle in which you live—I blush with shame, especially when I recall your reply. I'm very sorry I alarmed you, and I certainly won't in future. But more than ever I stick to my opinion that the best thing that a self-respecting man can do is to get away from this ugly sea of self-opinionated vulgarity, of debauched idleness and lies, lies, lies, which inundates the tiny islet of honest and industrious living which I have organised for myself, and get away to England, because only there is the freedom of the individual guaranteed—guaranteed for a peaceful and independent life and against every outrage.[2]

Goodbye; I kiss your hand, and beg you to forgive me for alarming you.

173. To COUNTESS A. A. TOLSTAYA

Yasnaya Polyana, 26(?) October 1872

My dear Alexandrine,

When I was writing my last letter[1] (and particularly when I was sending it off),

2. I have taken the liberty of correcting what appears to be an error in the Russian which reads '*for* every outrage'.

[173] 1. Letter 172.

173. To Countess A. A. Tolstaya

I felt I was doing something wrong, but when I got your reply I was amazed that I could have sent the letter at all. I beg you with all my heart to forgive me for causing you distress.

I wanted to write to you at length, but before leaving for Moscow I have written a whole lot of business letters and I feel I shan't be able to write what I wanted to write to you. I'll wait till another time. I'm sending this off to relieve my conscience a little. I kiss your hand.

Yours,
L. Tolstoy

You asked me about the business of the bull. The result was that the investigator *had made a mistake* in charging me. And having charged me, he had *made a second mistake* in extracting from me a signed undertaking not to leave my estate. And those who levied a fine on me *had also made a mistake*. And the fact that these proceedings had been begun at all was *a mistake* as well, because, after they had acquitted me, they began to charge my steward, to try to prove that there had been some sort of case; but it's so obvious that nobody was to blame, that no formal charge can possibly be brought against the steward. To justify myself a little, I may add that having finished my *Primer* I recently began to write the big story—I don't like to call it a novel—which I've been dreaming about for so long.[2] And when this folly, as Pushkin well called it, begins to take hold of you, you become particularly sensitive to the coarse things of life. Imagine a man in perfect stillness and darkness trying to hear the sounds of whispering and trying to see rays of light in the gloom, suddenly having stinking Bengal lights let off under his nose and having to listen to a march played on instruments that are out of tune. Very painful. Now once again I'm listening and watching in the stillness and darkness, and I only wish I could describe the hundredth part of what I see and hear. It gives me great pleasure. So much for my confession. You gave me a subject for my letter which I would like to write on—namely my children. Here they are:

The eldest is fair-haired—and not bad-looking. There is something weak and forbearing in his expression, and very gentle. When he laughs, it's not contagious, but when he cries I can hardly refrain from crying too. Everyone says he is like my elder brother. I'm afraid to believe it. It would be too good. My brother's chief characteristic was not egoism and not unselfishness, but a strict middle course. He didn't sacrifice himself for anybody, but he didn't get in anybody's way, far less do anybody any harm. He kept his joys and sorrows to himself. Seryozha is clever—he has a mathematical mind and a feeling for art, he's an excellent pupil, good at jumping and gymnastics; but he's gauche and absent-minded. There's little originality in him. He's dependent on the physical. When he's well he's a very different boy from when he's ill.

Ilya is the 3rd child. He's never been ill. He's big-boned, fair-skinned, ruddy-complexioned and glowing. A bad pupil. Always thinking about what he's told not to. Thinks up games himself. Neat and tidy; possessive; 'mine' very important to him. Hot-tempered, *violent*, pugnacious; but also tender and very sensitive.

2. A 'novel' about the times of Peter the Great.

173. To Countess A. A. Tolstaya

Sensual—fond of eating and having a quiet lie down. When he eats blackcurrant jelly and buckwheat porridge his lips smack. Original in everything. When he cries, he's angry at the same time, and unpleasant, but when he laughs everyone laughs too.

Everything forbidden has its attraction for him, and he gets to know about it at once. When still a little fellow he overheard my pregnant wife saying she could feel the movement of her child. For a long time his favourite game was to stuff something round underneath his jacket, stroke it with a tense hand and whisper with a smile: 'it's baby'. He would also stroke all the bumps where the furniture springs had broken and say 'baby'. Recently, when I was writing stories for my *Primer* he invented one of his own: 'A boy asked: "does God go to the lavatory?" God punished him, and the boy had to spend all his life going to the lavatory.'

If I die, the elder boy will turn out a splendid fellow, wherever he gets to, and will almost certainly be top at school, but Ilya will come to grief unless he has a strict supervisor and one he loves.

In summer we used to go bathing; Seryozha would ride himself, and I would put Ilya in the saddle behind me. I came out one morning and they were both waiting. Ilya was wearing a hat and carrying a towel, all neat and tidy and beaming, but Seryozha had come running up from somewhere, hatless and out of breath. 'Find your hat', I said, 'or I won't take you.' Seryozha ran hither and thither—but no hat. 'It's no good, I won't take you without a hat. It will be a lesson for you, you're always losing everything.' He was on the verge of tears. I set off with Ilya and waited to see if he showed any sympathy. None at all. He just beamed, and talked about the horse. My wife found Seryozha in tears. He'd looked for his hat and couldn't find it. She guessed that her brother, who had gone off early in the morning to fish, had put on Seryozha's hat. She wrote me a note to say that Seryozha was probably not to blame for losing his hat, and she was sending him on to me in a cap. (She had guessed rightly.) I heard rapid footsteps on the bridge leading to the bathing-place and Seryozha came running up (he'd lost the note on the way) and began to sob. Then Ilya did too, and so did I a little.

Tanya is 8. Everyone says she is like Sonya, and I believe it, even though it's a good thing to believe, but I also believe it because it's obvious. If she had been Adam's eldest daughter and there had been no children younger than her, she would have been an unhappy girl. Her greatest pleasure is to play with little children. She obviously finds physical enjoyment in holding and touching a child's body. Her avowed dream now is to have children. The other day we went to Tula to have her portrait done. She began to ask me to buy a penknife for Seryozha, then something else for another child and something else for a third. She knows exactly what will give most pleasure to each one. I didn't buy anything for her, and she never for a moment thought about herself. On our way home I said 'Tanya, are you asleep?' 'No.' 'What are you thinking about?' 'I'm thinking when we get home how I'll ask mama whether little Lev has been good, and how I'll give him a present, and somebody else a present, and how Seryozha will pretend he doesn't like it, but will really like it very much.' She's not very clever. She doesn't like to put her mind to work,

173. To Countess A. A. Tolstaya

but the mechanism in her head is sound. She'll be a splendid wife if God should give her a husband. And I'm prepared to give a huge prize to anyone who could make *a new woman* out of her.

The 4th—Lev. Good-looking, clever, a good memory, graceful. Any clothes fit him as though made for him. Anything other people do he can do too, and very cleverly and well. *I don't understand him* properly yet.

The 5th—Masha. Two years old, the one who nearly cost Sonya her life. A weak, sickly child; milk-white body, curly fair hair, large, strange blue eyes—strange because of their deep, serious expression. Very clever, and unattractive to look at. She's going to be an enigma. She'll suffer, and search and find nothing; but she'll go on searching for ever for what is most unattainable.

The 6th—Pyotr. A giant. An enormous, fascinating baby in a bonnet. He puts his elbows out and tries to crawl somewhere, and my wife gets agitated and excited and het up when she takes him in her arms, but I don't understand it at all. I know he has great physical reserves, but I don't know whether there is also anything for which they are needed. For this reason I don't like children less than 2 or 3 years old—I don't understand them. Did I tell you a strange observation of mine?

There are two sorts of men—those who hunt and those who don't. Those who don't, like little children, and can pick them up in their arms; those who hunt have a feeling of fear, disgust and pity for babies. I don't know any exception to this rule. Try it out on your friends.

174. To P. D. GOLOKHVASTOV

Pavel Dmitriyevich Golokhvastov (1838–92), a writer and historian. He contributed to *Russian Archives* and made a special study of the Russian byliny. He visited Yasnaya Polyana on several occasions, and offered to send Tolstoy some books on Peter the Great.

Yasnaya Polyana, 24 January 1873

I'm getting unscrupulous. No sooner did I turn down your offer than I found I needed 3 books. I consulted your next to last letter and two of them are there: Korb,[1] and Yesipov's book on the dissenters.[2] If it's not too much trouble, please send them. The third book is Kirillov's *Statistics*,[3] which Ustryalov[4] mentions. If

---

[174] 1. Johann Georg Korb, Secretary of the Austrian legation in Moscow in the early part of Peter's reign, whose diary, published in Vienna in 1700, came out in Russian translation in 1867.

2. G. V. Yesipov (1812–99), author of a book on the Russian dissenting sects in the eighteenth century (2 vols, 1861–3).

3. Ivan Kirillov (d. 1738), Secretary of the Senate and author of the first statistical survey of Russia, compiled in 1728, and edited in the nineteenth century by the historian Pogodin.

4. N. G. Ustryalov (1805–70), historian and author of a substantial *History of the Reign of Peter the Great*.

it's on sale, then (do forgive me) get it at Solovyov's when you are there, on my account, and send it me, please. I've now reached the stage in my study of the period (you have surely experienced it) when you begin to move round in an enchanted circle. Different parties repeat the same thing and you know where it comes from. Isn't that so?

I'm still hopeful about genealogies. Do you know if there is anything in that line, particularly the Sheremetevs and the Apraksins? On the other hand I've reached the stage when, having read a lot of descriptions of the times, always false and written from a vulgar European heroic point of view, you feel furious at the falseness of it, and in your desire to break this magic circle of falseness, you lose your composure and attentiveness which are so necessary.

Your letter was very welcome. In good moments I think more or less the same, but confirmation from outside is welcome.

I also want to give you some heartfelt advice; but mine will not be welcome, although you probably know yourself what I shall say. Don't live in Moscow. For people who have to do hard intellectual work there are two dangers; the journals and conversation. You are, I imagine, impervious to the first, but the second, I think, is dangerous for you. You talk well, and people are glad to listen to you because you have something to say: but that's the trouble. And the cleverer the people you talk to the worse it is. For the clever people, you take the filling out of the pie, and you shouldn't do so in case, like dogs, they should get a sniff of a meal which is being cooked for a holiday.

I shall probably be in Moscow soon; you must remind me of your address so that we can meet.

My address is still Tula.

Yours,
L. Tolstoy

175. To A. A. FET

Yasnaya Polyana, 30 January 1873

It's several days since I received your kind but sad letter, and I've only got round to answering it today.

It's sad because you write that Tyutchev is dying, because of the rumour that Turgenev is dead[1] and because you say your *mechanism is wearing out* and you want to think peacefully about *Nirvana*. Please let me know as soon as you can whether it's a false alarm. I hope so, and that in Marya Petrovna's absence you have mistaken some minor symptoms for the return of your terrible illness.

There is no need to laugh about Nirvana, far less to be angry. For all of us (at least for me, I feel) it's far more interesting than life, but I agree that however much I think about it, I can't think of any other conclusion but that this Nirvana is

[175] 1. Tyutchev did die in 1873, but Turgenev recovered from what was in fact an acute attack of gout.

175. To A. A. Fet

nothing. I only insist on one thing—religious respect—awe in the presence of this Nirvana.

There is nothing more important than that.

What do I mean by religious respect? I mean this. I recently visited my brother; a child of his had died and was being buried. There were priests, and a pink coffin, and everything there ought to be. My brother and I took the same view about religious rites as you do, and when we were together we couldn't help expressing to one another a feeling almost of revulsion at this ritualism. But then I began to think: well, what could my brother have done to carry the decomposing body of his child out of the house in the end? How should it have been carried out? By a coachman in a sack? And where should it be put, how should it be buried? What, generally speaking is a fitting way to end things? Is there anything better than a requiem, incense, etc.? (I, at least, can't think of anything.) And what about growing weak and dying? Should one wet oneself, s..., and nothing more? That's no good.

I would like to give outward expression to the gravity and importance, the solemnity and religious awe in the presence of this greatest event in the life of every human being. And I can think of nothing more fitting—and fitting for all ages and all stages of development—than a religious setting. For me, at least, those Slavonic words evoke exactly the same metaphysical ecstasy which you feel when you think about Nirvana. The remarkable thing about religion is that for so many centuries and for so many millions of people it has rendered a service, the very greatest service that any human thing can render on this occasion. With such a task, how can it be logical? It is an absurdity, but the one out of many millions of absurdities which is suitable for this occasion. There is something in it.

It's only to you that I allow myself to write such letters. But I felt like writing, and your letter somehow made me particularly sad.

Please write about your health as soon as possible.

Yours,
Lev Tolstoy

176. To COUNTESS A. A. TOLSTAYA

Yasnaya Polyana, end of January–beginning of February 1873

Thank you very very much, my dear Alexandrine, for your letter and for your intercession on Bibikov's behalf.[1] He was here with me when I got your letter, and it would have delighted you to see his kind, grey face flushed with emotion and joy when I told him of what concerned him.

I probably didn't write what I meant to if it turned out to be so stupid and

---

[176] 1. On 14 December 1872 Tolstoy wrote to A. A. Tolstaya on behalf of a neighbour, A. N. Bibikov, requesting her assistance in the legal process of the legitimisation of Bibikov and two of his brothers. She had previously assisted S. N. Tolstoy in his attempts to have his children legitimised.

comical. I meant to say something serious and welcome to you—that they told him in Petersburg that you—yes you—do a lot of good by your influence. I was glad when he told me this and wanted to tell you.

Your letter saying that you're reading *War and Peace* was very welcome (I'd like to pretend, but I won't), particularly since I'm now on the point of writing something again. And I'd give a lot to be able to hear the opinions of your listeners. I didn't laugh at all at the opinion you passed on to me, but reflected on it very gladly. I only hope there won't be these defects in what God allows me to write in future! These ones at least I shall probably avoid; but don't think I was insincere in saying that I find *War and Peace* utterly repugnant now. A few days ago I had to glance through it in order to decide whether to revise it for a new edition,[2] and I can't tell you the feeling of repentance and shame I experienced, as I scrutinised many passages! It's a feeling not unlike what a man experiences when he sees the remains of an orgy in which he has taken part. One thing consoles me—that I was carried away by this orgy heart and soul, and thought that nothing else mattered besides it.

Please don't look at my *Primer*. You haven't taught little children, you're far removed from the people, and you will see nothing in it. I've put more work and love into it than into anything else I've done, and I know that this is the one important work of my life. It will be appreciated in 10 years' time or so by those children who study from it.

I'd already heard about Tyutchev's illness, and you won't believe how much it affects me. I've met him about 10 times in my life; but I like him and consider him one of those unhappy people who stand immeasurably higher than the people they live among, and because of that are always lonely. How will he accept death, which in any case is close to him?

If he's better, get someone to give him my love. I kiss your hand. I don't think that fate will bring me to Petersburg, although I know what a joy that would be to me. Give my sincere friendly wishes to your people.

177. To N. N. STRAKHOV

[Not sent]

Yasnaya Polyana, 25 March 1873

How sad I was to read your letter, dear Nikolay Nikolayevich. If you had stayed on with us, none of this would have happened[1] and I could have taken advantage of your company for longer. Thank you for the promise;[2] I will count on it and remind you of it.

2. Tolstoy was looking over *War and Peace* in preparation for a new edition of his collected works, published in eight volumes in Moscow, in 1873. *War and Peace* was published in volumes V to VIII.

[177] 1. Strakhov was suffering from erysipelas on his return from Yasnaya Polyana.
2. The promise to spend his summer holidays at Yasnaya Polyana.

177. To N. N. Strakhov

You don't tell me whether you have started work again and whether your condition has been clearly diagnosed. Please write and tell me.

Two things in your letter made me very happy: (1) that you are just as well disposed to me as ever; and (2) that you have many friends (visiting you), friends who are close to your heart, and that your book is a success.[3]

As long as you don't plunge into the literary mire, all will be well.

Now I'll tell you about myself, but please, keep it a great secret, because nothing may come of what I have to say. Nearly all my working time this winter I have spent studying Peter, i.e. summoning up spirits from that time, and suddenly a week ago Seryozha, my eldest son, began to read *Yury Miloslavsky*[4] with enthusiasm. I thought he was too young, and read it with him, then my wife brought up *The Tales of Belkin*,[5] thinking she would find something suitable for Seryozha, but of course found he was too young. After work I happened to pick up this volume of Pushkin, and as is always the case, read it all through (for the 7th time, I think), unable to tear myself away and seemingly reading it for the first time. But more than that, it seemed to resolve all my doubts. Not only Pushkin, but nothing else at all, it seemed, had ever aroused my admiration so much before. *The Shot, Egyptian Nights, The Captain's Daughter*!!! And then there is a fragment *The guests were arriving at the country house*. Involuntarily, unwittingly, not knowing why and what would come of it, I thought up characters and events, began to go on with it, then of course changed it, and suddenly all the threads became so well and truly tied up that the result was a novel which I finished in draft form today, a very lively, impassioned and well-finished novel which I'm very pleased with and which will be ready in 2 weeks' time[6] 'if God gives me strength, and which has nothing in common with all that I've been wrestling with for a whole year. If I finish it, I'll publish it as a separate book, but I very much want you to read it. Will you undertake to read the proofs, with a view to its being published in Petersburg?

One more request: I've started to prepare a second edition of *War and Peace* and to strike out what is superfluous—some things need to be struck out altogether, others to be removed and printed separately.[7] Give me your advice if you have time to look through the last 3 volumes. And if you can remember, remind me of what is bad. I'm afraid to touch it, because there is so much that is bad in my eyes that I should want to write it again after refurbishing it. If you could recall what needs changing and if you could look through the arguments in the last 3 volumes and tell me that this and that needs to be changed, and that the arguments from page so and so to page so and so need to be cut out, you would oblige me very much indeed. Thanks to somebody bothering about what I write and letting the public know about it, I have received invitations recently from Nekrasov and

---

3. *The World as a Whole*, 1872.
4. A historical novel by M. N. Zagoskin.
5. Pushkin's *Tales of Belkin* was included in the fifth volume of Annenkov's edition of his works which Tolstoy was reading at the time.
6. *Anna Karenina*. The first draft was written between 18 and 25 March 1873.
7. The text of *War and Peace* published in Tolstoy's *Collected Works* in 1873 differed considerably from that published in 1868–9.

179. To P. D. Golokhvastov

Katkov to contribute to their journals, which I shall have to refuse and thereby annoy them, which is very disagreeable.

I hope this letter will find you well and that you will soon reply to me.

You thank me for getting Petya[8] to pay my belated debt to you, but I forgot to do what I intended to at Yasnaya Polyana: to tell you that in spite of the fact that the publication of the *Primer* is a thing of the past and that the *Primer* was a fiasco (I have not a whit the worse opinion of it for that), I never cease to thank you most sincerely for the help you gave me. Had it not been for you, it would perhaps still be sticking in my throat. Please forgive me for this incoherently written letter—I worked hard and with enjoyment this morning, finished what I was doing, and now this evening my head is swimming.

Yours,
L. Tolstoy

178. To P. D. GOLOKHVASTOV

[Not sent]

Yasnaya Polyana, 30 March 1873

[7 lines omitted]...You wouldn't believe that recently, after you had gone, I read *The Tales of Belkin* for the 7th time in my life, with an enthusiasm which I haven't experienced for a long time. A writer should never cease to study this treasure. My new study of it made a powerful impression on me. I'm working, but not at all on what I intended.

The other day I read Daudet's *Le Petit Chose*. Olga Andreyevna[1] was wrong to couple his name with that of Droz.[2] Poetry and firewood. But Cherbuliez's *Prosper Randoce*[3] is a very good thing—I advise you to read it. It's a remarkable thing that the English and the French don't lack poetry, but all the other Europeans, especially the Germans, have nothing. How do you fit this in to your theory of art? ...[3 lines omitted]

179. To P. D. GOLOKHVASTOV

Yasnaya Polyana, 9–10(?) April 1873

You are probably reproaching me, Pavel Dmitriyevich, for my sheer bad manners; I still haven't replied to your two most welcome letters and the parcel of books. I, at least, in spite of the certain knowledge that our good and friendly relations were strengthened by those wonderful days we spent together—I was horrified when I

---

8. P. A. Behrs, Tolstoy's brother-in-law.

[178] 1. Golokhvastov's wife.

2. Antoine-Gustave Droz (1832–95), a Parisian novelist and journalist. Tolstoy had recently read his novel *Babolain*.

3. Victor Cherbuliez (1822–99), a French writer of Swiss origin. The novel referred to was published in 1868, and ridicules a conceited and untalented writer.

179. To P. D. Golokhvastov

realised that I still hadn't replied to you, or thanked you for the books and particularly for coming to stay with us. The reason is that I did write a long letter to you about 10 days ago, but I wrote something in it which, on reflection, I decided it was better not to write, and I didn't send the letter, and haven't written another one till now.[1]

What I wrote and didn't send referred to me, and I didn't send it because it was premature. I am sincerely glad that you have torn yourself away from Moscow and have (probably now already) settled down to work. What work? Please let me know, it interests me very much. As you know, I have most sympathy for the story *in prose*, and then for the byliny for Shatilov, and I set least store by the drama.[2] However, that is a matter between you and your own soul. With your sincerity and the *purity* of your love for poetic activity, it should turn out well. Have you read Pushkin's prose recently? Do me a favour—read all the *Tales of Belkin* from beginning to end. Every writer ought to study them again and again. I did so recently and I can't tell you the beneficial influence this reading had on me.

Why is this study important? The field of poetry is as infinite as life, but all objects of poetry are distributed according to a definite hierarchy for all time, and the confusion of the lower with the higher, or the mistaking of the lower for the higher, is one of the main stumbling-blocks. With great poets like Pushkin, the harmonious rightness of the distribution of objects is brought to perfection. I know that this can't be analysed, but it is felt and assimilated. The reading of gifted, but inharmonious writers (it's the same with music and painting) irritates one and seems to spur one on to work and to broaden the field, but this is fallible; while the reading of Homer or Pushkin narrows the field, and if it stimulates one to work, it does so infallibly.

My wife thanks you for remembering her, and sends her regards. Please give my regards to Olga Andreyevna.

Yours,
L. Tolstoy

180. To N. N. STRAKHOV

Yasnaya Polyana, 11 May 1873

I haven't written to you for a long time, dear Nikolay Nikolayevich. I received your two letters at once; a wonderful one from the Crimea which touched me to the quick, and the other one, a sad one, from Petersburg. And wishing to answer them both, I was left like the famous donkey between two bales of hay. But I particularly wanted to answer the Crimean letter. You may not believe it and I may be mistaken,

---

[179] 1. I.e. Letter 178—although even allowing for the omissions, which mainly repeat what is said in this letter, it can hardly be called long. It is not clear what caused Tolstoy to have second thoughts, unless it is the veiled reference to his work on *Anna Karenina*.

2. This repeats what was said at the beginning of Letter 178, and omitted in the translation. Golokhvastov was preparing a popular collection of byliny about *Ilya Muromets* for publication by I. N. Shatilov. The drama presumably refers to *Alyosha Popovich*, a drama in 5 acts, based on old Russian byliny (1869).

but I find it just as easy to answer the question what is good—the essence of life—as I do the question what is the date today. I can answer it clearly and comprehensibly for myself, but is it clear and comprehensible to someone else? For it to be clear to someone else, it is necessary for that someone else to agree with me about the meaning of the question. Man cannot understand and express the objective essence of life—that's the first thing. The essence of life—what makes us live—is the need for what we wrongly call good. Good is only the opposite of evil, as light is of darkness, and as there is no absolute light and darkness, so is there no absolute good and evil. Good and evil are only materials out of which beauty is made—i.e. what we love without reason, without profit and without need. And so in place of the concept of good—a relative concept—I ask you to put the concept of beauty. All religions which have made it their task to define the essence of life have beauty as their basis—the Greeks of the flesh, Christians of the spirit. To turn the other cheek when you are struck on one is not clever or good, but senseless and beautiful—as beautiful as Zeus hurling bolts from Olympus. But let reason touch what is only open to the feeling of beauty, let it make logical conclusions about how one should make sacrifices to Zeus, or serve him or imitate him, or how one should celebrate mass or confess, and there is no longer beauty nor a guide through the chaos of good and evil. You say that you can understand me however incoherently I write; well, don't say so again! But I would very much like to have a talk with you about it. I'm writing a novel which has no connection at all with Peter the First. I've been writing for more than a month now, and have finished it in draft form. This novel—I mean a novel, the first in my life—is very dear to my heart and I'm quite absorbed by it, but in spite of that, philosophical problems have been occupying me very much this spring. In the letter which I didn't send to you[1] I wrote about this novel and about how it came to me unwittingly, thanks to the divine Pushkin whom I happened to pick up and reread with new enthusiasm. I'm still busy correcting *War and Peace*. I'm cutting out all the arguments and the French, and I would dearly like your advice.[2] May I send it to you to look through when I've finished?

Yours,
L. Tolstoy

[Postscript omitted]

181. To N. N. STRAKHOV

Yasnaya Polyana, 31 May 1873

I'm very, very grateful to you for your offer to look through *War and Peace*. You wouldn't believe how valuable it is to me. I've begun to look through it and have

[180] 1. Letter 177.
2. In addition to cutting out some philosophical chapters and replacing French by Russian, Tolstoy reassembled much of the reflective material on the philosophy of history in a separate section entitled 'Articles on the 1812 Campaign'.

181. To N. N. Strakhov

done the main thing, that is I've cut out some arguments altogether and separated off some others such as, for example, those about the battle of Borodino, the fire of Moscow, the epilogue etc., which I intend to publish as separate articles.

The other thing I've done is to translate *all* the French into Russian, but I haven't finished volumes 4, 5, and 6 yet, and I've been cutting out bad things here and there.

I would have sent you my corrected copy of those parts which are finished straightaway, but the books have gone to Samara with half our possessions. I'll very soon correct the rest in Samara and send it to you, taking advantage of your invaluable offer.

I'll find out in Moscow on my way through when the printing press will start printing *War and Peace* and then I'll write to you. In any case they have to finish in September according to the contract (they will probably be late) and so there isn't very much time.

I'm sending various instructions by this post to Petya Behrs about the *Primer*. The *Primer* is an inscrutable mystery to me: if I meet anyone, especially anyone with children, I hear genuine praise, and complaints that there's nothing of mine to read, but nobody buys the *Primer*, therefore nobody needs it. I've now thought of sending it to the zemstvos and having it sewn up in 12 small booklets. As you see from my letter, I'm in a very cold, practical frame of mind, which is always the case with me in summer; I'm worried about the sale of books, printing, the harvest etc. But in the early part of spring I would have given a lot to see you. What was occupying my attention was close to your own interests. My novel is also at a standstill, and I'm losing hope of finishing it by autumn. Moreover I have had two misfortunes which have thrown me out of my isolated working rut this winter and spring. One was the death of Tatyana Andreyevna Kuzminskaya's eldest daughter. We felt her death almost as if it were the death of one of our own; and the other dreadful thing was the fact that about a week ago a bull (not the same one as last year) gored a shepherd to death. The man died after three days, despite all my efforts and attention. This incredible coincidence was a terrible blow to me. I've lived for 45 years and I've never heard of any cases of people being done to death by bulls, and now two men have to be killed in one year. I can't get rid of the feeling of guilt and sadness. I've only come to life again today, having been busy with packing and posting and giving orders etc. One thing which practical activity is good for is to make you forget life, if it has turned its dark side towards you. We are going the day after tomorrow. I embrace you with all my heart. My wife sends her regards.

Please give me your advice: what parts of the *Primer* are worth including and should be included in the complete works? Please tell me your opinion.

182. To N. N. STRAKHOV

farm on the river Tananyka, 22 June 1873

I'm sending you, my most dear Nikolay Nikolayevich—I don't know whether to say a corrected, but certainly a dirty and torn copy—of *War and Peace*, and I beg you to look through it and help me by word and deed, i.e. look through my corrections and tell me in your opinion whether they are good or bad (if you find the corrections bad, I give you permission to do away with them and to correct what you know and see to be bad). I was sometimes sorry to do away with the French, but on the whole I think it is better without it. The military, historical and philosophical arguments which have been removed from the novel have, I think, lightened it, and they are not without interest on their own. However, if you still find any of them superfluous, cut them out. I am in two minds about the amalgamation of the 6 parts into 4; please decide which you think best—the old division or the new.[1] I'm afraid that the calligraphic side of things is bad and will be impossible for the printers—I couldn't do any better, what with the Samara flies and the heat. If you find it needs to be copied out, engage a copyist. Get the money from Petya Behrs. If you need a clean copy, I'll tell Solovyov to send one just in case. The printers need the original by the middle, or no later than the end of July. If you wish to, and can manage to do the corrections and look through it, please do so, and send it to Moscow addressed to Mikhail Nikolayevich Lavrov at Katkov's printing press; if not, simply send it to him as it is. I feel my request to you is quite unscrupulous, but I rely on your friendship towards me and your partiality for *War and Peace*, which has very seldom pleased me when I have reread it and for the most part has caused me shame and anger. I hope they will bring me a letter from you from Samara, and that I shall find out the answer to my question what parts of the *Primer* you advise me to include in the complete works. If you haven't written, please write.

We are enjoying life in the Samara steppes, thank goodness, despite the heat, the drought and the children's illnesses, which are not serious, but are a worry to us. The primitive state of nature here and of the people with whom we are in close contact have a good effect on my wife and children.

I look forward to your reply and your decision.

Your irredeemably indebted and sincerely affectionate,

L. Tolstoy

183. To COUNTESS A. A. TOLSTAYA

farm on the river Tananyka, 30 July 1873

I'm sending you a copy of my long letter to the newspapers about the Samara famine,[1] and a postscript from my wife. It sometimes occurs to me that with your

---

[182] 1. The novel was published in four parts in the 1873 edition, and all subsequent editions.

[183] 1. Tolstoy wrote a long and detailed letter to *The Moscow Gazette* on 28 July in which

183. To Countess A. A. Tolstaya

completely different interests—interests in a different sphere—which are very near to your heart, you'll say to yourself when your receive my parcel: oh, why can't *they* leave me in peace! But when you've read it all through, and felt it rather than thought about it, you'll put on the yoke like a good horse and merely say: 'Well, where shall I take you? How many of you are there? I'm ready.' So I'm simply responding to this readiness of yours, my dear Alexandrine.

With my characteristic inability to write articles, I've written a very cold, clumsy letter to the papers, and for fear of a polemic, I've presented the matter as less terrible than it really is, and I've written to some of my friends to get things moving, but I'm afraid that no headway will be made or that it will be slow, and I'm turning to you. If you wish to, and are able to interest the good and the mighty of this world, who are, fortunately, the same people, then headway will be made, and yours and my joy in success will be such insignificant grains of sand in that enormous good that will be done for thousands of people, that we won't even give it a thought. I don't like writing in a plaintive tone, but I've lived for 45 years in the world and I've never seen anything like it, and never thought it possible. When one pictures vividly to oneself what it will be like in winter, one's hair stands on end. Just now—I'd already written the letter—we learned that a young peasant—a reaper—had been taken ill with cholera. There's nothing to eat except bad black bread, and if this hadn't happened in our vicinity, it's very possible that this man would have died for lack of proper food for a weakened stomach. It's particularly shocking and pathetic to someone who is able to understand the Russian's forbearance and humility in suffering—his calmness, and submissiveness. There's no good food—well, there's no point in complaining. If he dies—it's God's will. They aren't sheep, but good, strong oxen ploughing their furrow. If they fall—they'll be dragged away, and others will pull the plough.

It's unlikely you'll understand me, and you'll probably think the comparison insulting. You've always lived in a world where there are ugly things, physical and moral deformities, sufferings, chiefly spiritual, but where there's no place for purely physical deprivation. Your Magdalens are pitiful, I know; but pity for them, as for all spiritual suffering, is more of the mind, of the heart, if you like; but one's whole being feels pity for simple, good people, who are physically and morally healthy, when they suffer from deprivation; when one looks on their suffering, one is ashamed and grieved to be a human being. So there, I put this important matter, dear to our hearts, into your hands. Thank you in advance for everything you may do.

Thank you for your last letter. I sympathise with all my heart with your anxieties and wish you happiness.

Your old and true friend,
L. Tolstoy

he appealed to the public to help to relieve the famine in the Samara province, which had just experienced crop failure for the third successive year. His appeal was echoed by other leading Russian newspapers, and after some prevarication the government eventually launched a public appeal for funds.

184. To N. N. STRAKHOV

Yasnaya Polyana, 23–4 September 1873

I'm very grateful to you, dear Nikolay Nikolayevich, for all you have done with *War and Peace*; I only regret that you didn't cut out or shorten the part you quite rightly found long-winded and inaccurate—*on power*.[1] I remember that this passage was long and cumbersome. XII paragraphs need to be cut out—I'll write today.[2] I'm also grateful for what you mentioned. I'm writing to Solovyov today to ask him to send you some money. And since I don't doubt for a moment that you would have liked to do it for nothing, don't you doubt either that I've been turning over a thousand times the question of how to reward you for the loss of time which for you, unfortunately, *is* money.[3] You would do best in my opinion to publish your article about the growth of organisms separately. To stick it in to some *Nature* or other, would be to bury it.[4] Or don't publish it all, but wait.

I've made good progress in my work, but I'll hardly finish it before winter—December or thereabouts. As a painter needs light for the finishing touches, so I need inner light, of which I always feel the lack in autumn. Besides, everything has been arranged so as to distract me: acquaintances, hunting, a court session in October with me as a juryman, and then the painter Kramskoy who is painting my portrait for Tretyakov. Tretyakov tried to send him to me a long time ago, but I didn't want him, but now this Kramskoy has come himself and talked me round, particularly by saying 'your portrait will be painted anyway, but it will be a bad one'. Even this wouldn't have persuaded me, but my wife persuaded him to do another portrait for her, instead of a copy. And now he's painting it, and very well according to my wife and friends. He interests me as the purest specimen of the latest Petersburg trend as it might be reflected in a very good and artistic nature. He's now finishing both portraits and comes every day and stops me working. During the sittings I try to convert him from the Petersburg to the Christian faith, and, I think, successfully. He was telling me today about the murder of Suvorina.[5] What a significant event!

Werther shot himself and so did Komarov and the schoolboy who found his Latin lesson difficult. The one is important and noble, the other sordid and pathetic. Write and tell me if you find out any details of the murder.

Goodbye. Yours truly affectionately,

L. Tolstoy

[184] 1. A reference to part of the second epilogue.

2. There is no record of Tolstoy having written to the printers, and the changes suggested by Strakhov were not made.

3. Strakhov had been obliged to ask Tolstoy for money for the work he had done, owing to his straitened circumstances.

4. The article was in fact published in the popular scientific journal *Nature* despite Tolstoy's advice.

5. Suvorina, the first wife of the publisher and journalist A. S. Suvorin, was shot in a hotel by a certain Komarov, a friend of the family, who then committed suicide.

185. To N. N. STRAKHOV

Yasnaya Polyana, 13 February 1874

Thank you, dear Nikolay Nikolayevich, for sending the article on Darwin;[1] I devoured it and felt that it was good and satisfying fare. It was confirmation for me of my vague musings on the same subject and the expression of what I would have liked to express. One thing is surprising. The article has been published and will be read. It's impossible to treat it with contempt and it's impossible not to agree with it. But will it make a scrap of difference to the general current opinion about any new word of Darwin's? Not at all. I always feel surprised and sorry, particularly sorry, about *articles*. A big work, particularly a positive, not a critical one, will be appreciated sooner or later, the shot will reach the target and strike home—possibly somewhere where we shan't know about it, but it will strike home. But criticism which you are so fond of is a terrible thing. Its only importance and justification is to guide public opinion, but this is the joke—when criticism talks rubbish it guides public opinion, but if it is the result of genuine and serious (ernst) thought it has no effect, and may just as well have never been written.

You guessed that I'm very busy and am working hard. I'm very glad that I didn't start publishing a long time ago when I wrote to you. I can't draw a circle except by joining it up and then straightening out the initial irregularities. And now I'm joining up the circle and straightening it out, and straightening it out... It's never happened before that I've written so much without reading anything to anybody and not even talking about it, and I terribly want to read it out. What I would give to have you here! But I know that that's mean and I'm only deluding myself. I'm tired of working—revising, putting the finishing touches—and I'd like someone to praise it and I don't want to work on it any more if possible. I don't know if it will be all right. I rarely see things in such a light that I like everything about them. But so much has already been written and polished up and the circle has been almost joined, and I'm so tired of revising, that I want to go to Moscow after the 20th and deliver it to Katkov's printing press.[2] I've changed my mind about troubling you. I'm very grateful to you but I must correct the proofs myself.[3]

Yours most cordially,
L. Tolstoy

186. To N. N. STRAKHOV

Yasnaya Polyana, 6 March 1874

I'm delighted, dear Nikolay Nikolayevich, that your affairs have been so arranged that your hands are free for congenial work, and I'm very grateful to you for

---

[185] 1. Strakhov's article 'On the Growth of Organisms', criticising Darwin's views.

2. Tolstoy went to Moscow on 2 March to deliver the first part of *Anna Karenina* to the printer's.

3. Tolstoy corrected the proofs with the help of Yury Samarin, owing to the fact that Strakhov lived in Petersburg while the novel was being published in Moscow.

187. To Countess A. A. Tolstaya

writing to tell me about it. I'm a very disorganised and fickle person, but not in my affections, and everything that concerns you as a man interests me keenly, not to mention the fact that I'm delighted about your freedom, since you won't need to debase the value of your currency.[1]

I came back from Moscow yesterday and delivered part of my manuscript—7 printer's sheets—to the press. There will be 40 altogether. I hope to have it all printed before May. When I was in Moscow I read a few chapters out for the first time to Tyutchev's daughter and Samarin. I chose them both as being very cold, intelligent, and shrewd people, and it seemed to me that it made little impression on them; but so far from being disenchanted, I set about revising and touching it up with even greater enthusiasm. I think it will be good, but it won't be liked and it won't be successful because it's very simple. Samarin has agreed to correct the proofs. I'm very glad about this, but I'll do some correcting myself as well.

About a month ago I received a diploma from the Academy of Sciences on my election as a member. I confess that I was flattered, despite the fact that Pushkin was not a member, but Pypin is. I think I must write a letter of thanks and send my works, especially as I see from the Proceedings and the *Bulletins* of the Academy which they send me that this is what is done. Please write me a draft letter if this is necessary; otherwise I don't know.

What are your plans for the summer? May we hope to see you at Yasnaya?

Yours,
L. Tolstoy

187. To COUNTESS A. A. TOLSTAYA

Yasnaya Polyana, 6 March 1874

Dear friend,

Even if I haven't written to you for so long, and didn't go to Moscow to see you, I still call you my dear and beloved friend just the same—and even more sincerely than ever—because of my feelings for you. A day hasn't passed without my thinking of you and talking to my wife about you during these recent times that have been so important and painful for you. I won't speak to you in this letter of your feelings, as I imagine them to be, but I'm sure that I guess them correctly, otherwise I wouldn't love you; but just the same, I would give a lot to hear confirmation from you that I'm not mistaken, and to understand new nuances which have perhaps eluded me. For a very long time I've been meaning to write to you just so that you should know that the... I won't say *sorrow* (I don't know what to call it), but the painful time of life that you have lived through and are living through has found an echo in my heart,[1] despite the fact that we see and write to

[186] 1. By writing for the newspapers. Strakhov had told Tolstoy of the recent improvement in his financial circumstances.

[187] 1. A. A. Tolstaya was upset by her separation from her pupil, the Grand Duchess Marya Alexandrovna, who married the Duke of Edinburgh in 1874.

187. To Countess A. A. Tolstaya

each other so rarely. This is how I see your situation: there is a machine which is very good and very useful etc., but a machine which is always operated by everyone by means of long steel handles, so that their fingers won't be hurt; yet this machine needs the sort of workers who can operate it with their hands too: and you undertook to be such a worker, and of course, being the way God created you, you went to work on the machine, not with your hands but with your heart, and your heart or a part of it was crushed. And I know that this is so, and from the bottom of my heart I'm sorry for you. If I were to have my doubts whether my friendship for you had changed, I would be completely reassured of it from the way I grieve for you. If you feel like it, write to me; if not, then don't. I returned from Moscow yesterday, and spoke about you to K. Tyutcheva, whom I'm always especially fond of, because she understands and loves you.

I didn't go to Moscow, especially since I was there only just before your arrival, and you can't imagine how it becomes more and more difficult for me to leave home—i.e. to discard from my life the days that I'm away from home; and the fewer of them that remain, the more difficult it is. This year sorrow has afflicted us. We lost our youngest son, the 6th child. Now we have 5 and are expecting another around Easter.[2] Of all the intimate losses we could have suffered, this was the easiest to bear—a little finger, but painful just the same, especially for my wife. Death never has a very painful effect on me (I felt this at the loss of a dearly loved brother). If you yourself don't approach nearer to your own death with the loss of a being you love, if you don't become disillusioned with life and don't cease to love it and expect good of it, then these losses must be unbearable; but if you submit to this approach to your own end, then it's not painful, but important, significant and beautiful. That is the effect death has on me, yes, and on everyone, I think. A small example. When burying Petya, I was concerned for the first time about where I am to be laid. And, apart from a mother's special, almost physical pain, it had the same effect on Sonya, despite her youth.

We're living in the same old way, so busy that there's never enough time. The children and their upbringing take up more and more of our time, and it's going well. I try not to, but I can't help being proud of my children. Besides that, I'm writing and have started publishing a novel which I like, but which is unlikely to be liked by anyone else, because it's too simple.[3]

See what details I write to you about myself; please write to me about yourself, about your life and about your great and good joys and sorrows and your silly little joys and sorrows. What are your people doing? Your mother and sister? Where are they? And how is Praskovya Vasilyevna?

What a charming representative of Russian womanhood you have chosen—Princess Vyazemskaya,[4] and what a pitiful example of Russian manhood—Koloshin.[5] When I think of him among the English lords, with their Olympian self-

2. S. A. Tolstaya gave birth to a son, Nikolay, on 22 April 1874.
3. The novel *Anna Karenina*.
4. A Maid of Honour, who accompanied the Grand Duchess to England after her marriage.
5. Tolstoy is mistaken: D. P. Koloshin did not accompany the Grand Duchess to England. This function was assigned to an official of the Ministry of Foreign Affairs, A. P. Ozerov.

satisfaction at their own narrow one-sided stupidity, I'm ashamed and I blush. He is just that very non-existent Russian man, mentally restless and aimless, weakly imitating the European outward form, without principles, without convictions, without character—just that very non-existent Russian man that foreigners in their scorn imagine the Russian to be.

I'm afraid I've caused a lot of trouble for you with the Samara famine. Ever since I was young, and more and more as I get older, I've valued one negative quality above all others—simplicity. We need our ugliness in order to understand the confusion that is caused—because of what? Because of the fact that people who are not starving, but are living luxuriously, want to give the starving a piece of bread. If you want to give—give, if you don't want to—pass on. You would think that there's nothing more to it. But no, it appears that if you give, this shows that you're an enemy of someone, and want to cause someone pain or to persuade someone, but if you don't give, you...

Good God! What does it mean? I've only just returned from Moscow, and although I avoid listening to all tales about the doers, I can't help returning with so much contempt and revulsion that it takes me a long time to calm down. Particularly when you have growing children, you so much want to share with them the same serious attitude to life, and it's so difficult where human affairs are concerned.

Goodbye; I kiss your hand.

Your old and faithful friend,
L. Tolstoy

188. To T. A. KUZMINSKAYA

Yasnaya Polyana, 15–22 March 1874

Tanya, my dear, do me a favour. Ask your brother Sasha whether I can include in the novel I'm writing the story he told me about the officers who rushed into a married woman's room instead of a mademoiselle's, and how the husband threw them out and they apologised.[1] The scene takes place in my book in a cavalry guards' regiment; the names, of course, are different, and anyway I don't know who the real people were, but the whole scene is just as it was.

The story is charming by itself, and moreover I need it. Please write. And my dear Sasha,—I'm addressing Alexander Mikhaylovich—please write as well. What are your plans and prospects and hopes in the service? Please write and tell me. It interests me very much, and you probably have something definite if you are so determined to abandon the delightful Caucasus (however much Tanya may abuse it).

We look forward to your return with great pleasure.

[188] 1. See *Anna Karenina*, Part II, ch. 5.

189. To N. N. STRAKHOV

Yasnaya Polyana, 18–19 April 1874

I received your letter in Moscow, dear Nikolay Nikolayevich. I go there as usual once every month or two, and no proofs in the world would make me live there. Furthermore, the proofs are being printed and sent to me extremely slowly, so that I don't know when the printing will be finished and whether it will be finished before summer. Besides, I've been recently occupied with something quite different —schools of literacy. The Moscow Committee on Literacy got me involved in the cause, and made the old pedagogical ferment rise in me again.[1] You'll probably read in the papers how people will abuse me and misquote my words, and it won't interest you; but I shan't read it, although it does interest me very much. I angled for a loach and caught a pike. The talk turned on literacy and I came up against such a monumental conglomeration of obtuseness that I couldn't walk calmly past. If you have connections in the literary world, give me un coup d'épaule so that people won't just rest content with the fact that Count L. Tolstoy is a reactionary and a Slavophile, but will make a bit of a fuss about it. People who know nothing and have no talents—who don't even know the people they have undertaken to *educate*—have got their hands on the whole business of public education, and what they are doing makes your hair stand on end. But don't forget your promise— come and see us in summer. There is something ironical about the tone of your last letter. Please don't allow this with me, because I love you very much.

190. To COUNTESS A. A. TOLSTAYA

Yasnaya Polyana, 23 June 1874

If I didn't immediately answer your long, kind, moving letter, it wasn't because I haven't been thinking of you ceaselessly. I'm writing now and I'm picking on you only so as to continue to feel my nearness to you. Yesterday I buried Auntie Tatyana Alexandrovna. You didn't know her, but your maman knew her, and you heard a lot about her from me. She died almost of old age, i.e. she faded away little by little, and had already ceased to exist for us 3 years ago, so much so that (I don't know whether this was a good or a bad feeling), I avoided her and couldn't see her without a feeling of agony; but now that she's dead (she died slowly, and painfully —like a childbirth), all my feeling for her has returned with still greater force. She

---

[189] 1. On 15 January 1874 Tolstoy had taken part in a discussion about elementary education at the Moscow Committee on Literacy and as a result had been persuaded to try to prove the superiority of his own educational methods over the established ones. For a period of seven weeks, different groups of children were instructed by different methods and a report made on their progress. The final report back to the Committee, however, was confused and inconclusive, and Tolstoy took his case to the press. He was further drawn into the educational arena when he attempted unsuccessfully through the Tula zemstvo to start a Teachers' Training College for the peasants, to be located at Yasnaya Polyana where the elementary schools ('schools of literacy') were still operating.

was a wonderful creature. Yesterday, when we were carrying her through the village, we were stopped at every door. The peasant or his wife would come up to the priest, give him money and ask him to say prayers for the repose of her soul, and take leave of her. And I knew that every stop meant the memory of many good deeds done by her... She lived here for 50 years, and never did anything unpleasant to anyone, let alone any evil. But she was afraid of death. She didn't say she was afraid, but I could see she was. What does this mean? I think that it's humility. I lived with her all my life; and I feel frightened without her. All's well with my family. You predicted a girl for me, but a boy was born, just like the one we lost, and although he's called Nikolay, we involuntarily call him Petya, like the other. I'm in my summer mood—i.e. I'm not occupied with poetry and have stopped publishing my novel and want to give it up, I dislike it so much.[1] Instead I'm occupied with practical things—with pedagogics, actually: I'm organising schools, writing projects and battling with the Petersburg pedagogics of your protégé, Dmitry Andreyevich,[2] who's doing terribly stupid things in the most important department of his administration—that of public education. I kiss your hand, my dear, dear friend; write to me sometime, as I write to you, about all that is close to your heart. Everything will find a true echo, without one false note.

Yours,
L. Tolstoy

191. To COUNTESS A. A. TOLSTAYA

Yasnaya Polyana, 15 August 1874

I'm very grateful to you, my dear Alexandrine, for your readiness to help me with the business of a governess. I prefer Swiss, and so if you still want to do me a good turn, please write to Switzerland. I repeat my requirements and the conditions. I need both a tutor and a governess. Either will do. Not to mention the fact that they must be good people, a good knowledge of French is desirable for the governess, and a knowledge of the classical languages is even more desirable for the tutor. The salary will be between 500 and 1,000 roubles each.

I was very glad...no, to be exact, I was just glad to hear news of you, and to hear good news: that you have spent a good 2 months with the Grand Duchess, and that you are still just as happy and have reason to love her.

A few days ago I got back from Samara where I had gone to have a look at the management of the estate I've bought there. You can have a completely clear conscience with regard to the part you took in helping the people there. The disaster would have been terrible if such friendly help hadn't been given to the people there. And I saw and recognised that although the process of distribution wasn't entirely free of fault, the help was nonetheless effective and in most cases intelligent.

[190] 1. *Anna Karenina.*
 2. D. A. Tolstoy, the Minister of Public Education, who sought to limit the spread of education, and to compel a return to more traditional subjects of study.

191. To Countess A. A. Tolstaya

In connection with this business, there happened to me one of those strange, direct interventions in my life by some mysterious hand that have occurred several times in my life. Three years ago I bought some land there—I sowed a very big area and for the first two years I suffered what was by my standards a very big loss —about 20,000. Last year you wrote to me, and indeed everyone tells me, that it was I who raised the whole business of the famine and was the apparent cause of the help that was given. This year there was a very abundant harvest throughout the whole Samara province, and, as far as I know, the only place in the whole Samara province that was missed by the rains was my estate, and I had again sowed a big area and again suffered a big loss. I went there and couldn't believe my eyes, and I felt hurt, as though I'd been put in the corner when I'd done nothing wrong. But later I came to my senses and realised that it was good and flattering to me.

I'm writing this to you because I'm sure that you'll either understand it as I do, or, if it's pride and impudence, that you'll forgive me. Goodbye; I kiss your hand.

Yours,
L. Tolstoy

192. To N. N. STRAKHOV

Yasnaya Polyana, 23 December 1874

How are you getting on, dear Nikolay Nikolayevich? Judging from your last letter, you're in a bad state. Probably, however, boredom and apathy precede a burst of mental energy with you, as they do with me. I hope and wish that it's so, and that this letter finds you in the throes of work.

I've delivered my novel to Katkov (verbally), and your advice to do so made me decide. As it was, I was hesitating. I'm still busy with the *Primer*, a Grammar, and the schools in the district, and I haven't the heart to get down to the novel. However, I must do so now, since I've promised. I read Solovyov's philosophical article and liked it very much.[1] He is one more man to swell the tiny number of Russian people who allow themselves to think their own minds. I've now counted 5 of them. In it, i.e. in the article, there is one flaw—the pernicious Hegelian phraseology. Suddenly at the end of the article some long familiar, and to me very repulsive spirit turns up out of the blue. Gladden my heart with your pearls—they are not scattered before swine when they are addressed to me. Everything is fine with me now. I'm happy and fit, and am working well. It would be good if you were too.

Yours,
L. Tolstoy

[192] 1. Vladimir S. Solovyov (1853–1900), the religious philosopher. Tolstoy refers to his Master's dissertation *The Crisis of Western Philosophy. Against the Positivists*.

193. To COUNTESS A. A. TOLSTAYA

Yasnaya Polyana, 15–30(?) December 1874

When I received your last kind letter which I was expecting, I immediately replied to you, but wrote something stupid in the letter, as so often happens with me, and had to tear it up. I rejoice with all my heart that you're returning to the work you abandoned, and however alien it is to me, I still sympathise, as I have always sympathised, with your attitude towards it.[1] You say that we are like a squirrel in a wheel. Of course. But you musn't say it or think it. I, at least, whatever I do, am always convinced that du haut de ces pyramides 40 siècles me contemplent,[2] and that the whole world will perish if I come to a stop. True, an imp sits there winking and saying that it's all just threshing the water, but I don't let him have his way, and you musn't either. However, as soon as a human soul is involved, and it's possible to love those we work for, then no imp can persuade us that love is a trifle. I've now moved over entirely from abstract pedagogics to a matter which is on the one hand practical and on the other hand very abstract—the matter of schools in our district. And I've again taken a great liking, as I did 14 years ago, to the thousands of children that I'm concerned with. I ask everyone why we want to educate the people; and there are 5 answers. Tell me your answer when you have a chance. This is mine. I don't reason about it, but when I enter a school and see this crowd of ragged, dirty, skinny children with their bright eyes and often angelic expressions, alarm and terror come over me, not unlike what I'd feel at seeing people drowning. Ah, goodness me!—how can I pull them out, and who should I pull out first and who next? And what is drowning here is what is most precious—just the very spiritual qualities that strike one so obviously in children. I want education for the people simply in order to save those drowning Pushkins, Ostrogradskys,[3] Filarets,[4] and Lomonosovs.[5] Every school is teeming with them. And my work is going well, very well. I see that I'm doing my job, and am progressing faster than I expected. I hope with all my heart that your work too might be as successful as mine has been lately. I very much want to come to Petersburg, and you know that to see you is a great attraction for me, but I'm busier now than ever, particularly since I'm in a good mood for working. I've promised to publish my novel in *The Russian Herald*, but so far I've been quite unable to tear myself away from living people in order to devote myself to imaginary ones.

Yours,
L. Tolstoy

[Postscript omitted]

[193] 1. A. A. Tolstaya had said that she was resuming her work as guardian of a charitable institution for prostitutes. Both she and Tolstoy referred to these women in their correspondence as 'Magdalens'.

2. Words attributed to Napoleon in a speech to his soldiers at the time of the Egyptian campaign.

3. A distinguished mathematician and a member of the Academy of Sciences.

4. The son of a village deacon, he eventually became Metropolitan of Moscow.

5. M. V. Lomonosov (1711–65), Russia's most versatile eighteenth-century scholar-scientist, philologist and poet. Moscow University is named after him.

194. To M. N. KATKOV

                                    Yasnaya Polyana, middle of February 1875

I am sending some proofs, dear Mikhail Nikiforovich. I'm very sorry that there are so few, especially as the next 5 or so printer's sheets are certainly ready, and I'll send them to you in a few days.

The second part is one of 6. I need this division because of the interval of time that has passed and the internal division of the book.

I can't touch anything in the latest chapter. *Vivid realism*, as you say, is the only tool, since I can't use either pathos or argument. And this is one of the passages on which the whole novel stands.[1] If it is false, everything is false. I tried to do the correcting so as to avoid setting up new type; I don't know if I've succeeded, but all the corrections are necessary.

                                                              Yours ever,
                                                              L. Tolstoy

195. To N. N. STRAKHOV

                                      Yasnaya Polyana, 16 February 1875

I'm very grateful to you, dear Nikolay Nikolayevich, for your brief but very heartening letter. Not only did I not expect success, but I confess I was afraid of the complete collapse of my reputation as a result of the novel. I tell you frankly that such a collapse—I was prepared for it—would not have affected me very much a month ago. I was completely immersed—as I continue to be—in school affairs, the *New Primer*,[1] which is being printed, a Grammar and an arithmetic book; but just very recently I conceived the idea of a new poetic work which gives me great pleasure and excitement, and which will probably be written if God gives me life and strength and for which I need my reputation.[2] And I'm very, very glad that my novel hasn't let me down. I don't believe it will be a great success. I know how much you want it to be a great success and you think it is. But I completely agree with the people who don't understand what there is to say about it. It's all—I don't say *simple* (simplicity, if it is there, is a tremendous virtue which it is difficult to attain), but low-grade. The idea is such a private one. It can't be, and it oughtn't to be a great success, particularly the first chapters which are decidedly weak. Besides, it's poorly finished. I can see that, and it hurts me. I've already sent everything off for the 2nd issue, and I shan't be late for the 3rd. But so far as I know, the editors of *The Russian Herald* won't print more than 3 issues this year, and then there will be

---

[194] 1. The passage where Anna and Vronsky first make love (Part II, ch. 11 in the definitive edition).

[195] 1. Tolstoy was working on a second Primer, as the first one had not been approved for use in schools. He finished it in 1875 and called it *The New Primer*.
    2. This evidently refers to a proposed adaptation of select passages from old Russian literature.

a break. And I'm glad of that. I have so much to do that I wouldn't have the time to correct it and get it all in proper order for printing.

I've been living in a strange and awful state of excitement this winter. In the first place I've had a cold all the time—toothache and a feverish condition—and I've been staying at home. Then there has been practical work—managing 70 schools which have been opened in our district and which are going wonderfully. Then the pedagogical work I spoke about. Then the older children whom I have to teach myself, since I haven't found a tutor yet. Then the printing of the novel, the proofs of the novel and of the *Primer*, which are urgent, and now at the same time a family sorrow and a new plan. The family sorrow is the terrible brain disease of our 9-month baby in arms.[3] For over 3 weeks now he has been going through all the stages of this hopeless disease. My wife is feeding him herself and is in despair one minute that he will die, and the next that he will live and be an idiot. And it's strange: I feel the need and the joy of work as never before. Goodbye: why do you write nothing about yourself?

I remember, you were staying with us this time three years ago.[4] How we enjoyed ourselves.

Yours,
L. Tolstoy

196. To BARONESS Y. I. MENGDEN

Baroness (by her second marriage) Yelizaveta Ivanovna Mengden (1822–1902), whom Tolstoy met during her first marriage in 1857, and who remained a friend of the Tolstoy family until her death. She was the hostess of a well-known Moscow salon where both the aristocracy and the literary world mixed, to the discomfort of some aristocrats. Baroness Mengden wrote her *Memoirs* which were published posthumously in 1913.

Yasnaya Polyana, 10–19 February 1875

I am replying on my wife's behalf, dear Lizaveta Ivanovna, because our youngest child is very dangerously ill, and she cannot think about anything else.

I reply to two points which interest me very much: a popular journal[1] and the translation of my works into English.[2] If I sympathise with a popular journal too little, it is only because I sympathise with it too much, and am convinced that those who undertake it will be à cent milles lieues away from what people need. I flatter

3. The Tolstoys' seventh child, who died a few days later.
4. In fact, two years previously.

[196] 1. Baroness Mengden had told Tolstoy of a mutual friend's intention to found a journal 'for the people', *The Russian Worker. A Spiritual Journal*. It was published from 1875 to 1886 with a break from 1880 to 1882, and specialised in articles of an evangelical nature, including many translated from English.

2. Baroness Mengden asked Tolstoy's permission to allow the Princesses Urusov to translate his works into English.

196. To Baroness Y. I. Mengden

myself with the hope that my demands are identical with those of the people, namely that a journal should be *intelligible*, but this one will not be. Intelligibility, comprehensibility, is not only a necessary condition if people are to read willingly, but is, I am firmly convinced, a check which prevents what is foolish, inappropriate or untalented from appearing in a journal. If I were the editor of a popular journal, I would say to my colleagues: write what you will, preach communism, the Flagellant faith, Protestantism, what you will, only in such a way that every word should be intelligible to the carter who takes the copies round from the press; and I am certain that the journal would contain nothing that is not honest, wholesome and good. I am not joking, and I don't wish to talk in paradoxes, but I know this well from experience. It is impossible to write anything bad in completely simple and intelligible language. Everything immoral will seem so ugly that it will be discarded at once: everything sectarian, whether Protestant or Flagellant, will appear so false if expressed without unintelligible phrases; everything would-be educational, popular-scientific, but not serious and for the most part false, which popular journals are always full of, also expressed without such phrases but in intelligible language, will seem so stupid and impoverished that it will also be thrown out. If a popular journal seriously wishes to be a popular journal, it only has to try to be intelligible and it is not difficult to achieve this. On the one hand it has only got to filter all the articles through the censorship of yardmen, cabmen and kitchen cooks. If the readers don't stop over a single word which they don't understand, the article is fine. But if after reading an article none of them can tell what they have read about, the article is useless.

I genuinely sympathise with the idea of a popular journal, and I hope you will partly agree with me, which is why I say all this. But I also know that 999 people out of a 1,000 will consider my words plain foolishness or the desire to be original, while I, on the contrary, regard a journal for the people published by ladies, and by ladies who neither think nor speak Russian and who have no desire to find out whether the people understand them, as a very strange and very funny joke. I said it is very easy to achieve intelligibility on the one hand—one has only to read something in manuscript or give it to the people to read; but on the other hand it is very difficult to publish an *intelligible journal*. It is difficult because there will be very little material. It will constantly be the case that an article considered charmant in editorial circles will be considered useless when read in the kitchen, or that out of 30 printer's sheets of *words* there will be only 10 lines of *action*

I respect you so much that I have allowed myself to be frank. I hope you will not condemn me for it.

I enclose a note about translation rights, and have left a space for the name.

Very truly and respectfully yours,
Count L. Tolstoy

197. To A. A. FET

Yasnaya Polyana, 22 February 1875

We have one sorrow after another. You and Marya Petrovna will certainly pity us, especially Sonya. Our youngest son, 10 months old, fell ill about three weeks ago with the terrible disease which is called water on the brain, and after 3 weeks' terrible torture died the day before yesterday, and we buried him today. I feel it hard on account of my wife, but for her, nursing him herself, it was very difficult. You praise *Karenina*, which pleases me very much, and other people praise her, so I hear; but assuredly there never was a writer so indifferent to his own success, si succès il y a, as I am.

On the one hand there are the school affairs, and on the other, strange to say, the subject for a new work which seized hold of me just at the very worst time of the child's illness, and then the illness itself and death.

Your poem[1] seems to me to be the embryo of a fine poem; as a poetic idea it is completely clear to me, but as a verbal composition it is completely obscure.

I have received from Turgenev a translation of *Two Hussars* printed in *Le Temps*,[2] and a letter in the 3rd person[3] asking me to let him know that I received it, and that M. Viardot[4] and Turgenev are translating some other stories, both of which things were completely unnecessary.

My wife and I will be very glad if, as we understand, you and Marya Petrovna wish to come and see us and give us a day of your time.

The money will be sent by 1 April. I'm very grateful to Pyotr Afanasyevich[5] for the horses' pedigree. I'm only afraid that the young stallion might be too difficult and fleet-footed. I would like the old one better.

Yours,
L. Tolstoy

198. To N. N. STRAKHOV

Yasnaya Polyana, 23–4 February 1875

I've just received the proofs for the 2nd issue[1] and there are many things I'm dissatisfied with. You have ruffled my author's self-esteem about the novel, dear Nikolay Nikolayevich, and so if you have the time and the inclination, please let me know anything intelligent you hear or read by way of criticism of these chapters. There are many weak passages in them. I'll mention them to you: Anna's return home, and Anna at home.[2] The conversation in the Shcherbatsky family after the

[197] 1. The poem beginning 'Why do you sit there pensive, darling?'
2. Translated by S. Rollin in *Le Temps* (1 February 1875).
3. Written by Annenkov at Turgenev's request.
4. The singer Pauline Viardot's husband, who translated works by Pushkin, Gogol, Turgenev and Tolstoy into French.
5. Shensin (Fet's brother).

[198] 1. The proofs of *Anna Karenina* for the February issue of *The Russian Herald*.
2. Part I, chs. 22–3.

198. To N. N. Strakhov

doctor's visit up to where the sisters have it out.[3] The Petersburg salon,[4] and others. If there are criticisms of these passages, please let me know. In the proofs you sent me there is the end of a drama by Averkiyev,[5] and when I read it I realised why my writing, so full of shortcomings, is successful. Some Russian prince or other has killed his mistress, and in the first moment of horror at what he has done he exclaims: 'Oh, unhappy me! It will be written in the chronicles that I am a murderer!' It's dreadful! As I read this abomination I realised what blank verse is for. Ostrovsky once made this reply to my question why he wrote *Minin* in verse: 'you need to distance yourself'. When a man is not personally involved in what he writes, he writes in blank verse, and then the falseness is not so grossly apparent.

I have a great favour to ask you. My brother-in-law Petya Behrs has got married and is completely absorbed in his honeymoon and has no time to devote to my *Primer*. Please be kind enough to take it under your protection...[9 lines omitted]

199. To ARCHIMANDRITE LEONID

Archimandrite Leonid (Lev Alexandrovich Kavelin, 1822–91) was Prior of the New Jerusalem Monastery and subsequently Superior of the Troitse-Sergiyev Monastery, where Tolstoy later met him. He had been an army officer before taking monastic vows and wrote extensively on archaeology and the history of old Russian literature.

Yasnaya Polyana, 16–20 March 1875

Your Holiness,

I felt great spiritual pleasure when I received your letter.[1] I read in it your expression of sympathy for views which are dear to me on a matter which is dear to me, and a far higher and deeper expression of those ideas which I had only vaguely imagined. An edition for the people of select passages from our ancient literature and actually on the big scale you propose seems to me such a good and important cause that I intend without fail to dedicate to it all the powers, knowledge and resources that I can. I shall make my own financial contribution to the cause, and I have begun to, and will continue to collect people, on your instructions, to form a society with such an edition as its object. The greatest difficulty is the selection and the editing, i.e. abridgements and explanations, if they are needed. The question is,

3. Part II, chs. 1–2.
4. Part II, ch. 6.
5. A reference to the end of the play *Princess Ulyana Vyazemskaya* by D. V. Averkiyev (1836–1905).

[199] 1. A belated reply to an earlier letter of Tolstoy's in which he had sought the Archimandrite's help in compiling a popular reader based on passages from the Lives of the Saints. The Archimandrite agreed to help on condition that he could select and edit the texts himself, but nothing came of the project.

200. To N. N. Strakhov

will you be willing to take on this task? If so, and if God gives us life and strength, the work will be done.

Needless to say the whole thing will need thorough discussion, for which I shall try to visit you; but at present I am only expressing the feelings and intentions which your letter aroused in me.

I am very grateful to you for such an interesting and splendid study of Silvester.[2] Judging by it, I can guess what treasures—the like of which no other people possess—lie concealed in our ancient literature. How sure is the instinct of the people, which attracts them to old Russian and repels them from the modern language.

Please accept my deep gratitude for your kind favour towards me and the assurance of my deep and sincere respect; I have the honour to be your obedient servant,

Count Lev Tolstoy

200. To N. N. STRAKHOV

Yasnaya Polyana, 5 May 1875

Don't be angry, dear Nikolay Nikolayevich, because this letter will be short. I've already written 8 letters and this—intimate—letter to you I was putting off to the end. And now there's no time. Still, better a short one than nothing at all. I know how nice it is when abroad to get letters from Russia.

I particularly want to reply to what you write about yourself. The state of your soul has been partly revealed to me, but that is all the more reason for wanting to penetrate further into it. And my wish is a legitimate one; it isn't based on intellectual interest, but on heartfelt attraction towards you. There are souls whose only doors lead straight into living rooms. There are big doors and small ones, open doors and closed ones, but some are at the end of entrance halls, back and front staircases and corridors. You have winding corridors, but your apartments are good, and the main thing is, I love them. And I always wanted to penetrate them. You always speak, think and write about the general—you are objective. And we all do this, but really it is only deceit, legitimate deceit, the deceit of decency, but still deceit, like clothing. Objectivity is decency, as necessary to the masses as clothing. Venus di Milo can go about naked, and Pushkin can talk frankly about his personal impression of her. But if Venus goes about naked and an old cook does as well, it will be disgusting. And so people decided that it would be better for Venus to be clothed too. She doesn't lose anything, and the cook will be less ugly. This compromise seems to me to exist in things of the mind too. Extremes, ugliness, surcharge[1] of clothing often do harm, but we are used to them. And you wear too much objectivity, and so spoil yourself, at least for me. What criticism, judgements,

---

2. Silvester was the author of the sixteenth-century *Domostroy*, a manual of Christian behaviour and household management.

[200] 1. The word 'surcharge' is in French in the original.

200. To N. N. Strakhov

or classifications can compare with an ardent, passionate search for a meaning for one's life? How strange that you are seeking out the monks and want to go to the Optina Monastery. That's just what I wanted, and still do.[2]

How can we see each other? I'm going to Samara with the family at the end of May and come back in August. If only you could come to see me!

In any case, please write to me. The address in Samara is: Samara (poste restante). I've sent something for the 4th issue[3] and won't touch it again till autumn.

Yours,
L. Tolstoy

201. To N. N. STRAKHOV

Yasnaya Polyana, 25 August 1875

Dear Nikolay Nikolayevich,

I've just read *The Last Idealist*[1] (the 2nd day after our return from Samara), and am very grateful to you for it. What with this and your last letters, you have told me everything you can and wish to say about yourself, and I confess I've learned a great deal that is new.

Above all I learned from your story what I have always guessed, namely that your sympathy for me, and mine for you, is founded on the exceptional affinity of our spiritual lives. I hope that this severance of the umbilical cord, this indifference to one side of life, is only the sign of another umbilical cord through which stronger juices are flowing, and I hope that neither you nor I would want to change places with the people we so envied some 20 or 25 years ago.

And how right you are that *A Hamlet of Shchigrov Province*[2] and the superfluous men were not the result of the fact that Nikolay Pavlovich[3] loved marching, as the Annenkovs would have us believe, and that they are not a lamentable weakness of a particular period of Russian life or even of Russian man in general, but are an enormous new force not comprehensible to Europe, but comprehensible to an Indian. I confess to you that I always felt what your hero and Hamlet felt, but I never complained about it, but was proud and rejoiced, and now the nearer I am to death the more I rejoice.

We arrived safely the day before yesterday. I didn't take up my pen for two months and am very pleased with my summer. Now I'm settling down again to dull, commonplace *Anna Karenina* and I pray to God just to give me the strength to get it off my hands as quickly as possible in order to clear a space—I need the leisure very much—not for pedagogical activities, but for others which are taking more

2. Tolstoy and Strakhov went there together in 1877.
3. The next instalment of *Anna Karenina*.

[201] 1. *The Last of the Idealists (A Fragment from an Unfinished Story)* published by Strakhov in 1866.
2. Turgenev's story about a superfluous man (1849), the hero of which was only one of many so-called superfluous men in Russian literature of the first half of the nineteenth century, in particular during the reign of Nicholas I.   3. Nicholas I.

and more of a hold on me.⁴ I love my pedagogical activities just as much, but I want to force myself not to pursue them.

What are you doing? Have you got over the sad impressions of your brother's death? Above all, are you working? And what on? My acquaintance with the philosopher Solovyov⁵ gave me a great deal of new material, stirred up the philosophical ferment in me very much and did a lot to confirm and clarify for me those thoughts of mine which are so necessary for the rest of my life and death, and which are so comforting to me that if I had the time and was able, I would try to pass them on to others.

Is there any hope of seeing you this year? Will you be going anywhere via Moscow? I could come to Moscow to see you, or you could come to me. I daren't, of course, invite you from Petersburg.

Yours,
L. Tolstoy

202. To A. A. FET

Yasnaya Polyana, 26(?) October 1875

I haven't written to you for so long, dear Afanasy Afanasich, because I've been unwell myself all this time and have been distressed to watch the illness in the family. Now both they and I are a little better, and I hope—I only hope—to settle down to work.

Our work is a terrible thing. Nobody knows this except us. In order to work it is necessary for scaffolding to be erected under your feet. And this scaffolding doesn't depend on you. If you start working without scaffolding, you will only waste material and make a mess of the walls and not be able to go on with them. You feel this particularly once the work has begun. You keep thinking—why not go on? And all of a sudden your arms fail you and you sit and wait. This is what I've been doing. But now, I think, the scaffolding has been erected and I'm rolling up my sleeves.

I've been reading a book recently, which nobody has any idea about, but which I've been revelling in. It's a collection of information about the Caucasian mountain tribes, published in Tiflis.¹ It contains the legends and poetry of the tribesmen and some remarkable poetic treasures. I would like to send it to you. As I read it, I was constantly reminded of you. But I'm not sending it because I grudge parting with it. I'm rereading it on and off. Here is an example for you:

> 'The earth will dry up on my grave, and you will forget me, my mother dear.'

---

4. I.e. religious writings. Tolstoy began an article on the meaning of religion in November 1875.
5. The philosopher Vladimir Solovyov visited Yasnaya Polyana at his own request in May 1875 and presented Tolstoy with his book, *The Crisis of Western Philosophy*.
[202] 1. Published in 1868. Tolstoy used some of the verses below in ch. 20 of *Hadji Murat*.

202. To A. A. Fet

> 'Grass will sprout on my grave in the cemetery, and the grass will choke your grief, my old father.'

> 'The tears will dry up in my sister's eyes, and grief will fly away from her heart.'
>
> . . .
>
> 'You are hot, bullet, and you carry death—but were you not my faithful slave? Black earth, you will cover me, but did I not trample on you with my horse? You are cold, death, but I was your master.'

> 'My body is the property of the earth.'

> 'Heaven will receive my soul.'

Marvellous!
Now the introduction to a poem:

> 'A white hawk on the wing overtakes its prey and catches it with its crooked claws. It catches it and pecks it raw.'

> 'A brindled panther swift of foot overtakes a fox and tears it with its strong claws.'

> 'The bold Khamzat leaves the Terek behind him and crosses over to the left bank with his brave Gikha horsemen...'

> 'Go outside, mother, and behold a wonder: the green grass is pushing up from beneath the snow on the mountain.'

> 'Go up to the roof, mother, to the very edge of the roof: a spring flower is showing through from beneath the ice in the ravine.'
>
> . . .
>
> 'The green grass is not pushing up from beneath the snow on the mountain. A spring flower is not showing through from beneath the ice in the ravine. You thought you saw the flower because you are in love.'

Will you like this?[2] Give my regards to Marya Petrovna and Pyotr Afanasich.
Yours,
L. Tolstoy

203. To N. N. STRAKHOV

Yasnaya Polyana, 8–9 November 1875

Dear Nikolay Nikolaich,

All this time—2 weeks—I've been looking after a sick wife who gave birth to a stillborn child and has been at death's door. But it's a strange thing—I've never

---
2. Fet in fact reworked some of the verses into a poem dedicated to Tolstoy.

204. To N. N. Strakhov

thought with such vigour about the problems which interest me as at this time. I read and reread carefully again the words of Wundt,[1] and understood for the first time the full force of the materialist outlook and for two days was an out and out materialist, but for the first and last time only. Now I rejoice all the more at your plan and challenge you to a correspondence. And so—to a meeting of minds.

My God, if only someone would finish *A. Karenina* for me! It's unbearably repulsive.

Yours,
L. Tolstoy

204. To N. N. STRAKHOV

Yasnaya Polyana, 30 November 1875

Your letter made such a strong impression on me, dear Nikolay Nikolayevich, that my nose twitched and tears came to my eyes. The expression of all that is genuine, 'Das Echte', which one meets so rarely, makes this impression on me. It also struck me because it asked the same things, or at least put questions from the same field in which I had just previously written answers for my own benefit to the questions which interested me.[1]

I am sending you what I have written by way of introduction to a philosophical work I have conceived. You will see from it that of Kant's 3 questions,[2] only the last one interests me and has done so since childhood (this is the difference in our characters)—'what can we hope for?'

The difference between you and me is only an external one. For every thinking man all three questions are inseparably joined into one—'what is my life, what am I?' But the instinct of presentiment, or the experience of the mind—as you like—tells each man which of these three locks on these doors opens most easily, which one he has a key for, or which of these doors, perhaps, is barred to him by life; but there is no doubt that it is sufficient to open one of these doors to penetrate into what is behind them all. I fully understood what you were saying, and although I would like to await your explanation of passive and active activity, and the borderline between them, I cannot refrain from the wish to state my answer to this 2nd question: 'what ought I to do?'

I know that it is very bold of me and may seem strange and frivolous to answer such a question on 2 small sheets of writing paper, but I have reasons for considering that I not only can but should do so. And I would do so even if I were not writing a letter to you, a close friend, but were writing my own profession de foi, knowing that all humanity was listening to me.

[203] 1. Wilhelm Max Wundt (1832–1920), German psychologist and one of the founders of experimental psychology.

[204] 1. Perhaps a reference to two contemporary fragments: *On a Future Life outside Space and Time*; and *On the Importance of the Christian Religion*.

2. Strakhov had said in his letter that of Kant's three questions in the *Critique of Pure Reason*: What can I know?, What ought I to do? and What may I hope for? he considered the most important to be the second.

204. To N. N. Strakhov

Here are my reasons:

(Please listen to me attentively, don't be angry at this digression and do correct what is not exact, explain what is not clear and refute what is untrue. This digression is essentially what is called an exposition of method.)

In every scientific exposition it is assumed that the science being expounded is unknown to the listener or reader. Even if something is known, the person who is expounding the science requires the reader to forget what he knows, and begins to define from the beginning, in his own way and in accordance with the objectives of science, every phenomenon known to the listener.

I assume that while reading this you have already provided examples yourself from mathematics or the natural and political sciences which confirm that this is the method and process of expounding all the sciences.

This method is natural and necessary in all the sciences because the results of knowledge (in any branch of science) cannot be known to the listener—he cannot understand them or believe in their reality unless his previous concepts about the phenomena in that particular field of knowledge have been corrected and he has been introduced step by step to explanations of primary phenomena.

A man cannot know the weight of the sun and believe in the accuracy of its calculation unless it has been demonstrated to him that the sun does not move; and he cannot believe in the Darwinian system unless the concept of the horse, the fish, etc. has been replaced for him by the concept of the organism and its functions.

It should be observed as well that in the exposition of all the sciences the method of exposition and the corrections made in the listener's concepts (i.e. the way of defining the simplest scientific phenomena) is not to follow a general law, but always to conform only with the latest results attained by science (results which, although known to the person expounding them, are unknown to the listener) so that the definitions of the simplest phenomena appear to be, and in fact are arbitrary or dependent on the level which science has attained. In ancient times people said fire was an element; in Newton's time they spoke of rays being emitted; now they speak of the motion of the ether. No science can proceed differently, for there are always scientific results known to the person expounding them, but unknown to the listener, which the listener must be convinced of.

Only philosophy (genuine philosophy, whose task is to answer Kant's questions, to explain the meaning of life) does not have this attribute of the other sciences which is to correct the simplest primitive concepts of the listener, offer him new definitions and then lead him to the latest results attained by science, which are known to the person expounding them but not to the listener. I say that philosophy (genuine philosophy) does not have this attribute, but nevertheless one has only to read all the books with 'philosophy' written on their covers to find precisely this attribute, which according to me is alien to philosophy, in all of them.

This is so, firstly because many of these books are not philosophy at all, like all those positivist works in which the scientific method is or can be applied with the utmost rigour, while others are truly philosophical books (Descartes, Spinoza, Kant, Schelling, Fichte, Hegel, Schopenhauer) but adopt in their exposition a

204. To N. N. Strakhov

method inappropriate to their subject. (Plato is sharply distinguished from all the others, in my opinion, by the correctness of his philosophical method. Schopenhauer is closest of all to him.) From this point of view, all philosophical works are for me subdivided into three categories:

1. Materialists and positivists, who set a low and therefore wrong objective for philosophy, apply the general scientific method with the utmost rigour, and fully achieve their objective; but by the essential nature of their objective remain outside philosophy.

2. Idealists and spiritualists, who set a comprehensive objective for philosophy, but adopt general scientific methods for its exposition, and then to a greater or lesser extent retreat from them according to the strength and depth of their thought. (Hegel never retreats, Schopenhauer does so continually.)

3. Plato, Schopenhauer and all religious teachings set a true objective for philosophy and in its exposition do not adhere to the scientific method, i.e. do not correct their listeners' simplest primitive concepts, but seek the meaning of life without dividing into their constituent parts the essential things which make up the life of every man.

You will perhaps ask me what right I have to make such a bold subdivision of all philosophical teachings on the basis of a proposition about the difference in method of philosophy and of all other sciences, when the need for this difference has not yet been proved.

The need for this difference is proved by the following:

1. If it is true that the scientific method of exposition consists in correcting the listener's concepts about certain subjects and replacing them by certain exact definitions with the object of leading him to a knowledge of general laws by means of these definitions, then it is evident that this method is not applicable to philosophy, because at the highest level of philosophical knowledge not a single one of the basic concepts which make up philosophical knowledge can be changed or understood differently, or defined differently. In astronomy the concept of a low winter sun has been replaced by an entirely different concept, that of a shift in the earth's position in its orbit, and in physics and chemistry the concept of a flame on a wick has been replaced by the concept of a chemical combination; but the basic concepts of philosophy, the elements of which it is composed, have never changed in the history of mankind and never can change—neither for a savage nor for a wise man. *My body, my soul, my life, my death, my desire, my thought, I feel pain, I feel bad, I feel good, I feel joyful,* they are always the same and they cannot be either more clear or more obscure for a savage or for a wise man. Consequently, the scientific method of correcting and redefining the concepts which make up science is inapplicable to philosophy, to a knowledge which has as its subject the soul, life, thought, joy, etc.

2. I base my proof that the scientific method is inapplicable to philosophy on the fact that every science begins by separating off from each phenomenon which comes under that science, that aspect which actually does come under it, summarily removing from its jurisdiction all other aspects of the phenomenon. And, as it

204. To N. N. Strakhov

travels along its path, each science generalises only one aspect of phenomena, not only not concerning itself about accord between the other aspects of phenomena and the facts deduced by it, but often exulting over this lack of accord as a proof of science's success. By its very purpose philosophy cannot reject any one aspect of those phenomena which concern it. The very subjects with which philosophy is concerned—life, the soul, the will, reason—are not amenable to dissection or the rejection of certain aspects. The phenomena which form the subject of the sciences are phenomena known by us indirectly in the outer world; the phenomena which form the subject of philosophy are all known by us directly in our inner world, and we can observe them in the outer world only because we know them from the inner world—and these phenomena can only form the subject of philosophy when they are taken in their entirety, i.e. as we recognise them directly. Take for example life, will, reason. As an activity of the organism, life can be the subject of physiology; as a phenomenon of the state it can be the subject of law or history; as a series of chemical processes it can be the subject of chemistry, as a series of physical processes —of physics; but life as the subject of philosophy is life in its entirety, i.e. what every living thing knows about itself. And so, if for the exposition of a science it is necessary to choose one aspect of phenomena and to reject all other aspects, then by the very nature of the subject of philosophy this method is not applicable to it.

3. A third proof is the fact that the cogency of the propositions advanced by each science lies, as Schopenhauer says, in their logical, physical, mathematical or moral necessity; in the fact that having rejected a certain aspect of a phenomenon and having explained only one aspect of it, the person expounding it leads the listener by means of a series of deductions to a belief in the general laws which can be deduced from this aspect of the phenomenon; and the listener is outwardly convinced incontrovertibly of the facts given to him in this manner, but inwardly remains completely free of his received convictions.

It is entirely different with the exposition of philosophy. With philosophical exposition it is impossible to redefine the concepts which make up philosophical knowledge; it is impossible to truncate these concepts, but they must be left in their entirety, since they are concepts acquired directly, and therefore it is impossible to construct any sort of causal chain out of them. None of these concepts obey a single one of Schopenhauer's propositions about adequate foundations. None of these concepts are subject to logical deductions; they are all equal among themselves and have no logical connection; consequently, the cogency of philosophical teaching can never be achieved by logical deductions, but is only achieved by the harmonious combination of all these illogical concepts into one whole, i.e. it is achieved instantaneously, without deductions and proofs, and has only one method of proof—that any combination other than the given one is senseless. Therefore, by a harmonious combination I mean only the best combination. In confirmation of this proposition I ask you to remember the ineffectiveness of scientific philosophical theories, and the effectiveness and strength of religions—and not only on crude and ignorant minds, as you yourself know.

Another confirmation of this proposition is the fact that philosophy is the know-

204. To N. N. Strakhov

ledge on which the whole of one's outlook on life, including all knowledge, is based, and that all branches of knowledge are encompassed in philosophy.

If knowledge, with all its infinite progress, is the walls of a cylinder, then there is no, and can be no philosophy; but if knowledge is the walls of a cone, then the top of the cone cannot be built in the same way as the walls are built.

And so the 3rd proof that the scientific method is inapplicable to philosophy is that the cogency of the sciences is based on logic and on deduction, while the cogency of philosophy is based on harmony.

While speaking about the different methods of the sciences and philosophy, I almost defined, involuntarily, what I mean by philosophy, and I am glad I did so and I shall try to define it even more precisely. As it is, we who love philosophy are very often not understood by, and do not understand other people. Either too much or too little is demanded of philosophy. The positivist says: you cannot logically prove the correctness of your outlook because it is unscientific and *unnecessary*. The believer says: you cannot confirm the correctness of your outlook because it is arbitrary.

For this reason, it seems to me we must clearly define what we mean by philosophy so that we shall not be told it is unnecessary, so that we shall not ask of it what it cannot give, and so that at the same time we can recognise that it is not something incidental.

Philosophy, in an individual sense, is the knowledge that gives the best possible answers to questions about the meaning of human life and death.

In a general sense, it is the combination in one concordant whole of all the fundamentals of human knowledge which cannot have logical explanations.

I can see the mass of omissions, obscurities and repetitions, as well as the repulsive didactic tone in all that I have written, but I stand by my basic idea about the method of philosophy which I hope you will understand amid all this confusion. This idea is necessary to me in order to begin the exposition of what I think about the questions which interest me. The basic idea is that everyone's (and therefore, my own) philosophical outlook derived from life is a circle or a sphere where there is no end, middle or beginning, nothing important or unimportant, but where everything is a beginning, everything a middle, everything equally important and necessary; and that the cogency and truth of this outlook depends on its inner concord and harmony, and that if I want to express this outlook, it is just as good if I begin with Kant's 2nd question about what one ought to do, which interests you, although this question of ethics seems to me to be one of the last ones in my plan.

You say: what ought I to do? A child at the breast doesn't ask what he ought to do; he sucks and wants to live—he loves himself; neither does a man who is dying from illness or old age ask this question. He wishes not to suffer, he wants to die, he doesn't love himself (he loves what is not himself). Why do you and I ask ourselves what to do? Only because we want to live and we want to die, at the same time. But we don't live from old age to childhood, but from childhood to old age.

204. To N. N. Strakhov

One must go with the stream in order to feel calmness, strength and inner satisfaction; one must want to die. What does it mean to want to live? To love oneself. To want to die is not to love oneself, or to love what is not oneself—which is the same thing.

If it were as clear to you as it is to me that loving, desiring, and living are the same thing, then I would say frankly that in childhood we desire the self, live in the self, love the self, but in old age we live not for the self, desire something beyond the self, love not the self, and that life is only a transition from love of the self (i.e. from the individual life, from this life) to love not of the self (i.e. to a general life, not this life), and therefore, to the question 'what ought I to do?' I would answer: 'Love not the self', i.e. I would resolve each moment of doubt by choosing the way in which I might satisfy love not of the self.[3]

Why am I writing this?

I am 47. Either because I have lived passionately or because this is the normal age for it, I feel that old age has begun for me. I call old age the inner spiritual condition in which all the outer phenomena of the world lose their meaning for me. It seems to me that I know everything people of our time know. If there is something I don't know, it seems to me that if I were to learn this unknown bit of knowledge it would have no interest for me: it would not reveal anything new to me, nothing new that I want to know. I desire nothing from the outer phenomena of the world. If a magician were to come and ask me what I wanted, I would not be able to express a single desire. If I have any desires, such as, for instance, to raise a breed of horses I dream of raising, or to bring 10 foxes to bay in one field, etc., or to have enormous success with my book, to acquire a fortune of a million roubles, to learn Arabic and Mongolian, and so on, I know that these are not true or lasting desires, but only remnants of habitual desires which appear at bad moments of my spiritual condition. At the moments when I have these desires, an inner voice tells me they will not satisfy me.

And so I have reached old age, that inner spiritual condition in which nothing from the outer world has any interest, in which there are no desires and one sees nothing but death ahead of one.

I have lived through the period of childhood, adolescence and youth when I climbed higher and higher up the mysterious hill of life, hoping to find at its summit a result worthy of the effort put in; I have also lived through the period of maturity during which, having reached the summit, I went on calmly and contentedly, resting deliberately and unhurriedly, searching all round me for the fruits of life which I had attained; and I have lived through the gradually growing doubt whether I made a mistake in assigning an unnatural importance to those fruits which I had attained, or whether the discrepancy between those fruits and the desire for their attainment was the general fate of man; and I have lived through the conviction that nothing of what I expected on this summit was there and that now, only one thing remained to me willy-nilly—to descend the other side to the place where I came from. And I have begun that descent. Not only do I no longer have

3. The letter continues in a different hand.

204. To N. N. Strakhov

the desires which so unobtrusively carried me up, but I have a contrary and unworthy desire to stop and clutch hold of something; I have moments of terror (even more unworthy) at what awaits me; and I go down, slowly and cautiously, recalling the path I have travelled, examining my present path and, from experience of the path travelled and from my observations of what surrounds me, trying to penetrate the mystery of the meaning of the life I have lived and the even greater mystery that awaits me in the place towards which I am involuntarily hurrying.

I call such a condition old age, and at the present moment I have reached that condition.

As I said, the first feeling I experienced when I reached old age was bewilderment, then terror, a deep feeling of despair that the smart phrase of the poet is not just a phrase, but that life really is a stupid and empty joke[4] which someone has played on us. But the awareness that my life cannot be a joke, the awareness which led Descartes to prove the existence of God and to express his conviction that God could not be playing a joke on us—this awareness made me resist, as it does with every man, the acknowledgment of the senselessness of a rational being's life. This awareness made me doubt if I had understood life's meaning reasonably. And indeed, if at a certain age it appears that all one's past life is senseless, then the lack of accord between this conviction and the demand for human nature to be reasonable can be resolved in two ways: either (i) by saying that all people's lives really are senseless and lead to despair in old age, or (ii) by saying that the meaning I attributed to life is incorrect, and that this incorrectness becomes evident at a certain age just as the deviation of a line from the parallel becomes noticeable at a certain distance.

Not to mention that inner awareness that always stubbornly resists the acknowledgment that life is a stupid joke, the second supposition (i.e. that I had misunderstood the meaning of life) was confirmed also by the fact that if one granted the first supposition, one would have to encounter in all people who reach old age a feeling of despair, while observation shows me that with few exceptions old people in our time and at all times, not only have not despaired but, on the contrary, have lived the calmest and quietest period of their lives in old age, and hold the clearest and calmest view of life and approaching death.

And so I began to search for a view of life which would do away with its apparent senselessness, being convinced that my despair did not come from an attribute of life itself, but from my view of it. The aim and content of what I am writing at present is to recount how I passed from a condition of hopelessness and despair to the clarification for myself of life's meaning, extending both to the part already lived by me and its source, and to the remaining part and its end.

I couldn't get all this copied out.[5]

What is to follow would lead a copyist into temptation. If, God willing, I should finish this, then of course I will send it to you. What is to follow explains how religions fully satisfy these questions, but how it is impossible with our

4. A quotation from Lermontov's poem: 'I am bored and sad...'
5. The letter continues in Tolstoy's own hand.

204. To N. N. Strakhov

knowledge to believe in the propositions of religions; then, how European peoples live without religion when religion is a necessary condition of life. Then I try to discover the religion of materialists, positivists and progressives in their outlook; but it is an incomplete religion—a religion of life but not a religion of death. Then I want to explain why Max Müller and Burnouf, whom I have only just read, and modern people in general, are completely wrong in opposing religion to science. The collection of scientific data of our time is the religion of our time. When people taught the Christian religion in ancient times they did not oppose it to science. It was the science of sciences, the truth, just the same as what is now called positivist science. Then I would like to expound this whole religious collection of scientific views of our time, to show the gaps and—forgive my boldness—without denying anything, to fill in these gaps. That is my bold plan. I ask for your help, most of all in the criticism of my propositions, in the very strictest criticism of them, and I also ask for your help in giving guidance and in indicating materials. For instance, I now need a book or books, or else your exposition of the entire general 'religious' (—in my opinion—'scientific' in their opinion) outlook of the materialists and positivists on God's world. Then I need to know how the authorities define science, religion, and philosophy.

In my opinion, science in the general sense, philosophy and religion are all the same thing.

Science is the aggregate of all human knowledge in subdivided form.

Philosophy is the combination and resultant of all knowledge without subdivisions, and with the repudiation of all other combinations of knowledge.

Religion is the combination and resultant of all knowledge without subdivisions, and without the repudiation of all other combinations.

Science is a false concept when taken as a single whole. Science is by its very nature a series of subdivisions. Philosophy and religion are distinguished only by the polemical character which is inherent in philosophy and alien to religion.

I shall now add a few explanations to the answer which I gave you to the question: what should be done? I say that 'to love', 'to want' ('to desire', 'the will') and 'to live' are the same thing, and at the same time not the same thing. This is one of the applications of the philosophical method which does not use logical deductions, but tries to convince by the rightness of its combinations and concepts.

I cannot say that I am living only because I want to, and that I want to only because I love, nor can I say that I love because I am living, and that I am living because I want to. Nor that I want to because I love, etc. I can and I cannot say all this. Rearranging them does not add to their cogency. But the juxtaposition of these concepts makes them cogent.

Speaking in philosophical jargon which only has a polemical object, I would say: to desire is a temporal concept, for one can only desire what will be.

To live is a spatial concept. When we say 'life', 'living', we are only thinking about a space encompassed by life.

206. To Prince Y. V. Lvov

To love is a causal concept, for one can only desire what one loves, and live only because one loves. However, I don't attach cogency to this, but to the harmonious juxtaposition, not only of these but of all other philosophical concepts.

I shall wait for your sequel, your replies and your objections in order to show you and myself the harmony and validity of the juxtaposition of the concepts of my religious (philosophical) outlook.[6]

Yours,
L. Tolstoy

205. To PRINCE S. S. URUSOV

Yasnaya Polyana, 21 February 1876

I thank you, dear friend, with all my heart for your visit to us, and still more for your letter, the like of which you don't often write. I was touched by this letter: you obviously love me sincerely and probably don't know how much I value it. I won't write to you now about my religious doubts, particularly because they are not so strong now as usual, and because your stay with us helped a lot, and particularly your letter: the fact that you don't want to refute or try to prove. You wouldn't believe what a great effect this has on us. You fortunate people who are believers enjoy spiritual eminence, tranquillity, and enormous strength of mind, and you say that you have this blessing but cannot hand it on to us, but only wish that we had it. I don't believe in prayer and cannot pray, but if it is true what you believe, then *you* can pray and your prayer can be heard; and so pray that God might give me the support of faith...[13 lines omitted]

206. To PRINCE Y. V. LVOV

Yevgeny Vladimirovich Lvov (1817–96), a landowner in the Province of Tula and the father of Prince G. Y. Lvov, Prime Minister of the Provisional Government in 1917.

Yasnaya Polyana, 29 February–1 March 1876

Your letter gave me great pleasure, dear Prince, and also made me sad. It gave me pleasure because you appreciated the form of my stories for the people, but made me sad because in the 5 years, I think it is, since these stories came out, you have never come across them and, like the public, you considered me either a speculator, writing for the people for money, or a 50-year-old fool talking about something he knows nothing about. I fought against German pedagogy precisely because I have devoted a big part of my life to this matter, because I know how the people and the people's children think and because I know how to talk to them, and this knowledge

---

6. Several more letters were exchanged, without any significant change of view on Tolstoy's part.

206. To Prince Y. V. Lvov

did not fall out of the sky because I have talent (a most foolish, nonsensical word), but because I acquired this knowledge by love and hard work. The stories and fables written in the booklets are what has been sifted out from a quantity of adapted stories 20 times as great, and each of them was revised by me as many as 10 times, and cost me more hard work than any passage in any of my writings. The *Primer* cost me even more hard work. I have been praised for everything I have written, but not a single word which is not abusive has been said in print about the one really good and useful thing that I have done, the *Primer* and these booklets. You read them and appreciated them because you write yourself, and want to write, and because you have taste and feeling. But anyone with taste and feeling reading these booklets could say: 'Yes, all right, simple and clear, but in places bad and false.' And anyone who read them and said this would be absolutely right. But if anyone tries to write stories like these he will see how hard to come by these negative virtues are, which consist merely in a thing being simple and clear and having nothing superfluous or false about it.

I am writing this to you because it seems to me that you understand it, and moreover because I think you are able to write like this and perhaps even better. Only you will see how long it takes and how little one can write that is good. Joseph de Maistre wrote a long letter to his king in 1812 about the war and about Petersburg and ended the letter like this: 'Je prie votre Majesté d'excuser la longueur de cette lettre. Je n'ai pas eu le temps de la faire plus courte.'[1]

And when you devote time to making things as short as possible (this is the first rule), you will see how difficult it is. I haven't received your book, though. I do beg you to send it to me. I need it very much.

I gave the Caucasian anthology[2] to a friend; I'll send it you when I get it back. Give my regards and my wife's to the Princess.

Please don't forget your promise to call and see us in summer. If I am in Moscow, I shall certainly visit you.

Yours,
L. Tolstoy

207. To P. D. GOLOKHVASTOV

Yasnaya Polyana, 17–20(?) March 1876

Thank you, dear Pavel Dmitrich, for remembering me—the only unfortunate thing is that you send me bad news about yourself—firstly the fact, as I see, that you are not working, that you are not up to your eyes in work. That's the only real way. I don't even want to know what you ought to be working at. That doesn't matter. I only know that there are things which you know and others don't—poetic or philological, scientific or artistic—and that only you ought to express

---

[206] 1. A letter from the *Correspondance diplomatique* of Joseph de Maistre, the Savoyard envoy in Petersburg from 1803 to 1815, written to the King of Sardinia in August 1812.
2. See Letter 202, note 1.

208. To Countess A. A. Tolstaya

these things, and that in order to do so you must immerse yourself up to your eyes in work. And you are not doing so, and that's bad. Secondly, the fact that you are living abroad, and in Italy. You wouldn't believe that I would rather live in Mamadysh[1] than in Venice, Rome or Naples; these towns and the life in them have such a conventional, and invariably identical, grandeur and elegance for everyone else, but such vulgarity for me, that it makes me sick to think about them, and it's unbearable to read about them (Strakhov recently sent me his article about Italy and art).[2]

But worst of all is the fact that Olga Andreyevna is ill. There can be no situation more awful for a husband's health than the illness of his wife. I have experienced this condition this year and continue to experience it. My wife has been dangerously ill. All winter she was sick and weak and now she is in bed again, and you tremble every moment lest the situation should get worse. This situation is particularly painful for me because I don't believe in doctors or in medicine, or in the fact that human remedies can make a scrap of difference to a person's state of health, that is to his life. Owing to[3] this conviction which I can't alter, I call in all the doctors, follow all their prescriptions and can't make any plans. It's very likely that we shall go abroad soon, and probably to Italy, which is so repulsive to me, but less so than Germany.[4] In Europe it seems to me that I could only live in England, but people go away from there for their health, and there's no point in going there. Generally speaking my wife's illness, the death of my aunt who died at our house this winter, and the death of our newly born little girl all made this winter very hard for me. The only comforts are the children who, thank goodness, are growing up nicely, and my work in which I'm immersed up to my eyes.

You don't have the first comfort, but you must provide yourself with the second.

But the main thing is, I wish Olga Andreyevna good health, for her sake as well as for your own.

Goodbye. Please write, if only occasionally.

Yours truly affectionately,
L. Tolstoy

208. To COUNTESS A. A. TOLSTAYA

Yasnaya Polyana, 20–3 March 1876

Alas! It's true that I mixed the letters up. Urusov's letter went to you, and yours, probably, went to him. I'm writing to him today to ask him, if that's the case, to put it in an envelope and forward it to you; and with a thousand apologies I ask you to do the same: *Prince Sergey Semyonovich Urusov, Troitse-Sergiyev District, Spasskoye Village.* He's a Sevastopol friend of mine, and we're very fond of each other.

[207] 1. A small town in the Kazan province, used by Tolstoy to mean any provincial backwater.   2. *A Trip to Italy* (1875).
3. Tolstoy presumably meant 'In spite of this conviction...'
4. The trip did not take place.

208. To Countess A. A. Tolstaya

It's strange that the letter in which I write to him of the longing for faith should come to you. Our preceding conversation was as follows. He was staying at my house and I read him a philosophical work of mine.[1] In it I talked about faith and, incidentally, about the fact that nothing used to repel me and turn me away from religion so much as when people tried to convert me by explaining religion to me. The more they explained, the more obscure it became to me. He was apparently struck by this, and wrote me a beautiful letter in which he said that God was punishing him by this for his pride, and that never again would he raise any objections or try to explain anything to me, but he asked me nevertheless to write to him about my spiritual condition. And I wrote to him, particularly after a meeting with Alexey Pavlovich Bobrinsky,[2] who struck me very much by the sincerity and ardour of his faith. And no one has ever spoken to me better about faith than Bobrinsky. He's irrefutable because he doesn't try to prove anything, but says that he just believes, and you feel that he is happier than those who don't have his faith, and above all you feel that it's impossible to acquire the happiness of his faith by an effort of thought, but that you have to receive it by a miracle. And this is what I want and this is what I wrote about to Urusov, and I'm very glad you've read it.

Do you know Radstock?[3] What impression did he make on you?

Thank you very much for praying for me. Although I'm unable to believe in the efficacy of prayer, I'm glad, because this proves your affection for me and because, although I don't believe, I can't say for sure that it's useless. And perhaps it's even true. In any case I know that the more I think, the less I'm able to believe, and that if I come to do so, it will be by a miracle. So please don't try to persuade me. There's no question but that I think ceaselessly about the problems of the meaning of life and death, and think just as seriously as it's possible to think. There's no question either but that I desire with all my heart to find solutions to the problems tormenting me, and don't find them in philosophy; but it seems to me impossible that I could believe.

Have you read Pascal's life—Blaise Pascal—his *Pensées*?[4] What a wonderful book, and his life too. I don't know of a better Life.[5]

I kiss your hand.

Yours,
L. Tolstoy

I didn't write in the other letter that I kiss your hand, and so Urusov, like you, might have been in doubt whether the letter was to him.

[208] 1. Possibly an article written in December 1875, *On the Soul and its Life outside the Life that We Know and Understand*.

2. Count A. P. Bobrinsky (1826–90), a landowner, and Minister of Communications. He was a disciple of the English Evangelical preacher, Lord Radstock, who visited Petersburg in 1874.

3. A. A. Tolstaya knew Lord Radstock well and, in general, responded favourably to his teaching, although disagreeing with him in many respects.

4. The book *Pascal, Pensées, précédées de sa vie par Mme. Perier, sa soeur...* is in the library at Yasnaya Polyana. Tolstoy was more impressed by Pascal's life than by his theology.

5. The Russian word here has a hagiographical flavour, being used of a Life of a saint.

209. To N. N. STRAKHOV

Yasnaya Polyana, 8–9 April 1876

Thank you, dear Nikolay Nikolayevich, for sending Grigoryev.[1] I read the introduction but—don't be angry with me—I feel that I could never read it all through if I were incarcerated in a dungeon. This is not because I don't appreciate Grigoryev —on the contrary—but because criticism is to me the most boring of all boring things in the world. In clever art criticism everything is the truth, but not the *whole* truth, and art is only art because it is *whole*.

I feel with alarm that my summer condition is coming on: I'm disgusted with what I've written, and now there are the proofs for the April issue and I'm afraid I shan't have the strength to correct them. Everything in them is bad, everything needs to be revised and revised—everything that's been printed—and I need to cross it all out and throw it away and disown it and say, 'I'm sorry, I won't do it again', and try to write something new, something not so clumsy and neither one thing nor the other. This is the condition I'm in now, and it's very pleasant. I'm afraid you won't be in the mood to answer this letter and that it won't interest you. In that case please don't write, but simply write now and again, as usual. And don't praise my novel. Pascal made himself a belt of nails which he pressed his elbows against everytime he felt that praise gave him pleasure. I need to make a belt like that. Be a true friend to me: either write nothing about my novel or only write and tell me everything that's bad about it. And if it's true, as I suspect, that I'm getting feeble, please write and tell me.

Our vile literary profession is corrupting. Every writer has his own atmosphere of flatterers which he carefully surrounds himself with, and he can have no idea of his own importance or the time of his decline. I wouldn't like to lose my way and have to turn back further on. Please help me in this.

Yours,
L. Tolstoy

And don't be inhibited by the idea that your stern criticism might upset the work of a man who has talent. Far better to stop at *War and Peace* than to write *The Watch*,[2] etc.

210. To COUNTESS A. A. TOLSTAYA

Yasnaya Polyana, 15–17(?) April 1876

[21 lines omitted]...I was also very glad to hear your opinion (if I've understood it correctly) that sudden conversions rarely or never happen, but that one has to pass through work and suffering. I'm glad to think so, because I've suffered and worked a lot, and in the depths of my soul I know that this work and suffering are better than anything else I've done in life. And this activity must have its reward—if not

[209] 1. The first volume of *The Works of Apollon Grigoryev*, with an introduction by Strakhov, the editor.   2. A story by Turgenev, first published in 1876.

210. To Countess A. A. Tolstaya

the comfort of faith, then the consciousness of the work which is its own reward. But the theory of grace descending on a man in the English Club or at a shareholders' meeting has always seemed to me not only stupid but immoral.

You say you don't know what I believe in. Strange and terrible to say: not in anything that religion teaches us; but at the same time I not only hate and despise unbelief, but I can see no possibility of living, and still less of dying, without faith. And I'm building up for myself little by little my religious beliefs, but although they are all firm, they are very undefined and uncomforting. When questioned by the mind, they answer well; but when the heart aches and seeks an answer, they provide no support or comfort. With the demands of my mind and the answers given by the Christian religion, I find myself in the position, as it were, of two hands endeavouring to clasp each other while the fingers resist. I long to do it, but the more I try, the worse it is; and at the same time I know that it's possible, that the one is made for the other...[5 lines omitted]

211. To N. N. STRAKHOV

Yasnaya Polyana, 23 and 26 April 1876

Our letters to each other have crossed, dear Nikolay Nikolayevich. I had just replied to your philosophical letter when I got your heartening reply to mine. You write: do you understand my novel correctly, and what do I think about your opinions? Of course you understand it correctly. Of course your understanding heartens me beyond words; but not everyone is bound to understand it as you do. Perhaps you are only an amateur at these things, just as I am. Just like one of our Tula pigeon-fanciers. He rates a tumbler-pigeon very highly, but whether the pigeon has any real merits is another question. Besides, the likes of us, as you know, are constantly leaping without any transition from despondency and self-abasement to inordinate pride. I say this because your opinion about my novel is true, but it isn't everything—i.e. everything is true, but what you said doesn't express everything I wanted to say. For example, you speak about two sorts of people. I always feel this—I know—but I didn't intend it so. But when you say it, I know that it's one of the truths which can be said. But if I were to try to say in words everything that I intended to express in my novel, I would have to write the same novel I wrote from the beginning. And if short-sighted critics think that I only wanted to describe the things that I like, what Oblonsky has for dinner or what Karenina's shoulders are like, they are mistaken. In everything, or nearly everything I have written, I have been guided by the need to gather together ideas which for the purpose of self-expression were interconnected; but every idea expressed separately in words loses its meaning and is terribly impoverished when taken by itself out of the connection in which it occurs. The connection itself is made up, I think, not by the idea, but by something else, and it is impossible to express the basis of this connection directly in words. It can only be expressed indirectly—by words describing characters, actions and situations.

211. To N. N. Strakhov

You know all this better than I do, but it has been occupying my attention recently. For me, one of the most manifest proofs of this was Vronsky's suicide which you liked. This had never been so clear to me before. The chapter about how Vronsky accepted his role after meeting the husband had been written by me a long time ago. I began to correct it, and quite unexpectedly for me, but unmistakably, Vronsky went and shot himself. And now it turns out that this was organically necessary for what comes afterwards.

That's why such a nice clever man as Grigoryev interests me very little. It's true that if there were no criticism at all, then Grigoryev and you who understand art would be redundant. But now indeed when 9/10 of everything printed is criticism, people are needed for the criticism of art who can show the pointlessness of looking for ideas in a work of art and can steadfastly guide readers through that endless labyrinth of connections which is the essence of art, and towards those laws that serve as the basis of these connections.

And if critics already understand and can express in a newpaper article what I wanted to say, I congratulate them and can boldly assure them qu'ils en savent plus long que moi.

I'm very, very grateful to you. When I read through my last dejected and humble letter, I realised that I was really asking for praise and that you had sent it to me. And your praise—sincere, I know, although, I'm afraid, too partial—is very, very dear to me.

I'm very annoyed that I made mistakes over the wedding, especially as I love that chapter.[1]

I'm afraid there may also be mistakes over the special subject which I touch on in the part which will come out now in April.[2] Please write and tell me if you or other people find any.

You are right that *War and Peace* grows in *my* eyes. I have a strange feeling of joy when people remind me of something from it as Istomin did recently (he'll be staying with you), but it's strange, I remember very few passages from it, and the rest I forget.

Goodbye; a thousand thanks once more. I still hope to finish. But I shall hardly have the strength. In summer I often feel the physical impossibility of writing.

Yours,
L. Tolstoy

26 April

I wrote this letter several days ago and didn't want to send it—so obtrusive was my author's flattered vanity. But I've just written 7 letters and needed to write to you again, and decided to send this.

Murder will out, and you know me through and through.

L.T.

---

[211] 1. *Anna Karenina*, Part v, chs. 4–5. Strakhov pointed out that the bride should arrive after the bridegroom, and that they should kiss the icons after the wedding ceremony. The corrections were made when the novel came out in book form.

2. Presumably the chapters in Mikhaylov's studio on the subject of art.

212. To A. A. FET

Yasnaya Polyana, 28–9 April 1876

I received your letter, dear Afanasy Afanasich, and from that short letter and from Marya Petrovna's words which my wife passed on to me and from one of your most recent letters in which I overlooked the phrase: 'I wanted to call you to witness my departure', written between calculations about fodder for the horses, and which I have only just understood, I was able to imagine myself in your condition, one that is very understandable and near to me, and I became sorry for you (both according to Schopenhauer and to our own understanding, compassion and love are one and the same thing), and I wanted to write to you. I'm grateful to you for thinking of calling me to witness your departure when you thought the time was near. I'll do the same when I'm ready to go *there*, if I'm able to think. The priests whom our wives will call at that moment won't help you and me; no one will be so necessary to me at that moment as you and my brother. In the face of death, contact with people who in this life look beyond its bounds is precious and heartening, and you and those few *real* people I have been close to in life, in spite of a healthy attitude to life, always stand on its very verge and see life clearly just because they look now at Nirvana, the illimitable, the unknown, and now at Sansara,[1] and that view of Nirvana strengthens their vision. But worldly people, priests etc., however much they may talk about God, are unpleasant to the likes of us, and must be a torment when one is dying, because they don't see what we see, namely the God who is more indeterminate, more distant, but more lofty and indubitable, as was said in that article.

The God of Sabaoth and his son, the God of the priests, is just as little and ugly and impossible a God—indeed far more impossible—than a God of the flies would be for the priests, if the flies imagined him to be a huge fly only concerned with the well-being and improvement of the flies.

You are ill and think about death, while I am well and never cease to think about the same thing and to prepare for it. Let's see who will be first. But various imperceptible facts suddenly revealed to me how deeply akin to mine is your nature—your soul (especially in relation to death), and I suddenly came to appreciate our relationship and began to value it far more than before.

However:

> Mourir vient de soi-même.
> N'en ayons point souci.
> Bien vivre est le problème
> Qu'il faut résoudre ici.[2]

And it can't be otherwise. I have tried to express much of what I thought in the last chapter of the April issue of *The Russian Herald*.[3]

[212] 1. In Buddhist philosophy, life on earth with all its cares, as opposed to Nirvana.
2. A quotation from Béranger.
3. *Anna Karenina*, Part v, ch. 20. entitled *Death*.

Please write and tell Petya Borisov to come and see me without fail and for at least three days or so.

I know that this is close to your heart, and I will look at him carefully, without haste, without any preconceived idea and without any wish to contradict, and will tell you my impression. My only preconceived idea will be a very strong desire to love him—for your sake.

Yours,
L. Tolstoy

I'm very grateful to you for sending *Hamlet*[4] I'll expect him soon.

213. To N. N. STRAKHOV

Yasnaya Polyana, 12–13 November 1876

[21 lines omitted]...Real knowledge, in my opinion and, I'm sure, in yours also, although you will express it better, comes from the heart, i.e. from love. We know what we love, that's all.

Your last question in our philosophical correspondence was: what is evil? I can answer it for myself. I'll give you an explanation of this answer another time, at Christmas, I hope. My wife and I are dreaming you will come; please do come. Well, the answer is as follows: *evil is everything that is rational.*[1] Murder, robbery, punishment—all this is rational and based on logical conclusions. Self-sacrifice and love make no sense...[7 lines omitted]

214. To N. N. STRAKHOV

Yasnaya Polyana, 17–18 November 1876

I've come to life a little, dear Nikolay Nikolaich, and have stopped despising myself, and so I feel like writing to you. 'That's a true friend', I couldn't help saying to myself when I saw your handwriting on your last letter enclosing Polonsky's.[1] I'm replying to him.

It was very disagreeable to me to read Avseyenko's[2] article on Grigoryev, especially because I know how this deliberate, though partly genuine, lack of understanding concealed beneath a show of scornfully-ironical superiority—how this hurts you. What an abomination literature is! The literature of newspapers and journals! Really I read just the same thing in all the papers, now that

---

4. A stallion bought from Fet.

[213] 1. Tolstoy uses *razumno* (literally 'rational', 'reasonable') to mean what may be intellectually justified without regard for moral considerations.

[214] 1. Polonsky was passing on the request of 'a certain lady', (in fact Princess Paskevich) for permission to publish her recent French translation of *Family Happiness*.

2. V. G. Avseyenko (1842–1913). His article entitled *Vagaries of Russian Thought* took sharp issue with Strakhov over his introduction to the *Collected Works of Grigoryev*.

214. To N. N. Strakhov

I've become interested in political events. The same half-contrived, half-genuine lack of understanding, concealing its obtuseness beneath the importance of having attitudes towards the most important phenomena of life. Literature is a terrible abomination, except for its highest manifestations—true scholarly work without any bias, philosophical impartiality of thought and artistic creativity which, I flatter myself with the proud hope, has descended on me these last few days.[3]

It's a pity that you publish your articles in *The Citizen*. It's true that all these newspaper firms with their different characters are equally repulsive, but *The Citizen* has a certain childishness about it because of its foolishness, though not its innocence, and at the same time a false enthusiasm and an aristocratic Christianity.

What will you say about Christmas? I shall await your reply anxiously. Only you will have to get up on a chair and decorate the Christmas tree and tie ribbons on to sweets.

It seems we shan't avoid the Golokhvastovs, and my wife has invited them—if this cup cannot pass—to come for Christmas. I say this not as an inducement for you, but so that you should know what to expect. He's nice, but she's intolerable; she is literature and a bit of *The Citizen*, only without the Christianity. 'All people are thieves, and the man who hasn't stolen is a negative thief.'[4] You wouldn't believe how much this example explained to me. Drop literature altogether and write philosophical books. Who for? But who else will say what we think?

And the Avseyenkos ought to keep silent, but if they do misinterpret things after their own fashion, they will only cover themselves with shame.

I hope to see you soon.

Most cordially yours,
L. Tolstoy

215. To A. A. FET

Yasnaya Polyana, 6–7(?) December 1876

Your letter with the poem[1] reached me by the same post as your collected works which I had ordered from Moscow.

The poem is not only worthy of you, but quite exceptionally good, with just that philosophically poetic character which I expected from you. It's splendid that it's spoken by the stars. And the last stanza is particularly good.

It's good, too, as my wife remarked, that on the same sheet on which the poem is written you give vent to feelings of grief that paraffin now costs 12 copecks.

That's a secondary, but sure sign of a poet.

I ordered Tyutchev, Baratynsky and Tolstoy[2] at the same time as your poems. I know that you'll be pleased to share the society of Tyutchev. Baratynsky won't

---

3. Tolstoy had resumed work on *Anna Karenina* after a long interval.
4. A slight paraphrase of a sentence by Strakhov in a previous letter to Tolstoy.

[215] 1. Fet's poem *Among the stars*.
2. A. K. Tolstoy (1817–75), poet, dramatist and novelist. The line quoted below is from his poem 'Darling, you cannot sleep...'

disgrace you by his company either, but Tolstoy is terrible. I opened him in various places, each worse than the last. For example, a picture of night: 'the steps do not creak in the vestibule'. Why not have said: 'the pigs do not grunt in the pig-sty?' And all in the same vein. And what an edition and what a lot of it. I packed it up as quickly as possible and sent it back.

Baratynsky is genuine, although there's not much beauty and elegance in him, but there are some splendid things. One line:
>'To love and cherish the illness of existence'[3]

is worth more than all Tolstoy's dramas.

I have begun a little writing and am content with my lot.

Unfortunately I haven't anyone in Moscow suitable for you.[4] Dyakov is staying with us now, but will be in Moscow, and will be seeing you.

Yours,
L. Tolstoy

216. To P. I. TCHAIKOVSKY

Pyotr Ilich Tchaikovsky (1840–93), the composer. Tolstoy first met Tchaikovsky through Nikolay Rubinstein, the then Director of the Moscow Conservatoire, in December 1876, while he was in Moscow delivering the manuscript of Part V of *Anna Karenina* to Katkov. This meeting took place on Tolstoy's initiative, at a time when he was particularly interested in music. Tchaikovsky, a great admirer of Tolstoy's literary works, persuaded Rubinstein to arrange the musical evening to which Tolstoy refers in his letter. Much impressed with the works by Tchaikovsky which were performed that evening, Tolstoy sent a collection of Russian folk-songs for him to arrange. Tchaikovsky replied, however, that the material sent was too far removed from its original form to be suitable for treatment as songs; he added that he hoped to use it as symphonic material.

These two letters constitute the whole of the Tolstoy–Tchaikovsky correspondence. Despite a favourable first impression, Tchaikovsky was offended by Tolstoy's persistent and outspoken criticism of Beethoven and the two men never met again.

Yasnaya Polyana, 19–21 December 1876

I am sending you the songs,[1] dear Pyotr Ilich. I have looked through them again. They will be a wonderful treasure in your hands. But for goodness sake, work them up and use them in a Mozart–Haydn style, and not in a Beethoven–Schumann–Berlioz–artificial style, striving for the unexpected. How much I left unsaid to you! I really said nothing of what I meant to say. There was simply no time. I did enjoy

---

3. Y. A. Baratynsky (1800–40), a close contemporary of Pushkin's. The line is from his poem to Delvig: 'In vain we dream of finding, Delvig...'

4. A reference to Fet's request for a home in Moscow for his niece.

[216] 1. A book of Russian folk songs collected by Kirsha Danilov.

216. To P. I. Tchaikovsky

myself. Indeed this last visit of mine to Moscow will remain one of my best memories.

I have never received such a valuable reward for my literary works as that wonderful evening. And what a nice man Rubinstein[2] is! Thank him once more for me. I liked him very much. In fact all those high priests of the highest art in the world, sitting down to their pie, left such a pure and serious impression on me. As for what took place in the round hall, I can't think of it without trembling.[3] Which of them may I send my works to—i.e. who doesn't have them and who will read them?

I haven't looked through your pieces yet,[4] but when I settle down to them, I will give you my opinion—whether you need it or not—and give it boldly, because I have grown to love your talent. Goodbye; I cordially press your hand in friendship.

Yours,
L. Tolstoy

What portrait was Rubinstein talking about? I'll be glad to send one to him, having asked him to do the same, but for the Conservatoire it is somehow not the thing.

217. To N. N. STRAKHOV

Yasnaya Polyana, 25–6 January 1877

Dear Nikolay Nikolaich,

I'm very grateful to you for the news about my wife and for your trouble on her behalf. I'm very pleased. Botkin found nothing dangerous in her condition, although, I must confess, I suffered such dreadful things in my imagination. She came back happy and full of life, and with such good news.

The success of the latest instalment of *Anna Karenina* also, I confess, gave me pleasure. I hadn't expected it, and really I'm surprised that such an ordinary and insignificant thing should be liked, and still more that, being convinced that such an insignificant thing is liked, I haven't started to write any old thing at random, but have been making a choice which is *almost* incomprehensible even to me. I say this frankly, because it's to you, and especially because, having sent off the proofs for the January issue, I have faltered over the February issue, and am only just getting back into my stride mentally. I haven't read the Turgenev, but judging from all I hear, I sincerely regret that this spring of pure and excellent water has been polluted

---

2. N. G. Rubinstein (1835–81), the brother of the more famous Anton Rubinstein, was also a fine pianist, and was the founder of the Moscow Conservatoire in 1864 and its director until his death.

3. A reference to the concert arranged by Rubinstein in the Moscow Conservatoire, in Tolstoy's honour, at which some of Tchaikovsky's chamber and vocal compositions were performed.

4. Tchaikovsky presented Tolstoy with some of his own compositions: 'The Storm', 'Winter Reveries' and a number of piano pieces.

by such trash.¹ If he had simply recalled in detail a day of his and described it, everyone would have been full of admiration.

However trite it is to say so, there is only one negative quality needed for everything in life, particularly in art—not to lie.

In life, lying is nasty, but it doesn't destroy life, it smears it over with its nastiness, but the truth of life is still there underneath, because somebody is always wanting something, something is always giving pain or pleasure; but in art, lying destroys the whole chain which links phenomena, and everything crumbles to dust.

What are you doing, i.e. writing? Send me your *Citizen* articles.² God grant you the leisure and the inclination to write.

I haven't for a long time been so indifferent to philosophical questions as this year, and I flatter myself with the hope that this is good for me. I very much want to finish what I'm doing quickly and begin something new.

Goodbye; my wife sends her regards.

Yours,
L. Tolstoy

218. To A. A. TOLSTAYA

Yasnaya Polyana, 5–9 February 1877

[8 lines omitted]...Thirdly, you offend me by supposing me to have fausse honte in problems of religion. I once wrote to Urusov, from the bottom of my heart, and I repeat it to you: the problem of religion is exactly the same for me as the one facing a drowning man—the problem of what to clutch at to save himself from the imminent death which he senses with his whole being. For a couple of years now religion has seemed to offer the possibility of salvation. And so there can be no question of fausse honte. But the point is that as soon as I clutch at the plank I go down with it. Somehow or other je surnage as long as I don't seize hold of the plank. If you ask me what stops me I won't tell you, because I would be afraid to shake your faith. And I know that that is the highest good. I know that you will smile at the idea that my doubts could shake you; but it's not a question of who can argue better, but of not being drowned, and so I won't tell you, but will rejoice for you and for all those who are sailing in the boat in which I am not a passenger. I have a friend, Strakhov, a learned man and one of the best people I know. We are very much alike in our religious views: we are both convinced that philosophy has nothing to offer and that it's impossible to live without religion, but we cannot believe. This summer we intend to go to the Optina Monastery. There I shall explain to the monks all the reasons why I cannot believe.

I kiss your hand. Sonya sends her regards.

Yours,
L. Tolstoy

[217] 1. Turgenev's novel *Virgin Soil*. See Letter 219.
2. *Three Letters on Spiritualism.*

219. To A. A. FET

Yasnaya Polyana, 11–12 March 1877

Dear Afanasy Afanasyevich,

I'm dictating this letter to Seryozha because I have a headache. I'm very glad that your opinion about Kulyabko's poetry was favourable, and almost the same as mine. I'll show him your words and encourage him to work. I know that for anything to come of him he'll need a lot of what you can't find out, not just from poetry, but even from the closest personal relationships. But there is at least one feature pointing to the poet in him, and it's not impossible. And that's a good thing.

I didn't receive your long letter, and you wouldn't believe how upset I am at the thought that it has gone astray. I started to write via Seryozha more as a joke. The children came in after lessons and I made Tanya take down a letter in French to Gautier,[1] and Seryozha turned up and I began dictating to him. It's true that I have a headache and it stops me working, which is particularly annoying, because the work is not just coming, but has come to the end. There's only the epilogue left. And that is occupying me very much.

I read through the first part of *Virgin Soil* and skimmed through the second. I was too bored to finish it. Eventually he makes Paklin say that it's Russia's misfortune in particular that all the people who are well are bad, and the good people are unwell.[2] That is my own, and his own, opinion of the novel. The author is unwell, and his sympathies are with people who are unwell, and he doesn't sympathise with those who are well, and so he calls what he is himself and therefore what he likes, good, and says: 'What a misfortune that all the people who are well are bad, and the good people are unwell.'

The one thing at which he is such a master that your hand shrinks from touching the subject after him is nature. Two or three strokes and you smell it. There are $1\frac{1}{2}$ pages of such descriptions all told, and nothing else. The descriptions of people are only descriptions of descriptions. When we read your letter with its promise to visit us in May my wife and I both said with a sigh, what a long time it was until May. But three days have passed, the birds and the streams have appeared, and it already seems like May outside. Our cordial greetings to Marya Petrovna.

Yours
L. Tolstoy

220. To N. N. STRAKHOV

Yasnaya Polyana, 21–2 April 1877

[12 lines omitted]...Please let's go as soon as possible to the Optina Monastery.

[219] 1. The owner of a French and English bookshop in Moscow where Tolstoy ordered books from abroad.
2. A not very accurate paraphrase of the original words—'if you are a full-blooded man with feeling and awareness you are certain to be ill'.

221. To the Editor of 'New Times'

You say in your last letter that you are cooling off towards your work.[1] I refuse to believe it. You wouldn't believe how necessary your ideas are to me. I wait for them like facts and figures which are necessary to confirm beyond doubt the conclusion I've already formed. I've been reading *The Herald of Europe*. Potekhin's story[2] is good; but what an abomination of Flaubert's[3] in Turgenev's translation. It's revolting stuff. Everybody runs V. Hugo down. But he says there, in a conversation between the earth and man:

                Man: Je suis ton roi.
                Earth: Tu es ma vermine.[4]

Well now, why couldn't they say that sort of thing?

I'm hurrying off to Tula for Seryozha's exam.

221. To THE EDITOR OF 'NEW TIMES'

Yasnaya Polyana, 10 June 1877

Dear Sir,

In the May issue of *The Russian Herald*, on page 472, there is a notice in the form of a completely inconspicuous footnote about the non-appearance in that issue of the last chapters of the novel *Anna Karenina*. This notice is so striking in its dutiful attitude towards the subscribers of *The Russian Herald*, its consideration towards the author of the novel and its masterly exposition, that I consider it would not be out of place to draw the attention of the public to it.

'In the previous issue, the words "to be concluded", were inserted at the foot of the novel *Anna Karenina*. But with the death of the heroine the novel proper finished. According to the author's plan a short epilogue of a couple of printer's sheets was to follow, from which the readers would learn that Vronsky, in grief and bewilderment after Anna's death, left for Serbia as a volunteer, and that all the others were alive and well, but that Levin remained in the country and was angry with the Slavonic committees and the volunteers. The author will perhaps develop these chapters for a special edition of his novel.'

The dutiful attitude towards subscribers was expressed by the fact that, having refused to publish the ending of the novel, the editor, in his concern to satisfy the curiosity of his readers, told them the content of the unpublished part, and tried to assure them that the novel proper was finished and that there was nothing important to follow.

The consideration towards the author was expressed by the fact that the editor not only did not allow the author to express harmful ideas, but indicated where his novel ought to end, and, without publishing the ending he wrote, artificially extracted and revealed to him and to others the essence of that ending.

[220] 1. His article *On the Basic Concepts of Psychology*.
  2. A. A. Potekhin (1827–1908), an author of stories and dramas based mainly on the life of the peasantry and the provincial gentry. The story referred to here is *In the Peasant Commune*.
  3. *La Légende de Saint Julien l'Hospitalier*.
  4. A slightly inexact quotation from Hugo's *L'Abîme*.

221. To the Editor of 'New Times'

The masterly exposition of the last, unpublished part of *Anna Karenina* makes one regret the fact that for three years the editor of *The Russian Herald* gave up so much space in his journal to this novel. With the same gracefulness and laconicism he could have recounted the whole novel in no more than ten lines.

But there is an error in this notice. It omits the fact that the last part of the novel was already set up and ready for printing in the May issue, but was not printed only because the author did not agree to cut out certain passages from it as the editor insisted, while the editor for his part did not agree to print it without their omission, although the author suggested that the editor might make any reservations he found necessary.

These last chapters of *Anna Karenina* are now being published separately.

I have the honour to be your obedient servant.

Count Lev Tolstoy

222. To N. N. STRAKHOV

Yasnaya Polyana, 10–11 August 1877

Dear Nikolay Nikolayevich,

I meant to write to you almost immediately after you left, but I haven't managed to do so until now. I've been hunting, and also to my brother's, and tomorrow I'm going hunting again a long way off for wolves. I'd like you to think of us as often and as kindly as we do of you, especially myself.

I was terribly sad that I had a cough again and so overslept the night you left. I came round 10 minutes after you had gone. There's now only the family here—just Styopa[1]—and I would like to begin work but I can't because of the war. Whether I'm in a good or bad frame of mind, the thought of the war overclouds everything for me. Not the war itself, but the problem of our insolvency which must be resolved at once, and the causes of this insolvency which are becoming clearer and clearer to me.

Styopa was talking to Sergey[2] about the war today, and Sergey said (1) it's good for young soldiers in the war to enjoy themselves at the expense of the Turkish women. And when Styopa said that that was a bad thing, he said 'Well, the women won't be any the worse for it. To hell with them.' This is the same Sergey who sympathised with the Serbs and who is quoted to us as evidence of the people's sympathy. But what he really only thinks about in the war is the Turkish women, i.e. the unbridling of his animal instincts. (2) When Styopa said that things were going badly, he said why don't they get hold of Mikhail Grigoryevich Chernyayev[3] (he knows his Christian name and patronymic)—he would take them down a peg. Turkish women and blind trust in a name, the new and the popular. I think we're on the verge of a great revolution.

[222] 1. S. A. Behrs.
2. Tolstoy's manservant, S. P. Arbuzov.
3. General Chernyayev (1828–98), a veteran of the Crimean War and the conqueror of Tashkent.

223. To N. N. Strakhov

Please write about what they are doing and saying in Petersburg.

Have you a book in which I could find an account of the present reign? Or is it possible to get newspapers for the last 20 years anywhere? Would it be expensive? Or is there a journal which has reviews of internal policy? If there is anything like that from which one could trace the internal history of the government's actions and the moods of society during these 20 years, let me know, and indeed send it.[4]

How have you settled down to your old life again? Are you bored? Have you got down to work? Goodbye; write more often. We all send our regards, and I embrace you most cordially.

L. Tolstoy

[Postscript omitted]

223. To N. N. STRAKHOV

Yasnaya Polyana, 19 October 1877

I'm very grateful to you, Nikolay Nikolayevich, for the books and especially the proverbs.[1] I'm delighted with them. Please send the articles, your own and Danilevsky's.[2] In the quietness of my backwater I'm a great reader. Finish off yours and send it to me.[3]

I'm ashamed to look at the last page of *Anna Karenina* which you copied out. Of course I agree with you and with the insertion.[4] Moreover, if the wedding scene hasn't been printed yet, could you send it to me; I want to correct the error about the bridegroom arriving at church before the bride. The information you gave about the war is very interesting and welcome. Obruchev, from all I've heard about him, is very nice.[5]

I'm still doing nothing except hunting and shooting hares, and feel ill physically and morally. I'm depressed. But still I often think about you, as always, and love you.

Yours,
L. Tolstoy

---

4. Tolstoy's interest in the reign of Alexander II was due to his wish to find out the reasons for Russia's military disasters. On Strakhov's advice he obtained A. A. Golovachov's *Ten Years of Reforms*.

[223] 1. Strakhov sent Thomas Carlyle's *Sartor Resartus* (in English) and Dahl's collection of Russian proverbs. In a previous letter to Strakhov, not translated here, Tolstoy had asked for several books, including Dahl's proverbs and an economic survey of peasant allotments and taxes.

2. N. Y. Danilevsky (1822–85); his articles on *The Present War* and *Europe and the Russo-Turkish War*.

3. *On the Basic Concepts of Psychology*.

4. Strakhov suggested that Tolstoy should restore some words spoken by Anna in her suicide scene which had been in the serial version in *The Russian Herald*, but which Tolstoy had deleted for the version in book form.

5. The information concerned new military appointments, including that of N. N. Obruchev to the Transcaucasian Army.

224. To N. N. STRAKHOV

Yasnaya Polyana, 6 November 1877

[15 lines omitted]...I know that it's wrong of me to complain, but I do so in my own heart, and to no one but you. It's agonising and humiliating to live in complete idleness and it's repulsive to console myself by saying that I'm sparing myself and waiting for inspiration. It's all petty and worthless. If I were alone I wouldn't be a monk, I would be a yurodivy,[1] i.e. I wouldn't value anything in life and wouldn't do anybody any harm.

Please don't try to console me, especially by saying that I'm a writer. I've been consoling myself like this for too long already, and better than you can, but it has no effect; just listen to my complaints and that will console me.

The other day I heard a priest giving some children a lesson on the catechism. It was all so disgraceful. The clever children obviously not only don't believe these words but can't even help despising them, so much so that I wanted to try to expound in catechism form what I believe in, and I've tried to do so.[2] And the attempt showed me how difficult it was for me, and, I fear, impossible.

And that made me sad and miserable.

Perhaps my letter will have an effect on you according to the principle that *similibus curantur*[3] and will rouse you to energy. God grant it may be so. But don't be angry with me for it.

Yours most cordially and affectionately,
L. Tolstoy

225. To N. N. STRAKHOV

Yasnaya Polyana, 26–7 November 1877

[9 lines omitted]...I feel that I shall start work soon, and with great enthusiasm, and shall forget myself. Many very important things have become completely clear to me, but I can't express them yet and I'm searching for words and a form. I'm very grateful for the books. But it's the later volumes of Lacroix I need.[1] Forgive me for troubling you. Have you a catalogue of books referring to the reign of Nicholas? Lacroix says in his introduction that Korf told him about such a catalogue.

What a pity about Popov.[2] I didn't know him well. He was very nice, I think. You are right, one needs to wait—it's like insomnia—wait until sleep comes and

---

[224] 1. Usually translated as a 'God's fool', or a 'fool in Christ', the *yurodivy* was a wandering beggar, often of very low intelligence, who was thought to embody the ideal of Christian poverty and asceticism, and even to possess the gift of prophecy.
  2. Tolstoy's *Christian Catechism* was begun, but never completed.
  3. More correctly *similia similibus curantur*—'like cures like'.

[225] 1. Paul Lacroix (1806–84), the French historian and bibliographer, and author of *Histoire de la vie et du règne de Nicolas I, empereur de Russie*, an unfinished work in 8 volumes which Tolstoy needed in connection with his work on *The Decembrists*.
  2. The Russian historian, A. N. Popov, who died in 1877.

226. To N. N. Strakhov

occupy the period of enforced wakefulness somehow. God grant you a fruitful year. I think you're in good, healthy spirits.

You suggest some philosophical books to me. I need books, only not philosophical ones—books on religion.

I would like to have Max Müller and Burnouf;[3] I did have them, but they weren't mine; then I'd like to know Strauss—not *The Life of Christ*, but his latest one where, if I remember, he propounds a new religion.[4] And then Renan.[5] Will all this be expensive? And do you know of anything else? Is there in philosophy any definition of religion and faith other than that it is a prejudice?

And what is the form of the purest Christianity? These, in vague form, are the two questions which I would like to find answers to in books.

I embrace you most cordially, my dear and only spiritual friend, Nikolay Nikolaich.

L. Tolstoy

226. To N. N. STRAKHOV

Yasnaya Polyana, 3 January 1878

[15 lines omitted]...I've got hold of *The Critique of Practical Reason*.[1] I'm sending off today to get your notice about it. However, I now have so many books and materials on two heterogeneous subjects that I'm getting lost among them.

3. Friedrich Max Müller (1823–1900), Anglo-German orientalist and Professor of Comparative Philology at the University of Oxford, whose main work was devoted to a comparative study of religions, especially Eastern religions. His *Introduction to the Science of Religion* was published in 1873, and the momumental work *The Sacred Books of the East* was published under his editorship from 1875 onwards.

Eugène Burnouf (1801–52), a French orientalist and professor who translated Buddhist and Zoroastrian texts and wrote an introductory study of Buddhist beliefs.

4. David Friedrich Strauss (1808–74), German theologian and biographer, author of *Leben Jesu* (published 1835–6). With Ernest Renan, Strauss applied the theory of myths to the study of Christianity, interpreting the growth of primitive Christianity in Hegelian terms and denying the historical basis of all supernatural elements in the Gospels. Tolstoy is referring to *Der alte und der neue Glaube* (1872), in which Strauss rejects Christianity in favour of scientific materialism.

5. Ernest Renan (1823–92), French Hebrew scholar, philologist, critic and historian of religion, author of *Les origines du christianisme* (1863–83), of which the first volume is *La vie de Jésus*. This book, his most famous, is an application of myth theory to Christianity, which is considered as a product of the popular imagination. Specifically, it is an attempt to reconstruct the life of Christ as realistically as possible. He termed Christ 'an incomparable man', which led to the frequent charge of atheism levelled against him; nevertheless, he claimed to retain a belief in 'the hidden God' to the end of his life. In his attempt to reconcile the two sides of the basic conflict of his time, religion versus science, Renan's contribution was to show that the church's teachings were incompatible with the findings of historical criticism. Tolstoy read *La vie de Jésus* in the spring of 1878 and wrote to Strakhov disagreeing fundamentally with Renan's approach to the Gospels. (See Letter 238.) He considered that Renan's historically based study added nothing to our understanding of the spiritual truth of the Gospels, and in fact detracted from its understanding by encumbering it with unnecessary details. In particular, he found the attempted 'day-to-day reconstruction' of Christ's life irrelevant.

[226] 1. A Russian translation was published in 1877.

226. To N. N. Strakhov

Please send me Solovyov's article in *The Citizen*.² The title is very alluring. 'Faith, knowledge and experience'. I met B. Chicherin in Moscow. He's writing a book on knowledge and faith.³ I have a mathematics teacher living with me, a postgraduate of Petersburg University, who spent two years in Kansas in America in a Russian colony of communists.⁴ Thanks to him I've now got to know the three best representatives of the extreme socialists—the very ones who are now on trial.⁵ These people have come to realise the necessity for stopping their reforming activity and seeking first of all a religious foundation. On all sides (I won't now mention who) all minds are turning to the very thing which gives me no peace.

I await your article impatiently.⁶ One sentence in your letter hurt me. You say you have sent off the last proofs and have settled down to your article. Unintentionally you admitted that this futile work interfered with your own.

Nekrasov's death made an impression on me. I was sorry for him, not as a poet and still less as a leader of public opinion, but as a character whom I won't try to describe in words, but whom I understand completely and even love—not with love, but with admiration.

I had a difficult few moments today—I had to dismiss our Swiss tutor—he had become intolerable because of his rudeness and bad character.

Is there anything in ancient Mongolian religion as elaborate as the Vedas, the Tri-Pitaka and the Zend-Avesta, and have they penetrated in that religion to the real, i.e. the sublime?⁷

Where did you take Lao-Tzu's words from?⁸

I embrace you most cordially, my dear friend, and wish you this year what I pray for each day, namely peace and quiet for working.

Yours,
L. Tolstoy

227. To COUNTESS A. A. TOLSTAYA

Yasnaya Polyana, 3 January 1878

[41 lines omitted]...For a long time now a plan has been going round in my head for a book which would be set in the Orenburg area in the time of Perovsky.¹ I've

---

2. *Faith, Reason and Experience.*
3. Chicherin's book entitled *Science and Religion* came out in 1879.
4. V. I. Alexeyev (1848–1919), see Letter 264.
5. Apart from Alexeyev, Tolstoy was referring to A. K. Malikov and A. A. Bibikov, and to the 'Trial of the 193'—one of a series of large-scale 'Populist' trials of students and others who had gone to the villages in the mid 1870s as teachers and propagators of socialism.
6. *On The Basic Concepts of Psychology.*
7. The scriptures of Hinduism, Buddhism and Zoroastrianism respectively.
8. Strakhov had quoted the words 'the unexpressed and the unthinkable are the only things that truly exist, as the Buddhists and the followers of Lao-Tzu recognise', from a French translation by St Julien.

[227] 1. V. A. Perovsky (1793–1857), a close friend of A. A. Tolstaya. He was military governor

now brought back from Moscow a whole pile of material for it. I don't myself know whether it's possible to describe V. A. Perovsky, and if it is possible, whether I could describe him; but everything about him interests me very much, and I'm bound to say that I find this person, as a historical figure and a character, very sympathetic. What would you and his relations say? Could you and his relations give me any papers and letters with the assurance that nobody except me would read them, that I would return them without copying them out, and that I would publish nothing from them? I would like to look a bit deeper into his soul.

228. To S. A. RACHINSKY

Yasnaya Polyana, 27 January 1878

I'm very grateful to you, Sergey Alexandrovich, for continuing to gladden me periodically with your letters and to give me news which I always find exciting about your continuing enthusiasm for your school. I am always glad on your account and envy you a little and feel affection for you. I'd be glad to follow your advice,[1] and it's true that I haven't started anything new yet, but I have some work which is turning my attention in a different direction.[2] However, your reminder had its effect on me, and a plan occurred to me yesterday which gladdened me very much, and which, if carried out well, would please you, and especially Terentyev and Anufriyev.[3] But it's better not to speak about it until I've made a start.

Your opinion about *Anna Karenina* seems to me wrong.[4] On the contrary, I'm proud of the architecture—the arches have been constructed in such a way that it is impossible to see where the keystone is. And that is what I was striving for most of all. The structural link is not the plot or the relationships (friendships) between the characters, but an inner link. Believe me, this is not unwillingness to accept criticism —especially from you whose opinion is always too indulgent; but I'm afraid that in skimming through the novel you didn't notice its inner content. I wouldn't quarrel with the man who said 'que me veut cette sonate',[5] but if you wish to speak about the lack of a link, then I can't help saying—you are probably looking for it in the wrong place, or we understand the word 'link' differently; but what I understand by link—the very thing that made the work important for me—this link is there— look for it and you will find it. Please don't think that I'm touchy—really, I'm not

---

of Orenburg for many years, and took part in many campaigns in what is now Soviet Central Asia. The eponymous hero of Tolstoy's fragment *Prince Fyodor Shchetinin* is thought to have been modelled on Perovsky. He was also an intimate friend of the poet V. A. Zhukovsky.

[228] 1. Rachinsky advised Tolstoy to write some more Readers now that he had finished *Anna Karenina*.

2. A novel about the Decembrists.

3. The names of some of Rachinsky's pupils.

4. Rachinsky had complained of a fundamental weakness in the construction of *Anna Karenina*. 'There is no architecture in it. Two themes are developed side by side, and developed magnificently, which are in no way connected with each other.'

5. A saying going back to Fontenelle implying impatience at having to listen to something uninteresting.

228. To S. A. Rachinsky

writing because of that, but because when I got your letter I began to think about all this and wanted to tell you. And the first impulse est le bon.

Perhaps this will provoke another letter from you and we shall have a talk again, which is a real joy for me.

Yours most cordially,
L. Tolstoy

When I got your letter I felt like going to see you. That was also a good impulse, but I didn't do so, and I won't do so just yet because I've had a cold and been unwell all winter.

229. To N. N. STRAKHOV

Yasnaya Polyana, 27(?) January 1878

Not receiving any letters from you for a long time, dear Nikolay Nikolayevich, I was constantly cheered by the thought that you were probably working (and so it turned out), but I missed your letters. I missed them so much indeed that I wrote to Styopa asking him to drop in on you to find out about you and to write to me. I shall reply point by point. Golokhvastov is probably in the country, you can write to him at New Jerusalem, I don't know the name of the town.

Fet is at his new property—Moscow–Kursk line, Budanovka Station. In his last letter he sent me a fine poem.[1]

Here are two couplets for you:

> The grass on your far distant grave
> Is fresher here in the heart, the older it grows.[2]

> Love has its words, and these words will not die.
> A special judgement awaits us both.

Nekrasov's funeral. There is nothing more terrible for me than such a spectacle.[3]

The shameless way of life in dens like your Petersburg has become so debauched that it wants to lay its hands on the phenomenon of death, to which it has no right. And most ridiculous of all, it wishes to apply to the mystery of death all its own special knowledge of propriety—in ceremonial fashion, according to rank; and it is precisely here that all its worthlessness and vileness hits you in the eye, if you have an eye to see it. As if not only Nekrasov's fame, but the fame of all great men, heaped on one head, could be decently commemorated over a dead body.

I was thinking about Nekrasov recently. In my opinion, his place in literature

---

[229] 1. *Alter ego.*

2. Tolstoy misquoted this verse, making the phrase 'the older, the fresher' refer to 'grass' rather than to 'the heart' as it does in the original.

3. Nekrasov's funeral took place on 30 December 1877. Tolstoy is reacting here to Strakhov's description of the massive demonstrations and speech-making which accompanied the funeral, turning it into an event of social and political significance. Among those who delivered speeches at the graveside were Dostoyevsky and G. M. Plekhanov, the outstanding Marxist intellectual of his day.

229. To N. N. Strakhov

will be the same as Krylov's. The same false folksiness, the same fortunate career—he appealed to the taste of his time—and the same unrefined, and unrefinable, genuine trace of gold, even though in small proportion and in a mixture not susceptible to purification.[4]

About the search for faith. You write that 'any compromise with thought is repugnant to you'. And to me too. You go on to write that 'for believers any nonsense is good as long as it *smacks of piety* (I would substitute: as long as it is permeated with faith, hope, and love).* They are just as at home in nonsense as a fish in water, and what is clear and definite is repugnant to them.' And I agree. I began to write about this and wrote rather a lot,[5] but I have now put it aside, distracted by other occupations.[6] But counting on your ability (*an unusual ability*) to understand others, I shall attempt to say in this letter why I think that what appears strange to you is not strange at all.

My reason says nothing to me, and can say nothing to me, on three questions which can easily be expressed by one: what am I? Some feeling in the depths of my consciousness gives me answers to these questions. The answers which this feeling gives me are confused, unclear, and inexpressible in words (the instrument of thought).

But I am not the only one to have searched, and to be still searching, for the answers to these questions. The soul of every man alive has been tortured by these same questions and each soul has received the same vague answers. Millions of vague but synonymous answers have given definition to these answers. These answers constitute religion. Viewed by reason the answers make no sense. They make no sense even, simply by the fact that they are expressed by words. But nevertheless, they alone answer the questions of the heart. In expression, in form, they make no sense, but in content they alone are true. I look solely at the form and the content slips away; I look solely at the content and the form doesn't concern me. I seek answers to questions which in essence are beyond reason, and require that they be expressed in words, the instrument of reason, and am then surprised that the form of the answers doesn't satisfy my reason. But you will say: therefore there can be no answers. No, you won't say this, because you know that there are answers, that it is only by these answers that people live and have lived, and that you yourself live. To say that these answers can't exist is just the same as saying, while crossing ice, that rivers can't freeze because bodies contract, not expand, with cold. To say that these answers make no sense is the same as saying that I am incapable of understanding something about them. And what you are incapable of understanding, it seems to me, is this: answers are required not to questions posed

---

* Faith—what I may know, love—what I ought to do, hope—what I may hope for. [Tolstoy's footnote]

4. Compare Tolstoy's more favourable judgement of Nekrasov as a man in his earlier letter to Strakhov on 3 January 1878 (Letter 226).
5. A reference to Tolstoy's unfinished work *Interlocutors*, intended as an exposition of arguments for and against faith, which would ultimately show the necessity for faith.
6. *The Decembrists*.

229. To N. N. Strakhov

by reason, but to other questions. I call them questions of the heart. As long as mankind has existed, people have answered these questions not by words, the instrument of reason, a part of the manifestation of life, but by the whole of life, by actions, of which words are only one part. All those beliefs which I hold, and you and the whole people hold, are based not on words and arguments, but on a series of human actions and lives which directly influence one another (like a yawn) starting with the lives of Abraham, Moses, Christ, and the holy fathers—even by their external actions: genuflecting, fasting, observing feast days and so forth. In all the countless mass of actions by these people, certain actions for some reason stood out and constituted a whole tradition, serving as a single answer to the questions of the heart. And therefore, for me, there is not only nothing nonsensical in this tradition, but I don't even understand how one can apply the test of sense and nonsense to these phenomena. One test to which I subject, and always will subject these traditions is whether the answers given are in accord with the vague, solitary answers outlined in the depths of my consciousness (which I spoke about earlier). And therefore when this tradition tells me that I must drink wine which is called the blood of God at least once a year, I—understanding this act in my own way or not understanding it at all—perform it. There is nothing at all in it which could conflict with my vague consciousness of things. I also eat cabbage on certain days and meat on others, but when tradition (distorted by rational struggles with various interpreters) says to me: let us all pray for more Turks to be killed, or even says that the man who doesn't believe that this is real blood...etc., then, consulting not my reason, but the indisputable voice of my heart, vague though it is—I say: this tradition is false. Therefore I swim just like a fish in water, in actions which make no sense, and only refuse to submit when tradition tells me to perform actions to which it has assigned a meaning, but which do not correspond to the fundamental irrationality of that vague consciousness which exists in my heart. If you understand my thought despite my inaccuracy in expressing it, please write to say whether you agree or not, and why. I am ashamed to say this, but I will say what I feel: I am so convinced of what I say, and this conviction is so joyful for me, that I don't want your opinion for my own sake, but for yours. I would like you to experience the same tranquillity and the same spiritual freedom which I am experiencing. I know that every mind has its own ways of understanding even formal, mathematical truths, and it must be far more so with understanding metaphysical truths, but it is so clear to me (as a trick which has been demonstrated) that I can't understand how the trick can be incomprehensible to others. I know also that if, in order to get to Moscow, I need to go north and to board a train in Tula, this can in no way be a general rule for people in all corners of the earth who wish to get to Moscow—especially you—because I know that you carry with you a great deal of luggage (your knowledge and past works) while I travel light; but I can assure you that I am in Moscow, that I can't wish to travel anywhere else, and that it is very good in Moscow. I have written and told you how I arrived and, not knowing exactly where you are, I ask you to verify my route—is it of any use to you? When you have time, please write to me and explain whether there is any difference

230. To Countess A. A. Tolstaya

between my proposed route and yours, and where mine is inaccurate in your opinion. And please write and criticise me a bit more crudely, so as to say more in fewer words.

I have just had a daring idea. If you are free and the expense of the journey is insignificant for you, and if you love us as much as you used to, what about coming to visit us for Shrovetide for a few days?

Forgive me if this invitation is too bold. I extend it in the hope that you won't be angry and if there is 1 chance in 100 that it's possible, why not take a chance on what could be such a joyful occasion? We wouldn't talk about religion. Perhaps I shall be in Petersburg. But in Petersburg I won't see you.

Yours,
L. Tolstoy

[Postscript omitted]

230. To COUNTESS A. A. TOLSTAYA

Yasnaya Polyana, 27(?) January 1878

Your doubts, my dear, about my recent recovery were unfortunately too justified: I'm still ill and I only recently got up—about four days ago—and that's the reason why I haven't replied to you and your brother for such a long time. I'm very, very grateful to you for your promise to give me information about Perovsky.[1] Your promise would have been a great temptation for me to travel to Petersburg if I hadn't already had a very strong desire to visit Petersburg in any case. This desire has already reached its *maximum*; now a jolt is needed... But there is no jolt, or rather there are jolts in reverse, in the form of my illness... I shall wait. You define Perovsky's personality quite correctly—à grands traits, just as I imagine him; and such a figure filling the canvas on its own—a biography of him—would be crude; but with other contrasting, finely drawn, small-scale and gentle characters like Zhukovsky whom you apparently knew well—with others and particularly with the Decembrists—this large-scale figure as a shadow of Nikolay Pavlovich, the largest figure à grands traits, fully expresses the time. I am now entirely engrossed in reading from the period of the 20s, and I can't express to you the delight I feel in imagining that time to myself. It's strange and pleasant to think that the time which I remember, the 30s, is already history. And so you see the figures in the picture are ceasing to waver, and everything is coming to rest in the solemn peace of truth and beauty...I'm experiencing the feeling of a cook (a bad one) who has gone to a rich market, and after looking over all the vegetables, meat, and fish at his disposal, dreams of what a dinner he could make! And so I dream on, although I know how often I've had splendid dreams and then spoiled the dinner or done nothing. Once you have overcooked the grouse, you can't do anything to remedy it. And cooking is difficult and frightening...But washing and laying out the provisions is great fun!

[230] 1. See Letter 227, note 1.

230. To Countess A. A. Tolstaya

I pray to God to allow me to do at least approximately what I want. This business is so important to me that however capable you may be of understanding everything, you can't imagine how important this is. It's as important to me as your faith is to you. And even more important, I'm tempted to say. But nothing can be more important. That is the most important thing of all.

I kiss your mother's hand, and press your own in friendship.

Yours,
L. Tolstoy

231. To A. A. FET

Yasnaya Polyana, 27 January 1878

[5 lines omitted]...Thank you for not punishing me for my silence, but actually rewarding me by letting us be the first to read your poem.[1] It's splendid! It has that special character which your latest, all too rare poems have. They are very compact, and the radiance from them is very far-reaching. Evidently a very great deal of poetic stock is expended on them. It accumulates for a long time before it crystallises out. The Stars[2] is another of your latest ones of the same kind. Here is a point of detail. When I read it, I said to my wife: 'Fet's poem is charming, but one word is bad.' She was nursing and running about, but over tea, when she had settled down, she began to read it, and she immediately pointed to the word which I considered bad: 'like gods...'[3] [4 lines omitted]

232. To P. N. SVISTUNOV

Pyotr Nikolayevich Svistunov (1803–89), a Decembrist and a member of both the Southern and Northern Societies, was sentenced for his participation in the uprising to life imprisonment—later reduced to ten years' hard labour and permanent exile in Siberia. After the amnesty of 1856 he returned to European Russia and settled in Kaluga, where he took part in implementing the peasant reforms in a minor official capacity. In 1863 he moved to Moscow where he met Tolstoy in 1878. At the time Tolstoy was gathering material for a projected novel about the Decembrists, and he found Svistunov a valuable witness to the uprising and its aftermath. He visited Svistunov twice, in February and March 1878, and listened to his reminiscences and those of A. P. Belyaev, another Decembrist who had been sentenced to hard labour and exile in Siberia for his part in the rising of 1825. A correspondence with Svistunov followed, of which four letters have survived from each man.

[231] 1. *Alter ego*.
2. *Among the stars* (*sredi zvyozd*).
3. From the fourth stanza of *Alter ego*:
    And I know, having looked at the stars at times,
    That you and I gazed at them like gods.

233. *To N. N. Strakhov*

Yasnaya Polyana, 14 March 1878

Dear Pyotr Nikolayevich,

When you are talking to me, it probably seems to you that everything you say is very simple and ordinary, but to me your every word, opinion and thought seems extraordinarily important and unusual; and not because I particularly value the factual information which you are giving, but because your talk transports me to a height of feeling which is very rarely encountered in life and which always touches me profoundly. I am writing these few words just to tell you this and to make two requests: (1) to pass on the enclosed letter to A. P. Belyaev (I don't know his address) and (2) to take advantage of the permission you gave me to ask questions and to ask whether you have that religious work or journal of Bobrishchev-Pushkin's which he wrote in Chita, and the reply of Baryatinsky's.[1] If not, can you recollect and tell me what they were both about?

I have been to the Peter and Paul Fortress, and was told there that *one* of the criminals threw himself into the Neva and then ate glass. I can't express the strange, powerful feeling I experienced when I knew it was you. I experienced a similar feeling there too, when they brought me the manacles and irons of 1825.

With sincere and deep respect,
Count L. Tolstoy

One more question: what sort of person was Commandant Sukin?[2]

233. To N. N. STRAKHOV

Yasnaya Polyana, 16 March 1878

I'm very grateful to you, dear Nikolay Nikolayevich, for sending Semyovsky's notebook.[1] I have read it through and sent it back and am requesting another book —namely Bestuzhev's memoirs.[2]

One more request: The Travels of the Monk, Parfeny,[3] and of the Old Believer priest Avvakum,[4] and anything else about the Old Believers—only not refined, but

[232] 1. P. S. Bobrishchev-Pushkin, a Decembrist, and member of the Southern Society. He was banished to Siberia for life, and lived for a time with Svistunov in Tobolsk. He returned to the Tula province after the 1856 amnesty. Both his own religious work and the atheistic rejoinder by his fellow Decembrist A. P. Baryatinsky are unknown.
  2. The commandant of the Peter and Paul Fortress in 1825.

[233] 1. In connection with Tolstoy's work on *The Decembrists*, M. I. Semyovsky, the historian and editor of *Russian Antiquities*, had sent a volume of letters by the Decembrist N. A. Bestuzhev, who died in Siberia in 1855.
  2. The memoirs of N. A. Bestuzhev's brother, M. A. Bestuzhev, also a Decembrist. He returned to Moscow from Siberia in 1867.
  3. *The Tale of the Travels and Pilgrimages of Parfeny, a monk of Mt Athos, through Russia, Moldavia, Turkey and the Holy Land.*
  4. *The Life of Avvakum.* The Archpriest Avvakum was the leader of the conservative reformers within the Orthodox Church whose intransigent beliefs led to the Nikon-Avvakum controversy and to permanent schism after his condemnation by the Church Synod in 1667. His *Life* (1672–3) is the most famous of the Old Believer writings, and an outstanding work of literature in its own right. He was burnt at the stake in 1682.

233. To N. N. Strakhov

the raw material. If there is anything, or if you find out about anything, please send it to me. I'm urgently requesting Stasov,[5] as a member of the Committee, etc., on Nicholas I, to find out if he can, and explain how the hanging of the five was decided on, who insisted on it, and whether there were any vacillations and discussions between Nicholas and those closest to him.

Küchelbecker[6] is touching, as are all people of his type—not poets, but people convinced that they are poets, and passionately devoted to that illusory calling. Besides, 15 years in prison!

I am mentally following your work from here and am afraid that Styopa might disturb you, and for this reason alone I'm afraid to encourage you to visit Countess Tolstaya. I would like you to become acquainted with her so that I may know the mutual impressions of people who are close to me.

However much Solovyov irritates me, I don't wish you to write about him.[7] It definitely isn't worth it. Your opinion that he concludes *a priori* what he has found out *a posteriori* is absolutely right. I also made inquiries about Sophia.[8] She is represented in ancient Russian icon painting as a woman raising her hands to heaven, *in prayer*.

Yours most cordially,
L. Tolstoy

234. To I. S. TURGENEV

Yasnaya Polyana, 6 April 1878

Ivan Sergeyevich,[1]

Lately, when recalling my relations with you, I felt to my great surprise and joy that I bore no hostility towards you. God grant that the same is true of you. To tell the truth, knowing how good you are, I am almost certain that your hostile feeling for me disappeared even before mine did.

If this is so, then please let us extend our hands to each other and, please, forgive me once and for all for everything for which I was to blame towards you.

It is so natural for me to recall only what is good about you, because there was so much that was good in your relations with me. I remember that I owe my

---

5. V. V. Stasov was a member of a committee set up to collect material relating to the reign of Nicholas I.

6. V. K. Küchelbecker (1797–1846), poet and literary critic, a contemporary and schoolfellow of Pushkin. He joined in the Decembrist conspiracy and spent the last twenty years of his life in prison and in exile in Siberia.

7. This is in response to Strakhov's unfavourable opinion of one of the public lectures given by the religious philosopher Vladimir Solovyov.

8. A reference to Solovyov's mystical doctrine of the Saint as the embodiment of divine wisdom.

[234] 1. This is the first letter between Tolstoy and Turgenev for seventeen years, breaking the silence which followed their quarrel in 1861. According to Annenkov, Turgenev cried when he read it. Turgenev replied positively and warmly in his letter of 8 May 1878 to the idea of re-establishing friendly relations. On 8 August of the same year, Turgenev paid a visit to Yasnaya Polyana.

literary renown to you, and I remember how you loved both my writings and myself. Maybe you will also find similar recollections about me, because there was a time when I sincerely loved you.

Sincerely, if you can forgive me, I offer you all the friendship which I am capable of. At our time in life, there is only one good—affectionate relations with people. And I will be very happy if such relations can be established between us.

Count L. Tolstoy

Address: Tula

235. To A. A. FET

Yasnaya Polyana, 6 April 1878

I have received your wonderful, long letter, dear Afanasy Afanasyevich. Don't praise me. Really you see in me too much good, and in others too much evil. One thing that is good in me is that I understand you and therefore love you. But although I love you as you are, I'm always angry with you because Martha is troubled about many things: but one thing is needful.[1] And that one thing is very strong in you, but somehow you are disdainful about it, and prefer to organise a game of billiards. Don't think I mean poems. Although I'm actually waiting for them, I'm not referring to them—they will come in spite of the billiards—I'm referring to a conception of the world which would make it unnecessary to be angry at human stupidity. If you and I were to be pounded together in one mortar and then moulded into a pair of people, we should make a wonderful pair. But as it is, you are so strongly attached to the things of this life that if some day some of these things should suddenly cease, it would go hard with you, whereas I am so indifferent to them that I have no interest in life, and I am a trial to others by continually milling the wind. Don't think that I've taken leave of my senses. It's just that I'm out of sorts, and I hope you'll love me, even when I'm black. I'll come to see you without fail.

Your plans for Pyotr Afanasyevich[2] won't please him, however good they are. Our regards to Marya Petrovna.

Yours,
L. Tolstoy

236. To COUNTESS A. A. TOLSTAYA

Yasnaya Polyana, 6 April 1878

What a wonderful letter you wrote to me, my dear Alexandrine, so gay and sparkling. I don't need to ask about you: you are surely well and have no sorrows. Please don't deprive me of the great pleasure of receiving your letters on the pretext that I'm very busy; firstly, I'm not busy with anything, and secondly, such

[235] 1. A reference to Luke 10, 41–2.　　2. Fet's brother.

236. To Countess A. A. Tolstaya

cautious treatment terrifies me with the responsibilities it lays upon me and, above all, it puts the evil eye on me. I think in general that nothing will come of my undertakings. I lack the energy delusion gives, which is necessary for all worldly affairs, or else a jolt from above. My brother Sergey had an old manservant to whom he suggested bathing in his bathhouse in summer. 'No thank you, Sir, I've already had my fill of bathing.' So too, it seems, have I had my fill of writing.

I'm in a depressed state, and there are several reasons for this: the first and most important is that Sonya and the child are unwell and have been getting worse and worse for over a week now. The child is wasting away, Sonya torments herself and the child gets even worse. Today we're getting a wet-nurse in order to try different milk; and if there's no improvement, she'll go to Moscow.

Another reason is: our governor in Tula is a certain Ushakov, a frivolous but very kind man, and he has a wife, the mother of four children, a splendid woman who supports her husband and the whole family. I knew them slightly and had a high opinion of her. The day before yesterday I was in Tula with the children to have their portraits done and some clothes made. When leaving, I learned that a horse had badly hurt Ushakova and that she was seriously injured. Over dinner at home we learned that Ushakova had been killed. She is being buried today. No matter how long we've known this, i.e. that we are in the hands of God, it's always new and amazing.

The third reason is your Petersburg affairs. You write that la politique est noire, comme l'encre de l'excellent Aksakov, but in my opinion, elle est rouge, comme le sang du vilain Trepoff. To me, an outsider at a great distance from the struggle, it's clear that the animosity of the two extreme factions towards each other has reached bestial proportions. For Maydel[1] and the rest, all these Bogolyubovs[2] and Zasuliches[3] are such trash that he doesn't see them as people and can't feel pity for them; while for Zasulich, Trepov and the rest are dangerous animals who can and must be killed like dogs. And it's no longer a case of indignation, it's a fight. All those who acquitted the murderer and sympathised with the acquittal know very well that for their personal safety one cannot and must not justify murder, but for them the question is not 'who is right?' but 'who will win?' It seems to me that all this heralds much misfortune and much sinfulness. But in both camps there are good people. Can't conditions exist in which they could stop being beasts and become people again? God grant that I'm mistaken, but it seems to me that all these Eastern Questions and Slavs and Constantinoples are trifles compared to

[236] 1. The commandant of the Peter and Paul Fortress who showed Tolstoy round the Fortress in 1878 and served as the prototype for Baron Kriegsmuth in *Resurrection*.

2. Bogolyubov was the pseudonym of A. P. Yemelyanov, a member of the revolutionary movement in the 1870s. He was sentenced to fifteen years' hard labour for his part in a demonstration in Petersburg. In 1877, when in prison awaiting trial, he was subjected to corporal punishment following a clash with General Trepov, the Governor of Petersburg. As a protest, Vera Zasulich fired a shot at Trepov and wounded him.

3. Vera Zasulich (1849–1919) was one of the first women members of the social-democratic movement in Russia. Although clearly guilty of wounding Trepov, she was acquitted at her trial.

238. To N. N. Strakhov

this. Ever since I read about this trial and about all this commotion, I can't get it out of my head.

I'm ending with a request. You said that you have a store of governesses: we need an English girl who knows French and is well-educated of course. Salary up to 1,000 roubles. Apart from the most important moral qualities, it's desirable for the girl to have as few fads as possible about material comfort, as we don't have much of it. I kiss your hand. Kiss Auntie's hand for me, and give my regards to your people.

237. To N. N. STRAKHOV

Yasnaya Polyana, 8 April 1878

[12 lines omitted]...To tell you the truth, however, you are right when you say you ought to keep silent because you can't see the proper road to take. But I'm surprised that you can't see it. When I think about you and weigh you up according to your writings and conversations, I always suppose from your well-known speed, power and sense of direction that you have already gone very far towards the place you are going to; but when I meet you or read (some of) your letters, I almost always find you, to my surprise, in the same place. There is something wrong here. And I'm waiting and hoping that you will put it right, and that I shall lose sight of you—so far away will you have gone. Similarly on the other hand, when we are young we see people pretending that they *know*. And we begin to pretend that *we* know, and seem to find ourselves in harmony with people, and don't notice the greater and greater lack of harmony with ourselves which we experience as a result. The time comes (and has already come for you since I got to know you) when harmony with oneself is the most precious thing of all. If you will boldly discard all human pretence at knowledge, of which science is the most evil pretence, and establish this harmony with yourself, you will come to know the road. And I'm surprised that you can fail to know it.[1]

The Zasulich affair is no joke. It's a nonsense, a folly which afflicts people, and not for nothing. These people are the first terms in a series which we don't understand, but it's an important folly. The Slavonic business was the precursor of war; this could be the precursor of revolution...[3 lines omitted]

238. To N. N. STRAKHOV

Yasnaya Polyana, 17–18 April 1878

There is no person I respect more than you, or would wish to please more, and

---

[237] 1. A reference to Strakhov's failure to see eye to eye with Tolstoy over religious questions. Relations between the two men were rather strained at this period, and Strakhov was hurt by some of Tolstoy's bluntly expressed criticisms.

238. To N. N. Strakhov

suddenly I have gone and caused you pain. I don't know how it happened. I was talking about myself, and saying that when I ceased pretending that I knew and understood what cannot be known, I found harmony with myself, and suddenly I linked this idea with the expectation of something big and important from you (this expectation is shared by all who love and understand you), and I transferred it to you and probably made a mistake and, more important, expressed myself unclearly and abruptly.

You write: 'In a state of bewilderment I sift through all sorts of opinions by people, ancient and modern, and I search with diligent care and can find nothing.' Again: 'I can't understand your reproach of pretence (at knowledge) and of lack of harmony with myself.'

But it's precisely this sifting through of other people's opinions and searching among them that I call (inexactly) pretence at knowledge—i.e. I mean that by imitating other people's views you pretend you know, and forfeit harmony with yourself. You have lived ⅔ of your life. You have been guided by something, you have known somehow what is good and what is bad. Well then, without asking what other people have said, tell yourself, and tell us.

You say that you are free of science, and that's true. And then you say that you apparently have no thoughts and feelings which need this freedom. That's not true. In order to do all the work of liberation which you have done, you needed much strength of thought and feeling, and this strength is intact but, surprised by its liberation, it has not yet found an application. Or else obedience to the forms of other people's thoughts has survived from habit—and this is what I'm more inclined to think. I recently found two things to confirm this. The first was your splendid exposition of the ideas of Solovyov in your last letter but one. But I was hurt on your account because you lowered yourself to the point of carefully scrutinising such rubbish. Wasn't it obvious to you at once that it was all childish nonsense? So why do you have to think about it?

The second thing was that I fasted today and started to read the Gospels and Renan's *Vie de Jésus*,[1] and read it all through, and all the time I was reading I was amazed at you. I can only explain your partiality for Renan by the fact that you were very young when you read him. If Renan has any ideas of his own, they are the two following ones: (1) that Christ didn't know about l'évolution et le progrès, and in this respect Renan tries to correct him and criticises him from the superior position of this idea (pp. 314, 315, 316). This is terrible, at least to me. Progress in my opinion is a logarithm of time, i.e. nothing, an establishment of the fact that we live in time; and suddenly it becomes the judge of the highest truth we know. The superficiality or unscrupulousness of such an outlook is amazing. Christian truth—i.e. the highest expression of absolute good—is the expression of the very essence —it is outside the framework of time, etc. But the Renans confuse its absolute expression with its expression in history, and reduce it to a temporal manifestation and then discuss it. If Christian truth is elevated and profound, it is only because it

[238] 1. The book was banned in Russia at the time, but Strakhov had obtained a duplicate copy for Tolstoy from the Petersburg Public Library.

is subjectively absolute. But if one looks at its objective manifestation, it is on a level with the Code Napoléon, etc.

The other new idea of Renan's is that if Christ's teaching exists, then some man or other existed, and this man certainly sweated and went to the lavatory. For us, all degrading realistic human details have disappeared from Christianity for the same reason that all details about all Jews, etc. who ever lived have disappeared, for the same reason that everything disappears that is not everlasting; but what is everlasting remains. Sand which is not necessary is panned off and gold remains, according to an immutable law. It would seem that all people have to do is to take this gold. But no; Renan says: if there is gold, then there was sand, and he tries to find what this sand was like. And he does so with a most profound air. But what would be even more funny if it were not so terribly stupid is the fact that he doesn't find any sand at all, and only asserts that it must have been there. I read it all through and searched for a long time and asked myself: 'well, what new thing have I learned from these historical details? Think hard and admit—*nothing*, absolutely *nothing*.' I'm proposing to supplement Renan and to calculate what sort of physical functions were exercised, and how. It's all progress, all évolution. Perhaps in order to get to know a plant you need to know its *environment*, and even to get to know a man as a political animal you need to study environment, movement and development, but in order to understand beauty, truth and goodness, no study of the environment will help, nor has it anything in common with what is being examined. In the former case there is movement along a plane, but in the latter there is a completely different direction, inwards and upwards. Moral truth can and must be studied, and there is no end to the study of it, but this study, as practised by religious people, moves inwards while the other is a childish, base and vulgar prank.

I would very much like you to agree with me. And I'm sure you won't be angry with me. My whole offence is that I am too fond of your mind and your soul, that I expect too much of it, and have been too hasty in deciding the reason why you don't satisfy the demands I make of you.

Write to me as soon as possible. Shall we see each other? You don't answer our request in my last letter. I look forward to getting Parfeny from you.

Yours,
L. Tolstoy

239. To V. V. STASOV

Vladimir Vasilyevich Stasov (1824–1906), an art and literary historian, music and art critic, and archaeologist. From 1872 he was Head of the Fine Arts department of the Petersburg Public Library, where he met Tolstoy in 1878. His major work of literary historical scholarship was *The Origin of the Russian Byliny*, in which he argued that there was nothing specifically Russian about the *byliny*, but that they incorporated Eastern themes and motifs brought to Russia by the Mongols. Stasov

239. To V. V. Stasov

visited Tolstoy many times at Yasnaya Polyana and in Moscow, and was a devoted admirer of his fiction, though severely critical of his religious views. The correspondence between the two men spanned a period of twenty-eight years; 97 of Tolstoy's letters have survived and 121 of Stasov's.

Yasnaya Polyana 8–9 June 1878

I don't know how to thank you, Vladimir Vasilyevich, for the document you made available to me.[1] It is a key which has opened for me not so much a historical, as a psychological door. It is the answer to the main question which worried me. I consider myself eternally indebted to you for this favour. I can vouch for my discrétion. I have not even shown it to my wife, and have now copied out the document and torn up the copy in your handwriting.

But so far I have only thanked you selfishly for the benefit which the document you made available has been to me, but believe me, quite apart from my own profit, I am very grateful to you for your sympathy and your favourable disposition towards me and the work of my dreams.[2]

I understand from what was told to me by Styopa (Behrs) that you are displeased with me for my indifference to the correspondence of Ivashov.[3] My insufficient interest in Ivashov's correspondence is due to the fact that of the whole Decembrist saga, it is Ivashov's story which has become fashionable: Dumas wrote about it[4] and all the ladies recount it, and one gentleman sent me a story made up of the authentic correspondence of Ivashov and Le Dantu, and there is mention of it again in some papers I have from Kazan. I'm not very interested, not because it has become commonplace—the commonplace is often important too—but because there is a lot that is false and artificial in it; and unfortunately for that reason only it has become so commonplace. More precious to me is the fact that there is a man like you who is willing and able to help me, and that I can always turn to you, assured of sympathy. May I? I thank you most cordially, and press your hand in friendship.

Yours,
L. Tolstoy

Everything you wrote about and sent me is of course necessary to me, and I'm very grateful to you, but I can't begin anything new before August.

Here is another request. I was and still am particularly interested in who particularly insisted on the death penalty. Svistunov, a Decembrist, told me that it was

---

[239] 1. A memorandum of Nicholas I concerning the procedure for the execution of the Decembrists. Stasov had obtained it privately and sent Tolstoy a handwritten copy via S. A. Behrs, asking him to be particularly discreet and to destroy the copy. Tolstoy did so, but his own copy of Stasov's copy survived and was discovered in 1948.

2. The novel *The Decembrists*.

3. V. P. Ivashov (1794–1839), sentenced to hard labour and exile for his part in the Decembrist conspiracy, was married to a Frenchwoman, Camille Le Dantu, who followed him into exile.

4. Dumas père's novel, *Le Maître d'Armes*, in fact tells the story of another Decembrist, I. A. Annenkov, and another Frenchwoman.

240. To N. N. Strakhov

Karamzin who particularly insisted and argued it was necessary.[5] Is that true? Is there any evidence? Where?

240. To N. N. STRAKHOV

Tula(?), 5 September 1878

Dear Nikolay Nikolaich,

While waiting for a letter from you I meant to forestall you so that you should find a letter from me in Petersburg, but I still haven't got into the swing of the winter's intellectual work and I haven't managed to because of hunting, croquet and guests. Thank you for your letter and for your visit to us and for your unfailing friendship.[1] I didn't say anything to you about your poems.[2] I didn't like them. I don't understand anything about poems, you know, and even you yourself don't take them very seriously, so don't be angry with me on that account. Your letter is all interesting, but the most interesting thing of all for me was Kavelin's opinion which you had copied out about your book.[3]

It's impossible to devise any worse tortures on this earth than to make a man write and express with the utmost effort all the depth and complexity of his ideas and at the same time to make him read, as the opinions of an authority, such pronouncements as those of Kavelin. If I were tsar, I would make a law that a writer who uses a word whose meaning he can't explain should be deprived of the right to write and receive 100 strokes of the birch. From the beginning you analyse things and demonstrate that people who say certain words invariably mean such and such a thing by them; but Kavelin considers that your opinion is not binding for him, and that science rejects dualism. And nobody says that Kavelin is either an unscrupulous man or a madman, but everyone says: Kavelin is a philosopher. Your profession is a difficult, thankless and painful one, but he who endures to the end will be saved. Kavelin's argument that Strakhov is wrong because he thinks (if I understand him correctly) that all *science* rejects dualism is the same as the argument that it is incorrect that a husband and wife are two separate people, because the church recognises them as one.

Again, if I were tsar, I would give 100 strokes of the birch to a person who uses the very popular argument, common to learned books, namely: according to my researches and observations, i.e. according to science, it turns out that a mushroom is a mushroom but a horse is a horse, that a body is a body but a soul is a soul, electricity is electricity but heat is heat, and therefore the legitimate conclusion according to science would be that things are different, but according to my secret

5. Soviet commentators point out as proof that Svistunov's allegations are false, the fact that Karamzin died before the end of the trial, although this need not, of course, invalidate them.

[240] 1. Good relations between the two men had been restored during the summer.

2. Six poems by Strakhov which he had written in 1878 and copied out for Tolstoy during his stay at Yasnaya Polyana.

3. K. D. Kavelin (1818–85), a moderate liberal historian and publicist, had accused Strakhov of dualism in his book, *On the Basic Concepts of Psychology*.

240. To N. N. Strakhov

desire (and according to the *purpose* of science) it would be better if everything were one. And then the following jump is made: science, science itself, is left aside, and the course of science, the history of science is brought into the reckoning, as if the future course of science could be intelligible to the man who knows no science; and it is assumed that only some little trick is needed to achieve what we desire.

Forgive me for jabbering about something you understand better than I do, but I'm so fond of studying the physiology of delusions that I can't help it. I'm truly glad and proud that my advice to you to write your life interests you. I'm very interested to know how it has been taking shape. I would have to tell you too much that was flattering in order to explain why it was actually you I advised to do this. Your poems have precisely the good in them that I expect from your confession.[4]

Our children have been ill, the older ones with tonsilitis and Seryozha with pleurisy; they are getting better now.

Turgenev has been again[5] and was just as nice and brilliant, but—between ourselves, please—rather like a fountain of piped water. You were afraid all the time that he would soon run out and dry up. As soon as you had left, we sat down at the table and I said: 'well, go on and abuse him'. I wish you could have heard Tatyana Andreyevna's tone of voice when she said: 'it's impossible now' and heard the general chorus of assent and seen my feeling of self-satisfaction at this, as if it were something creditable on my part. God grant you may get on with your difficult philosophical work, and in such a way that it will satisfy you more from within than from without. Wish me the same. I very much want to write and I'm gradually making a start.

I wrote to Stasyulevich to say that I have entrusted everything to do with *The Russian Library* to you.

241. To A. A. FET

Tula(?), 5 September 1878

[3 lines omitted]...You mention your article.[1] Please don't attach any importance to my opinion—firstly because I'm a bad judge when listening and not reading to myself, and secondly because I was in a very bad mood that day for physical reasons. When you revise it, don't forget to improve the methods for linking the individual parts of the article. One often finds superfluous preambles in your work, such as, for example, 'Now we shall turn to', or 'let us look at', etc. The main thing of

---

4. Strakhov had mentioned to Tolstoy his intention of writing something in the nature of a confession, but he never did so.

5. Turgenev visited Yasnaya Polyana on two occasions in the summer of 1878—8–9 August and 2–4 September.

[241] 1. When visiting Yasnaya Polyana in August, Fet had read to Tolstoy and Strakhov an article of his which he subsequently entitled *Our Intelligentsia* and which attacked nihilism and left-wing trends in Russian social thought from the point of view of philosophical idealism. Tolstoy disliked it, and although Fet took some account of Tolstoy's criticisms when revising it, it was never published.

course is the positioning of the parts in relation to the focus, and when they are correctly positioned, all that is unnecessary and superfluous falls away of its own accord and the whole thing gains enormously...[15 lines omitted]

242. To I. S. TURGENEV

Yasnaya Polyana, 27 October 1878

I'm entirely to blame towards you, dear Ivan Sergeyevich. I meant to write to you immediately after your departure, but I've even neglected answering your letter until now. All is well here, thank God, but I haven't written because lately I've been (to put it quite accurately) intellectually unwell: I've been hunting and reading, but I've been literally incapable of any kind of original intellectual activity—even the writing of a letter with any sense in it. This happens to me occasionally and you are surely familiar with it or, if you aren't familiar with it, you probably understand it. For this reason I haven't replied to Ralston either, but I hope to reply to him today.

Schuyler has sent me his English translation of *The Cossacks*, and it seems very well translated.[1] But it's been translated into French by Baroness Mengden whom you saw here, and probably badly.[2] Please don't think that I am being affected but, really and truly, even a cursory rereading or a mention of my writings produces an unpleasantly complex feeling in me, the greater part of which is shame and fear that people are laughing at me. The same thing happened to me while I was compiling the biography.[3] I realised that I couldn't, and wanted to get out of it.

Much as I love you and believe that you are well-disposed towards me, it seems to me that you too are laughing at me. So let's not talk about my writings. You know that every person blows his nose in his own way, and, believe me, I like to blow my nose this way, as I put it. I rejoice with all my heart that you are in good health and that all is well with your people, and I continue to marvel at the freshness of your old age. In the 16 years[4] when we didn't see each other, you only got better in every respect, even physically.

All the same, I can't help wishing you what for me constitutes the greatest happiness in life—hard work—with the assurance of its importance and excellence. I don't in the slightest believe you when you say that you've stopped writing, and I don't want to believe you because I know that the best is still in you, as in a bottle which people have tried to decant too abruptly. One only needs to find the position in which it will pour smoothly. I wish this both for you and for myself.

[242] 1. Eugene Schuyler, American consul in Moscow and Petersburg in the 1860s and 1870s, had translated *The Cossacks* on Turgenev's recommendation. It was published in London in 1873.
2. Published in 1878 in *Le journal de St Petersbourg*.
3. A request had been made, through Turgenev, for an autobiographical sketch from Tolstoy to accompany a volume of his works to be published in *The Russian Library* series. His wife compiled it with his help.
4. In fact seventeen years, not sixteen.

242. To I. S. Turgenev

The autumn here is marvellous and I've been hunting a great many hares, but there've been no woodcocks.

What is Tchaikovsky's *Yevgeny Onegin* like? I haven't heard it yet but it interests me very much.

I cordially embrace you. My wife sends her greetings and thanks you for remembering her.

Yours,
L. Tolstoy

243. To WILLIAM SHEDDEN RALSTON

William Shedden Ralston (1821–89), a librarian in the British Museum from 1853 to 1875, who played an important part in building up its Russian collection. He was an accomplished translator from Russian to English, his publications including a Turgenev novel, an edition of Krylov's fables, a collection of Russian folk songs and an anthology of folk-tales. He also wrote a series of introductory lectures on early Russian history. Ralston visited Russia several times but never met Tolstoy.

This letter which Tolstoy wrote in English is a reply to Ralston's request for biographical information about him in connection with an article he was writing. Failing with Tolstoy, Ralston succeeded in getting the information he wanted from Turgenev. The article appeared in the journal *Nineteenth Century* in April 1879, under the title 'Count Leo Tolstoy's Novels'.

[Original in English]

Yasnaya Polyana, 27 October 1878

Dear Sir,

I am very sorry not to be able to give you a satisfactory answer to your letter. The reason of it is that I very much doubt my being an author of such importance as to interest by the incidents of my life not only the Russian, but also the European public. I am fully convinced by many examples of writers, of whom their contemporaries made very much of and which were quite forgotten in their lifetime, that for contemporaries it is impossible to judge rightly on the merits of literary works, and therefore, notwithstanding my wishes, I cannot partake the temporary illusion of some friends of mine, which seem to be sure that my works must occupy some place in the Russian literature. Quite sincerely not knowing if my works shall be read after a hundred years, or will be forgotten in a hundred days, I do not wish to take a ridiculous part in the very probable mistake of my friends.

Hoping that on consideration of my motives you will kindly excuse my refusal,

I am Yours faithfully,
Count L. Tolstoy

244. To P. N. SVISTUNOV

Yasnaya Polyana, 25 December 1878

[14 lines omitted]...My work tires and torments me, gives me joy, sometimes puts me in a state of rapture, sometimes of doubt and despondency; but the thought of it never leaves me for a moment, day or night, ill or well. You allowed me to put written questions to you too. I am now choosing the ones which are most important to me.

What sort of man was Fyodor Alexandrovich Uvarov, who was married to Lunina?[1] I know he was a brave officer, wounded in the head at the battle of Borodino. But what sort of man was he? When did he marry? What was his attitude to society? How did he disappear? What sort of woman was Katerina Sergeyevna? When did she die? Were there any children?

In what duel—with whom and what for—was Mikhail Sergeyevich Lunin wounded in the groin?

Having written down all these questions I feel conscience-stricken. Please don't answer if it is a nuisance for you, or if you have no time, but if you do answer even a few of them, I shall be very grateful. If all you know about it is too long, write and tell me—I will come and listen to you talk.

In any case I entrust myself to your good favour, and only ask you to believe that the work which is occupying me is nearly as important to me now as my own life, and furthermore that I value my relations with you as much for the help you have given and can give me, as for the sincere and profound respect I have for your person.

Count L. Tolstoy

Do you remember any Decembrists who escaped and disappeared?

245. To N. N. STRAKHOV

Yasnaya Polyana, 18–19 January 1879

After you had left, dear Nikolay Nikolayevich, I became quite ill, so much so that I was in bed for several days. I'm now almost fit again and have started work, but I haven't been out yet and I have a cough. I was very glad to learn that you had spent a day with dear Fet and got back home safely, and that you don't regret having been to see us. I was very glad to see you.

I have two requests to make to you: (1) There is a story translated by P. Behrs. Can it be published in *Family Evenings*?[1] It's no worse than some others, and I

[244] 1. Tolstoy was particularly interested in F. A. Uvarov, who had distinguished himself in the War of 1812, and was married to the sister of the Decembrist M. S. Lunin, because of his sudden and unexplained disappearance in 1827. It has since been suggested that Uvarov may have been the Fyodor Kuzmich whom legend claimed to be Alexander I in disguise.

[245] 1. The story *It's me!* was published with Strakhov's assistance in *Family Evenings* in 1879. S. S. Kashpireva was the editor of the journal, which was designed for children and for family reading.

245. To N. N. Strakhov

would be very grateful to you and Mrs Kashpireva. The second impudent and importunate request is one that I have no right to make to you; but really it is *urgently* necessary, and essential. The thing is this: Prince Nikolay Ivanovich Gorchakov,[2] my great-grandfather, who died in 1811, had three sons: Mikhail, Vasily (Major-General, married Stromilova. He had a daughter, Katerina, who married Uvarov and Perovsky) and Alexander. One of these Gorchakovs was tried for some wrongdoings and was sent to Siberia.[3] He was probably tried at the end of the century—no earlier than the '80s, since he was born about the year '60. And he was probably tried in the Senate. Can you find the case about him?

The ex-War Minister Alexey Ivanych (Gorchakov) was also tried at the beginning of this century—in case you should be misled.

Can Semyonov[4] help you? Do you need to approach Dmitry Obolensky?

Can Count Ilya Andreich Tolstoy be of any use? He's a senator. And can you find out whether one can approach Prince Alexander Mikhaylovich, the Chancellor? He is the eldest of the Gorchakovs, and the one I'm looking for is his uncle. If one can approach Gorchakov, through whom does one approach him, or can one write?

You have probably noticed my capacity for being absorbed in reading something and imagining that some piece of information I lack is particularly important to me, and then forgetting all about it. For goodness sake don't think this is the case now. This information is exceptionally important to me. This person is the key to the whole thing. These Gorchakovs have no heirs except us. And I need to know what can be known. If it's nothing, then I have a free hand. I don't know the ways of finding out about this case, but you will surely find them. If anybody needs to be approached, or if it's necessary to go to Petersburg, write and tell me. Please, please do this. I embrace you most cordially.

Yours,
L. Tolstoy

246. To COUNTESS A. A. TOLSTAYA

Yasnaya Polyana, 25–8 January 1879

Are you and all your people alive and well, dear friend?

For our part we are alive and are more or less well, although only recently; before that we've been constantly ill—first the children, then me.

I have a request to make to you: is there a biography, even a very short one, of

---

2. Prince Nikolay Ivanovich Gorchakov (1725–1811), a wealthy army officer and landowner, whose estate of Nikolskoye-Vyazemskoye subsequently came into Tolstoy's possession.

3. It was in fact Vasily Nikolayevich Gorchakov who was exiled to Siberia at the beginning of the nineteenth century for importing forged banknotes from abroad in a piano! He was to have been the hero of a story, *Those who Labour and are Heavy Laden*, of which four drafts exist, but which was never finished.

4. N. P. Semyonov (1823–1904), a member of the Senate active in the cause of peasant reform.

Lev Alexeyevich Perovsky?[1] I need to know where he worked and where he lived from 1816 to 1833. And above all, I really need to know *when, how* and *where* he married Katerina Vasilyevna Uvarova (the widow of Dmitry Petrovich Uvarov), née Princess Gorchakova. I know that she had a very bad life with him and died in 1833, but every detail of his marriage and relations with her would be valuable to me. I wanted to write directly to Boris Alexeyevich,[2] but I don't know his address, I don't know whether he's a count or not, and however ashamed I feel about writing to you with a request, I'm still glad that it makes me write to you. As always, be sweet and kind and all-forgiving, and do this for me, please. And while I'm about it, I've one more request. I'm told that the original Decembrist files with biographies and portraits of all the Decembrists are in Petersburg. Only Bogdanovich, the historian, has been allowed access to these files. Is there any hope of my gaining access to them? If there is, whom should I apply to, and how?[3] Well, come what may! I'll be very lucky if you don't say 'Well, I've rarely met such an unscrupulous egoist as Lev Tolstoy!'

Thank you very much for the trouble you took over the English governess; she didn't suit us and I think it's our own fault for loading her with too many duties.

Please kiss Auntie Praskovya Vasilyevna's hand particularly tenderly and respectfully for me. Please write about yourself—is your health better than last year, and are you calmer in spirit? Despite my egoism, I love you sincerely.

I kiss Sophie's hand and embrace Count Ilya Andreich.

Yours,
L. Tolstoy

I'll send V. Perovsky's papers to you by the next post.

247. To A. A. FET

Yasnaya Polyana, 31 January–1 February 1879

Dear Afanasy Afanasyevich,

It's about a week since I got your particularly good last letter and the very good, though not outstanding poem,[1] and I didn't reply at once because, would you believe it, I still haven't recovered from my indisposition and it's only today that I feel better and my head is clearer, although I haven't been out yet. *Truth is what is*

---

[246] 1. L. A. Perovsky (1792–1856), a statesman in the reign of Nicholas I and brother of V. A. Perovsky. He married Tolstoy's relative Y. V. Uvarova (*née* Gorchakova). Tolstoy's interest in Perovsky and Uvarova was connected with his work on his new story *Those who Labour and are Heavy Laden*.
2. Perovsky.
3. Permission for Tolstoy to have access to the archives was refused.

[247] 1. *Never*. The subject of this poem is the poet's return from the grave to an uninhabited world, and his realisation that life without human ties is futile and unbearable—'For whom has the grave returned me? With what is my consciousness linked?...Where shall I go when there is no one to embrace?' His despair is such that he begs death to return him to the grave.

247. To A. A. Fet

true, not what is proven, etc.[2] That is the greatest truth of all. But truth, just the same as this truth, can be tracked down even if it can't be proved—you can get to it and see that you can't go any further, and that that's where one must start from. Your last poem I didn't like as much as the previous one,[3] either for the form (it's not so tight as the other), or for the content which I don't agree with, as one can only disagree with such an impossible assumption. Verne has a story of a trip round the moon. They find themselves at a point where there is no force of gravity. Is it possible to jump up and down at that point? Learned physicists have given different answers. Similarly there must be different answers to your assumption, because the situation is impossible, and not human. But the spiritual problem is finely put. I answer it differently from you. I wouldn't want to go back into the grave. All is not over for me, even with the destruction of all life except my own. There still remain my relations with God, i.e. relations with the force which created me, attracted me towards it and will destroy me or change me.

The poem is good because I read it to the children, some of whom are concerned about the plague,[4] and it answered their fears and moved them. My wife didn't see Marya Petrovna in Moscow and was very sorry. She asks me to send her regards, and I do too.

God grant you health, peace of mind and the recognition of the need for relations with God, the absence of which you so vividly reject in this poem.

Yours,
L. Tolstoy

248. To COUNTESS A. A. TOLSTAYA

Yasnaya Polyana, 25(?) March 1879

I've been so long in replying to you, my dear, because I've been in Moscow these past days, and as always I was worn out by the bustle of town life which I find so terrible.

I don't understand the word 'cross'—'the cross that we bear'—in the same way as you do. If what I am planning finds favour with God, you will read it;[1] it's also possible to speak about it in words, but it's impossible to write about it. I'll merely say that 'Take up your cross', by itself, has no meaning in my opinion, since to take up or not to take up the cross doesn't depend on our will; it is laid upon us; but we mustn't take on anything else as well—anything that is not the cross. And

---

2. A reference to a phrase in a letter of Fet's about the main point of Schopenhauer's *Die Welt als Wille und Vorstellung*, which Fet was reading with a view to translation.
3. *Death*.
4. The fear of an epidemic of the plague proved groundless.

[248] 1. In February 1879 Tolstoy started work on a new novel set in the eighteenth century and reflecting his increasing interest in religion. It was to portray the conflict between egoism and the demands of the conscience, between the gratification of one's desires and adherence to religious teachings. He gave the general title of *One Hundred Years* to the work. Several fragments have survived from February and March 1879.

we mustn't carry the cross just anywhere, but following Christ, i.e. fulfilling His commandment of love of God and of one's neighbour. Your cross is the Court, mine is the labour of thought—bad, proud, and full of temptations...But enough of that...

I have two requests to make to you, i.e. through you, to the Emperor and the Empress. Don't be alarmed. I hope that the requests are so slight that you won't need to refuse me. The request to the Empress is such that I'm sure she will even be grateful to you. The request through her to the Emperor is on behalf of three old men, schismatic bishops[2] (one is 90 years old, the other two are around 60—a fourth died in prison), who have been imprisoned in a Suzdal Monastery for 22 years. Their names are Konon, Gennady and Arkady.

When I heard about them, I found it hard to believe—as you too, no doubt—that four old men should be kept in strict confinement for 23 years for their religious convictions...You know better than I do whether it's possible or not to intercede for them and to free them. How good it would be to free them at this time...It seems to me that intercession for such people well becomes our kind Empress.

My other request to you is that I be given access to the secret archives from the time of Peter I, and the Empresses Anna Ioannovna and Elizabeth. The main reason for my being in Moscow was to work on the archives (I'm no longer interested in the Decembrists now, but in the eighteenth century—the early part), and I was told that I wouldn't be given access to the secret archives without the highest authorisation; and they contain everything that is of interest to me: the pretenders, the brigands, the schismatics...How can I get authorisation? If it's not tedious, difficult or inconvenient for you, then help me and enlighten me on this—but if for some reason it should be the least bit disagreeable to you, please don't do anything and forgive me my indiscrétion.

How are you, and how do you feel? Your letters are always a joy to me. The older one gets, the more strongly one feels old friendship. God grant you the very best of everything! I kiss your hand. Sonya thanks you for your love, and sends you hers.

Yours,
L. Tolstoy

249. To A. A. FET

Yasnaya Polyana, 16–17 April 1879

There is a prayer which says: 'reward us not according to our merits, but according to Thy mercy'. I've received another good long letter from you. I'll certainly go to Kiev and Vorobyovka soon, and then I'll tell you everything, but just now I'll simply reply to your apprehensions: goodness knows where my Decembrists are now; I don't think about them, and if I were to think about them and to write, I

2. 'Old Believers'. Tolstaya failed to obtain their release, and it was only in 1881 that, at Tolstoy's instigation, the Governor of Tula succeeded in doing so.

249. To A. A. Fet

flatter myself with the hope that my breath alone which the book would smell of, would be unendurable to those who shoot people for the good of mankind.[1]

How right you and the peasants are. [1 line omitted; meaning obscure] But I must say that I conscientiously refrain from reading the newspapers, even now, and I consider it my duty to wean everybody from that pernicious habit. There's a good old man sitting in Vorobyovka who smelts 2 or 3 pages of Schopenhauer in his brain and pours them out in Russian, has a game of billiards, kills a woodcock, admires a foal from Zakras, sits drinking excellent tea with his wife, and smoking, loving everyone and loved by everyone. Then suddenly somebody brings him a smelly, damp sheet of newspaper, harmful to the hands and harmful to the eyes, and his heart is filled with the malice of condemnation, a feeling of alienation, a feeling that I love nobody and nobody loves me, and he begins to talk and talk and gets angry and suffers.

You should give it up. It will be much better.

I hope to see you. Our regards to Marya Petrovna.

Yours,
L. Tolstoy

250. To A. A. FET

Yasnaya Polyana, 27–8 July 1879

Thank you for your last good letter, Afanasy Afanasyevich, and for the apologue about the falcon, which I like, but which I wish could be more fully explained. If I am that falcon, and if, as it appears from what follows, my too distant flights mean that I reject real life, then I must justify myself. I neither reject real life nor the labour necessary to support this life, but it seems to me that the greater part of my life and yours is taken up with satisfying needs which are not natural, but have been artificially inculcated in us by education, or have been invented by us and become habitual, and that 9/10 of the labour which is put into satisfying these demands is idle labour. I would very much like to be absolutely sure that I give people more than I take from them. But since I feel myself very inclined to set a high value on my own labour and a low one on other people's, I do not hope simply by intensifying my own labour and choosing what is most burdensome (I invariably assure myself that the labour I like most is the most necessary and the most difficult) to be sure that other people's accounts with me will not suffer; I would like to take as little from others as possible and to labour as little as possible for the satisfaction of my own needs, and I think this is the easiest way to avoid going wrong.

I'm very sorry that your health is still uncertain, but I'm very glad that you are well in spirit, as is apparent from your letters. I confess that I'm very much looking forward to seeing Strakhov. I cordially embrace you, and ask you to give our regards to Marya Petrovna.

Yours,
L. Tolstoy

[249] 1. A reference to terrorist acts and an attempt on the Tsar's life in 1879.

251. To A. A. FET

Yasnaya Polyana, 30–1 August 1879

Dear Afanasy Afanasyevich,

Of course I'm to blame again towards you, but not, of course, from any lack of love for you or thoughts about you. Strakhov and I have been continually talking about you—judging and disposing of you as we all judge one another, and as God grant that others may judge me. Strakhov is very pleased with his visit to you and even more so with your translation.[1] I won't reply to the provocative points in your letter about the murder of the Duc d'Enghien because I think you are wrong, and you know it better than I do. I managed to recommend you to read *The 1,001 Nights* and Pascal; both of them you liked, and even found congenial. Now I have a book to suggest to you which nobody has read, and which I read the other day for the first time and continue to read with exclamations of joy; I hope it will also prove congenial, especially as it has much in common with Schopenhauer: it is the *Proverbs* of Solomon, *Ecclesiastes* and the *Book of Wisdom*. It would be difficult to read anything more modern than this, but if you read it, read it in Slavonic. I have a modern Russian translation. This translation (I'm ashamed to call it a translation) is interesting because it shows plainly the stupidity, ignorance, and effrontery of our priests. The English translation is also bad. If you had the Greek, you would see what it is like. Give my regards to Petya Borisov and advise him from me to read it in Greek and compare the translations. I've just been for a walk and was thinking about Petya. I don't know what else he needs to learn, but I do know that with his knowledge I could suggest to him the choice of about four tasks which need a lifetime's devotion, and even the partial success of which would earn him the eternal gratitude of every Russian, as long as Russians exist.

Since Strakhov's visit we have had one guest after another, theatricals, and all hell let loose. 34 sheets were in use for the guests, there were 30 people at dinner, everything went off well, and everybody, including myself, enjoyed themselves.

Our cordial greetings to Marya Petrovna.

When can we hope to see you, and how is your health?

Yours,
L. Tolstoy

252. To N. N. STRAKHOV

[Not sent]

Yasnaya Polyana, 19–22 November 1879

Dear Nikolay Nikolayevich,

You write as if to provoke me. I know you value my opinion as I do yours, and so I'll say everything I think. Only please don't listen to my words as though they were the words of a living person with whom there may be scores to settle,

[251] 1. Of Schopenhauer's *Die Welt als Wille und Vorstellung*.

252. To N. N. Strakhov

relationships, rivalries—the possibility of being offended by my words or flattered by them—regard them as the sympathetic, loving echo of a human soul which has suffered and still suffers, I won't say no less than yours, but suffers *its own* grief. Someone else's is easier to see. And I can see you clearly. Your letter distressed me very much. I felt a great deal and thought a great deal about it. In my opinion you are spiritually ill. And your illness amounts to this, that you have two natures in you—one of the spirit and one of the flesh. There are people who live by the flesh alone and don't understand how it is possible to shift one's centre of gravity to the spiritual life. By shifting one's centre of gravity to the spiritual life I mean guiding one's activity by spiritual aims. There are people who live by the flesh and understand—only understand—the spiritual life. There are fortunate people—our peasants, or the Buddhists about whom you spoke, you remember—who live the full life of the flesh until they are 50 and then suddenly shift to the other foot, the spiritual one, and stand on it. There are still more fortunate people for whom doing the will of the Father is true meat and drink and who have stood on this spiritual foot since they were young. But there are unfortunate people like you and me whose centre of gravity is in the middle and who have forgotten how to walk and stand. In the world in which we live, everything is so confused—all the things of the flesh are so clothed in spiritual attire, all the things of the spirit so plastered over with those of the flesh—that it is difficult to distinguish them. I am worse than you, and therefore more fortunate in this misfortune. The passions of the flesh were stronger in me and it is easier for me to shake myself free and to distinguish the one from the other, but you are completely confused. You want the good, but regret that there is not more evil in you; that you have no passions. You want the truth, but regret and seem to feel resentful that there is nothing rapacious about you. But what is good, and what is bad? You evidently don't know well enough not to be afraid of making a mistake in doing good.

You oughtn't to write your life. You don't know what has been good or bad in it. And one must know. If you knew how to walk earlier on in childhood and if other people can walk, then you must walk, and if you can't walk, it means you are drunk or ill, and you need to sober up or have treatment. You can't arrive at anything but despair along the path you are going, so the road is the wrong one and you must turn back.

In Christ's teaching I found one particular feature distinguishing it from all other teachings. He teaches and explains why the meaning of our life is the one he gives to it. But he always says besides that one must carry out what he says and then you will see whether what he says is true. Either: light was given to the world but men loved darkness because their deeds were evil. Or: whoever believes in the Son of Man, the same will do God's deeds. Here is the metaphysical knot, and it can't be untied by reason but by one's whole life.

Believe me, transfer your centre of gravity to the spiritual world, and all the aims of your life, all your desires will stem from it, and you will then find peace in life. Do God's works, carry out the will of the Father, and you will then see the light and understand...[8 lines omitted]